Discover God's
Blessings

Discover God's
Blessings

A One-Year Bible Reading Plan and Devotional

Originally published as *The Best of Bible Pathway*,
by Dr. John A. Hash (1993 edition)

UPDATED BY ROBBI CARY

HILLTOP
HOUSE PUBLISHING

Discover God's Blessings: A One-Year Bible Reading Plan and Devotional

Copyright © 2022 by Robbi Cary Hilltop House Publishing (HHP)

Originally published as *The Best of Bible Pathway*, by Dr. John A. Hash © 1991. Revised printing 1993. ISBN 1-879595-02-8

Dr. John Hash granted permission to Robbi Cary (Hilltop House Publishing, HHP) for reprinting and updating *The Best of Bible Pathway*, 1993 edition. HHP published a first reprint titled *Building Faith with Bible Pathway* (2009). This second reprint, which has been retitled *Discover God's Blessings*, includes expanded introductions to a number of books of the Bible and added helpful information on reading the Bible.

For more information, see the back resource, "How I Came to Love Reading the Bible and to Publish This Book."

Printed in the United States of America

ISBN: 978-0-9893754-4-3 (softcover)
ISBN: 978-0-9893754-5-0 (e-book)

For reprint permission concerning any portion of this book, please contact:
Robbi Cary, P.O. Box 718, Fort Myers, FL 33902
Email: RobbiCary@outlook.com Website: RobbiCary.com

All Scriptures in quotation marks are from the King James Version (KJV) of the Holy Bible. Scriptures in *italics* and *without* quote marks are paraphrases, with verses indicated.

Note: This book uses the pronoun "he." We trust that you will allow for the intent of *he* and *she* where appropriate.

Cover and interior design: Katherine Lloyd, TheDeskOnline.com
Cover and interior illustrations: Love Watercolor Store, Creative Market
Editors: Marilyn A. Anderson, Michele Schiavone, and Ken Walker

May you know God better,
grow in faith,
and
live well.

Contents

About Bible Pathway Ministry and the Reading Plan

Bible Pathway is the world's most widely read through-the-Bible devotional commentary.

The ministry began modestly in 1973 when Dr. John Hash, knowing the value and importance of reading the Bible to change lives and destinies, posted an ad offering a free-subscription guide to help people read through the Bible in one year. One thousand requests poured in, not only for reading guides, but for Bibles, as well. Inquiries continued to come in from all over the world, including from mission fields and Third World countries, which compelled the ministry team to translate the popular study guide into many languages.

Christian leaders and educators in all major denominations throughout the world endorsed and recommended the plan, further promoting it. The first book edition, *The Best of Bible Pathway*, was published in 1991.

More than 90 million publications were sent to 186 nations in 35 languages from 1973 through 1993 (the year this book edition was first published).

The purpose of Bible Pathway publications is to encourage people to read God's Word through in one year. The reading plan benefits anyone who desires to grow in God's Word—whether first-time readers or longtime Christian servants. The guide is an aid for reading the Bible, not a substitute, for to only read the guide would be to miss the whole aim of the Bible Pathway Ministry.

Bible Pathway Ministry believes in the authority and reliability of the Bible, and that it is God-inspired (2 Tim. 3:16). All the Bible is essential for life and one's relationship with God. It reveals God to us, discloses life's purpose and meaning, and enables us to live well and grow spiritually.

We encourage you to find ways to study God's Word further, but study begins with reading. Many books teach us about the Bible, but no book can replace God's Word. Our prayer is that, at a minimum, you devote thirty minutes every day toward reading through the Bible once a year, beginning with Genesis.

Each day's text includes the Bible chapters to read, a "verse for the day," and thoughts for personal application. In addition, the Old Testament readings include a glimpse of *"Christ Revealed"* from the daily Scripture passage.

Importance and Purpose of God's Word

BY DR. JOHN HASH

God, who created us, has plans and purposes for this world and mankind. He has allotted to each of us just one lifetime to accomplish our purposes and responsibilities. We are to:

- Begin to know God, for this is eternal life (John 17:3).
- Prepare ourselves to be the people God wants us to be (Jer. 29:11).
- Accomplish the purposes for which He created us (Eph. 2:10).

Think how tragic it would be to fall short of fulfilling God's perfect will—wasting our few short years achieving material gains or social recognition—only to fail at achieving the purpose for which God created us.

Our ability to please the Lord and gain strength for our spiritual lives will be in exact proportion to the time we set aside to thoroughly read and study the Bible. There are no shortcuts to spiritual maturity. No one's growth is complete without a comprehensive, working knowledge of all Scripture, and certainly no Christian worker is fully effective without a basic knowledge of the purpose and application of each book of the Bible. We are all dependent upon the Holy Spirit to reveal God's will, and to help us read God's Word (Luke 24:45; 1 Cor. 2:12; Col. 1:9), but the Holy Spirit will not reveal that which we do not avail ourselves of in the first place from His Word.

We all have just one life to live. May we make the most of how we invest our time, so that we, too, may one day hear those words: *"Well done . . . good and faithful servant"* (Matt. 25:21).

A Few Tips for Reading the Bible and Using This Plan

Developing a daily Bible-reading routine and prayer time takes persistence and effort.

- Know that reading through Scripture sometimes won't be easy, especially in the beginning. Be persistent and don't give up. Your effort will be worth it. (You may find my story regarding this helpful, which is in Appendix B.)
- Decide on a consistent, specific time of day that you will read. Allot time in your daily schedule for reading.
- Choose a Bible translation you enjoy.

It's important to understand that in God's Word you will encounter both truth *and* grace.[1] God's truth includes the serious and hard aspects that we are accountable to Him; He has high, righteous standards; and one day we will stand before God and give an account of our lives to Him.

God created us in His image and for fellowship with Him. We are to honor Him. Transgressing against His commands is called sin, and He declared that the "sentence" for sin is death (Gen. 2:15-17; Rom. 6:23). Because sin is brokenness from God, it brings strife, pain, and difficult, unforeseen consequences. However, God loves us greatly.

In God's love and mercy, He has provided a way of salvation for us through Jesus's life, death, and resurrection. As we turn to God and receive His Son, Jesus, into our lives, we are granted forgiveness, grace, new life, peace, and blessings! Scripture declares it this way:

> *"For the wages of sin is death; but the gift of God is eternal life through Jesus Christ our Lord"* (Rom. 6:23).

> *"For God so loved the world, that he gave his only begotten Son, that whosoever believeth in him should not perish, but have everlasting life"* (John 3:16).

> *God's law was given to us by Moses, but **grace and truth** came by Jesus Christ* (John 1:17).

---

1 This key element is additionally shared in Appendix C: A Brief Overview of the Bible and Helpful Tips for Reading It.

"The Word [Jesus] *was made flesh, and dwelt among us, (and we beheld his glory, the glory as of the only begotten of the Father,) full of **grace and truth**"* (John 1:14).

But now, through Jesus, we have been released from the law and its penalty; we are free from what had bound us [the law, condemnation, and sin]; *now we are able to serve God with a new spirit* (Rom. 7:6).

As you read God's Word, seek to recognize both truth and grace. Let yourself be moved by God's righteousness; His love and mercy; and His power to save and help.

Because the Bible can seem overwhelming, it also helps to know that God's foundational truths are repeated and given to us in various ways, through various stories and examples, and through different kinds of literature in its pages.

Options for beginning this plan anytime during the year

While the plan offered in this book starts with a January 1 reading date, following are two options for beginning any time of year:

- If you want to start reading with Genesis later during the year and follow along with this plan, visit my website (https://www.blessings andgrace.com/one-year-Bible-reading-plan-checklist/) and print out the checklist, which begins with Genesis. You can keep the list in your book and track your readings. Mark down your beginning date. Read every day and aim to finish in one year.
- Whatever month of the year it is, check this plan and see what day the next book of the Bible starts. Mark this date down on your calendar, and when it arrives, begin reading. This will allow you to stay on track with this book's readings and plan.

◆ Please note that the first day's reading on January 1 is longer than most because Genesis covers a number of foundational truths. Most daily readings are substantially shorter.

Old Testament

January

 # GENESIS

The word Genesis means origin and this book gives us the origin of mankind. Genesis, and especially the first several chapters, reveal key truths that are built upon throughout the Bible. Genesis helps us learn about God, our purpose in life, and about sin, its consequences, the suffering it brings, and sin's remedy.

The first three chapters declare that God is the supreme Creator of the universe and sovereign over all (Gen. 1:1; Col. 1:16). Throughout the Bible, God is honored as Creator (Gen. 1:1; Col. 1:16). Through the beauty and glory of the heavens and earth, every day we are to experience some of God's goodness, wisdom, and glorious power (Rom. 1:20). God claims the glory, rights, and privileges of Maker (Gen. 1-3; Ps. 8; Isa. 44:24; 45:7-18; Jer. 5:22-24). In the last book of the Bible, Revelation, God is again praised as Maker of the universe's wonders. *"Thou art worthy, O Lord, to receive glory and honour and power: for thou hast created all things, and for thy pleasure they are and were created"* (Rev. 4:11; and Rev. 4:10; 10:6; 14:7).

Genesis shows that God takes pleasure in the goodness of His creation. He beheld what He brought into being, and six times called it good. After creating mankind, He beheld creation and declared it *"very good."* God then fellowshipped with those He created. He walked and talked with them.

Genesis reveals that God *spoke* everything into existence. His words contain power. (God didn't snap His fingers or use any other method.) He created everything that exists by the power and authority of His Word. Whatever God says—happens. This is the reason that all of God's Word, and every promise of Scripture, is filled with power.

When God created mankind, He created men and women in His own image for fellowship with Himself, and to rule over and care for His wonderful creation (Gen. 1:26-31; 2:4-25; 3:8-10). In addition, He created Adam and Eve (and all mankind) with a free will, along with instructions to obey, and warnings regarding consequences for not doing so (Gen. 2:16-17).[1]

When Adam and Eve disregarded God's command, their rebellion broke their relationship with God, the giver of life, so that sin and death began to reign over mankind (Gen. 2:16-17; 3:1-24; Rom. 5:12-14). Adam and Eve's rebellion

---

1 Scripture additionally reveals that God made us with a body, soul, and spirit (1 Thess. 5:23).

resulted in the tragic fall. Ever since, mankind's offspring carries this same sinful nature (a rebellious, independent spirit) and broken fellowship with God.

Sin continued to fill the hearts and minds of people with hate, murder, and violence. Eventually, God in judgment brought a great flood upon the world and reduced mankind to one family—that of godly Noah. But again, sin grew and prevailed, and the people decided to build the huge Tower of Babel in defiance of God (Gen. 11:1-9).

Chapters 1–11 record approximately the first two thousand years of man's history. During that time, four major events took place: the creation of all things, Adam and Eve's fall, the great flood, and the building of the Tower of Babel.

Chapters 12–50 cover about three hundred years and focus on four men—Abraham, Isaac, Jacob, and Joseph (and their families). Through these men and their families, God shows His love, protection, and provisions for those who walk with Him. God begins by choosing and calling Abraham into a special covenant relationship, promising Abraham that, as he walks with God, God will greatly bless him and his descendants (Gen. 17). This promise, woven throughout Scripture, states that everyone who believes and follows the Lord is counted in Abraham's family and receives the blessings promised to him (Gen. 12:1-3).[2]

The New Testament quotes Genesis more than sixty times, and includes Jesus's teaching from Genesis, which confirms the book's reliability and truth. Jesus declared Genesis to be vital to one's faith, saying to the people that *"had ye believed Moses, ye would have believed me: for he wrote of me. But if ye believe not his writings, how shall ye believe my words?"* (John 5:46-47). Some of the additional topics from Genesis that Jesus spoke on include: *creation* (Matt. 19:4-6; Gen. 2:21-24); *Noah* (Matt. 24:37-38; Gen. 6:5, 13; 7:6-23); *Abraham* (Matt. 3:9; Gen. 17:1-16); and *Sodom and Gomorrah* (Matt. 10:15; Gen. 19:24-25).

January 1: Read Genesis 1–3

Verse for Today: *"Now the serpent was more subtil than any beast of the field which the Lord God had made. And he said unto the woman, Yea, hath God said, Ye shall not eat of every tree of the garden?"* (Gen. 3:1).

God created Adam and Eve, placed them in a perfect environment, and supplied their every need. He said they could eat from all the trees, except one. Eating the fruit from this one tree was forbidden in order to test their loyalty and obedience to Him.

---

2   Galatians 3:29 states, *"And if ye be Christ's, then are ye Abraham's seed, and heirs according to the promise."* Other Scripture references regarding this promise of blessing include Gen. 15:1-19; 17:1-19; Rom. 4:13-25; Gal. 3:7-29.

Surprisingly, we also find Satan, God's enemy, in the garden. Since the early days of history, Satan not only personally rejects God's authority, but he seeks to separate man from his creator and inspire confidence in self. He seeks to destroy all those he can and keep them from God. While we learn much about this Evil One throughout Scripture, this account reveals some of his primary methods that he still uses to cause people to doubt and distrust the Lord.

Satan first caused Eve to question the Word of God, asking, *Can it really be that God has said you shall not eat of every tree in the garden? . . . God knows that when you eat the fruit from this tree, you will be like Him, knowing what is good and what is evil* (Gen. 3:1, 5). The devil implied that God was holding back something good from them, raising doubt about whether He cared for their best interests. Once Eve questioned the goodness of God in providing what was best, Satan had won a major victory.

Satan's next move was to undermine Eve's reliance on the truth of God's Word by contradicting it: *You shall not die.* Questioning God easily leads to contradicting His Word. Satan then appealed to her natural desires, and worked through her to cause Adam to sin (Gen. 3:4-6). Satan led Adam and Eve to think that they knew what was best. They believed Satan's lie, rather than what God said. As a result of sin, mankind became self-seeking, self-centered, and self-willed.

When Adam and Eve disobeyed God, sin and death entered the world. With these came all the evil, suffering, and sorrow that we have today. Because every person born after Adam and Eve is now created in *their image*, everyone sins (Rom. 5:12), and begins to grow old and die.

Because sin is deceptive, destructive, and deadly, it brings unforeseen, unimaginable consequences. Adam and Eve could not have imagined the sorrow and trouble that came with their single act of disobedience. Adam and Eve learned that we are not independent creatures free to do things our own way without regard for God's Word. We are His creation and His Word is absolute.

Satan often appears as an *"angel of light"* (2 Cor. 11:14) and deceives many by quoting a portion of Scripture that, by itself, sounds reasonable. He even quoted Scripture to Jesus in an attempt to cause Him to sin (Luke 4:1-13). Reading and knowing *all of God's Word* is our remedy for being restored to God and His blessings, and it is our safeguard against making wrong decisions.

"Thou art worthy, O Lord, to receive glory and honour and power: for thou hast created all things, and for thy pleasure they are and were created" (Rev. 4:11).

Thought for Today: Our eternal destiny is determined by choice, not chance.

Christ Revealed: As Creator (Gen. 1:1; John 1:1-4; Col. 1:15-17; Heb. 11:3). Also, as the seed of woman (Gen. 3:15; Isa. 7:14; 9:6-7; Gal. 4:4).

January 2: Read Genesis 4–6

Verses for Today: *"And the LORD said, My spirit shall not always strive with man. . . . And God saw that the wickedness of man was great in the earth, and that every imagination of the thoughts of his heart was only evil continually"* (Gen. 6:3, 5).

After Adam and Eve sinned, God showed his mercy and grace by providing a covering for their sin. He also told of the coming Savior, who would defeat Satan, the source of sin (Gen. 3:15; Heb. 10:12-14).

As time passed, mankind became more and more evil. Although God was *grieved at heart* about their rebellion (Gen. 6:6), He did not leave mankind to their own destruction—He gave many warnings to keep them from going to hell.

God raised up great men of faith, such as Enoch, and preachers of righteousness, such as Noah (Heb. 11:5-7). Added to this, God's own Holy Spirit spoke to the consciences of men (Gen. 6:3). But the people continued to ignore His message.

The Spirit of God moves in the heart of every person, convicting of sin and seeking to turn each one to God. The allotted time for each of us is sufficient to accept God's message of love and receive Christ as Savior and Lord. Continual rejection of God's mercy causes a person to become so hardened that he no longer hears the voice of the Holy Spirit. The striving of God's Spirit eventually comes to an end—not because God is no longer willing to help, but because of the hard-heartedness of those who refuse to yield their wills to His will.

Today, if you will hear His voice, do not harden your hearts (Heb. 3:7-8).

Thought for Today: Either you will yield to Satan's influence and become hardened to the things of God, or you will yield to God's Spirit and become more like Jesus.

Christ Revealed: Through Abel's blood sacrifice (Gen. 4:4-7). Jesus is the Lamb of God sacrificed for our sins, so that we might be saved from God's judgment (John 1:29; Heb. 9:22; 11:4). Man's best achievements can never take the place of Christ's atonement on our behalf.

January 3: Read Genesis 7–9

Verse for Today: *"And Noah builded an altar unto the Lord . . . and offered burnt offerings on the altar"* (Gen. 8:20).

Upon leaving the ark, Noah built an altar, offered a sacrifice, and worshiped God. These actions were a proclamation and confession of Noah's faith in God, and his gratitude for God's saving mercy and care. The sacrifice he made acknowledged that he was undeserving of mercy before a Holy God. The sacrifice also represents Christ and that we need someone other than ourselves to pay our penalty and be our substitute for the judgment against our transgressions.

Noah's trust in God is a great example of faith, which is highlighted and esteemed in the great hall-of-faith chapter in the New Testament (Heb. 11).

By faith Noah, when warned by God about things not yet seen, in holy fear prepared an ark to save his household. Through this action of faith, he condemned the unbelief of the rest of the world and became the possessor of the righteousness that results from faith (Heb. 11:7).

Thought for Today: It is not *things* that we need, but *Christ.*

Christ Revealed: Through the ark (Gen. 7:1-7). Christ is our ark of safety and will protect believers from the waters of judgment (Acts 4:12; 1 Pet. 3:20).

January 4: Read Genesis 10–12

Verse for Today: *"Say, I pray thee, thou art my sister: that it may be well with me for thy sake; and my soul shall live because of thee"* (Gen. 12:13).

God spoke to Abram, saying, *Leave your country and your relatives, and go to a land that I will show you* (Gen. 12:1). Abram expected God's blessings as He walked toward the Promised Land but, instead, he faced severe famine, which caused him to go down to Egypt. There, God exposed weakness in Abram's faith through his deceptive agreement with his wife, Sarai.

Fearing that someone might kill him to have his beautiful wife—Abram and Sarai agreed that if anyone asked who Sarai was, they would say she was his sister (Gen. 12:10-13). Abram reasoned with Sarai that *my life will be spared because of you.* This reasoning expressed a lack of faith in God's ability to protect him and exposed a greater concern for his own well-being than for Sarai's chastity and safety. The unbelieving Pharaoh rebuked Abram's act. Surely, Abram had to feel that he had dishonored God. But these trials were necessary to perfect his faith.

Abram had a threefold weakness that God exposed—an unwarranted fear of man, a foolish reliance on his own schemes, and a sinful desire to please himself at the expense of the welfare of others. God could not bless Abram until he gave up his reliance on human wisdom and selfish reasoning.

Abram's experience is a reminder that we must take God at His Word and, in faith, depend wholly upon Him.

Lord, direct my life according to Your Word; and let no sin rule over me (Ps. 119:133).

Thought for Today: Christians who commit foolish acts of unbelief leave themselves open to Satan's destructive power.

Christ Revealed: As the Seed of Abraham (Gen. 12:1-3; 18:18). Jesus's genealogy reveals His lineage as coming from Abraham (Matt. 1:1; Acts 3:25-26; Gal. 3:16). In addition, Abraham was a type of Christ, who leads the way to a better land (John 14:2-4; Heb. 11:8-16).

January 5: Read Genesis 13–15

Verse for Today: *"And the Lord said unto Abram, after that Lot was separated from him, Lift up now thine eyes, and look from the place where thou art northward, and southward, and eastward, and westward"* (Gen. 13:14).

God had promised to give Abram all the land of Canaan (Gen. 12:7). Abram, though, generously waived his rights and surrendered his claim to the land in an attempt to end the strife that had developed between his herdsmen and Lot's herdsmen. In contrast, Lot exposed his greediness as he chose all the well-watered plains, especially at the expense of losing daily fellowship with Abram, the father of the faithful.

What a difference between Lot and Abram! Lot sought worldly, material gain, but soon lost it. Abram, however, looked toward a faithful God. He willingly gave up the best land to maintain peace with his fellow man, and God blessed him. Abram's desire was to please the Lord and, in doing so, he received eternal riches and rewards.

The Lord is able to compensate Christians for the loss of all the sacrifices that we make for His sake. He knows, when no one else does, what we willingly give up for Him.

"But seek ye first the kingdom of God, and his righteousness; and all these things shall be added unto you" (Matt. 6:33).

Thought for Today: Our relationship with God can grow closer and dearer as we trust Him in all things.

Christ Portrayed: By the high priest, Melchizedek (Gen. 14:18-20). Christ is our High Priest today, interceding in prayer for us (Heb. 4:14-16; 5:5-10; 7:1-4, 25).

January 6: Read Genesis 16–18

Verses for Today: *"And Abraham drew near, and said, Wilt thou also destroy the righteous with the wicked? . . . Shall not the Judge of all the earth do right?"* (Gen. 18:23, 25).

Angels visited Abraham and told him of God's coming judgment upon the wicked city of Sodom—the city in which his nephew Lot lived. When the angels left, Abraham prayed earnestly to God (Gen. 18:22-33). Abraham's prayer, the first long prayer recorded in Scripture, is also the first example of intercessory prayer—praying for others.

It would have been an example of forgiving love had Abraham prayed for Lot to be spared, but to plead for a wicked city where he had no personal interest at stake—for lost souls in whom he had nothing personal to gain—brings to light the compassion and mercy of this man of faith.

Six times Abraham offered his intercessory prayer, and each time God's gracious answer gave him encouragement to continue asking. Although Sodom was not spared in answer to Abraham's prayer, God graciously saved Lot's family, which doubtless included all the righteous in the city.

Here is an example to teach us to pray for the unsaved. Guilty, lost souls have been spared because Christians have asked God to save them. The greatest need today is for intercessors. Few people are ever saved until someone begins to pray for them by name. Check your prayer list. Are you praying for loved ones and those within your mission field by name? Pray, and keep praying, that God will grant them life and salvation.

Whatever you ask in prayer, if you have faith and believe, you will receive (Matt. 21:22).

Thought for Today: We can intercede for others and change their lives and eternity. What a privilege and responsibility!

Christ Revealed: As the Seed of Isaac (Gen. 17:19). Jesus was a descendant of Isaac (Luke 3:34; Heb. 11:18).

January 7: Read Genesis 19–21

Verses for Today: *"Then the Lord rained upon Sodom and upon Gomorrah brimstone and fire from the Lord out of heaven. . . . But his [Lot's] wife looked back from behind him, and she became a pillar of salt"* (Gen. 19:24, 26).

It does not appear that the inhabitants of Sodom had any warning of their sudden destruction. Lot's sons-in-law scoffed at Lot's warning and were typical of the people in Sodom whose hearts were hardened beyond repentance.

Lot's wife had known Abraham for many years. Through him, she had learned of the one true God and His guidance. Added to this, angels had come to her home and urged her to leave the city. Although she had taken steps toward salvation, she was destroyed with the wicked because her heart still longed for the things she was leaving behind.

God's dealing with Lot's wife shows us how He regards sin—how so few people escape the corruption that is in the world and are saved. Many people just want one more look, one more act of sin, one more object of self-satisfaction. But just as the people of Sodom were destroyed by fire and brimstone because of wickedness, Jesus taught that there will be a final judgment of eternal fire, where all the unsaved will be cast—a place of torment, with weeping and wailing and gnashing of teeth (Matt. 13:42).

These chapters in Genesis also bring us the story of Lot's daughters, who scheme and sleep with their father so that they might have a child. Surely, all of us can think of times we have schemed to get what we want. The Bible is right when it says, *We all, like sheep, have wandered off, and have turned to our own way, and God in mercy has laid on Jesus the iniquity of us all that we might be saved* (Isa. 53:6).

In Jesus, we are offered salvation from sin, judgment, and death. Once we have accepted Jesus, let us remember Lot's wife as an example. We are not to look back with longing to our old life (Luke 9:62; 17:32), but we are to look to Jesus (Heb. 12:2).

Our Lord is a *"rewarder of those who diligently seek Him"* (Heb. 11:6).

Thought for Today: Sin seeks to attract, control, and eventually destroy the soul, but Jesus sets us free and gives us new life.

Christ Portrayed: By Isaac, the promised son (Gen. 21:12)—in contrast to Ishmael, the son of a bondwoman (Gal. 4:22-31). Life in Christ sets us free from the bondage of sin, the law, and death (Rom. 6:14; 8:2; Gal. 4:5)!

January 8: Read Genesis 22–24

Verses for Today: *"And he said, O Lord God of my master Abraham, I pray thee, send me good speed this day, and shew kindness unto my master Abraham. . . . And let it come to pass, that the damsel to whom I shall say, Let down thy pitcher, I pray thee, that I may drink; and she shall say, Drink, and I will give thy camels drink also: let the same be she that thou hast appointed for thy servant Isaac"* (Gen. 24:12, 14).

Abraham was determined that his son Isaac would not marry a woman from the families of Canaan. For this reason, he sent his most-trusted servant (probably Eliezer) on a five-hundred-mile journey to choose a wife for Isaac in Mesopotamia, the land of Abraham's origin.

Eliezer undertook his mission with every desire to satisfy his master, as well as Almighty God. In reverent humility, Eliezer interceded in prayer on behalf of Isaac and Abraham, asking God to lead him to the woman He wanted Isaac to marry. When the young woman, Rebekah, came to the well, she did not know that God had led her to be the answer to Eliezer's prayer.

Eliezer of Damascus was an intercessor. He had nothing to gain for himself—simply a desire to fulfill God's will and bring blessings to others.

The Lord is seeking men and women who will intercede in prayer, making any sacrifice necessary in order to reach lost souls, and please the Master. Little do we realize how God can use us to be the answers to someone else's prayers as we simply go about our ordinary tasks and daily lives.

The earnest [passionate, heartfelt, continued] prayer of a righteous man can bring powerful results (James 5:16).

Thought for Today: God answers prayers of faith when we desire to please Him.

Christ Revealed: Through the sacrifice of Abraham's only son Isaac, whom he loved, and through Isaac's willingness to be offered (Gen. 22:7-10). God's demand of Abraham (to sacrifice his son) is shocking. Has God not given us this account in Scripture, so that we will pause and consider His willing and loving sacrifice of His son, Jesus, for us (John 10:11-18)?

January 9: Read Genesis 25–27

Verse for Today: *"And Esau said, Behold, I am at the point to die: and what profit shall this birthright do to me?"* (Gen. 25:32).

As the firstborn son, Esau was entitled to the family birthright that gave him the privilege of being the leader of the tribe and serving as priest. But this worldly minded man placed no importance on his spiritual inheritance and responsibilities. Consequently, he sold his birthright for one meal, thus exposing his lack of concern for the covenant promise that God had given to his grandfather, Abraham.

Two different ways of life are evident with these brothers. Esau lived to satisfy present desires, while Jacob had an intense desire to please God. As a result, Jacob not only became a great man of faith, but he additionally obtained the privilege of being an ancestor of Christ, the Messiah.

Even though some of Jacob's actions seem questionable, he did believe in the promises of God. In fact, as we read the history of Jacob, we might think that he did not deserve to become Israel—one of the great spiritual leaders of the people of God—but no child of God ever deserves or earns a right to His blessings. It is due to God's great mercy and love that we receive His gifts.

Jacob's life is a reminder that we are not to criticize the actions of other Christians because we have no way of knowing their hearts and how much they desire to please the Lord. Neither do we know how the Lord is working in the life of another. That person may be another Jacob, whom God is able to use for great purposes.

Who are we to judge someone else's servant? It is the master who will decide whether one succeeds or fails. And that person will succeed because the Lord is able to make the servant succeed (Rom. 14:4).

Thought for Today: We must not judge by mere appearances.

Christ Revealed: As the spiritual Seed (Gen. 26:4). All believers in Jesus are the children of promise (John 1:12-13; 1 John 3:9).

January 10: Read Genesis 28–30

Verse for Today: *"And, behold, I am with thee, and will keep thee in all places whither thou goest, and will bring thee again into this land; for I will not leave thee"* (Gen. 28:15).

Jacob feared that Esau would kill him as he threatened. So Jacob left his home in Beersheba and went to live five hundred miles away in Padan-aram, the land of his mother's family.

Stopping near Bethel along the way, Jacob, a lonely man, received God's comforting promise that He was with him. Following the miraculous revelation of God's never-failing presence, Jacob left Bethel and journeyed on to Padan-aram. There at the well, where the shepherds had gathered to water their sheep, he met Rachel, the daughter of Laban, his mother's brother. The Lord had brought him to this place to meet the woman who was to become his wife.

It was no accident or chance happening that Jacob stopped at the exact well where Rachel watered her father's flocks, or that she came by at that very hour. Unknown to either Jacob or Rachel, God worked out the details for His desired outcome.

The way before us may seem long and wearisome but, if we live to please God, we have His promise that He is protecting us and directing our path.

"For this God is our God for ever and ever: he will be our guide even unto death" (Ps. 48:14).

Thought for Today: There are no chance happenings or accidents in the lives of those who have placed their faith in Jacob's God.

Christ Revealed: As the Lord, whose unseen presence protects (Gen. 28:13-16; John 10:28-30; Rom. 8:28; 2 Thess. 3:3-5; 2 Tim. 4:18; Heb. 13:5-6).

January 11: Read Genesis 31–33

Verse for Today: *"I am the God of Bethel . . . where thou vowedst a vow unto me: now arise, get thee out from this land, and return unto the land of thy kindred"* (Gen. 31:13).

Jacob's life was filled with many fears and disappointments, but his greatest fear had haunted him for twenty years. Now he was forced to face his brother, who had vowed to kill him. Although Jacob had gone to great expense and made many plans in preparing to face Esau, he finally realized that his only hope rested in God and not his own efforts (Gen. 32:24-30).

Like Jacob, many Christians struggle in the energy of the flesh. We scheme, plan, and strive, all in an effort to accomplish victories. But God's mercy leads us to realize that to truly be victorious, we need God's guidance and help.

"Not by might, nor by power, but by my spirit, saith the Lord of hosts" (Zech. 4:6).

Thought for Today: We can depend on God to supply us with the answer that satisfies—Jesus.

Christ Revealed: As the angel of God, who guides (Gen. 31:11-13). Studies of Scripture reveal that *"the angel of God"* speaks not merely in the name of God, but as the Lord our God (Gen. 16:7-14; 22:12-15).[3]

January 12: Read Genesis 34–36

Verse for Today: *"And God appeared unto Jacob again, when he came out of Padan-aram, and blessed him"* (Gen. 35:9).

At least ten years passed since Jacob left Padan-aram and began his five-hundred-mile journey back to Bethel, the place where God had promised to bless him. He was off to a good start, but became sidetracked along the way by the beautiful valleys of Succoth.

He built a home there and settled down near Shechem, where he and his family became associated with their heathen neighbors. Jacob also failed to destroy the idol that his favorite wife, Rachel, had taken from her father. Jacob's failure to separate his family from ungodly influences and his other compromises resulted in the rape of his daughter, Dinah, and the cruel crimes of his sons. Not until then did he exert his parental authority and insist that his family get rid of

---

3   Following are links to two brief articles about the angel of the Lord: https://www.blueletterbible .org/faq/don_stewart/don_stewart_26.cfm;   and   https://www.gotquestions.org/angel-of-the -Lord.html.

all idols (Gen. 35:2, 4), purify themselves, leave their home near Shechem, and travel to Bethel.

Just as Jacob had to leave Succoth, each of us must separate ourselves from everything that prevents us from fulfilling God's will for our lives. Failure to separate ourselves from the world—its enticements, lusts, and desires—always ends in disaster.

Friendship with the world means enmity against the Lord (James 4:4). *Stop loving this evil world and all that it offers, for when we love other things, we show that we don't really love the Lord. Pride, power, possessions, and prestige—are not from God. They are from this evil world. This world is fading away, and these evil, forbidden things will go with it, but whoever keeps doing the will of God will live forever* (1 John 2:15-17).

Jesus declared, *"Ye are my friends, if ye do whatsoever I command you"* (John 15:14).

Thought for Today: The Lord's mercies are new every morning (Lam. 3:22-23). Let us rejoice that we can commit ourselves afresh to Him today!

Christ Revealed: As God Almighty (Gen. 35:11). Jesus said, *Before Abraham was born, I am* (John 8:58).

January 13: Read Genesis 37–39

Verses for Today: *"And Joseph's master took him, and put him into the prison, a place where the king's prisoners were bound: and he was there in the prison. But the Lord was with Joseph, and shewed him mercy, and gave him favour in the sight of the keeper of the prison"* (Gen. 39:20-21).

As a teenager, Joseph was misunderstood by his family and friends, cruelly mistreated, hated, betrayed, sold by his brothers as a slave, and taken to Egypt by Ishmaelite traders. In Egypt, Joseph was once again sold in the slave market. Then he was cast into prison. None of these events happened because of sin, for he had high moral integrity.

As a homesick prisoner, Joseph remained shut up for many years. During that time, his feet were injured by the cruel treatment he received (Ps. 105:17-18). Without a doubt, his faith was tested. Although he was innocent, he suffered as if he were a guilty criminal, bearing shame and physical cruelty. Still, Joseph did not complain and continued to live honorably.

God had not forgotten Joseph. In God's timing, He brought Joseph to the favorable attention of Pharaoh, through a serious of unusual events, and Pharaoh quickly made him a top official in the land of Egypt.

This was God's plan for Joseph from the beginning. Joseph was finally exalted to a position from which he could provide for the great needs of God's people in a time of famine. *God is the one who lifts us up out of the pit and miry clay and establishes us* (Ps. 40:2).

When we seek Him, the Lord works in our circumstances for good purposes. He allows events to come into our lives that we may not understand. But, through all that happens to us, He is able to test and purify our faith in Him, perfect our character, and reveal His salvation and glory.

And we know that all things work together for the good of those who love God and are called to His purpose (Rom. 8:28).

Thought for Today: As *"the Lord was with Joseph,"* He is with those who love Him and remain faithful to Him.

Christ Portrayed: By Joseph, who was rejected and struck down, but was then raised up by God to be a great ruler (Gen. 37:28)—all in fulfillment of prophecy. Joseph depicts Jesus, who was rejected, and will one day rule over all (Isa. 9:6-7; Eph. 1:20-21).

January 14: Read Genesis 40–42

Verses for Today: *"And Pharaoh said unto Joseph, Forasmuch as God hath shewed thee all this . . . Thou shalt be over my house. . . . And he made him to ride in the second chariot which he had; and they cried before him, Bow the knee: and he made him ruler over all the land of Egypt"* (Gen. 41:39-40, 43).

Satan used Potiphar's wife to cause Joseph to be put into prison (Gen. 39), but God was behind the scenes, guiding and protecting His servant until He was ready for Joseph to be exalted. It was no accident that Pharaoh had a dream, nor was it an accident that Pharaoh's butler remembered how Joseph had interpreted his dream two years earlier. God's time had come for Joseph to be released from prison and given a position of high honor and responsibility.

After Joseph interpreted Pharaoh's dream, Pharaoh made him ruler over the land of Egypt—second only to Pharaoh himself. What a marvelous change took place in Joseph's circumstances—from shame to glory, from prison to palace, from slave to honored ruler! This was his reward for faithfulness to the Lord.

In a number of ways, Joseph's life parallels the life of our Lord. He was dearly loved by his father; he suffered cruel treatment at the hands of those who should have loved him; he was wrongly accused and sentenced; and, in God's time, he was highly exalted. The day is coming when Jesus will be the highly glorified ruler over all the earth. Every knee shall bow and everyone will confess Him as Lord

(Rom. 14:11). However, before that day arrives, Jesus lovingly invites everyone who will *to come to Him and be saved* (Matt. 11:28).

"For the same Lord over all is rich unto all that call upon him. For whosoever shall call upon the name of the Lord shall be saved" (Rom. 10:12-13).

Thought for Today: Even when our situation seems hopeless, God will, in His time, deliver us.

Christ Revealed: Through Joseph's interpretation of Pharaoh's dream (Gen. 41:16-40). Jesus is the true interpreter of all circumstances and mysteries of life (Matt. 13:11-43; Eph. 1:9).

January 15: **Read Genesis 43–45**

Verse for Today: *"And Joseph said unto his brethren, Come near to me, I pray you"* (Gen. 45:4).

During the great famine, Jacob sent his sons to Egypt to buy food. As they stood before the great ruler of Egypt, asking for grain to carry back to their father, they were not aware that the ruler was Joseph, the brother whom they had sold into slavery about twenty years earlier.

After questioning them about their family, Joseph had them put into prison for three days—not for revenge, but to give them time to think. Joseph had not revealed his identity to them, but God caused them to realize that they were in prison because of their sin in selling Joseph.

When Joseph heard them confess how evil they had been in selling their brother (Gen. 42:21-23), he secretly wept and fully forgave them. He invited his brothers to come near him (Gen. 45:4), and fellowship was restored. There was no more barrier to be broken down and no aloofness—simply sweet fellowship and peace.

This is the way the Holy Spirit works in the hearts of lost sinners. He brings us to a place where we no longer try to defend ourselves, but we simply confess that we've sinned and ask for mercy and forgiveness. Then Christ draws closer to us and reveals Himself further. As we seek the Lord's mercy and forgiveness, He gives us new life, grace, and abundant blessings that we are to share with others.

Therefore, as God's chosen people, holy and dearly loved, know and exhibit compassion, kindness, humility, gentleness, and patience (Col. 3:12).

Thought for Today: There is no peace with God until sin has been confessed and forsaken.

Christ Revealed: Through Joseph's dealings with his brothers as Christ deals with us. The Lord helps us recognize God's mercy and forgiving love, and His sovereignty over the affairs of life (Gen. 45:5-8, 15; 2 Pet. 3:9).

January 16: **Read Genesis 46–48**

Verse for Today: *"And he blessed Joseph"* (Gen. 48:15).

Joseph, from early in his life, set his heart on pleasing the Lord, and God richly blessed him as a result of his faithfulness. In addition to this, before Joseph's father (Jacob) died, God led him to bestow a covenant blessing upon Joseph that carries down through his descendants and through the generations.

Oh, that Christians today would realize the rich rewards that God bestows upon all who put Him first and abandon worldly attractions! Alluring voices sound everywhere, demanding attention and seeking to draw Christians away from the Word of God. Far too often, the desire to satisfy self overrules one's desire to please the Lord.

God's greatest blessings, though, are bestowed upon faithful, steadfast followers—those who seek to faithfully serve the Lord, even when it interferes with what they personally would like to do.

Since future victory is sure, continue to remain firm and unmovable, and continue to faithfully devote yourselves to working for the Lord. Work without limit for you know that nothing you do for the Lord is ever wasted (1 Cor. 15:57-58).

Thought for Today: Have you set your heart on pleasing the Lord or self? Ask the Lord to help you to live to please Him.

Christ Portrayed: By Joseph, who was a great ruler able to sustain life and give needed bread and blessings to those under His care (Gen. 47:15). Jesus said, *For the Bread of God is He who comes down from heaven and gives life to the world* (John 6:33).

January 17: **Read Genesis 49–50**

Verse for Today: *"Joseph is a fruitful bough . . . whose branches run over the wall"* (Gen. 49:22).

When Jacob called his sons together and foretold God's blessing upon them, he emphasized the abuse Joseph had suffered: *"The archers have sorely grieved him, and shot at him"* (Gen. 49:23; 40:15; Ps. 105:17-18).

Joseph's difficulties began with his spiritual insight and God-given dreams that caused him to be sold into slavery by his brothers. Once Joseph had the dream from God, no record exists that Joseph complained or doubted God, even when his circumstances seemed to be taking him in the opposite direction. And at the end of his difficulties, he forgave his brothers, who had sold him into slavery. Through every event, God had been preparing Joseph to become the man He could use to protect and provide for His people in Egypt.

Perhaps the initial and most vital step toward fulfilling God's will is being convinced of His overruling hand and care in every situation. It is easy to manifest the characteristics of a Spirit-filled life—love, joy, and peace—when life is going well and with those we love. But as we allow Christ to rule our hearts, He enables us to go beyond painful feelings in trials. With Jesus, we can have peace in difficulties, and let go of feelings of ill will, jealousy, and resentment toward those we feel have wronged us. We can love the unlovely. In ourselves, we do not have the ability to cope with our emotions, but what we cannot do on our own, Christ can do for us, if we ask Him.

"For if ye forgive men their trespasses, your heavenly Father will also forgive you: but if ye forgive not men their trespasses, neither will your Father forgive your trespasses" (Matt. 6:14-15).

Thought for Today: It is always the responsibility of the innocent person to be forgiving.

Christ Revealed: A number of truths regarding Jesus are given in this verse: *"The sceptre* [right to rule] *shall not depart from Judah . . . until Shiloh* [Rest or Peace-Giver] *come"* (Gen. 49:10). Jesus is the Messiah, who descended from Abraham and came through the tribe of Judah (Luke 3:33). Jesus is the *"Prince of Peace"* (Isa. 9:6). He said, *"I will give you rest"* (Matt. 11:28). Christ will one day rule over the heavenly kingdom (Rev. 11:15).

 # EXODUS

The book of Exodus is a continuation of the history of the descendants of the twelve sons of Jacob. The last chapters of Genesis tell how Jacob and his family went to live in Egypt during the time Joseph was serving as a high official under Pharaoh. Because of Joseph, Pharaoh gave the Israelites the land of Goshen, the most productive land in Egypt. At that time, Jacob's family consisted of seventy people, but with God's hand of blessing on them, they grew into a nation.

After Joseph died, the prestige that the Israelites once enjoyed in Egypt gradually disappeared, to the extent that they became slaves in Egypt and endured great persecution. Exodus, which means "the way out" or "departure," is the story of their deliverance from captivity.

Chapters 1–11 cover the oppression of the Israelites and relate how God raised up Moses to lead His people out of Egypt and bring them back from exile—a great task. At the time they were released from slavery, it is estimated the

Israelites and "mixed multitude" (Ex. 12:37-38) numbered well over two million people. Moses, through the Lord's direction, pronounced a series of ten increasingly destructive plagues upon Egypt's land and the people.

Chapters 12–13 recount the Israelites' miraculous rescue and departure from the country. Deliverance was made possible by their faith and obedience in following God's directives, which included sacrificing an innocent lamb, applying its blood to their doorposts, and eating this Passover lamb. Their escape includes the harrowing, but miraculous and safe passage of the people through the Red Sea.

Chapters 14–18 provide an account of the Israelites' pilgrimage from the Red Sea to Mount Sinai. This journey lasted approximately fifty days.

Chapters 19–40 take place at Mount Sinai. God gave Moses the Ten Commandments (or first law), along with detailed instructions for constructing the tabernacle, worshiping God, and offering sacrifices, in order that the people would be able to experience the Lord's presence.

Exodus is a thrilling, accurate story in itself, but it is also given to us to reveal deep spiritual truths regarding our relationship with the Lord. From the time a priest entered the tabernacle court's gate and fenced enclosure until he entered the Holy Place, each procedure reveals Christ and a believer's relationship with Him. Ultimately, God filled the tabernacle with His glory and presence.

Renowned Bible teacher Dr. J. Vernon McGee wonderfully summarizes this incredible book: "Exodus begins in gloom and ends in glory."[4]

Exodus truly highlights God's great love for people; His ability to protect and provide for us, no matter how great our difficulties; and His desire to fellowship with us and bring us into His glorious presence.

January 18: Read Exodus 1–4

Verse for Today: *"Now therefore go, and I will be with thy mouth, and teach thee what thou shalt say"* (Ex. 4:12).

When God called Moses to lead the Israelites to freedom, Moses made excuses as to why he could not do the task. He was afraid to go alone, even when God

---

4   Dr. J. Vernon McGee (1904-1988) was a gifted pastor, theologian, Bible teacher, and radio minister. He possessed a memorable voice, folksy personality, and unique teaching style. In the 1940s, while pastoring a church in Pasadena, California, he began a weekly radio broadcast, called the *Open Bible Hour*. His radio program evolved, and in 1967, he launched *Thru the Bible,* a systematic study of each book of the Bible, from Genesis to Revelation. It eventually became a five-year study, which has been translated into more than one hundred languages, and is broadcast worldwide every weekday on Trans World Radio. Searching online provides easy access to many media options for Dr. McGee's materials. The quote on Exodus is from https://www.blueletterbible.org/Comm/mcgee_j_vernon/notes-outlines/exodus/exodus-outline.cfm.

said He would be with him. Moses could not be persuaded until the Lord permitted Aaron to be the spokesman.

Although Aaron's eloquence added nothing in the way of spiritual power, Moses was willing to go when God assured him that Aaron, a mere human like himself, would be with him.

Oh, how prone we are to trust something or someone other than the living God! We may step out boldly when we are supported by other people—even though they are mere humans, like ourselves. Christians should boldly act upon God's Word, knowing that His Spirit indwells every believer (John 14:17).

Many Christians have failed to obey the Lord, giving the excuse that they are inadequately prepared for an effective ministry. But all the schooling in the world is useless unless the Lord guides the Christian and instructs that person in what to say. God is able to give us what to say and how to say it (Luke 12:12). As we abide in Jesus, we can bear good fruit and accomplish much for Him (John 15:4).

For what this world considers to be wisdom is nonsense in God's sight (1 Cor. 3:19).

Thought for Today: God is more concerned with willingness than He is with eloquence.

Christ Revealed: As the *"I AM THAT I AM,"* who commissioned Moses (Ex. 3:13-14). *"Jesus said unto them, Verily, verily, I say unto you, Before Abraham was, I am"* (John 8:58). *Jesus is the same yesterday, today, and forever* (Heb. 13:8).

January 19: Read Exodus 5–7

Verse for Today: *"Then the Lord said unto Moses, Now shalt thou see what I will do to Pharaoh: for with a strong hand shall he let them go, and with a strong hand shall he drive them out of his land"* (Ex. 6:1).

Although Moses had just blamed God for the added suffering that had come upon the Hebrew slaves, the Lord did not answer Moses's impatient, faultfinding questions. God merely reaffirmed His purpose to free His people.

Pharaoh defiantly refused to let the Israelites leave Egypt (Ex. 5:2), but the God of creation declared that Pharaoh *would* let them go. In fact, God added that Pharaoh himself would drive them out of the land.

Moses became frustrated with the Lord when the Egyptian officials *increased* the people's burdens and suffering, and the Israelites angrily criticized him, but Moses did the right thing and went back to the right place for answers. He went back to God, who again confirmed His Word. God would keep His promise. Moses's faith was strengthened, and he stayed faithful to God and the task.

No matter how much others may criticize, threaten, or persecute us, they will not succeed against the purposes of God. *No wisdom, insight, or plan can succeed against the Lord* (Prov. 21:30). Not even the Evil One's fiery darts of suffering, disappointments, or opposition can prevail. *God has assured us that His Word will accomplish what He intends for it to accomplish* (Isa. 55:11).

God's Spirit that is in us is more powerful than the spirit that is at work in the world (1 John 4:4).

Thought for Today: Don't look at the problems you face, but look to God's Word and promises.

Christ Revealed: As the Redeemer from the bondage of sin. *"I will bring you out . . . I will redeem you"* (Ex. 6:6). *"Christ hath redeemed us from the curse of the law"* (Gal. 3:13; 1 Pet. 1:18-25).

January 20: Read Exodus 8–10

Verse for Today: *"And Pharaoh said, I will let you go, that ye may sacrifice to the Lord your God in the wilderness; only ye shall not go very far away: intreat for me"* (Ex. 8:28).

Egypt was the most powerful kingdom on earth at the time the Israelites were in bondage. Her idols and gods were considered equally powerful. Consequently, when Moses requested that the Israelites be permitted to worship the one true God, it was an insult to Pharaoh, who was considered one of the gods of Egypt.

Pharaoh did not refuse Moses's request to let the people worship Jehovah God, but he disagreed with the way they should worship. He wanted them to compromise what God had told them to do. By studying Pharaoh's three efforts to cause Moses to compromise the Word of God, we can learn several reasons why people experience spiritual defeat.

First, *"sacrifice to your God in the land"* (Ex. 8:25). Worship your God, but do not leave Egypt; be one of us. This is typical of how a Christian is tempted to stay enmeshed in worldly activities and fail to live a separated life. There are many people who consent to worship God, but do not intend to forsake their sins or worldly interests (2 Cor. 6:16-17).

Second, *"ye shall not go very far"* (Ex. 8:28). Just be lukewarm; don't become too involved in serving the Lord. Lukewarm Christians want to worship in their own way, cooperate with the world, and avoid any service for Jesus that conflicts with their own desires. They don't want to stand out for Christ.

Third, *"Go . . . only let your flocks and your herds be stayed"* (Ex. 10:24). Keep your Christian testimony and your work separate. Keep yourself entangled with the world in your business associations and relationships.

Satan seeks to deceive us into thinking that it is enough to simply believe in God. Yet, our worship is unacceptable to God unless it is according to His Word.

"He that saith, I know him, and keepeth not his commandments, is a liar, and the truth is not in him" (1 John 2:4).

Thought for Today: In seeking worldly advantages, it is easy to lose sight of God's will.

Christ Revealed: As a Light to His people: *"There was thick darkness in all the land of Egypt . . . but all the children of Israel had light in their dwellings"* (Ex. 10:22-23). Jesus declared, *"I am the light of the world: he that followeth me shall not walk in darkness"* (John 8:12). *"The Lord will lighten my darkness"* (2 Sam. 22:29).

January 21: **Read Exodus 11–13**

Verses for Today: *"For I will pass through the land of Egypt this night, and will smite all the firstborn in the land of Egypt. . . . And when I see the blood, I will pass over you"* (Ex. 12:12-13).

Many of the Israelites probably were skeptical of the peculiar method of deliverance from Egypt. Their only hope of escape from the death angel, however, was to kill a lamb and apply the blood to the lintel and the two side posts of their doors.

Some could have protested, expressing their distaste for the sight of blood above and around their doors. The "more enlightened" may have wanted to pay a guard to protect their homes from intruders, but deliverance from the death angel could not be bought. No amount of gold could replace the blood. Nor was there a family so good that its members did not need to apply the blood of a lamb as God said. God had only one plan, and His divine command had to be obeyed.

Just as the blood of the Passover lamb was the only possible means of saving the life of the firstborn, so the blood of Jesus is the sole means by which sinful man can receive eternal life. Many people believe that as long as they are sincere, some other means will satisfy God, but they are still eternally lost.

Because Christ was sinless and offered himself as an eternal and spiritual sacrifice to God, His blood is much more powerful and makes our consciences clear. Because we no longer do things that lead to death, and our consciences are cleansed from dead works, we are truly able to serve the living God (Heb. 9:14).

Thought for Today: Our assurance of eternal life is only through personal acceptance of Jesus Christ as Lord and Savior.

Christ Revealed: Through the sacrifice of lambs without blemish. Not one of the lamb's bones was to be broken (Ex. 12:5, 46). It was foretold of Jesus: *"He keepeth all his bones: not one of them is broken"* (Ps. 34:20; John 19:36). We are redeemed *"with the precious blood of Christ, as of a lamb without blemish and without spot"* (1 Pet. 1:19).

January 22: Read Exodus 14–16

Verse for Today: *"Then sang Moses and the children of Israel this song unto the Lord . . . for he hath triumphed gloriously"* (Ex. 15:1).

Soon after the Israelites left Egypt, Pharaoh decided to go after them and bring them back. God miraculously parted the Red Sea, and all the Israelites escaped to the other side, but Pharaoh's army was drowned when the soldiers attempted to cross.

The Israelites sang praises to the Lord for the wondrous deliverance from Pharaoh and his armies (Ex. 15:1-19). They did not praise Moses, their great leader; nor did they attribute their victory to their own wisdom, strength, or good fortune. They recognized that this was the hand of God, and they praised Him for His power, holiness, glory, mercy, and supremacy.

This song of Moses and the Lamb will continue in heaven for all eternity. This first song presented in the Scriptures is mentioned again in the last book of the Bible (Rev. 15:3). Combining judgment and grace, destruction and deliverance, this song sets forth God's final victory over all enemies—a victory that all Christians will celebrate in heaven.

All who overcome shall inherit His blessings: He will be their God, and they will be His people (Rev. 21:7).

Thought for Today: How sweet will be the heavenly song when all the travails of life and the enemies of the soul are forever defeated!

Christ Revealed: Through the bread (manna) from heaven (Ex. 16:15). Jesus declared, *"I am the living bread which came down from heaven"* (John 6:35, 41, 48, 51).

January 23: Read Exodus 17–19

Verse for Today: *"And the people thirsted there for water . . . and said, Wherefore is this that thou hast brought us up out of Egypt, to kill us and our children and our cattle with thirst?"* (Ex. 17:3).

From the time the Israelites left Egypt to the time they reached the border of the Promised Land, they were so concerned with satisfying their immediate needs that they always found fault and murmured when they faced problems. They even spoke against God Himself (Ps. 78:17). Therefore, that generation never experienced the satisfaction and blessings of fulfilling God's purpose—conquering the Promised Land.

Every thought of unbelief in the wisdom and goodness of God is evidence of a self-centered person who believes that he—not God—knows best and should control the affairs of his life.

At times, it may seem that God has not met our needs, but when we praise the Lord during times of testing, it expresses faith, helps our attitude, honors God, and is the key to victory and greater blessings from Him (1 Thess. 5:18). The Christian's faith is not based on favorable circumstances, but in a person—the Lord Jesus Christ.

God has promised to supply your every need according to His riches in glory by Christ Jesus (Phil. 4:19).

Thought for Today: Peace comes when we accept our circumstances as from the Lord, and seek to please Him in them.

Christ Revealed: As the Rock, and the Water that came forth (Ex. 17:6). *"For they drank of that spiritual Rock that followed them: and that Rock was Christ"* (1 Cor. 10:4).

January 24: Read Exodus 20–22

Verses for Today: *"And God spake all these words, saying, I am the Lord thy God. . . . Thou shalt have no other gods before me"* (Ex. 20:1-3).

The Ten Commandments were *"written with the finger of God"* (Ex. 31:18). These commandments reveal the absolute perfection of God's holy nature, and they reveal the terrible sinfulness of mankind.

If the Lord had given or commanded anything less than what is perfect, He would have been compromising—which He cannot do. Humanly speaking, though, a person cannot keep the law perfectly—whereby the mind, body, and spirit are in total agreement and obedient to the law—because *the natural mind is not capable of obeying God's Law* (Rom. 8:7). No one, except Christ Himself, has ever been able to live without sinning.

This points out how far mankind fell when Adam sinned and how true Scripture is, which states that *all have sinned and come short of God's glorious ideal* (Rom. 3:23). Everyone bears the characteristics of the fallen nature—*there is none that seeks God's will* (Rom. 3:11).

However, by accepting Jesus as our Savior, we receive His nature, and *"the Spirit of God"* indwells us (Rom. 8:9). Then our spirit agrees with the Lord that His Word is good, right, holy, and just; and our inward desire is to do what He has commanded (1 John 4:5-6).

For what the law could not do, ineffective as it was through the flesh (the entire nature of man without the Holy Spirit), God did. He sent His own Son in the likeness of sinful flesh and as an offering for sin. He condemned sin in the flesh, in order that the requirement of the law might be fulfilled in us, who do not walk according to the flesh, but according to the Spirit (Rom. 8:3-4).

Thought for Today: Are you seeking to know the Lord and follow His will as you read His Word?

Christ Revealed: The Ten Commandments portray the nature and character of Jesus (Ex. 20:1-17). He fulfilled the commandments perfectly, and He is without sin (Heb. 4:15). Christ gave us a New Commandment— *"That ye love one another; as I have loved you, that ye also love one another"* (John 13:34).

January 25: Read Exodus 23–25

Verse for Today: *"And he said unto Moses, Come up unto the Lord, thou, and Aaron, Nadab, and Abihu, and seventy of the elders of Israel; and worship ye afar off"* (Ex. 24:1).

God Himself summoned these men into His very presence. Never before had Jehovah—the God of creation—met with a group of men. Since God is absolutely holy, and man is defiled by sin, they had to worship Him from a distance. To do otherwise would mean instant death. Yet, they seemed at ease for they ate and drank in His presence (Ex. 24:11).

Notice what made it possible for them to be able to eat and drink in His presence. Moses had arisen early, built an altar, offered burnt offerings, and sacrificed peace offerings of oxen to the Lord (Ex. 24:4-5). These actions were in obedience to what the Lord had said to Moses (Ex. 20:24). The shedding of blood made it possible for the people to have a new relationship with God.

After the blood was applied, Moses, Aaron, Nadab, Abihu, and seventy of the leaders of Israel went up the mountain and feasted in the presence of the God of Israel (Ex. 24:8-10).

These events point out the importance of the blood of Jesus and the wonderful privileges it obtains for all who have acknowledged themselves as lost sinners and received Him as their Savior.

"For Christ also hath once suffered for sins, the just for the unjust, that he might bring us to God, being put to death in the flesh, but quickened by the Spirit" (1 Pet. 3:18).

Thought for Today: Because of Christ's sacrificial death on the cross, each of us has the privilege of being in His presence through prayer and hearing Him speak to us through His Word.

Christ Portrayed: By the servant who voluntarily bound himself to his master, although he was free to do whatever he wished (Ex. 21:5-6). This is a picture of Jesus's devotion to the Father. *"I delight to do thy will, O my God"* (Ps. 40:8).

January 26: Read Exodus 26–28

Verse for Today: *"And thou shalt rear up the tabernacle according to the fashion thereof which was shewed thee in the mount"* (Ex. 26:30).

God gave detailed instructions for the design of the tabernacle because His purpose was to have a place where He could reveal Himself to His people and dwell among them. The tabernacle, furnishings, and enclosure reveal much to us about God's holiness and His desire to commune with mankind, and they portray Jesus.[5]

The enclosure contained only one entrance (Ex. 27:16). This illustrates our Lord as the only way to God's presence. Jesus declared, *I am the door: whoever enters in by Me shall be saved and find freedom and pasture* [peace, provisions, and security] (John 10:9).

Once inside the courtyard, the worshiper approached the brazen altar (or altar of burnt offering). The sacrifices offered on it were a type of Christ's death (Heb. 13:10-12). Just as the ram was wholly burned upon the altar, Jesus (being fully dedicated to God) gave His life on the cross for our sins. Jesus is *the Lamb of God, who takes away our sin* (John 1:29). In addition, He is *our High Priest* (Heb. 4:14).

"Now of the things which we have spoken this is the sum: We have such an high priest, who is set on the right hand of the throne of the Majesty in the heavens" (Heb. 8:1).

Thought for Today: God no longer lives in a tabernacle; He dwells within the heart of every believer.

Christ Revealed: Through the brazen (bronze) altar, where the sacrifices were burned (Ex. 27:1-8). Jesus is our Sacrifice (Eph. 1:7).

January 27: Read Exodus 29–31

Verse for Today: *"This shall be a continual burnt offering throughout your generations at the door of the tabernacle of the congregation before the Lord: where I will meet you, to speak there unto thee"* (Ex. 29:42).

---

5   Studying a tabernacle diagram can increase our understanding of many spiritual truths. Two helpful website links are https://www.goodseed.com/diagram-of-the-tabernacle-and-basic -layout.html and https://www.youtube.com/watch?v=Ah4h-SQw9XQ.

When the Israelite worshiper brought an acceptable sacrifice to the brazen altar to present a burnt offering, the priest killed the animal and prepared the sacrifice on behalf of the worshiper. The *"continual burnt offering"* provided a way for the Israelite to be reconciled to a holy God. Through the burnt offering, God promised: *"I will meet you, to speak there unto thee."* The Lord wants to meet and speak with His people!

Some people assume that as long as their outward conduct is good, God is pleased with them. Mere obedience to the law does not soften and warm the heart, though, since the letter of the law leads to death. It is the indwelling Spirit of God that gives life (2 Cor. 3:6).

When we acknowledge our sinful, lost condition and turn to Christ—the One who became an acceptable offering for our sins—our hearts will be filled with His presence. The Bible will become more than "dos and don'ts," and we will grow in His great love for us!

It is the indwelling Holy Spirit that enables a Christian to worship God acceptably and fellowship with Him (Luke 1:67-68; John 4:23-24; Eph. 5:18-20).

Thought for Today: The power of victorious Christian living is experienced through prayer and hearing what God has to say as we read His Word.

Christ Revealed: Through the laver. (The laver was a large basin set upon a pedestal in the court of the tabernacle that contained water for the cleansing of the priests and washing of the sacrifices in the temple service.) Jesus is our container and the dispenser of *"Living Water"* (Ex. 30:18; John 4:10; 1 Cor. 10:4; Heb. 10:22).

January 28: Read Exodus 32–34

Verse for Today: *"And the Lord said unto Moses, I have seen this people, and, behold, it is a stiff-necked people"* (Ex. 32:9).

While Moses was on Mount Sinai, waiting for the Lord's instructions regarding the way they were to worship the holy God, the Israelites were at the foot of the mountain, proclaiming *"a feast to the Lord."* They presented burnt offerings and made a golden calf as an object of worship (Ex. 32:5-10).

The golden calf stands as a symbol of human intellect, which devises a system of worship apart from divine direction. It bears out the fact that when people turn from the Lord and ignore His Word, they will worship the works of their own hands (Acts 7:41; Rom. 1:21, 23).

True worship occurs when we live and worship in obedience to His Word. When we understand all that Christ has done for us, the relationship God desires to have with us, and the blessings He wants to give us, our hearts are moved to love Him and follow Him. He enables us to worship and fellowship with Him, and live according to His Word.

Jesus said, *Why do you call me "Lord" and do not practice what I tell you?* (Luke 6:46).

Thought for Today: We are given grace, provisions, and assistance, so that we may live to please Him.

Christ Revealed: As the One who is ever-present. *"My presence shall go with thee, and I will give thee rest"* (Ex. 33:14; Matt. 11:28; 28:20).

January 29: Read Exodus 35–37

Verse for Today: *"The candlestick also for the light, and his furniture, and his lamps, with the oil for the light"* (Ex. 35:14).

After the priest had washed his hands and feet at the laver, he proceeded toward the tabernacle and entered the only door to the Holy Place.

On the left was the seven-branched, golden candlestick, which provided the only source of light in the Holy Place. Without this light from the golden candlestick, the room would have been in total darkness. The golden candlestick represents Christ, who bestows light to make Himself known through God's Word (John 1:1; 8:12).

On the right was the table of showbread with its twelve loaves sprinkled with incense. The "showbread" was to always be shown, or constantly before, and in the presence of God. This bread was only to be eaten by the priests and only in the Holy Place. None of it could be removed and eaten elsewhere. The showbread, or "bread of presence," suggests more than bodily nourishment. It represents the need to stay in the presence of God—gaining spiritual insight and strength that are not obtainable in any other way. Beyond our ability to explain, the Holy Spirit enlightens, empowers, and transforms the lives of those who prayerfully continue to "eat" the Bread of Life.

Jesus said, *I am the living bread that came down from heaven. Whoever eats of this bread will live forever* (John 6:51).

Thought for Today: Christ is the Bread of Life, the Sustainer of each individual believer.

Christ Revealed: Through the *"candlestick"* [lampstand] (Ex. 35:14). Jesus is *"the Light of the World"* (John 9:5; Luke 1:78-79).

January 30: Read Exodus 38–39

Verse for Today: *"Thus was all the work of the tabernacle of the tent of the congregation finished: and the children of Israel did according to all that the Lord commanded Moses"* (Ex. 39:32).

The word tabernacle means *"to dwell."* Absolutely nothing about the tabernacle was left to human planning, for God had an exact design for the tabernacle—His holy dwelling place.

Ever since Adam and Eve sinned in the garden, God continued to draw people back into a new, close, spiritual, and loving relationship with Himself based on His righteousness and mercy. God had walked with Adam in the garden of Eden; He had spoken to Abraham; and He had given His Law to Moses, but the tabernacle in the wilderness was God's first dwelling place on earth.

Later, God the Son came to earth to *dwell* among people. Scripture declares that the Word was made flesh and dwelled (lived or tabernacled) among us (John 1:14).

After Jesus ascended into heaven, He sent His Spirit to indwell each one who receives Him as Lord and Savior. Believers are *dwelling places for His Holy Spirit!* (See 1 Cor. 6:19 and Eph. 2:21-22.)

No true child of God can plead ignorance to the fact that God wants him to live a different kind of life from the way the world lives. The life He would have us live is more than keeping the Ten Commandments, and is never the result of human wisdom. It is made possible by the indwelling Holy Spirit, who enlightens our understanding as we read the Word of God and seek Him. *"The Spirit of truth . . . will guide you into all truth"* (John 16:13).

> *"And I saw a new heaven and a new earth: for the first heaven and the first earth were passed away. . . . And I heard a great voice out of heaven saying, Behold, the tabernacle of God is with men, and he will dwell with them, and they shall be his people, and God himself shall be with them, and be their God"* (Rev. 21:1, 3).

Thought for Today: Have you ever sensed God's Spirit and presence in your life? Are you seeking to grow in being aware of Him and listening and watching for Him?

Christ Revealed: The golden altar and the incense represent prayers continually going up to heaven (Ex. 39:38). The New Testament reveals that Jesus ever lives and intercedes for us in prayer! He *"is able also to save them to the uttermost that* come unto God by him, seeing he ever liveth to make intercession for them" (Heb. 7:25; see also John 17:9).

January 31: Read Exodus 40

Verses for Today: *"Set up the tabernacle. . . . And thou shalt put therein the ark of the testimony"* (Ex. 40:2-3).

The ark of the testimony was about four feet long, two feet wide, and two feet high (Ex. 25:10; 37:1-5). It was made of wood and overlaid with gold, both within and without, so that nothing but the gold was seen. It was the visible symbol of God's presence.

The ark typifies the Lord Jesus. The wood and the gold represent the two natures of our Lord—the human and the divine. The two stone tablets preserved inside the ark picture Christ as the Word (Ex. 25:21-22; 31:18; Deut. 10:1-2; John 1:1-2). Also within the ark was a golden pot of manna—food that God gave to the Israelites for their journey to the Promised Land after their release from bondage. This manna foreshadows Jesus as the Bread of Life—the food of His faithful people. In addition, the ark held Aaron's rod that budded (Num. 17)—a symbol of the resurrection of Jesus Christ.

After leaving Mount Sinai, the ark of the testimony went before the Israelites (Num. 10:33)—a type of Christ as the leader of His pilgrim people. When they reached the Jordan River, the ark of the Lord's presence entered, dividing the waters for Israel to pass over on dry ground. This symbolizes our Lord Jesus Christ making possible the impossible to be *"more than conquerors"* (Rom. 8:37).

The ark of the testimony led the way as Israel marched around the walls of Jericho. This teaches us that strongholds of Satan will fall when the people of God are faithful to His Word.

The man who has received My commands and obeys them is the one who loves Me. My Father loves whoever loves Me; I too will love him and show Myself to him (John 14:21).

Thought for Today: Are you seeking to have Christ lead you and reveal Himself to you?

Christ Portrayed: By the high priest (Ex. 40:13). *"But Christ being come an high priest. . . . now to appear in the presence of God for us"* (Heb. 9:11-24, and entire chapter). Other references regarding Jesus as our High Priest include Ps. 110:4; Zech. 6:13; Heb. 2:17; 4:14-16; 5:6; 6:20; 7:23-28; 10:12.

February

 ## LEVITICUS

In Leviticus, God gave instructions to the Israelites regarding how to live holy lives. *"Be holy, because I am holy"* is a key statement for the entire book (Lev. 11:44-45). The word *"holy"* was not given in Genesis, but now, it appears about ninety times in the book of Leviticus.

Scripture reveals that our enjoyment of God's presence is based upon our trust in Him and our obedience to His Word. Obedience brings us into harmony with His holy nature, thereby imparting His peace. The word *"peace"* is mentioned more times in Leviticus (in the King James Version) than it is in any other book of the Bible.

Leviticus lays out laws for worship and religious ceremonies, and to regulate all of life. Instructions were given for sacrificial offerings that made it possible for God's people to draw near to Him. Direction was given for five sacrifices, which represent different aspects of Christ, the Lamb of God, giving Himself as a sacrifice for lost sinners. Scripture also reveals that Jesus is our High Priest.

The events in the book of Leviticus possibly took place in just one month, beginning with God speaking from the erected tabernacle (Ex. 40:1-2; Num. 1:1). As God continues to restore mankind's broken relationship with Him, He draws nearer to the Israelites. No longer was God speaking from Mt. Sinai, but now, He speaks from the mercy seat within the holy of holies in the tabernacle.

Chapters 1–7 relate instructions for the sacrificial offerings.

Chapters 8–10 relate details of the priesthood; the ordination of Aaron and his sons; and the tabernacle.

Chapters 11–15 provide regulations for holy living.

Chapter 16 is devoted to the Day of Atonement.

Chapters 17–27 include God's instructions for the five feasts and the laws governing holiness and worship.

As the people distinguished between the holy and the common (Lev. 10:10) and obeyed all of God's instructions, His glory appeared to them (Lev. 9:6, 23-24). His glory was so wonderful, fearful, and spectacular that it made the people shout for joy and fall down (Lev. 9:24).

February 1: Read Leviticus 1–3

Verse for Today: *"And he shall offer of the sacrifice of the peace offering an offering made by fire unto the Lord"* (Lev. 3:3).

The peace offering was the last one presented because there could be no peace or fellowship with God until all the regulations of the sin and trespass offerings had been obeyed. The peace offering was a *"sweet savor offering,"* giving to God that which satisfied Him. The bread used in this sacrifice had to be made without yeast, which was symbolic of sin. The withholding of yeast in the offering represented the removal of any corruption.

This peace offering naturally follows the other sacrifices and illustrates completeness and restored fellowship between God and man. It was different from the burnt offering and the meal offering in a number of ways. The peace offering was a joyful occasion of thankfulness for God's blessings and always shared with others. As the priest, the worshiper, and family and friends ate this meal, they were conscious of the presence of God, and were grateful for His ability and faithfulness to protect His people and supply their needs.

Many Christians never experience the full meaning of the peace offering. They have been delivered from the power of sin (Rom. 6:22; Jude 1:24) and have *peace with God.* They may even desire to present their bodies as a living sacrifice as represented in the burnt offering—but they know little of the *peace of God,* which goes beyond human understanding (Phil. 4:7).

We can ask for nothing greater than having the God of peace ruling our hearts! As we spend time in His presence and seek His guidance for everything, His truth, loving-kindness, and power enable us to rid ourselves of ill will, jealousy, envy, and strife (all things that destroy our peace).

Let the peace of God, which comes from Christ, be always present in your hearts and lives for this is your responsibility and privilege as members of His body. And always be thankful (Col. 3:15).

Thought for Today: As we yield our lives to the Lord of peace, we experience His peace.

Christ Revealed: Through the grain (meal) offering made without yeast, which symbolizes the removal of sin (Lev. 2:11). Christ is without sin (Heb. 4:15).

February 2: Read Leviticus 4–6

Verse for Today: *"And he shall bring the bullock unto the door of the tabernacle of the congregation before the Lord; and shall lay his hand upon the bullock's head, and kill the bullock before the Lord"* (Lev. 4:4).

The sin offering was the first sacrifice presented to God. Each person was required to bring one's own animal to offer upon the altar before the tabernacle. With other offerings, the Israelite came as a worshiper; but when offering a sin or trespass offering, he came confessing himself as a sinner. The offerer placed his hands upon the head of the animal as an act of passing his sins to the innocent animal. The animal was then put to death, instead of the sinner. The priest sprinkled the blood before the Lord, and the worshiper's sins were covered (but his sins were not fully removed until Christ died on the cross—Heb. 10:9-14).

The sin offering was a testimony not only to the fact that the worshiper was a sinner, but that God provided the way for him to be acceptable to God.

When Jesus shed His blood on the cross for the sins of mankind, there was no longer any need for animal sacrifices. *"For he hath made him to be sin for us, who knew no sin; that we might be made the righteousness of God in him"* (2 Cor. 5:21).

The Lord Jesus Christ not only presented Himself as a sacrifice to God, but He also fulfilled the position of the priest, becoming our great High Priest who *"ever liveth to make intercession"* for us (Heb. 7:25). Thus, He became both the sacrifice for our sins and the mediator between God and man (Heb. 2:17; 4:15).

"If we confess our sins, he is faithful and just to forgive us our sins, and to cleanse us from all unrighteousness" (1 John 1:9).

Thought for Today: Christ, who is in the presence of God, intercedes on our behalf when we pray (Heb. 7:25).

Christ Revealed: Through the body of the young bull, which was burned outside the camp (Lev. 4:12). This pictures Jesus as He suffered *outside the gate* (Heb. 13:11-12).

February 3: **Read Leviticus 7–8**

Verse for Today: *"In the place where they kill the burnt offering shall they kill the trespass offering: and the blood thereof shall he sprinkle round about upon the altar"* (Lev. 7:2).

The trespass offering was brought for specified acts of wrongdoing, either against God or man. The offender was just as guilty before God for trespasses committed in ignorance because ignorance is due to willful neglect of His Word (Lev. 5:15-6:7).

The trespass offering was part of the sin offering. God demanded that anyone who had committed a trespass bring an offering, restore what had been taken, plus give an additional 20 percent to the one wronged. The offerer did not eat any of this trespass offering, as with the peace offering. The sacrificer came as one unworthy, and the purpose for the offering was to restore fellowship with God.

Our Lord has provided mankind with His Word—the Bible. It sets forth the moral and spiritual principles necessary to maintain harmony with God and man. All who neglect to read the Bible, or having read it refuse to live according to its revelation, will face the judgment of God.

"For if we sin wilfully after that we have received the knowledge of the truth, there remaineth no more sacrifice for sins" (Heb. 10:26).

Thought for Today: How foolish it is to depend on one's conscience for guidance without having enlightenment from God's Word.

Christ Portrayed: By Moses consecrating the priests, who presented themselves for the work (Lev. 8:23-24). Through Christ, we offer ourselves for God's service (Rom. 12:1).

February 4: Read Leviticus 9–10

Verses for Today: *"The glory of the Lord appeared unto all the people. And there came a fire out from before the Lord, and consumed upon the altar the burnt offering and the fat: which when all the people saw, they shouted, and fell on their faces"* (Lev. 9:23-24).

God's law required the Israelites to bring sin and trespass offerings. Additionally, public burnt sacrifices were offered each morning and evening. A burnt offering could be brought by one who felt the need to humbly come before the Lord with deep gratitude for His mercy, and to confess any offenses and failings that were not specifically mentioned by the law. This burnt offering signified deep dedication and consecration to God.

The offering sacrifice could be a young bull, ram, goat, or sheep. The very poor could bring a pair of turtledoves or two young pigeons (Luke 2:24), having assurance that their offerings would be as fully acceptable to God as the costly gifts of their more prosperous neighbors.

Whatever was chosen for the offering, it was to be the most excellent of its kind—*"a male without blemish"* (Lev. 22:19). It would have been highly offensive to God to offer anything that was lame, blind, diseased, or in any other way imperfect. This offering was a type of our perfect Savior—the Lamb of God, who was *"without blemish and without spot"* (1 Pet. 1:19).

This is a reminder that we are to offer our best to God. We should offer the best of our tithes, talents, and time. Many people think that they can meet their needs first, and then consider what they will give to God from what remains.

This approach might agree with worldly economics, but it is spiritually unsound. No person is too poor to give. We cannot shirk our responsibilities to give and serve, by rationalizing that someone else will do it, or can do it, better.

Give according to what you have purposed to give, not grudgingly, or of necessity, for God loves a cheerful giver (2 Cor. 9:7). *Bring all your tithe, so that there may be provisions in your house; prove me in this, for I will open the windows of heaven, and pour out on you a blessing* (Mal. 3:10).

Thought for Today: Are you offering your finances, resources, and your personal service to God for His glory and kingdom work?

Christ Revealed: Through the sacrifice of a lamb without defect (Lev. 9:3). Jesus is the perfect Lamb of God (John 1:29; 1 Pet. 1:19).

February 5: Read Leviticus 11–13

Verses for Today: *"And the leper in whom the plague is, his clothes shall be rent, and his head bare, and he shall put a covering upon his upper lip, and shall cry, 'Unclean, unclean.' All the days wherein the plague shall be in him he shall be defiled; he is unclean: he shall dwell alone; without the camp shall his habitation be"* (Lev. 13:45-46).

The word *"leper"* struck terror in the heart of an Israelite for a number of reasons. Leprosy was feared because there was no known cure for it and it spread to other people. The individual with leprosy became an outcast from society. The person was forced to leave home, family, friends, and place of worship and live outside the camp. When anyone drew near, the leper had to cry out, "Unclean, unclean."

Leprosy is symbolic of the horrible, destructive nature of sin. Without a remedy, sin destroys life, body, and soul. Sin, like leprosy, separates us from worshiping and being in God's presence (2 Thess. 1:8-9). It affects our relationship with others, and it spreads its destructiveness to others.

Don't blame God for the wickedness and miseries all around us; blame Satan, the one who brought all sin and death into the world. God has given us Christ, through whom we receive forgiveness of sins; new and eternal life; and spiritual blessings.

"The thief [Satan] cometh not but for to steal and to kill, and to destroy: I am come that they might have life, and that they might have it more abundantly" (John 10:10).

Thought for Today: When Jesus forgives our sins, He cleanses our hearts.

Christ Revealed: Through the clean food of the believer (Lev. 11:47). Our Lord is the *Bread of Life* (John 6:35) and *Living Water* (John 4:14).

February 6: Read Leviticus 14–15

Verse for Today: *"And the priest shall offer the burnt offering and the meat offering upon the altar: and the priest shall make an atonement for him, and he shall be clean"* (Lev. 14:20).

The Hebrew word used here for *meat offering* means *"meal offering."* The priest burned a handful of meal offering on the altar, which consisted of fine flour, oil, and frankincense (Lev. 2:1). The wheat represents Christ in His earthly perfection. Just as the grain in the meal offering had to be ground into flour before it could be used, Jesus was broken by His death on the cross to become the Bread of Life for His people.

The meal offering had to be made without leaven (or yeast). Yeast was not acceptable to God as it represents the moral impurity and evil that corrupt a person's heart. This is a serious reminder to us. We cannot expect the Lord's blessings if we don't remove the moral impurities from our hearts and lives.

Don't you realize that if even one person is allowed to go on sinning, soon all will be affected? So let us leave entirely behind us the cancerous old life, with all its hatreds and wickedness. Let us feast, instead, upon the pure Word of God and live in sincerity and truth (1 Cor. 5:7-8).

Thought for Today: For our lives to be an expression of the meal offering, the leaven of sin and self-will must be removed and cleansed.

Christ Portrayed: By the priest, who made atonement for the leper (Lev. 14:20). Christ has atoned (made the necessary payment) for our sin (Rom. 5:11).

February 7: Read Leviticus 16–18

Verses for Today: *"And he shall take a censer full of burning coals of fire from off the altar before the Lord, and his hands full of sweet incense beaten small, and bring it within the vail: and he shall put the incense upon the fire before the Lord, that the cloud of the incense may cover the mercy seat that is upon the testimony, that he die not"* (Lev. 16:12-13).

The altar of incense was *"before the Lord"* in the Holy Place. This altar of incense was smaller than the brazen altar in the outer court (where the sacrifices were offered). The altar of incense was covered with gold and placed in front of the curtain that led to the holy of holies (or Most Holy Place).

The high priest offered incense on it morning and evening, symbolizing the offering of prayer to God *"without ceasing"* (1 Thess. 5:17). When the priest lit the lamps in the evening, and again when he trimmed them in the morning, he burned incense on the golden altar, using live coals from the altar of burnt offering. This signifies that all acceptable prayer has its foundations in the redeeming love of a forgiving God.

The incense ascending toward heaven is symbolic of the desires of the heart of the worshiper, reaching upward to God. It gives meaning to the Scripture, *"Pray without ceasing"* (1 Thess. 5:17).

What a privilege we have as believers today. We are invited, summoned even, to come freely to God's throne of grace and mercy and ask for what we need. We are to bring to Him everything that troubles us. God's Word helps us pray and instructs us how to pray. What a privilege and a responsibility we have—to offer prayers to God day and night—praying for our needs and the things that the Holy Spirit lays upon our hearts.

"And all things, whatsoever ye shall ask in prayer, believing, ye shall receive" (Matt. 21:22).

Thought for Today: We have the privilege of communicating with God through prayer and Bible reading. Are you taking your needs to Jesus, and asking Him for help and wisdom?

Christ Revealed: Through the two goats used on the Day of Atonement (Leviticus 16:7-10). The first goat slain foreshadows Jesus's death that brings forgiveness of sins and restores our peace with God. The release of the second goat into the wilderness represents God's precious mercy in forever removing from His sight the sins of His people *"as far as the east is from the west"* (Ps. 103:12; Heb. 10:17).

February 8: Read Leviticus 19–21

Verses for Today: *"And the soul that turneth after such as have familiar spirits, and after wizards . . . [I] will cut him off from among his people. . . . If man also lie with mankind, as he lieth with a woman . . . they shall surely be put to death"* (Lev. 20:6, 13).

If God's people are to receive the Lord's blessings, they are required to purify themselves from thoughts and actions that He calls sin. Sin that God calls detestable includes worshiping false gods, seeking knowledge from spirit mediums, and participating in sexual perversions and homosexuality.

When people don't know Christ and His Word, or when they have rejected Him, they run after other things to bring meaning to life and to assuage their fears and confusion. Many people (either trying to find answers to life's troubles and perplexities, or simply thinking they are fun and harmless) turn to astrology, fortune-tellers, palm readers, and spirit mediums. These counterfeit guides cause millions of people to be deceived. The Lord gave us life, and He alone is the authority on the way we should live.

Many more people are deceived because they do not understand that God has a beautiful design for men and women, and for marriage and family. Jesus foretold that the immorality and sexual perversions occurring in Sodom at the time of Lot would become prominent prior to His return (Luke 17:28-32). Participation in these sins constitutes a serious offense against the Lord.

The works of the flesh are very evident—adultery, fornication, uncleanness, lasciviousness, idolatry, witchcraft . . . and such like. Those who take part in such things will not inherit the kingdom of God (Gal. 5:19, 21).

Thought for Today: Are you seeking to know God more, and allowing Him to transform you and make you new in His image?

Christ Revealed: We are to flee from evil counterfeits and guidance through spiritualist mediums (Lev. 20:6-8), and from all sexual sins. Jesus proclaimed, "*I am the way, the truth, and the life*" (John 14:6).

February 9: Read Leviticus 22–23

Verses for Today: "*Speak unto Aaron and to his sons. . . . Whosoever . . . goeth unto the holy things . . . having his uncleanness upon him, that soul shall be cut off from my presence*" (Lev. 22:2-3).

Priests were to be consecrated and clean because they were united to God, and they were His representatives. If a priest was defiled, he could not perform his priestly duties or partake of the priestly food until he was cleansed (Lev. 22:4-6). Priests were to separate themselves from worldly things that would keep them from having a pure relationship with the Lord. Likewise, the animals offered to God were to be without blemish.

God tells us that because of Jesus's sacrifice, believers today are considered His priests (1 Pet. 2:5-9; Rev. 1:6; 5:10). We must be careful to follow God's instructions and remain clean so that we are not disqualified from serving God and from giving our sacrifices. Christians should be quick to remove wrong actions and attitudes in order to worship the Lord acceptably. As we give our tithes, offerings, talents, and service to the Lord, we should examine our attitudes. We are not to give carelessly to God, or with the motive of desiring our own glory or praise from others.

No matter the size of our gift, we need to offer it with a humble, thankful attitude. Let us examine ourselves for any unholy attitude that would make us unclean and unfit to properly worship and praise the Lord.

"First be reconciled to thy brother, and then come and offer thy gift" (Matt. 5:24).

Thought for Today: The Christian who serves the Lord acceptably will seek to be clean in body, mind, and spirit.

Christ Revealed: The seven great religious feasts (Lev. 23) all reveal various aspects of Christ. The feasts are the Passover, Feast of Unleavened Bread, Feast of Firstfruits, Feast of Pentecost, Feast of Trumpets, Day of Atonement, and Feast of Tabernacles (or Booths).[6]

February 10: Read Leviticus 24–25

Verses for Today: *"Bake twelve cakes thereof. . . . And thou shalt set them in two rows . . . upon the pure table before the Lord. And thou shalt put pure frankincense upon each row, that it may be on the bread for a memorial, even an offering made by fire unto the Lord"* (Lev. 24:5-7).

The twelve loaves on the table in the Holy Place were called *"showbread,"* or *"Bread of Presence."* The table was never to be without bread, for God had said, *"Thou shalt set upon the table shewbread before me alway"* (Ex. 25:30). Much could be studied about the meaning of the *Bread of Presence.* It is representative of God's provision for all His people (twelve loaves and twelve tribes) and of Christ, who is *"the Bread of Life"* (John 6:32-51). It was to be *eaten* by the priests, a picture of believers partaking of Christ (Mark 14:22; John 6:51). It was to *"always be present"* as Jesus and His Spirit are always present with us.

Pure frankincense was put on each of the two rows of bread, symbolizing how closely the bread and the altar of incense (prayer) were united. Putting incense on the bread demonstrated that the bread did not become acceptable food for the priests until God's blessing rested upon it. After this, the bread became holy and acceptable to God.

Just as the priests ate the Bread of Presence, we are to partake of our spiritual food. We are to partake of God's Word and Christ, and accompany these with prayer, so that we may receive spiritual strength and nourishment.

"Our sufficiency is of God; Who also hath made us able ministers . . . not of the letter, but of the spirit: for the letter killeth, but the spirit giveth life" (2 Cor. 3:5-6).

---

6 The topic of Jesus's fulfillment of the Jewish feasts is a worthwhile and fascinating study. A brief article on this topic can be found at https://www.gotquestions.org/Jewish-feasts.html.

Thought for Today: Our faith grows as we allow God's Word to work in our lives daily.

Christ Portrayed: By the kinsman-redeemer (Lev. 25:47-55). Christ is our kinsman-Redeemer (Isa. 60:16; Heb. 2:17).

February 11: Read Leviticus 26–27

Verse for Today: *"Ye shall make you no idols nor graven image, neither rear you up a standing image, neither shall ye set up any image of stone in your land, to bow down unto it: for I am the Lord your God"* (Lev. 26:1).

All the nations surrounding ancient Israel were idolatrous nations. The Israelites, however, walked with the one true God and worshiped Him. They were to be a people who loved and honored God, and be a testimony to other nations regarding God's truth and power. Therefore, it was vital that the Israelites follow God's command and destroy every idol upon entering the Promised Land (Ex. 23:24; 34:13; Num. 33:52; Deut. 7:5).

Throughout the Bible, believers are warned to not have any idols in their lives or homes. Most people think of idols as statues, or images, which they can be. But idols can also be anything that takes the place of God and our love for Him. He must be our focus. One of today's most subtle, deceptive forms of idolatry is the pursuit of money and possessions. Scripture declares that *we cannot serve both God and money* (Matt. 6:24).

Christians are to consider the examples of Jesus and His early disciples, who did not seek worldly treasures but, rather, sought to know and do God's will. The great apostle Paul, who wrote much of the New Testament, *counted it a privilege to suffer the loss of all things*, so that he might instead know Christ (Phil. 3:8). Barnabas, an early disciple, *"Having land, sold it, and brought the money, and laid it at the apostles' feet"* (Acts 4:37).

Do not trust in earthly riches, but in God. Aim to "be rich in good works," help the poor, and lay up for yourselves treasures in heaven* (Luke 12:33; 1 Tim. 6:17-19).

Thought for Today: The Lord promises not only to sustain those who trust Him, but to one day reward the sacrifices that we make for His sake.

Christ Revealed: As the One who will dwell among us (Lev. 26:11). Our hope of glory is Christ in us (Col. 1:27).

NUMBERS

The book of Numbers begins in the second year after the Israelites' exodus from Egypt. It makes plain that God is able to care for His people and lead them to the Promised Land. The name of the book is derived from two different numberings of the people taken during their journey (chapters 1 and 26). The book includes famous biblical accounts and key truth.

While they camped in the Sinai wilderness, God gave instructions to Moses and the people for the care of the tabernacle, for the Passover, and for camping and traveling toward the Promised Land. However, when the people continually complained to Moses and opposed his leadership, God dealt with those who grumbled and rebelled.

The Israelites traveled to the plains of Moab on the border of the land that God promised to give them. When they neared Canaan, God told them to send out twelve spies to assess the land (Num. 13). Ten spies returned with a bad report, saying the people were too large, like giants, and there were too many to be conquered. Joshua and Caleb, however, reported that with God's assistance, they could take the beautiful, fruitful land. The Israelites accepted the bad report. They shrank back in fear, refusing to believe they could conquer the Promised Land.

Because of their unbelief and defiance, along with their past grumbling in the desert, God declared that the adult generation would not enter the land. Instead, they would wander in the wilderness for forty years and die in the desert. Years passed as the older generation died (except Joshua and Caleb), and the new generation grew up.

In the fortieth year after the Israelites left Egypt, in the plains of Moab, the second census was taken of the new generation (Num. 26:1-65). Before entering the land, the people assembled for a new commitment to God. They also received instructions regarding the conquest and occupation of Canaan.

The book of Numbers is a solemn reminder of what happens when we do not believe, trust, and obey God. The New Testament, highlighting this example, reminds us that *the people were not able to enter the land of promise and blessing because of their "unbelief"* (Heb. 3:19).

God wants us to know His forgiveness (Num. 14:18); He wants us to know Him as our personal God (Num 15:41); He wants us to experience His glory (Num. 14:21); and He wants to pour out blessings upon us. One of the beautiful passages of Scripture (which has been turned into a number of songs) is found in Numbers:

"The Lord bless thee, and keep thee:
The Lord make his face shine upon thee, and be gracious unto thee:
The Lord lift up his countenance upon thee, and give thee peace.
And they shall put my name upon the children of Israel, and I will bless them."
(Num. 6:24-27)[7]

February 12: Read Numbers 1–2

Verse for Today: *"As the Lord commanded Moses, so he numbered them in the wilderness of Sinai"* (Num. 1:19).

This was the second numbering of the people. Nine months earlier, they were registered for the purpose of collecting atonement money from every male who was twenty years and older (Ex. 30:11-16; 38:25-26). The reason for this numbering was to organize an army. God had promised to give the Israelites the land of Canaan, but they were required to battle their enemies and conquer them.

This numbering was conducted about eleven months after their arrival in the desert of Sinai (Ex. 19:1; Num. 1:1; 10:11) and one month after the tabernacle was set up (Ex. 40:2, 17). Nearly an entire year had elapsed since their arrival. We may wonder, with so great a destiny as the Promised Land, why the long delay? God is always at work, preparing and testing His people, but quite often the delay is from our own slackness.

There are times in a Christian's life when the years pass, opportunities come and go, and life hastens toward its close, but so little progress seems to be made in the transformation of our character, and so little eternal work is accomplished. Are our wasted years evidence that much in us of the old nature is not yet buried? The fruitless years of the past need not be in vain. Let us recognize "desert experiences" as the means of dying to unbelief, and as His divine design to prepare us for spiritual service.

"Know ye not, that to whom ye yield yourselves servants to obey, his servants ye are to whom ye obey; whether of sin unto death, or of obedience unto righteousness?" (Rom. 6:16).

Thought for Today: The Lord is working in every circumstance to prepare His people for their promised inheritance.

Christ Portrayed: By Moses as he led the people (Num. 1:54). Jesus taught, *"I am the good shepherd, and know my sheep"* (John 10:14).

---

7   To search online for various song renditions from this Scripture, it is helpful to use several of the following phrases: "Numbers 6:24-27 songs"; or "The Blessing song"; or "The Lord Bless Thee and Keep Thee song"; or "The Lord Bless You and Keep You song."

February 13: Read Numbers 3–4

Verses for Today: *"As for the sons of Merari. . . . this is the charge of their burden"* (Num. 4:29, 31).

Just the three Levite families (the Kohathites, Gershonites, and Merarites) were appointed to transport the tabernacle and its furnishings throughout the wilderness journey. The tabernacle and furnishings may have weighed several tons. There were boards, posts, cords, metal sockets, furniture, skins, hangings, and more. Each family was responsible for specific items.

The Kohathite family was responsible for only the few items of furniture. The Gershonites were in charge of the hanging curtains, the coverings of the tabernacle, and the instruments of the service. But the Merarites had to carry all the pillars, boards, bars, sockets, and the heavier parts of the tabernacle; consequently, four wagons and eight oxen were provided to them (Num. 7:8).

Although there were fewer Merarites, their burden was much heavier than that of the other two Levite families. The Gershonites and Kohathites may have felt fortunate that their assignments were not so burdensome. But the Lord is looking for workers, like the family of Merari, who don't complain because their job seems heavier or less desirable than the tasks of others. The completion of any worthwhile project is often dependent upon a few who count it a privilege to do the Lord's work.

"And I will very gladly spend and be spent for you" (2 Cor. 12:15).

Thought for Today: How much we are permitted to accomplish for the Lord is determined not by our strength, but by our willingness.

Christ Portrayed: By Aaron, the high priest, whom the Levites served (Num. 3:6). We serve Christ, our great High Priest (John 12:26; Heb. 4:14).

February 14: Read Numbers 5–6

Verses for Today: *"The Lord bless thee, and keep thee: the Lord make his face shine upon thee, and be gracious unto thee: the Lord lift up his countenance upon thee, and give thee peace"* (Num. 6:24-26).

The laws presented in Numbers chapter five concerned any who *"trespass against the Lord"* (Num. 5:6), while the instructions in chapter six were given for the few who desired to go beyond what was required and be fully committed to Him. This was the Nazarite vow, which could last for any set period of time, from a month to a lifetime. Samuel, Samson, and John the Baptist were lifelong Nazarites.

When individuals took the Nazarite vow, they abstained from eating or drinking anything prepared from the vine *"from the kernels even to the husk"* (Num. 6:4). This sacrifice revealed a willingness to deny every physical satisfaction. Although grapes and raisins were good food, a Nazarite was more concerned about full dedication and pleasing the Lord than in indulging in the pleasures of life.

In addition, Nazarites refrained from cutting their hair. The *"consecration of his God is upon his head"* (Num. 6:7) indicated that the person's power came from God. This truth is seen in the story of Samson, who declared, *"If I be shaven, then my strength will go from me."* However, at one point in his life, Samson allowed himself to be tricked, his hair was cut, and he lost his strength. Later, when *"the hair of his head began to grow again,"* his strength returned, and *"the dead which he slew at his death were more than they which he slew in his life"* (Judg. 16:17-31).

Nazarites would also refrain from approaching a dead body, even if it were a close family member, for fear of defiling themselves and missing the priceless privilege of hearing the Lord say, *"The Lord bless thee, and keep thee: the Lord make his face shine upon thee, and be gracious unto thee: the Lord lift up his countenance upon thee, and give thee peace"* (Num. 6:24-26).

May we aim to be like a Nazarite and seek to go beyond what we think is necessary to "just be a Christian." May we gladly release what we hold dear, and seek to please our heavenly Father.

"For though I be free from all men, yet have I made myself servant unto all, that I might gain the more" (1 Cor. 9:19).

Thought for Today: We can ask the Lord for help and strength to deny ourselves, and to please and serve Him.

Christ Revealed: As the One who blesses us and keeps us (Num. 6:24-26; Jude 1:24-25).

February 15: Read Numbers 7

Verses for Today: *"The princes of Israel . . . brought their offering before the Lord"* (Num. 7:2-3).

The princes (leaders) of the tribes could not participate in the duties of the tabernacle; yet, through their offerings, they were able to assist the Levites in their God-appointed responsibilities. Because these leaders could not hold the position of prominence, as the Levites did, they could have shown contempt or a spirit of jealousy, and given little or nothing to help them. However, they willingly brought generous, sacrificial gifts to supply the needs of the Levites—*to every man according to the work he had to do* (Num. 7:5).

Since the offerings from each of the princes were exactly the same, it may seem monotonous to read all the details for each one. The repetition, though, reveals the significance God places on every sacrifice given to support His work.

Our individual offerings may seem small and unimportant, but God gives equal notice to every gift given, regardless of its size. Let us give with faith and joy to the Lord's work.

Give, and it shall be given unto you. A good measure—pressed down, shaken together, and running over—shall be given to you. For with the same measure that you use, it will be measured back to you (Luke 6:38).

Thought for Today: God records every act of service done in His name—even *"a cup of cold water"* (Matt. 10:42).

Christ Revealed: Through the offerings of the leaders (Num. 7). Every offering is carefully noted, just as Jesus noticed the widow's offering (Mark 12:41-44).

February 16: Read Numbers 8–9

Verse for Today: *"And Moses spake unto the children of Israel, that they should keep the passover"* (Num. 9:4).

The Passover Feast and the Feast of Unleavened Bread were considered the most important of all the feasts.

The Passover Feast served as a memorial of the Israelites' deliverance from Egypt by the blood that satisfied God and protected them from death. Christ has become our Passover Lamb, sacrificed for us, so that we might be delivered from the bondage of sin (1 Cor. 5:7) and receive eternal life (John 6:47-48; 1 John 5:11).

The Feast of Unleavened Bread was celebrated on the second day of the eight-day Passover Feast. It foreshadowed Jesus as our *Bread of Life.* Through Him and God's Word, we are strengthened and sustained throughout life's journey.

Christians today proclaim the true meaning of the Passover, when we celebrate all that Jesus secured for us on the cross. Jesus instructed His disciples in how they were to commemorate these events (Luke 22:14-20), which Bible-based churches still follow. We share the Lord's bread and cup in the part of the service that we call *Communion.* Other names for it include Holy Communion, the Lord's Supper, the Eucharist, the breaking of the bread, and the Lord's Table. It is our reminder and celebration that Jesus is our Passover Lamb and provides us with forgiveness and new life.

But God proved His love for us by the fact that while we were still sinners, Christ died for us. Much more, then, now we have been pronounced righteous by virtue of the shedding of His blood; it is far more certain that through Him we shall be saved from God's anger (Rom. 5:8-9).

Thought for Today: For all who are saved by Christ, His resurrection is assurance of victory over death.

Christ Revealed: The Passover serves as a beautiful illustration of the redemption Jesus accomplished at Calvary (Num. 9:2; 1 Cor. 5:7). John the Baptist declared on seeing Jesus, *"Behold the Lamb of God, which taketh away the sin of the world"* (John 1:29)!

February 17: **Read Numbers 10–11**

Verses for Today: *"And when the people complained, it displeased the Lord. . . . And the mixt multitude that was among them fell a lusting: and the children of Israel also wept again, and said, 'Who shall give us flesh to eat? We remember the fish, which we did eat in Egypt freely. . . . But now . . . there is nothing at all, beside this manna'"* (Num. 11:1, 4-6).

The Israelites were always complaining about something. It seems the *"mixed multitude"* originated the complaints that spread through all the people. They failed to comprehend that every problem, or disappointment, was an opportunity to seek God and trust Him (Phil. 4:19).

Praise and thankfulness should have been their attitude. Instead, they complained that manna was *"nothing at all,"* compared with the variety of food they had enjoyed in Egypt. God gave them their demands, but it resulted in leanness (lack of spiritual depth) and in years of trouble (Ps. 106:15).

The Lord frequently allows His people to face trials and disappointments to test and deepen our faith in Him as the All-Sufficient One. Prayer and thankfulness enable us to grow in faith and peace and experience victory.

"Be careful for nothing; but in every thing by prayer and supplication with thanksgiving let your requests be made known unto God. And the peace of God, which passeth all understanding, shall keep your hearts and minds through Christ Jesus" (Phil. 4:6-7).

Thought for Today: God is at work within each Christian, giving the believer a desire to obey the Lord.

Christ Revealed: The two trumpets made of silver (Num. 10:2). Silver in the Bible stands for truth (Ps. 12:6). Christ is *"the way, the truth, and the life"* (John 14:6).

February 18: Read Numbers 12–13

Verses for Today: *"We came unto the land whither thou sentest us, and surely it floweth with milk and honey. . . . Nevertheless the people be strong that dwell in the land, and the cities are walled, and very great. . . . We be not able to go up against the people; for they are stronger than we"* (Num. 13:27, 28, 31).

Twelve leaders of Israel were chosen to explore the land of Canaan (Num. 13:3, 17). God had promised Abraham the land of Canaan hundreds of years earlier in Hebron (Gen. 13:14-17), yet ten of the spies failed to believe God's promise. They saw only the high walls and "giants." Only Joshua and Caleb spoke in faith when they said, *the Lord is with us; do not be afraid* (Num. 14:9).

The people refused to trust the Lord and exercise faith in Him. Instead, they believed the bad-news report of the ten spies. They decided the enemy was too powerful to defeat, and did not attempt to act upon the Word of God.

Depending only on human reasoning and physical strength before committing oneself to the Lord's work reveals a lack of faith in God's ability to fulfill His pledges. Unbelief in God's sufficiency keeps many from experiencing the fulfillment of His abundant promises. Many become frightened at the "giants" of difficulties, but no one can prevent God's will from being accomplished when we follow Him. Even the weakest Christian who will trust in God's strength can accomplish a great deal with the Lord's help (Phil. 4:13).

Without faith, man cannot please God because those who draw near to Him must believe that God exists and that He rewards those who seek Him (Heb. 11:6).

Thought for Today: Spiritual accomplishments are never obtained without a battle.

Christ Portrayed: By Moses, the servant (Num. 12:8). Jesus is the Servant chosen by God (Matt. 12:18).

February 19: Read Numbers 14–15

Verse for Today: *"Wherefore hath the Lord brought us unto this land, to fall by the sword?"* (Num. 14:3).

It seems strange indeed that the people who had been miraculously delivered from Egyptian slavery and the death angel would say, *We should choose a leader and go back to Egypt* (Num. 14:4).

Little did they realize how their tenth act of rebellion marked the transition of the nation from *pilgrims,* being led by God for two years, to *wanderers* in the desert for the next thirty-eight years. They made no further progress toward the Promised Land during this time.

When God pronounced judgment upon their unbelief, they confessed, *"We have sinned."* Then they actually tried to enter the Promised Land without God's direction and blessing (Num. 14:40-45).

Just like the Israelites, all too many Christians are determined to guide their own lives. They refuse to submit to God's Word and consequently know nothing about letting Him direct them.

"Trust in the Lord with all thine heart; and lean not unto thine own understanding. In all thy ways acknowledge him, and he shall direct thy paths" (Prov. 3:5-6).

Thought for Today: Grumbling is a form of unbelief in the Lord's goodness, power, and care. Instead, He calls us to grow in praying for every need we have. As we pray, our trust in God, and our peace, thankfulness, and joy will all increase.

Christ Revealed: As God's glory (Num. 14:22). Jesus Christ is the radiance of God's glory (Heb. 1:3).

February 20: Read Numbers 16–18

Verses for Today: *"Two hundred and fifty princes of the assembly, famous in the congregation, men of renown . . . gathered themselves together against Moses"* (Num. 16:2-3).

Korah, the cousin of Moses, opposed him and his leadership, gained the confidence of the majority of the nation's leaders, and led them in resisting Moses. These people felt they should have a voice in making the decisions for the nation and that the majority should rule.

Even though Korah and his followers may have thought they had good intentions, God had placed Moses in the position of leadership. God commands us to honor our leaders (Rom. 13:1, 7; 1 Pet. 2:13-18). Therefore, they were not opposing Moses, but the Lord.

A tendency exists to magnify the natural weaknesses and inabilities of God's leaders. However, those with spiritual insight recognize that the Lord places leaders in positions of authority—regardless of their shortcomings—and we are to honor them. God is able to accomplish His work through them. What often may appear to be shortcomings or weaknesses are the means by which a person learns to rely on God, and the means by which the Lord shows His strength and power. Rather than criticizing those who are in authority over us, we are to pray for them.

"I exhort therefore, that, first of all, supplications, prayers, intercessions, and giving of thanks, be made for all men; for kings, and for all that are in authority; that we may lead a quiet and peaceable life in all godliness and honesty. For this is good

and acceptable in the sight of God our Saviour; Who will have all men to be saved, and to come unto the knowledge of the truth" (1 Tim. 2:1-4).

Thought for Today: God desires and commands us to honor our parents, secular leaders, and church leaders.

Christ Revealed: Through the first ripe fruits (Lev. 23:9-14; Num. 18:13). *Jesus has been raised from the dead as the first of those who are asleep in death* (1 Cor. 15:20). Christ's resurrection is a promise of the resurrection to come (John 11:25-26).

February 21: **Read Numbers 19–20**

Verses for Today: *"And the Lord spake unto Moses, saying . . . speak ye unto the rock. . . . And Moses lifted up his hand, and with his rod he smote the rock twice: and the water came out abundantly"* (Num. 20:7-8, 11).

During Israel's first year in the wilderness, God commanded Moses to strike the rock, and an abundance of water came out (Ex. 17:1-6). To the Israelites, the water that gushed out of the rock was just plain water, but the New Testament reveals its spiritual significance: *They continued to drink from the supernatural Rock that went with them; and that Rock was Christ Himself* (1 Cor. 10:4).

Throughout Scripture, the Lord is revealed as living water (Song 4:15; Isa. 49:10; 55:1; John 4:10-14; Rev. 7:17; 21:1-8; 22:17). Additionally, He is our strong Rock of refuge, to which we can always go (Deut. 32:31; 1 Sam. 2:2; 2 Sam. 22:32; Ps. 18:2, 31; 95:1).

The first striking of the rock was done in obedience to God's Word—and symbolic of Christ—who was stricken by God for our sins (Isa. 53:4-5). On this occasion, about forty years later, the Lord told Moses to *speak* to the rock (Num. 20:8). But Moses (in anger at the people) *struck* the rock. This implied that one sacrifice was not enough and contradicted God's Word: *"He died unto sin once"* (Rom. 6:10).

Moses could not comprehend the magnitude of his disobedience at the time he struck the rock a second time. His failure to enter the Promised Land because of disobedience emphasizes to us the seriousness of obeying all God's commands.

Jesus stated, *"If ye keep my commandments, ye shall abide in my love; even as I have kept my Father's commandments, and abide in his love"* (John 15:10).

Thought for Today: Obedience to God's will is an expression of our faith in Him.

Christ Revealed: Through the rock that was struck (Num. 20:8-11). Jesus, our Rock, was struck once through His death on the cross, and does not need to be struck again (Rom. 6:10; 1 Cor. 10:4).

February 22: Read Numbers 21–22

Verses for Today: *"And the Lord sent fiery serpents among the people. . . . And Moses made a serpent of brass, and put it upon a pole, and it came to pass, that if a serpent had bitten any man, when he beheld the serpent of brass, he lived"* (Num. 21:6, 9).

As a spirit of contempt prevailed in the camp of Israel, the Israelites bitterly *"spake against God, and against Moses"* (Num. 21:5). Finally, the Lord withdrew His protection from the people. Up until this time in the desert, there was no record that anyone had been bitten by a serpent (Deut. 8:15). Now, fiery serpents bit thousands of people and they died. The Israelites, once again, recognized their great need for the Lord.

The Lord instructed Moses to make a brazen snake to resemble the poisonous ones. Although the dying Israelites did not deserve to be healed, if they believed in God's provision and *"beheld the serpent of brass,"* they lived.

Years later, Jesus referred to this incident when He spoke with Nicodemus about being spiritually born again. While speaking about this passage, Christ confirmed the historical accuracy of Scripture, taught about Himself, and revealed to Nicodemus the way to be saved (John 3:1-21). *"And as Moses lifted up the serpent in the wilderness, even so must the Son of man be lifted up: That whosoever believeth in him should not perish, but have eternal life"* (John 3:14-15).

This world is just like the camp of Israel. Mankind was poisoned by *"that old serpent, called the Devil"* (Rev. 12:9), and the painful bite torments its victims unto death. *"And sin, when it is finished, bringeth forth death"* (James 1:15). Sin's poisonous bite brings eternal death, but salvation is provided as we look to Jesus.

God sent *"his own Son in the likeness of sinful flesh, and for sin, condemned sin in the flesh"* (Rom. 8:3; 2 Cor. 5:21).

Thought for Today: Eternal life is available in Jesus.

Christ Portrayed: By Moses, the intercessor (Num. 21:7). *Christ always lives and makes intercession for us* (Heb. 7:25).

February 23: Read Numbers 23–25

Verse for Today: *"Let me die the death of the righteous, and let my last end be like his!"* (Num. 23:10).

When the Israelites were drawing near to entering the Promised Land, they peacefully passed the borders of the Moabites, in the plains of Moab. King Balak and the Moabites were distressed when the Israelites were near their borders.

They had heard that the Israelites had overcome the powerful Egyptian empire, along with the nearby Amorites. In their fear, they believed the Israelites were a threat to their future safety. Consequently, Balak tried to bribe the prophet Balaam with great rewards of honor and wealth if he would curse the Israelites.

At first, Balaam resisted, saying, *"How shall I curse, whom God hath not cursed?"* (Num. 23:8). But Balaam's covetous desire for wealth caused him to compromise what he knew was God's will. In spite of God's warning, Balaam attempted to pronounce a curse on the Israelites. However, each time he opened his mouth to curse the Israelites, he spoke words of blessing from God. Humiliated, but determined to gain the riches and fame that Balak offered him, Balaam went to the Midianites with a plan to lead the Israelites to sin against God. In this way, he hoped the Lord would judge Israel and he would gain favor with Balak.

Balaam is typical of many people who know God and the Holy Scriptures, and long to *"die the death of the righteous,"* but are unwilling to live the life of the righteous. The Bible strongly warns us to beware of those who *"hold the doctrine of Balaam, who taught Balac to cast a stumblingblock before the children of Israel . . . to commit fornication"* (Rev. 2:14; Jude 1:11). *They have forsaken the right way and have gone astray, having followed the way of Balaam the son of Beor, who set his heart on dishonest gain* (2 Pet. 2:15).

Scripture is filled with instructions, and also with examples and warnings to prevent us from going astray.

These things happened to them as examples for us and to warn us accordingly (1 Cor. 10:11). *For the Holy Scriptures are able to make you wise for salvation through faith in Christ Jesus. They are God-breathed and given to us to be used for teaching, rebuking, correcting, and training in righteousness, so that God's people may be thoroughly equipped for every good work* (2 Tim. 3:15-17).

Thought for Today: Those who fight against God's people oppose God Himself.

Christ Revealed: As the Star and Scepter (Num. 24:17). Jesus is coming to reign in great glory, not only over Israel, but over all mankind (Rev. 19:15-16).

February 24: Read Numbers 26–27

Verses for Today: *"And Moses did as the Lord commanded him: and he took Joshua . . . and gave him a charge, as the Lord commanded"* (Num. 27:22-23).

Moses's usefulness to God as a great leader is revealed by the often-repeated words, *"And Moses did as the Lord commanded him."* Scripture additionally declares, *There has never been a prophet in Israel like Moses, whom the Lord spoke with face-to-face* (Deut. 34:10).

However, Moses sinned. Though he prayed afterward to be allowed to see the fertile land on the other side of the Jordan River (Deut. 3:25), God said he could not enter the Promised Land.

Just one recorded sin kept Moses from the earthly Promised Land. He represented the perfect Law, which could not allow one exception. God is perfect and holy, and justice demands that whoever keeps the whole Law (which is one piece), yet makes only one mistake, is guilty of breaking all of it (James 2:10).

Many people are deceived into thinking that if they try to keep the Ten Commandments, God will be satisfied, and they will go to heaven. But the question is not how good we think we are. The question is simply—guilty or not guilty?

All of us have sinned and broken God's law many times. We deserve not only to be cut off from God and His life, but we also deserve the punishment He decreed. We all stand in need of a Savior.

"And be found in him, not having mine own righteousness, which is of the law, but that which is through the faith of Christ, the righteousness which is of God by faith" (Phil. 3:9).

Thought for Today: May we rejoice that we have a great, merciful, and loving Savior.

Christ Portrayed: By the man who would lead the people like a shepherd (Num. 27:17). Jesus said, *"I am the good shepherd"* (John 10:11).

February 25: Read Numbers 28–29

Verse for Today: *"And on the fifteenth day of the seventh month . . . ye shall keep a feast unto the Lord seven days"* (Num. 29:12).

The Feast of Ingathering (also called the Feast of Tabernacles or Booths) was the last of the annual festivals held under the old covenant. It marked the completion of harvest and of the Jewish sacred year (Num. 29:12-40).

Far more sacrifices were offered during this feast than during any other feast. Thirteen bullocks were offered the first day. One less bullock was sacrificed every day after that. A total of seventy bullocks, fourteen rams, ninety-eight lambs, and seven goats were sacrificed. In addition, there were daily burnt offerings and meal offerings. All these sacrifices were a means of offering praise and thanksgiving to God for the abundant harvest.

The prolonged, detailed account reveals how important our offerings, sacrifices, and praises are to the Lord. He takes note of each and every one.

Through Jesus, let us continually offer to God a sacrifice of praise—the fruit of lips that openly profess His name. And do not forget to do good and to share with others because with such sacrifices God is pleased (Heb. 13:15-16).

Thought for Today: Acceptable praise includes praising the Lord for His greatness, kindness, and blessings.

Christ Revealed: Through the peace (or fellowship) offerings (Num. 29:39). We experience peace and fellowship with God through our Lord Jesus Christ (Rom. 5:1).

February 26: Read Numbers 30–31

Verse for Today: *"And Moses spake unto the people, saying, Arm some of yourselves unto the war, and let them go against the Midianites, and avenge the Lord of Midian"* (Num. 31:3).

The Midianites caused Israel to sin through Balaam's influence. Twenty-four thousand Israelite men died because of their sins of idolatry and immorality. However, the day came when God issued the command to *"avenge the Lord of Midian."* So, Moses sent the priest Phinehas and a thousand men from each tribe to battle. They took with them the silver trumpets. Israel's confidence rested in the promise of God: *"If ye go to war . . . blow an alarm with the trumpets . . . and ye shall be saved from your enemies"* (Num. 10:9).

The Lord gave Israel an overwhelming victory, without the loss of a single Israelite. *"And they slew the kings of Midian . . . Balaam also the son of Beor they slew with the sword"* (Num. 31:8).

The same Balaam, who once declared, *"I cannot go beyond the word of the Lord my God"* (Num. 22:18), died as he had lived—in fellowship with the heathen Midianites.

"Mortify . . . evil concupiscence, and covetousness . . . for which things' sake the wrath of God cometh on the children of disobedience" (Col. 3:5-6).

Thought for Today: God's spiritual laws are absolute! If we choose to live in sin, we die in sin.

Christ Revealed: As the ruling One, who will righteously judge the wicked (Num. 31:1-12; 2 Thess. 1:7-9).

February 27: Read Numbers 32–33

Verses for Today: *"And Moses said unto the children of Gad and to the children of Reuben, . . . wherefore discourage ye the heart of the children of Israel from going over into the land which the Lord hath given them?"* (Num. 32:6-7).

Down through the years, God's people looked forward to the fulfillment of His promise to Abraham, which stated that his descendants would inherit the land of Canaan. When the time arrived for these blessed people to enter the Promised Land, the tribes of Reuben and Gad and half the tribe of Manasseh said, *Do not take us across the Jordan* (Num. 32:5, 33).

They evidently believed they would have greater opportunity for material success in the beautiful fertile plains and valleys they had won from the Amorites than they would in the land God had chosen for them. But they were the first of the Israelites that the enemy nations defeated (1 Chron. 5:25-26).

Many have suffered defeat because they chose their way instead of God's way. The Lord's direction for our lives is often different than what we initially anticipate, but the spiritually minded are not as concerned about obtaining their desires as they are about following God's will and pleasing Him.

An unsaved person does not accept what the Holy Spirit teaches because spiritual truth can be understood only through spiritual insight (1 Cor. 2:14). *When we turn to God (and away from our sins), and are baptized in the name of Jesus Christ for the remission of sins, we receive the gift of God's Holy Spirit* (Acts 2:38).

Thought for Today: It is impossible to gain God's best when our hearts are set on the things of the world.

Christ Revealed: Through the blessings of the Promised Land. *"In Christ"* we are protected and given abundant spiritual blessings (Eph. 1:4-6).

February 28: Read Numbers 34–36

Verse for Today: *"These are the commandments and the judgments, which the Lord commanded by the hand of Moses unto the children of Israel in the plains of Moab by Jordan near Jericho"* (Num. 36:13).

The *"commandments and the judgments"* (Numbers 27–36) that were given reveal the importance of God's Word, so that the people might live a holy life pleasing to Him.

The new generation of Israelites was *"near Jericho"* and about to take possession of the Promised Land but, before they did, Moses reviewed the happenings of the past forty years in light of the Lord's commandments. He reminded them that because of grumbling and unbelief, their father's had not been allowed to enter Canaan. Moses emphasized the importance of having God Himself guide them if they were to possess the Promised Land.

Grumbling, whether in our conversations or thoughts, is a serious blight to the Christian life! We must build ourselves up in the holy faith (Jude 1:20-25), so that we do not fall victim to faultfinding or fearful unbelief and fail to receive the Lord's blessings.

"Take heed, brethren, lest there be in any of you an evil heart of unbelief, in departing from the living God" (Heb. 3:12).

Thought for Today: Seek to bless others, especially in the church; do not be counted among the faultfinders, who tear down the church.

Christ Revealed: As our *"city of refuge"* (Num. 35). In Jesus, we are protected from God's judgment and the curse of the law (Phil. 3:9; Heb. 6:18).

March

 # DEUTERONOMY

The first five books of the Bible are linked and considered a unit. They are referred to by a variety of names. The original Hebrew word, Torah, is rich with layers of meaning, but briefly means law, instruction, and doctrine. Other names for this grouping include the books of Moses; the books of the Law; and the Pentateuch (a Greek word meaning five books).

Deuteronomy reveals that as we follow God's commands, He is able to bless us. We can recognize the importance of this book, because the New Testament references it more than eighty times. This includes Jesus teaching from Deuteronomy, which he referenced more than any other book of the Old Testament.

Deuteronomy is the fifth and final book and means *"second law."* It was given by Moses (the mediator-representative of God) to the new generation of Israelites—those who were either unborn or under twenty years of age at the time of the exodus.

In chapters 1–4, Moses reviewed the Israelites' history from the first year after they came out of Egypt to the close of the forty years of wandering in the wilderness. After the Israelites arrived at Mt. Sinai, they received the Ten Commandments and other laws, and built the tabernacle. One year later, they were guided to Kadesh-barnea, where they appointed twelve spies to survey Canaan—the Promised Land (Num. 13; Deut. 1:19-28). However, ten of the spies convinced the people that the Canaanites were too powerful to overcome, and that they could not possess the Promised Land. The people believed this false report. After this action of unbelief, God declared that the adult generation would die in the wilderness (except for Joshua and Caleb).

Chapters 5–26 deal with Israel's obligation to obey God's Word. Before this new generation could enter the Promised Land, Moses reminded them of God's covenant relationship with the people, which meant they needed to commit themselves to Him, in return. Consequently, obedience is the central message of Deuteronomy. Some form of the words *"obey"* and *"do"* occurs an average of five times in each chapter. Except for the large book of Jeremiah, the word "obey" occurs more times in Deuteronomy than in any other book of the Bible.

Through Moses, God reminded the people again of His perfect, holy nature and His great love for them. God chose the Israelites because He loved them and was keeping the promise He had made to their ancestors. By choosing the fewest and most helpless of all people, God let the world see that it was not brilliance, power, or goodness on the part of the Israelites that brought them Jehovah's blessings and prosperity. Rather, it was the mercy of a mighty God who rules the affairs of earth and is able to bless those who walk in harmony with His laws. Therefore, Moses urged them—*"Set your hearts unto all the words which I testify among you this day, which ye shall command your children to observe to do, all the words of this law. . . . because it is your life: and through this thing ye shall prolong your days in the land"* (Deut. 32:46-47).

Moses reminded the people of Jehovah's love spanning from time past to the future (Deut. 4:37; 7:8, 13; 23:5). Chapters 27–30 are a prophetic revelation of Israel's future.

Chapters 31–34 end with the song of Moses, his final blessings upon Israel, and his death and burial. In Moses's final commission to Joshua, he said: *"Be strong and of a good courage: for thou must go with this people unto the land which the Lord hath sworn unto their fathers to give them; and thou shalt cause them to inherit it"* (Deut. 31:7).

This book reveals the principles still in place to receive abundant blessings from God. We are to know and follow God's Word. We are only cheating ourselves when we live in disobedience to Him.

March 1: Read Deuteronomy 1–2

Verse for Today: *"On this side Jordan, in the land of Moab, began Moses to declare this law"* (Deut. 1:5).

The adult generation of Israelites who left Egypt had not recognized that the hardships of the desert were not accidental or caused by poor leadership; they were the plan of God. Their wilderness journey should have caused them to exercise faith in His power—not only to provide for their needs but also to guide them into the Promised Land. But instead, they complained and murmured. As a result of their sin of unbelief, they could not possess the land. They wandered in the wilderness for thirty-eight more years—perhaps on the plains of Moab, just outside the border of the Promised Land.

After the older generation died (except Joshua and Caleb), Moses began to "declare" the original message that God had given the Israelites forty years earlier on Mt. Sinai. *"To declare this law"* meant more than merely repeating the law; it meant "to dig in"—to delve deeply into God's Word—reading, studying, understanding, and enjoying its rich treasures. A fresh revelation of God's love for His people was given and repeated three more times (Deut. 4:37; 7:7-8; 10:15; 23:5). This added assurance of God's love was to strengthen the new generation's faith in Him to lead them into the land of blessing.

Likewise for the Christian, the desire and effort to "dig in"—to go deeply into God's Word—will reveal the never-ending love of God and strengthen one's faith to trust Him for whatever lies ahead.

"Blessed are they that do his commandments, that they may have right to the tree of life" (Rev. 22:14).

Thought for Today: The Lord and His Word become more precious each day when we read the Bible with a desire to obey its truth.

Christ Portrayed: By Moses, who spoke to the children of Israel according to all that the Lord had commanded him (Deut. 1:3). Jesus very faithfully declared to others everything God told Him to say (John 8:28).

March 2: Read Deuteronomy 3–4

Verse for Today: *"Ye shall not fear them: for the Lord your God he shall fight for you"* (Deut. 3:22).

Before the people of Israel crossed the Jordan River, they traveled northward to the fertile and vast region east of the Sea of Galilee, where they faced the powerful king of Bashan. The Lord had encouraged them through Moses, saying, *"Ye shall not fear them: for the Lord your God . . . shall fight for you."*

To automatically trust the Lord when we are faced with overwhelming problems is not natural for anyone, but faith *"cometh by hearing, and hearing by the word of God"* (Rom. 10:17). As we read Scripture with a willing heart to obey it, and we act upon it, the Holy Spirit makes the Word *"quick and powerful"* (active and life-giving). As the Bible's truths become a living reality in our lives, our faith increases.

God's people often face seemingly impossible situations, but the Lord has provided the Christian with His Word, which is the *"sword of the Spirit"* and the *"shield of faith."* His Word is able to protect us from Satan's *"fiery darts"* that are aimed at us (Eph. 6:16-18).

"Now unto him that is able to keep you from falling . . . be glory and majesty, dominion and power, both now and ever. Amen" (Jude 1:24-25).

Thought for Today: It is our faith in God—not our strength or wisdom—that leads us to victory.

Christ Portrayed: By Joshua, who led the Israelites into the Promised Land that God gave them as an inheritance (Deut. 3:28). Through Jesus, we receive forgiveness of sin, and we are given a spiritual inheritance of abundant blessings for this life and eternity (Acts 26:18).

March 3: **Read Deuteronomy 5–7**

Verses for Today: *"Hear, O Israel: The Lord our God is one Lord: and thou shalt love the Lord thy God with all thine heart"* (Deut. 6:4-5).

The Israelites believed that what Moses spoke was the Word of God. But, for them to believe with all their hearts meant they would need to obey the Lord with their actions and have a right attitude.

The commandment to *"love God with all thy heart"* is not only repeated many times in Scripture, but Jesus declared it to be the Greatest Commandment (Deut. 10:12; 11:1, 13, 22; Matt. 22:37). Jesus further revealed that our love for God should include not only *"all thy heart . . . all thy soul . . . all thy strength,"* but also *"all thy mind"* (Mark 12:30; Luke 10:27). To love the Lord with our minds means that our innermost thoughts should reflect our love for Him. We are to *know* His great love for us, and love Him in return.

We must become aware of our actions and our attitudes since it is possible to have bitter thoughts while doing kind deeds. It's possible to say loving words while having wrong attitudes and motives. Our relationship with God, and with others, goes much deeper than word or deed; it goes to the very heart of our thoughts, for they reveal who we really are and to whom we belong.

"Casting down imaginations, and every high thing that exalteth itself against the knowledge of God, and bringing into captivity every thought to the obedience of Christ" (2 Cor. 10:5).

Thought for Today: Loving God with *"all thy heart"* means that we will desire to please Him and know His Word.

Christ Revealed: Through the land flowing with milk and honey (Deut. 6:3). This land is a picture of our rest, provisions, and blessings that we have in Christ (Heb. 3:18).

March 4: Read Deuteronomy 8–10

Verse for Today: *"And he humbled thee, and suffered thee to hunger, and fed thee with manna . . . that he might make thee know that man doth not live by bread only, but by every word that proceedeth out of the mouth of the Lord doth man live"* (Deut. 8:3).

The thirty-eight years of desert wanderings permitted the older generation of Israelites to die, and taught the new generation not to trust in their abilities, but to daily depend upon God for help and strength.

Christians today need day-by-day strength and help from God's Word. Jesus, the Living Word, is our Bread of Life. He is our source of spiritual nourishment. Neglecting the Word of God results in spiritual malnutrition and defeat.

When Jesus had His time of testing in the desert, Satan tempted Him three times, and each time Jesus spoke God's truth that came from the book of Deuteronomy.[8] After the third testing, Satan left the Lord (Matt. 4:1-11). The Lord's victory over Satan is an example of the power of God's Word to overcome, resist, and rebuke the enemy. We must follow the example of our Lord and know and use God's promises as a shield and sword.

"It is written, Man shall not live by bread alone, but by every word that proceedeth out of the mouth of God" (Matt. 4:4).

Thought for Today: God's Word brings comfort, healing, power, and protection as we meditate on it and declare it.

Christ Revealed: Through the acacia (*"shittim"*) wood (Deut. 10:3). Acacia wood, a desert growth, is symbolic of Jesus in His human form as *a root out of dry ground* (Isa. 53:2).

March 5: Read Deuteronomy 11–13

Verse for Today: *"A blessing, if ye obey the commandments of the Lord"* (Deut. 11:27).

Throughout the Israelites' history, they were reminded that obedience to God's Word was the only way they could be assured of God's presence and blessings. The Lord had directed Moses to tell the people, *"If ye will obey my voice indeed, and keep my covenant, then ye shall be a peculiar treasure unto me above all people"* (Ex. 19:5). When instructions for building the tabernacle (God's dwelling place) were given (Ex. 38–40), obedience was emphasized nineteen times.

---

8   The verse references are Deut. 8:3 and Matt. 4:4; Deut. 6:16 and Matt. 4:7; Deut. 6:13 and Matt. 4:10.

After the forty years of wandering in the wilderness and the dreadful history of disobedience, the new generation was about to enter Canaan. As Moses stood in sight of the Promised Land, he said, "*I set before you this day a blessing and a curse; a blessing, if ye obey . . . and a curse, if ye will not obey*" (Deut. 11:26-28).

Under the covenant of grace, the Christian receives God's greatest blessings—forgiveness and new life in Christ. Yet, even today, "*a blessing, if ye obey*" is still the key to enjoying abundant life in the Lord. As we abide in Him, we grow in receiving our spiritual inheritance.

"*And he that keepeth his commandments dwelleth in him, and he in him*" (1 John 3:24).

Thought for Today: It is the obedient ones who enjoy God's presence.

Christ Revealed: Through the burnt offerings, which typified Christ's offering of Himself unto death (Deut. 12:6; Heb. 10:5-7).

March 6: Read Deuteronomy 14–16

Verses for Today: "*Beware that there be not a thought in thy wicked heart . . . and thou givest him nought; and he cry unto the Lord against thee. . . . For the poor shall never cease out of the land: therefore I command thee, saying, Thou shalt open thine hand wide unto thy brother, to thy poor, and to thy needy*" (Deut. 15:9, 11).

Giving to the poor was recognition that all the Israelites' possessions actually belonged to the Lord. They were merely stewards of God's love, distributing to the less fortunate.

When we give to someone who needs our help, we are loaning to the Lord. He gives His Word as security: "*He that hath pity upon the poor lendeth unto the Lord; and that which he hath given will he pay him again*" (Prov. 19:17).

God has always identified Himself with the poor and the helpless. Giving a cup of cold water in His name is the same as giving to the Lord: *I was hungry, and you gave me food; I was thirsty, and you gave me drink; I was a stranger, and you took me in; naked, and you clothed me* (Matt. 25:35-36). Because the sufferings of distressed people touch the heart of God—our hearts should be moved, as well.

"*But whoso hath this world's good, and seeth his brother have need, and shutteth up his bowels of compassion from him, how dwelleth the love of God in him?*" (1 John 3:17).

Thought for Today: The Christian does not give because of the law, but because of love.

Christ Revealed: Through the year of release, which typifies Christ's forgiveness of our sins (Deut. 15:1). Jesus instructs us to pray: *Forgive us our sins, as we forgive those who sin against us* (Luke 11:4).

March 7: Read Deuteronomy 17–20

Verses for Today: *"I will raise them up a Prophet from among their brethren, like unto thee, and will put my words in his mouth; and he shall speak unto them all that I shall command him. And it shall come to pass, that whosoever will not hearken unto my words which he shall speak in my name, I will require it of him"* (Deut. 18:18-19).

Moses interceded for the Israelites in prayer and God delivered them (Deut. 9:25-26). Moses, though, was only a prophet. He received and proclaimed God's will and truth to the people, yet he was powerless to change the hearts of God's followers. Moses served God and the people faithfully for forty years, but he could not control the people.

Blessedly, Jesus is our mediator of a *better* covenant established upon *better* promises (Heb. 8:6). Although every lost sinner is cursed by the law and condemned by conscience, anyone who will *"call on the name of the Lord"* will receive forgiveness (Acts 2:21) and salvation.

Additionally, Jesus is the manifestation of God's character and indwells the life of every believer. He has the sovereign right *"as a son over his own house"* (Heb. 3:6) to be Master in His house—not merely an honored guest—while we retain the keys and the control. No! The keys belong to Him, and He must have control. The Lord dwells within *"his own house,"* as a life within a life, permeating and transforming our whole being. As He rules *"over his own house,"* He maintains His possessions.

"For the law made nothing perfect, but the bringing in of a better hope did; by the which we draw nigh unto God. . . . Wherefore he is able also to save them to the uttermost that come unto God by him, seeing he ever liveth to make intercession for them" (Heb. 7:19, 25).

Thought for Today: Jesus intercedes for all (His house) who come to the Father through Him.

Christ Revealed: Through the Old Testament sacrifices, which were without blemish or defect (Deut. 17:1). Jesus is our pure and perfect sacrifice, freeing us from all sin and appearance of evil (1 Pet. 1:19).

March 8: Read Deuteronomy 21–23

Verse for Today: *"Thou shalt not sow thy vineyard with divers seeds: lest the fruit . . . be defiled"* (Deut. 22:9).

God chose Israel to be *"a holy people,"* who belong fully to Him. He established laws, such as not sowing *"divers seeds,"* which may appear to the casual observer to be unnecessary restraints. These laws, though, were given to protect the Israelites from being corrupted by the surrounding nations. The laws were given to protect the people's relationship with God, preserve their witness, and enable them to fulfill God's plan.

In the New Testament, this principle is declared for all believers in a variety of ways: *"Wherefore come out from among them, and be ye separate, saith the Lord, and touch not the unclean thing"* (2 Cor. 6:17). *"Be ye not unequally yoked together with unbelievers"* (2 Cor. 6:14). *"A friend of the world is the enemy of God"* (James 4:4). These Scriptures all reflect God's question: *"Can two walk together, except they be agreed?"* (Amos 3:3).

A single-hearted love for God is the secret to victorious Christian living for *"no man can serve two masters"* (Matt. 6:24). There is room for only one Lord in our lives, and we must decide who that will be.

The child of God is not *of* the world, but is *in* the world as a witness against its evil influences. We must live as God's children, who have the *"Light of the World"* (Matt. 5:14-16; John 1:4-5).

"Be not ye therefore partakers with them. For ye were sometimes darkness, but now are ye light in the Lord: walk as children of light" (Eph. 5:7-8).

Thought for Today: Do you blend in with the world around you, or do you reflect God's image? Ask the Lord to help you speak with truth and grace, and to enable you to make a difference in the lives of others.

Christ Revealed: Jesus died on the cross in our place, taking the curse on Himself, and submitting to the penalty of death imposed by the law for our sins. In the evening, He was taken down from the cross, a token that God's Law was satisfied (Deut. 21:23; John 19:31; Gal. 3:13).

March 9: Read Deuteronomy 24–27

Verses for Today: *"Thou shalt not have in thine house divers measures. . . . But thou shalt have a perfect and just weight . . . that thy days may be lengthened. . . . For all . . . that do unrighteously, are an abomination unto the Lord thy God"* (Deut. 25:14-16).

The Israelites were taught that all business transactions should reflect the integrity and justice of God. A number of laws were given regarding the seriousness of unfair dealings between a buyer and a seller. It is of utmost importance in our relationships that we do not take advantage of others or misrepresent facts in our dealings.

If we are to manifest a true Christian spirit, we will conduct every transaction in a way that conforms to the character of our heavenly Father. This includes paying to others what we owe them. One of the most cruel business dealings is for someone to refuse to pay what is owed to another person.

"Therefore all things whatsoever ye would that men should do to you, do ye even so to them: for this is the law and the prophets" (Matt. 7:12).

Thought for Today: Honesty is truly the best policy.

Christ Revealed: Through the deliverance of the Israelites from Egypt and Pharaoh (Deut. 26:8). Jesus left His home in heaven to deliver us from Satan, sin, and death.

March 10: Read Deuteronomy 28

Verses for Today: *"If thou shalt hearken unto the voice of the Lord thy God. . . . The Lord shall open unto thee his good treasure"* (Deut. 28:2, 12).

The Israelites' enjoyment of *"his good treasure"* was inseparably linked with willing obedience to God's Word. It is an inflexible spiritual principle. God bestows *"his good treasure"* of blessings on those who desire to know and follow His Word.

This passage means that we need to do more than simply read the Scriptures for knowledge. As we read, we should desire to know Him and His will in order that we *"might walk worthy of the Lord unto all pleasing, being fruitful in every good work, and increasing in the knowledge of God"* (Col. 1:10).

Obeying merely to fulfill our responsibility does not qualify us to receive *"his good treasure."* But when we delight in His ways, we experience the greatest satisfaction.

"Open thou mine eyes, that I may behold wondrous things out of thy law" (Ps. 119:18).

Thought for Today: Love the Lord your God with all your heart, mind, body, and soul (Matt. 22:37).

Christ Revealed: As the One from whom our blessings come (Deut. 28:1-2; Matt. 25:34; Acts 13:48; Eph. 1:4-13).

March 11: Read Deuteronomy 29–31

Verses for Today: *"I have set before you life and death . . . therefore choose life . . . that thou mayest love the Lord thy God, and that thou mayest obey his voice, and that thou mayest cleave unto him: for he is thy life"* (Deut. 30:19-20).

Moses concluded the covenant blessings and curses with an appeal to *"choose life"*—to love the Lord, obey Him, and remain loyal to Him. A determination and choice rest within each individual.

Moses had an intense desire for the people's welfare. He described two possible courses of life, one of which every person must take; a third option does not exist. The first option is life: a right-heart relationship with God—to *"love the Lord."* The alternative is constant warfare with God, which leads to eternal destruction—*"Ye shall surely perish"* (Deut. 8:19).

Everyone gradually hears only what they wish to hear. The majority, like the Israelites, have made themselves deaf to God's voice—*"And worship other gods"* (Deut. 8:19). God has proclaimed, *"And it shall be, if thou do at all forget the Lord thy God, and walk after other gods, and serve them, and worship them, I testify against you this day that ye shall surely perish"* (Deut. 8:19).

It's vital to understand that *"life"* is more than physical existence, and *"death"* is not equivalent to nonexistence. Every unbeliever is in a state of "eternal death"—and soon "eternal punishment" (Matt. 25:46; John 3:36). But *"eternal life"* is provided through faith in Jesus Christ (Gal. 3:26-27; Eph. 2:8-9). We will be in His presence for eternity and enjoy wonderful blessings.

How strange that between such alternatives there should be a moment's hesitation.

"God hath given to us eternal life, and this life is in His Son. He that hath the Son hath life" (1 John 5:11-12).

Thought for Today: Christ came that we might have life, and have it in abundance (John 10:10).

Christ Revealed: As Life. Jesus is the Resurrection and the Life (Deut. 30:15; John 11:25).

March 12: Read Deuteronomy 32–34

Verse for Today: *"My speech shall distil as the dew, as the small rain upon the tender herb"* (Deut. 32:2).

Like dew in the dark of night, God's Word refreshes and provides growth to those who *"thirst after righteousness"* (Matt. 5:6). Dew comes unobserved, refreshing the grass and crops, especially in dry seasons. It descends gently and softly. Who hears the dew fall or sees the formation of water take place? Yet, in the morning, the grass is revived and prepared for the heat of the day.

Only living things benefit from the dew. It does nothing for stones, but refreshes plants that the afternoon sun has wilted. The heat of the sun and the dew of the night may seem far apart and even opposed to each other but, unaided by human hands, God has arranged for them to work together to produce the harvest.

Though we may not be aware of any great change, God's Word is able to refresh and direct the heart of every sincere Bible reader. We often don't notice the steady growth. Daily meditation on His Word nourishes and sustains as gently as the dew that appears following the darkest night.

"Blessed are they which do hunger and thirst after righteousness: for they shall be filled" (Matt. 5:6).

Thought for Today: Nothing compares with the fresh insight and comfort gained through feeding on God's Word.

Christ Revealed: *"For their rock is not as our Rock"* (Deut. 32:31). *"And did all drink the same spiritual drink: for they drank of that spiritual Rock that followed them: and that Rock was Christ"* (1 Cor. 10:4).

JOSHUA

The book of Joshua is a continuation of Deuteronomy. This book begins with God's commission to Joshua after the death of Moses. It covers approximately the first fifty years of Israel's history in the Promised Land of Canaan, and ends with the conclusion of Joshua's ministry.

The Israelites' entrance and settlement in the land are evidence of God's faithfulness. He was keeping His covenant promise that He made with Abraham and, then, Joshua (Josh. 1:1-6; 21:43-45).

During the wilderness years, very few battles ensued. But now, God intended for the people to rise up in faith and fight for possession of the land and their inheritance. Victory was assured because *"the Lord God of Israel"* fought for them (Josh. 10:42). Though Canaan was a place of conflict, ultimately God's people were to experience victory and conquest. Each tribe was assigned specific territory to claim and reign over. As the Israelites conquered the terrain, they were to occupy farther into the Promised Land.

The land of Canaan is symbolic of the spiritual victory and spiritual rest that every believer is to enjoy. In Christ, we are not to fear failure. Rather, through faith, we are to fight against Satan and evil, and to enlarge God's kingdom. With God's help, we are to battle and win the victory against the *"giants"* in our lives. These include sins such as jealousy, greed, hatred, lust, and other works of the flesh (1 John 5:4).

Just as Joshua was given the responsibility of leading the tribes to victory, so Christ, the Captain of our salvation, grants victory to those who act on the Lord's promises.

March 13: Read Joshua 1–3

Verses for Today: "*I will not fail thee, nor forsake thee. . . . Be strong and of a good courage; be not afraid, neither be thou dismayed: for the Lord thy God is with thee whithersoever thou goest*" (Josh. 1:5, 9).

Joshua was born during the period of Egyptian slavery. God chose him during the desert trials to be Moses's coworker. Joshua displayed great faith in God, urging the Israelites to advance into Canaan. But the former generation wanted to stone him to death (Num. 14:6-10).

To be "*brought out*" of Egypt was one thing, but it was altogether another thing to "*go over this Jordan*" and thus become committed to fighting against the powerful Canaanite army of giants, with their chariots of iron (Josh. 1:2). To move forward was to commit themselves to a course of action that ten out of twelve spies condemned when they reported about the land forty years earlier. From simply a human viewpoint, it was a risk of losing everything—even their lives. The crossing of "*this Jordan*" was a major step of faith, which the former generation had refused to take.

All Christians face a similar choice of faith. Will there be a once-and-for-all abandonment of self to the will of God, so that the Lord is truly first in one's life? It is one thing to be brought out of Egypt (a type of the unregenerate life), and to join God's redeemed by faith, but it is another thing entirely to cross over Jordan and "*present your bodies a living sacrifice. . . . And be not conformed to this world*" (Rom. 12:1-2). It is one thing to take Christ as Savior from one's sins, but it is another thing to take Him as Master of one's will and life.

When the Lord leads the way, we can be victorious. Whether it is overcoming a Pharaoh, a Red Sea, a wilderness, or "giants" in our lives, victory is assured. The Lord's grace and strength are sufficient for us.

"*And they overcame him by the blood of the Lamb, and by the word of their testimony; and they loved not their lives unto the death*" (Rev. 12:11).

Thought for Today: Our victories in life depend upon whether or not we desire to do His will as revealed in His Word.

Christ Revealed: Through the scarlet cord in the window, which saved Rahab and her household (Josh. 2:21). The scarlet cord represents the saving blood of Jesus (Heb. 11:31; James 2:25; 1 John 1:7).

March 14: Read Joshua 4–6

Verse for Today: "*At that time the Lord said unto Joshua, Make thee sharp knives, and circumcise again the children of Israel the second time*" (Josh. 5:2).

When the estimated two million Israelites crossed the Jordan River, the Canaanite inhabitants were gripped with terror (Josh. 2:9). It may have seemed like the perfect time to rush into battle and claim the land God had promised them, but they were not in a right relationship with the Lord to take possession of the Promised Land. During the forty years of wilderness wanderings, the Israelites had ignored the practice of circumcision, a symbol of their covenant relationship with God (Jer. 9:25-26).

Before Moses could rule as the Lord's appointed leader of His covenant people, it was vitally important that Moses's own son be circumcised (Ex. 4:24-26; Gen. 17:7-14). In addition, the people were to keep the covenant God made with Abraham and therefore the entire new generation had to submit to the humbling rite of circumcision. Their obedience ensured them of the Lord's continued protection and direction.

We may assume that God is in a hurry for us to do something for Him, but it is vital that we first humbly examine ourselves to consider if we are in submission to His Word.

Through our union with Jesus, we once received not a hand-performed circumcision, but one performed by Christ, in stripping us of our lower nature for we were buried with Him in baptism and raised to life with Him through our faith in the power of God, who raised Him from the dead (Col. 2:11-12).

Thought for Today: God's delays and instructions are always more profitable than our haste.

Christ Revealed: As the Captain of the host of the Lord (Josh. 5:14; Rev. 19:11-16).

March 15: Read Joshua 7–8

Verse for Today: *"So there went up thither of the people about three thousand men: and they fled before the men of Ai"* (Josh. 7:4).

The Israelites had seen the Lord roll back the waters of the Jordan River and overthrow the mighty walled city of Jericho. Yet in their battle at Ai, a much weaker city, they suffered humiliation and defeat, and thirty-six Israelites were killed.

Nine times in the first six chapters of the book of Joshua, the Bible records how the Lord directed Joshua (1:1; 3:7; 4:1, 8, 10, 15; 5:2, 15; 6:2). This time, though, Joshua and his committee, not the Lord, unanimously decided what action they would take, and it resulted in failure (Josh. 7:2-5). Joshua had not sought counsel from the Lord prior to going to battle, but instead accepted the instruction of his spies and made his own decision.

Even though Joshua was ignorant of the sin of Achan, which brought defeat at Ai, Joshua should have asked the Lord before going to battle instead of after the death of thirty-six men (Josh. 7:5-11).

Instructions had been given as to where Joshua was to get direction from God: *"And he shall stand before Eleazar the priest, who shall ask counsel for him"* (Num. 27:21). Jehovah Himself was their Captain, their Commander in Chief. He alone could issue orders that would result in success (Josh. 5:13-15).

God's people are never in greater danger of supposing they no longer need to pray for guidance than when the Lord has just brought them victory, answered prayer, or greatly blessed them.

"Be careful [anxious] for nothing; but in every thing by prayer and supplication with thanksgiving let your requests be made known unto God" (Phil. 4:6).

Thought for Today: The most honored of God's servants fail when they fail to pray!

Christ Revealed: Through the uncut stones of the altar (Josh. 8:31). Daniel saw Jesus as a stone that was not cut by human hands (Dan. 2:34).

March 16: Read Joshua 9–10

Verses for Today: *"Then spake Joshua to the Lord in the day when the Lord delivered up the Amorites before the children of Israel, and he said in the sight of Israel, Sun, stand thou still upon Gibeon; and thou, Moon, in the valley of Ajalon. And the sun stood still, and the moon stayed, until the people had avenged themselves upon their enemies"* (Josh. 10:12-13).

Biblical scholars believe the purpose of the miracle in prolonging daylight *"about a whole day"* (Josh. 10:13) was to dishonor the Canaanites' sun god, Baal, and their moon goddess. It was also confirmation of the Lord's promise to Joshua that He would *"magnify thee in the sight of all Israel, that they may know that, as I was with Moses, so I will be with thee"* (Josh. 3:7).

Books have been written to explain how the miracle of the sun standing still was performed, but they are of little consequence. The process of stopping the rotation of the earth and preventing all the adverse reactions would be as easy for God to accomplish as it was for Him to make the earth and the heavens (Gen. 1–3); part the Red Sea (Ex. 14); or bring Lazarus back to life when he had been dead for several days (John 11:38-44).

Which of Scripture's miracles is the most miraculous? Jesus Himself responded to the people, *"Whether is easier, to say, Thy sins be forgiven thee; or to say, Arise, and walk?"* (Matt. 9:5).

There should be no doubt about Joshua's long day for the believer, who looks forward to that eternal day when the sun and moon will no longer exist, and we shall be with the Lord forever (Rev. 22:5).

With God, nothing is impossible (Gen. 18:14; Job 42:2; Jer. 32:17; Matt. 19:26; Mark 9:23; 10:27; 11:24; Luke 1:37; 18:27).

Thought for Today: Any of our worthwhile accomplishments are the result of God working through us.

Christ Revealed: As the One through whom we have victory (Josh. 10:25; 1 Cor. 15:57; 2 Cor. 2:14).

March 17: Read Joshua 11–13

Verses for Today: "*Joshua was old and stricken in years; and the Lord said unto him, Thou art old and stricken in years, and there remaineth yet very much land to be possessed. This is the land that yet remaineth*" (Josh. 13:1-2).

The communication between God and Joshua closed with the dividing of the remainder of the land of Canaan. Many years had passed since Israel crossed over Jordan into the Promised Land. However, the Amorites, Jebuzites, and Hittites were still in possession of Canaan, and the Israelites still lived for the most part in the mountainous regions. The cities in the valleys had not yet been conquered.

God reminded the Israelites to move forward and claim their inheritance. They were not to be satisfied with past victories. If all the land of promise was to be possessed, it must be taken without compromise.

The older generation who had first entered and defeated many nations within Canaan should have led the way for final conquest. Often, Christians who have been useful in the Lord's service become inactive and satisfied with past achievements, when years of experience and spiritual discernment could enable them to render the church a more valuable service than ever. The Lord never promised His children an easy time in serving Him or told them to look forward to retirement.

While the aged often feel they have done their share, the young are prone to presume they have plenty of time. But every Christian is to take seriously what Christ said: "*The night cometh, when no man can work*" (John 9:4).

An anonymous poet aptly wrote:

"Only one life—'twill soon be past;

Only what's done for Christ will last."

"*Whatsoever thy hand findeth to do, do it with thy might*" (Eccl. 9:10). *Wake up, and rise from the dead, and Christ will shine on you* (Eph. 5:14).

Thought for Today: Make the most of each opportunity to bring glory to the Lord.

Christ Portrayed: By Moses, the servant of the Lord (Josh. 12:6). Jesus is the servant of God (Matt. 12:18).

March 18: Read Joshua 14–16

Verse for Today: *"And they drave not out the Canaanites that dwelt in Gezer: but the Canaanites dwell among the Ephraimites unto this day, and serve under tribute"* (Josh. 16:10).

Why did the Ephraimites fail to defeat the Canaanites in Gezer? Was it because of cowardice and a lack of belief in their ability with God's help, or something else? Perhaps their financial gain was more important to them than being obedient to God. We have no record that the tribe of Ephraim even attempted to claim that territory. They had no zeal and disobeyed the Lord's command. The Ephraimites were powerful enough to dominate the Canaanites, so they had no excuse for allowing the idol-worshiping Canaanites to live among them. Ultimately, it was the result of unbelief.

Ephraim's unbelief gave way to a spirit of compromise. Instead of the Canaanites being defeated, they *"dwell among the Ephraimites unto this day, and serve under tribute."* It is no surprise that the Ephraimites eventually followed the ways of their heathen neighbors, became idolaters, and worshiped other gods.

Many complain and give up when their circumstances seem difficult or not in their best interest. But God always honors the faith of those who rely upon His Word.

"But now I have written unto you not to keep company, if any man that is called a brother be a fornicator, or covetous, or an idolater, or a railer, or a drunkard, or an extortioner" (1 Cor. 5:11).

Thought for Today: Since we are greatly influenced by our friends, it's important that we choose ones who don't hinder our walk with the Lord but, rather, encourage us in our journey with Him and spur us on to love and good deeds (Heb. 10:24).

Christ Portrayed: By Caleb, who fully followed the Lord (Josh. 14:14). Our Savior declared, *Behold, I have come . . . to do Thy will, O God* (Heb. 10:7).

March 19: Read Joshua 17–19

Verse for Today: *"And there remained among the children of Israel seven tribes, which had not yet received their inheritance"* (Josh. 18:2).

The Israelites had crossed over the Jordan River, destroyed Jericho and, finally—after seven years of war—had control of the Promised Land. Yet, not all the Canaanites had been conquered. Joshua questioned them, *How long will you wait before you take the land that the Lord, the God of your ancestors, has given you?* (Josh. 18:3).

What was true of the tribes of Israel is true of Christians today. A general indifference to obeying God's Word prevails. We must *"press toward the mark"* (Phil. 3:14). This means to deny self and sacrifice pleasures that would otherwise prevent us from doing what the Lord instructs us to do.

Christians should not be satisfied with past victories and accomplishments. We should seek to know and do His will. This involves more than simply reading the Bible and enjoying new truths. We will receive transforming power as we seek to understand God's Word, meditate on it, and have a sincere desire to obey Him.

Fight the good fight of faith; take hold of eternal life, to which you are called (1 Tim. 6:12).

Thought for Today: To postpone doing God's will robs us of our usefulness and often causes us to be a stumbling block to others.

Christ Revealed: Through Shiloh. *"The children of Israel assembled together at Shiloh, and set up the tabernacle"* (Josh. 18:1). Shiloh, which was the dwelling place of God's presence, was prophetic of our coming Lord, as foretold in Genesis 49:10—*"until Shiloh come."*

March 20: Read Joshua 20–21

Verses for Today: *"Appoint out for you cities of refuge, whereof I spake unto you by the hand of Moses: that the slayer that killeth any person unawares and unwittingly may flee thither: and they shall be your refuge from the avenger of blood"* (Josh. 20:2-3).

Cities of refuge were established to protect those who accidentally killed someone, but the original command God gave was still in force: *"Whoso sheddeth man's blood, by man shall his blood be shed: for in the image of God made he man"* (Gen. 9:6). However, a definite distinction was made between the person who intentionally murdered someone and the one who accidentally killed another. Instead of a person being put to death for unintentionally killing another, he could flee to one of the cities the Lord appointed for shelter and protection.

Murder is a crime against God since man was created *"in the image of God."* Because of this fact, Scripture states that *"the land cannot be cleansed of the blood that is shed therein, but by the blood of him that shed it"* (Num. 35:33).

When parents and those in authority are lax to correct and rebuke, people's schemes to do wrong only increase (Eccl. 8:11). Sin and wrongdoing must be punished. For the welfare of many, the Lord commands those who willfully murder another to *"be surely put to death"* (Ex. 21:12). A nation that persistently ignores this fact will face God's judgment.

But we are also to remember Jesus's warning that hatred and slandering others are as sinful as murder. How vital it is that we flee to Jesus—our refuge—and ask for His mercy, forgiveness, and His wisdom!

"Whosoever hateth his brother is a murderer: and ye know that no murderer hath eternal life abiding in him" (1 John 3:15).

Thought for Today: Gossip creates divisions and hinders our being a blessing to others.

Christ Portrayed: By Eleazar, the chief priest (Josh. 21:1). Christ is our *"High Priest"* (Heb. 3:1).

March 21: **Read Joshua 22–24**

Verse for Today: *"And the children of Reuben and the children of Gad and the half tribe of Manasseh returned, and departed from the children of Israel out of Shiloh, which is in the land of Canaan, to go unto the country of Gilead"* (Josh. 22:9).

The people of the tribes of Reuben, Gad, and the half tribe of Manasseh asked to live on the east side of the Jordan River, where they could take advantage of the rich grazing land of Gilead. Moses consented to their request if they would first help the other tribes conquer the Promised Land.

These 2½ tribes united with the other tribes in achieving great victory. Then, after seven years of conquest, they returned to their rich grazing land on the other side of the Jordan River. But living outside the God-protected Promised Land, they were the first tribes to sink into idolatry, and the Assyrians eventually destroyed them (1 Chron. 5:26).

God has a definite plan for each one of us. He may permit us to go our own way, as He did the 2½ tribes; but, when we do, we are in danger of being trapped by worldliness, defeated by compromise, and ensnared by the devil. May we not become weary and discouraged and quit because we believe the war is too long and the conflict is too difficult.

"Know ye not that they which run in a race run all, but one receiveth the prize? So run, that ye may obtain" (1 Cor. 9:24).

Thought for Today: God's Word may not satisfy our fleshly desires, but we can be confident that He alone knows what is best for His children.

Christ Revealed: Through the peace offering (Josh. 22:27). Jesus offered Himself to God as our means of peace with the Father (Rom. 5:1).

JUDGES

The book of Judges covers between three and four hundred years of Israel's history—from the beginning of the period of the judges until Samuel the prophet.

Judges is a sad contrast to the book of Joshua. As long as Joshua was alive and leading the people, they followed the Lord. But after Joshua's death, *"there arose another generation after them, which knew not the Lord. . . . and they forsook the Lord, and served Baal and Ashtaroth"* (Judg. 2:10, 13). This was the national condition after Joshua's death (chapters 1–2), and it marked the turning point in the conquest and control of the Promised Land.

Civil wars broke out as self-interest weakened national unity (Judg. 12:1-6; 20). The people's independent spirit was summarized by the words, *Everyone did that which was right in his own eyes* (Judg. 17:6; 18:1-28; 21:25).

To avoid war, the Israelites compromised with the Canaanites and thus failed to fully obey God's command to drive out the Canaanites (Josh. 17:18). Soon the Israelites were participating in Canaanite-idol worship. Because of this, the Lord withdrew His protection, and the Israelites were attacked by invading nations. But, each time the children of Israel prayed, God raised up a judge who delivered them (chapters 3–16).

The book of Judges centers on six particular times when *"the children of Israel did evil in the sight of the Lord."* Although twelve judges are mentioned, the book focuses on the five judges God raised up when the Israelites prayed, and around Abimelech's violent rule.

The death of Samson marked the close of the long period of the judges. What follows in the remaining chapters is not a continuation of Israel's history, but an illustration of the moral and spiritual level within the Promised Land (chapters 17–21).

The book of Judges is more than a record of battles between the Israelites and their enemies. It is a "book of wars" where God was contending with sin in the hearts of His people. The main purpose of the book is to reveal what inevitably results when man rejects God as his King and becomes his own judge.

March 22: Read Judges 1–2

Verses for Today: *"And an angel of the Lord came up from Gilgal to Bochim, and said, I made you to go up out of Egypt, and have brought you unto the land which*

I sware unto your fathers; and I said, I will never break my covenant with you. And ye shall make no league with the inhabitants of this land; ye shall throw down their altars: but ye have not obeyed my voice: why have ye done this?" (Judg. 2:1-2).

The deliverance from Egypt, the miracles of the wilderness, and the long period of discipline in the desert were all designed to prepare the Israelites to fight for their full inheritance in Canaan. After Joshua died, however, all the tribes settled within their territories, defeating—but not destroying—the Canaanites. *"And it came to pass, when Israel was strong, that they put the Canaanites to tribute, and did not utterly drive them out"* (Judg. 1:28). Instead of fully obeying the Lord, the tribes thought it was wiser (or easier) to make slaves of the Canaanites and collect taxes.

God is either Lord of all or not Lord at all; therefore, it is no surprise to read that Israel soon worshiped idols. In the midst of this crisis, the Lord Himself appeared, saying, *"Why have ye done this?"* Then, *"the people lifted up their voice, and wept"* (Judg. 2:2, 4). Although they offered sacrifices to God, they still did not defeat the enemy or destroy the idols. However, no amount of tears or sacrifices can substitute for full obedience.

Since you call on God your Father, and you know He judges each person's work impartially, conduct yourselves in reverent fear while you sojourn on this earth (1 Pet. 1:17).

Thought for Today: Many of our heartaches can be avoided if we obey God's Word.

Christ Revealed: By *"an angel of the Lord."* "Angel" means messenger sent from heaven with a message of God's love. It was the Lord Himself who led them *"up out of Egypt"* (Judg. 2:1).

March 23: Read Judges 3–5

Verse for Today: *"And Deborah said unto Barak, Up; for this is the day in which the Lord hath delivered Sisera into thine hand"* (Judg. 4:14).

Because *"they did evil,"* the Lord delivered the Israelites into the hand of Jabin, king of Canaan. During the next twenty years of captivity, no record exists that anyone prayed to the Lord for deliverance.

Still, the day came when God raised up Deborah to speak His Word, bring deliverance to His people, and free them from oppression. Through her spiritual leadership, God brought peace to the land for forty years (Judg. 5:31).

God's Word and intercessory prayer have the power to bring freedom. For Scripture declares, *"He sent his word, and healed them, and delivered them from their destructions"* (Ps. 107:20).

The Lord is seeking Christians today who will intercede in prayer on behalf of others (Isa. 59:16). God tells us to ask Him to *send out laborers* (Matt. 9:37-38), and to *open the hearts and ears of people,* so they may be saved (1 Tim. 2:1-4).

"And I sought for a man among them, that should . . . stand in the gap before me for the land, that I should not destroy it" (Ezek. 22:30).

Thought for Today: Afflictions become blessings when they cause us to turn to the Lord.

Christ Portrayed: By Othniel, a deliverer upon whom the Spirit of the Lord rested (Judg. 3:9-11). Moreover, the Spirit of God is upon Jesus, our Deliverer (Matt. 3:16; Rom. 11:26).

March 24: **Read Judges 6–7**

Verse for Today: *"And the Lord looked upon him [Gideon], and said, Go in this thy might, and thou shalt save Israel from the hand of the Midianites: have not I sent thee?"* (Judg. 6:14).

The Lord called Gideon, a God-fearing man from the half tribe of Manasseh—where Baal worship was popular—to *"go in this thy might"* against an invading army of 135,000 Midianite soldiers. Exactly what was *"this thy might"*? Surely, God was not speaking about Gideon's tribe, for it was the smallest of all; nor could it be his family, because it was the poorest. Gideon's strength—*"this thy might"*—rested in one thing alone: *"I sent thee."*

But before Gideon could deliver the people from the Midianites, the altar of Baal had to be destroyed and the worship of Jehovah restored. Once Gideon accomplished this feat, he issued a call to the tribes of Israel to defend their country. Out of many thousands who volunteered to go to war, God instructed Gideon to reduce his forces to merely three hundred men. This way, God alone could receive the praise and honor for the victory.

Like Gideon's small army of three hundred men, the number of men and women who are dedicated to accomplishing God's will at any cost is amazingly small. The Lord's faithful servants refresh themselves in His strength, and remind themselves that their victory comes from Him.

"For the weapons of our warfare are not carnal, but mighty through God to the pulling down of strongholds" (2 Cor. 10:4).

Thought for Today: God can use the weakest, smallest, and most unlikely person in people's eyes to perform His work.

Christ Revealed: As the angel of the Lord (Judg. 6:11). This expression implies the presence of Deity, considered to be the Lord Himself.

March 25: Read Judges 8–9

Verse for Today: *"And Gideon made an ephod thereof, and put it in his city, even in Ophrah: and all Israel went thither a whoring after it: which thing became a snare unto Gideon, and to his house"* (Judg. 8:27).

Gideon's great faith shines as a star on the pages of Scripture (Heb. 11:32). At the angel's command, he destroyed the altar of Baal at his own father's house (Judg. 6:28-29). With implicit obedience, he reduced his army to three hundred men to fight the vast armies of Midian *"without number, as the sand by the sea side for multitude"* (Judg. 7:12). Furthermore, when Gideon was urged by all, *"Rule thou over us,"* he immediately rejected the tempting proposal, saying that *"the Lord shall rule over you"* (Judg. 8:22-23).

Yet, *"Gideon made an ephod."*

The high priest alone was commissioned to wear the ephod (Ex. 28:6-12). The ark, containing the commandments—the dwelling place of God—was in Shiloh, the God-appointed center for Israel's worship. But Shiloh was located in the tribe of Ephraim, and they had shown themselves hostile to Gideon. Perhaps this godly man of faith thought that since so much hypocrisy existed in Shiloh, he was justified in making the ephod and in establishing a worship center. Even if he did have good intentions, his act was wrong, and he lost a battle of great importance. Not even a godly Gideon—no, not even Moses—was permitted to alter the Word of God.

"For they being ignorant of God's righteousness, and going about to establish their own righteousness, have not submitted themselves unto the righteousness of God" (Rom. 10:3).

Thought for Today: Only if God blesses and directs our efforts will anything of eternal value result.

Christ Portrayed: By Gideon, who delivered the Israelites from Midian (Judg. 8:22). The Lord Jesus has delivered us from sin, Satan, and death.

March 26: Read Judges 10–11

Verses for Today: *"And Gilead's wife bare him sons; and his wife's sons grew up, and they thrust out Jephthah, and said unto him, Thou shalt not inherit in our father's house; for thou art the son of a strange woman. . . . And it came to pass in process of time, that the children of Ammon made war against Israel. And it was so, that when the children of Ammon made war against Israel, the elders of Gilead went to fetch Jephthah out of the land of Tob"* (Judg. 11:2, 4-5).

People do not all begin life with the same advantages. Some are born of parents with great wealth and influential friends. But a far greater number of people are born among the poor, who must work long hours for the necessities of life; still others are born under the shadow of reproach and face strong prejudice.

So it was with Jephthah, who was rejected by his own brethren. As an illegitimate child, he was forced into exile for eighteen years. Jephthah, however, did not use this fact as an excuse to hate those who rejected him or blame God and turn to idols. Instead, he allowed this rejection to deepen his faith and trust in God. If Jephthah had become bitter and resentful because everyone was against him, he would never have risen in life to be a judge in Israel and be commended by God, having his name associated with Samuel, David, and other heroes of the faith (Heb. 11:32).

All those whom the Lord uses will experience a time of preparation, when it may seem that one's efforts result in disappointments and troubles. Accept with gratitude everything that God allows through friends or enemies—by failures and humiliations—as a means to see yourself as nothing and to recognize your need of full dependence upon Him. Then will come the time of fulfillment, when your faith will be rewarded.

"Humble yourselves therefore under the mighty hand of God, that he may exalt you in due time" (1 Pet. 5:6).

Thought for Today: Recognize that the Lord allows trials to build your faith in Him.

Christ Portrayed: By Jephthah's only child as she submitted to her father's will (Judg. 11:34-40). Jesus, God's only Son, stayed faithful to God's will (Matt. 26:39).

March 27: Read Judges 12–14

Verses for Today: *"And the woman bare a son, and called his name Samson: and the child grew, and the Lord blessed him. And the Spirit of the Lord began to move him at times"* (Judg. 13:24-25).

Each time the children of Israel had *"cried unto the Lord,"* God prepared a deliverer. They had now been slaves of the Philistines for forty years; but still, there was no national prayer for deliverance.

Israel had forsaken Jehovah, but God in mercy *"began to move"* upon Samson, who could have delivered them. However, the people had still not prayed for deliverance and consequently remained powerless under the control of the Philistines.

Sadly, Samson was more concerned about pleasing himself than he was about pleasing God. This was evident when he insisted on having a Canaanite wife, saying, *"Get her for me; for she pleaseth me well"* (Judg. 14:3). The three women in Samson's life represent the attractions of the pleasure-living world, which rob Christians of the power they could otherwise receive from God.

"Ye ask, and receive not, because ye ask amiss, that ye may consume it upon your lusts" (James 4:3).

Thought for Today: Many lives are empty because the Lord is not asked to fill them.

Christ Portrayed: By Jephthah, who showed a loving spirit to the nation that rejected him (Judg. 12:1-3; Matt. 18:15).

March 28: Read Judges 15–17

Verse for Today: *"Every man did that which was right in his own eyes"* (Judg. 17:6).

The Israelites were set apart as a holy nation under God's leadership, but they soon ignored the laws given on Mt. Sinai by their true King and no longer looked to Him for daily direction.

Samson was a typical example of Israel's condition. What was wrong with him was wrong with the nation. It is recorded in the book of Judges that everyone *"did that which was right in his own eyes"* (Judg. 17:6; 18:1-28; 21:25). No one was concerned with knowing and doing God's will.

The same deceptive reasoning is popular today. Many individuals conform to their own chosen external standards of doing whatever they want to do, supposing that it doesn't matter what a person believes as long as one is sincere. But this path leads to eternal ruin.

Let us seek the Lord and His ways. For He is able to save us, and to transform hearts and lives!

Now flee from youthful lusts, and pursue righteousness, faith, love, and peace with those who call on the Lord from a pure heart (2 Tim. 2:22).

Thought for Today: The person who lives to satisfy self cannot fulfill God's purposes for his life.

Christ Revealed: In the strength of Samson. *"I have been a Nazarite unto God"* (Judg. 16:17). A Christian's spiritual strength is faith in Christ and consecration to God (1 Pet. 1:5).

March 29: Read Judges 18–19

Verse for Today: *"The tribe of the Danites sought them an inheritance to dwell in"* (Judg. 18:1).

The tribe of Dan numbered more than 64,000 men, but they had not succeeded in driving the Amorites from their territory (Num. 26:42-43). Rather, the Amorites forced the Danites into the mountains (Judg. 1:34).

The Danites' failure to claim their inheritance was a faith failure. Whether they thought themselves too weak or didn't want to devote the effort, they became dissatisfied with the territory God had allotted to them and moved north. As a result, their spiritual condition continued to decline.

We, too, decline spiritually when we become dissatisfied with the blessings we have, and when we fail to walk in God's promises.

"Be not slothful, but followers of them who through faith and patience inherit the promises" (Heb. 6:12).

Thought for Today: Worldly compromise is a silent witness of unconcern about what the Lord has to say.

Christ Portrayed: *"In those days there was no king in Israel"* (Judg. 18:1). Jesus was rejected as King of Israel (John 19:14-15).

March 30: Read Judges 20–21

Verse for Today: *"In those days there was no king in Israel: every man did that which was right in his own eyes"* (Judg. 21:25).

Because the Israelites failed to recognize God as King, they were constantly defeated by the Canaanites, whom God had intended for them to drive out. God was to be Israel's true King (1 Sam. 12:12), but four times in the book of Judges, these or similar heartbreaking words were recorded: *"In those days there was no king in Israel, but every man did that which was right in his own eyes"* (Judg. 17:6; 18:1; 19:1; 21:25).

When everyone does that which is right in his own eyes, there will be lawlessness, immorality, deception, false teaching, chaos, and strife. When God's Word is ignored, as by the tribe of Dan (Judg. 18), people are without a true guide.

Man was created with a desire to worship the Lord. However, unless he worships God according to His Word, he will turn to some form of false worship.

"Holding faith, and a good conscience; which some having put away concerning faith have made shipwreck" (1 Tim. 1:19).

Thought for Today: Man was not created to be master of his own will.

Christ Revealed: As our Deliverer (Judg. 20:26, 28). When we pray and seek the Lord's will, He delivers us from all evil forces (1 Cor. 10:13).

 # RUTH

The events in the book of Ruth occurred during the period of the judges. The purpose of the book is to reveal how God's mercy and providential care extend far beyond man's limited sight and faith.

God used even the unbelief of Elimelech to bring Ruth, the Gentile Moabitess, to Bethlehem, where she married Boaz, a Bethlehemite from the tribe of Judah. Their union was blessed by a son named Obed. Through him, Ruth and Boaz became the great-grandparents of David (Ruth 4:16-17; 1 Chron. 2:12-15), and the ancestors of Jesus (Matt. 1:5-6; Luke 3:31-32).

Little could the gracious and godly Boaz realize what would be accomplished when he accepted his responsibility as a "*near kinsman*" (Ruth 3:11-12; Lev. 25:23-25). Through his marriage to Ruth, God united Jew and Gentile in the ancestry of David, the greatest king of Israel, and in the genealogy of our Lord, the Messiah.

March 31: Read Ruth 1–4

Verse for Today: *"Why then call ye me Naomi, seeing the Lord hath testified against me, and the Almighty hath afflicted me?"* (Ruth 1:21).

Because of a famine, Elimelech took his wife, Naomi, and their two sons and left Bethlehem (which means *"house of bread"*). This family crossed the Jordan River and sojourned in the land of Moab, the place of God's curse (Num. 24:17; Amos 2:1-3). What they thought would be an escape from starvation by a temporary "sojourn" became a long-term dwelling place for they remained there about ten years (Ruth 1:1-4). During that time, both sons married women of Moab.

Eventually, Elimelech (which means *"my God is King"*), and both his sons, died and were buried there. God was no longer King of this family that failed to trust Him for *"bread"* in Bethlehem. Naomi, whose name means *"pleasant,"* was left empty and felt she no longer had anything worth living for.

News that *"the Lord had visited his people in giving them bread"* caused Naomi to return to Bethlehem, taking Ruth with her (Ruth 1:6). Naomi expressed her deep sorrow, saying, *"Call me not Naomi, call me Mara"* (meaning *"bitter"*—1:20). She confessed, *"I went out full, and the Lord hath brought me home again empty"* (Ruth 1:21). But this wasn't the end of the story.

The thrilling conclusion is that Ruth stayed by Naomi's side, and God used Naomi to bring the Gentile Moabitess, Ruth, to Boaz, which brought the Gentiles into the ancestry of the Messiah.

This story provides us with encouragement and hope in times of despondency. The Lord is able to bring good out of every circumstance as we stay faithful to Him (Rom. 8:28).

"Nay, in all these things we are more than conquerors through him that loved us" (Rom. 8:37).

Thought for Today: Out of our most bitter experiences, God can bring blessings to many if we are willing to let Him.

Christ Revealed: Through Bethlehem, which means *"house of bread."* Jesus is the Bread of Life, who satisfies the spiritual hunger of all who come to Him (John 6:35).

April

1 SAMUEL

The book of 1 Samuel is a continuation of the book of Judges and covers Israel's history from the time of Eli (chapters 1—5) to the death of King Saul (chapter 31). It records Israel's transition from the period of the judges to the monarchy. During that period of time, the Israelites were often oppressed by the Philistines. Samuel the prophet and Saul, Israel's first king, lived during this corrupt, backslidden era.

Through Samuel the prophet, the tribes were united as a kingdom (chapters 5–8). However, as Israel gained strength and Samuel grew old, the Israelites demanded a king to rule over them (1 Sam. 8:5; Acts 13:21). Samuel knew that if the people chose a man to rule them, they would place their faith in him and no longer depend on God for leadership; therefore, he was strongly opposed to their request. But because of their continued demands, God instructed Samuel to anoint Saul as king of Israel (1 Sam. 8:22; 10:1).

Saul's forty-year reign is best expressed by his own words, *I have been a fool* (1 Sam. 26:21). Because of his disobedience and pride, *"the Spirit of the Lord departed from Saul"* (1 Sam. 16:14), and God commanded Samuel to anoint David as king.

David's journey, though, to fulfilling his anointed position took place only after many years of trials, testing, and waiting. He started out as a young shepherd boy, who killed a bear and a lion while protecting his father's flock. After this, he killed Goliath, a giant from the Philistine army, with a slingshot and a single stone (1 Sam. 17), which brought the defeat of the Philistine army. David became a mighty warrior (1 Sam. 18:7) and very popular with the people. King Saul became increasingly jealous and pursued David, trying to kill him. David was forced into hiding from Saul until the time of Saul's death in the tragic battle on Mt. Gilboa (chapters 16—31).

David is a prominent and key figure in the Bible for a number of reasons. He was Israel's third and most important king, and helped establish God's earthly headquarters in Jerusalem. David's throne and earthly reign are linked to God's covenant promise of blessing to all people through Abraham, and to God's throne and Jesus's reign. (While these truths are woven throughout Scripture, a few key verses include Gen. 22:17-18; Ps. 89:3-4; Matt. 1:1; Luke 1:32; and Acts 2:29-36.)

Other key notes about David:
- He is the second most frequently mentioned person in the Bible (after Jesus).
- He wrote many of the psalms, some of which contain prophecies about Jesus (Ps. 16 and Acts 2:25-28; Ps. 22; 110).
- Although he had a period of moral failing, he had such great faith and zeal that God called David a man after God's own heart (1 Sam. 13:14; Acts 13:22).

The book of 1 Samuel points out that faithfulness to God brings success, while disobedience brings disaster (1 Sam. 2:30).

April 1: Read 1 Samuel 1–3

Verse for Today: *"And the word of the Lord was precious in those days; there was no open vision"* (1 Sam. 3:1).

Eli's two sons, Hophni and Phinehas, along with Samson, grew up together in Shiloh, performing their duties in the tabernacle. Because Eli was slack in disciplining Hophni and Phinehas, they were indifferent to God's Word (1 Sam. 3:12-13). But Samuel was careful to do God's will (1 Sam. 3:9-10) and grew in favor with the Lord (1 Sam. 2:26).

The ark of the covenant and the tabernacle, which represented God's Word and His presence among them, had been at Shiloh since Joshua placed them there hundreds of years earlier. However, a lack of interest in God and His will prevailed. *"There was no open vision"* means little was known about the will of God; and *"the word of the Lord was precious"* means there was seldom a prophetic revelation from God. The sins of Eli and his sons are brought to our attention as the reason for the spiritual blindness among the people.

The Word of the Lord was not clearly understood for the same reason it is not clearly understood today. We cannot understand God's Word or His will if we do not read the Bible with a desire to *know* and *do* God's will. We cannot keep His commandments if we are not concerned about knowing what they are.

In the hectic pace of our culture, countless thousands of *words* fill our minds every day from newspapers, magazines, books, television, radio, and the internet. There is a serious neglect, though, of setting aside time to read the Bible—the only written Word from God to mankind.

We must *let Christ's teaching remain as a rich treasure in our hearts in all wisdom* (Col. 3:16).

Thought for Today: Sin can keep you from the Word, or the Word can keep you from sin.

Christ Revealed: Through Samuel's miraculous birth (1 Sam. 1:5, 11, 20). Jesus's birth was even more miraculous because He was born to a virgin and is God's only begotten Son (Luke 1:27, 31-32).

April 2: Read 1 Samuel 4–7

Verse for Today: *"And Samuel spake unto all the house of Israel, saying, If ye do return unto the Lord with all your hearts . . . serve him only: and he will deliver you out of the hand of the Philistines"* (1 Sam. 7:3).

The Israelites had been defeated by the Philistines twenty years prior. When Israel was again threatened by war with the Philistines, Samuel appealed to the people to put away their idols and serve the Lord only. After Samuel offered a sacrifice and prayed, God intervened. The Philistines were so badly defeated that they did not attack Israel again during Samuel's lifetime (1 Sam. 7:7-13).

One's confession of faith may be as bold as the *"great shout"* that accompanied Phinehas and Hophni when they brought the ark into Israel's camp before they were slain (1 Sam. 4:5), but truly triumphant faith, like that of Samuel, is experienced by those who worship the Lord only and follow Him.

"Then saith Jesus unto him, Get thee hence, Satan: for it is written, Thou shalt worship the Lord thy God, and him only shalt thou serve" (Matt. 4:10).

Thought for Today: Serving the Lord acceptably requires single-hearted love for Him.

Christ Revealed: Through the rock called Ebenezer, which means *"the stone of help"* (1 Sam. 7:12). Jesus is the Rock of our salvation. He is the One who is able to help (Ps. 18:2; 121:2).

April 3: Read 1 Samuel 8–11

Verse for Today: *"And ye have this day rejected your God, who himself saved you out of all your adversities and your tribulations; and ye have said unto him, Nay, but set a king over us"* (1 Sam. 10:19).

Samuel, along with a number of the ruling judges of Israel, desired to please God—their invisible King. These leaders were chosen by God and received direction from Him. However, the majority of people openly rejected God as King when they persistently asked to have a king like other nations. This decision constituted rebellion against God.

The Lord was to be their Leader, but the nation insisted, saying, *"Nay; but we will have a king over us . . . [to] go out before us, and fight our battles"* (1 Sam. 8:19-20). Samuel called a national assembly at Mizpeh and again warned the people of their serious mistake in demanding a king. But the people wanted Saul. They were happy that he *looked* like a king, and were satisfied with his external appearance. All of these things were examples of the nation's spiritual failures.

We are not to judge by external appearances and trappings, because God looks on a person's heart (1 Sam. 16:7; 1 Kings 8:39; 2 Chron. 16:9; Luke 16:15; John 7:24; Acts 1:24; 2 Cor. 10:7). Neither are we to look to others, but we are to seek God first. Desiring to be like the majority has caused many to ignore the Bible and seek counsel from others. The Lord leaves the choice to us. Each person decides whether to accept or reject His leadership.

"He that rejecteth me, and receiveth not my words, hath one that judgeth him: the word that I have spoken, the same shall judge him in the last day" (John 12:48).

Thought for Today: Unless we call on the Savior, and turn from our sins, we will face eternal consequences.

Christ Revealed: Through the favored food set before Saul (1 Sam. 9:24). The shoulder denotes strength; the breast denotes affection. Jesus loves us, and He is our food, imparting strength to all who seek Him (John 6:51, 56).

April 4: Read 1 Samuel 12–14

Verses for Today: *"Only fear the Lord, and serve him in truth with all your heart. . . . And Saul said, Bring hither a burnt offering to me, and peace offerings. . . . And Samuel said to Saul . . . thou hast not kept the commandment of the Lord thy God"* (1 Sam. 12:24; 13:9, 13).

King Saul had been commanded to wait until Samuel returned, who alone was qualified to offer sacrifices. But his failure to wait until Samuel arrived at the *"appointed"* time (1 Sam. 13:8) revealed his lack of submission to God's Word.

Saul was not as concerned about God having authority over him, as he was with God making him successful in the eyes of the people. This was more than poor judgment on the part of Israel's first king; it revealed the self-will of his heart.

Saul tried to justify his impatience and self-will as an act of worship when he made the peace offering himself. Because the enemy could attack at any hour, and many of his soldiers deserted, he did not wait for Samuel the prophet. By violating *one* spiritual principle (waiting on God) and performing *another* (offering sacrifices), Saul assumed he could bring victory to Israel.

But the faith that God honors is followed with surrender and doing His will. This is the faith that makes our service and sacrifices acceptable.

"Sacrifice and offering thou didst not desire; mine ears hast thou opened: burnt offering and sin offering hast thou not required. Then said I, Lo, I come: in the volume of the book it is written of me, I delight to do thy will, O my God: yea, thy law is within my heart" (Ps. 40:6-8; Heb. 10:7).

Thought for Today: Obedience to God's Word is better than sacrifice.

Christ Portrayed: By Samuel, the intercessor (1 Sam. 12:23). Even now, Jesus lives and intercedes for every believer (Heb. 7:25).

April 5: Read 1 Samuel 15–16

Verses for Today: *"And Samuel said, How can I go? If Saul hear it, he will kill me. . . . But the Lord said unto Samuel, Look not on his countenance, or on the height of his stature; because I have refused him: for the Lord seeth not as man seeth; for man looketh on the outward appearance, but the Lord looketh on the heart"* (1 Sam. 16:2, 7).

Israel was suffering from the misrule of a king who would not be ruled by God. Consequently, God chose to use Samuel to bring about change. At first Samuel questioned God, wondering how he could complete the task, for surely he would be killed.

Those who are instruments of God have their moments of fear and of wondering what God is asking of them. Everyone has an opportunity to shrink back from the work the Lord calls us to do because His ways are not our ways. God's methods in using His servants for instruments of good are sometimes perplexing and painful.

When Moses was called to stand before Pharaoh, he initially resisted and said he was not qualified (Ex. 4:14). Thankfully, though, with both Moses and Samuel, their reluctance was merely a momentary failure of full confidence in God. Neither Moses nor Samuel attempted to *"flee . . . from the presence of the Lord"* as Jonah did (Jonah 1:3). Instead, Moses and Samuel made known their fears to the Lord, and He strengthened them. The Lord increased their faith, so they were able to accomplish His purposes.

We, too, can be encouraged to know that Elijah, who called down fire from heaven, was *a man subject to like passions as we are, and he prayed* (James 5:17). God's most honored servants in all the ages have had their time of fear. Failure comes when we continue looking at the problem, ourselves, or others. Instead, we must trust the Lord for answers.

"Let us therefore come boldly unto the throne of grace, that we may obtain mercy, and find grace to help in time of need" (Heb. 4:16).

Thought for Today: When God gives you a task to do, remember that He is with you.

Christ Revealed: Through David's name (1 Sam. 16:13), which means *"beloved."* When John baptized Jesus, and Jesus came up out of the water, *"There came a voice from heaven, saying, Thou art my beloved Son, in whom I am well pleased"* (Mark 1:11).

April 6: Read 1 Samuel 17–18

Verses for Today: *"Saul hath slain his thousands, and David his ten thousands. . . . And Saul eyed David from that day forward. . . . David behaved himself wisely in all his ways; and the Lord was with him"* (1 Sam. 18:7, 9, 14).

David became very popular with the people after his victory over Goliath, the Philistine. However, his victory was too much for the pride-filled King Saul. As it became evident to Saul that another man was gaining the influence and honor that he once held, he became obsessed with a jealous spirit. Self-centered King Saul ruled Israel with one thought: "How will this affect me?" He only thought about himself.

Many individuals are like Saul. They are happy serving God, as long as they receive recognition. "Success," though, can lead to a sense of self-sufficiency and cause us to boast about what we accomplish, rather than praising the Lord for what He has accomplished.

God allows us to choose His ways or our ways. Those who remain self-willed and refuse to yield to Him are left on their own like Saul—destitute in the hour of crisis.

"Pride goeth before destruction, and an haughty spirit before a fall" (Prov. 16:18).

Thought for Today: True success in life comes from humbly knowing and obeying God's Word—not in seeking popularity or the praise of others.

Christ Portrayed: By Jonathan, whose love for David was as deep and as close as a brother's love (1 Sam. 18:3-4). We are called Jesus's brothers and sisters when we keep His commands (Rom. 8:29; Heb. 2:11).

April 7: Read 1 Samuel 19–21

Verse for Today: *"And Saul spake to Jonathan his son, and to all his servants, that they should kill David"* (1 Sam. 19:1).

David's success and victory over Goliath led him to become extremely popular with the people, which enraged King Saul. Blinded by self-interest and pride, Saul set out to destroy David at any cost. Saul was driven from one desperate act to another even though he knew that David was chosen by God (1 Sam. 24:20). However, Saul's obsession to destroy David only ended in his own demise (1 Sam. 31:3-6).

Like Saul, many have brought about their own downfall while attempting to destroy another. When we are controlled by pride, we no longer recognize God's sovereign right to arrange the affairs of earth and to rule the heart of every person.

"But he giveth more grace. Wherefore he saith, God resisteth the proud, but giveth grace unto the humble" (James 4:6).

Thought for Today: To some people, worldly popularity and power appear as a dazzling, giant prize to be gained at any price.

Christ Portrayed: By David, whom Saul rejected (1 Sam. 19:2). *Jesus came to His own, but they refused to receive Him* (John 1:11).

April 8: Read 1 Samuel 22–24

Verse for Today: *"I will not put forth mine hand against my lord; for he is the Lord's anointed"* (1 Sam. 24:10).

Saul made a great mistake when he said that God had delivered David into his hand (1 Sam. 23:7). This shows how man can be deceived in his interpretation of providential events, especially when he is not living in subjection to God.

Such a misinterpretation of circumstances is more than poor judgment. Saul was so determined to have his own way that he gave no thought to the wishes of a sovereign God (1 Sam. 24:6). Living outside of God's will makes us easy prey for Satan and leads us to make more poor decisions.

When David knew that Saul wanted to kill him, he did not know which way to turn. Even those whom David had trusted turned against him. Though the way seemed more uncertain each day, David continued to pray for help and guidance (1 Sam. 23:10-12).

At times, because of our circumstances, we may think that God does not care; but, like David, we can be confident in the unchanging, eternal Word of God. Our all-wise heavenly Father often allows us to experience times of trials and distress in order to develop in us a greater faith in Him. The Lord cares, and He stands ready to answer our call for help when we seek Him and submit to His ways.

Everyone born of God overcomes the world, and this victory is through faith (1 John 5:4; and 2 Cor. 5:7).

Thought for Today: We can praise God because the victory is the Lord's, and He shares it with us (Rom. 8:37; 1 John 5:4)!

Christ Revealed: In David's refusal to take the kingdom by force before the appointed time set by God (1 Sam. 24:10-13). Jesus refused to become King of Israel by force, even though the people wanted to make Him an earthly king before the appointed time (John 6:15).

April 9: Read 1 Samuel 25–27

Verses for Today: *"Then said Abishai to David, God hath delivered thine enemy into thine hand this day: now therefore let me smite him, I pray thee, with the spear. . . . And David said to Abishai, Destroy him not: for who can stretch forth his hand against the Lord's anointed, and be guiltless?"* (1 Sam. 26:8-9).

David had opportunities to remove the only person blocking him from becoming king over Israel. Not only did his men strongly urge him to do so (1 Sam. 24:4) but, on one occasion, Abishai insisted that *God has delivered your enemy into your hands this day; now therefore let me kill him.*

But David refused to harm King Saul because he knew Saul was the Lord's anointed (1 Sam. 24:6). David was willing to wait until the Lord Himself removed Saul from the throne.

Although the prophet Samuel had anointed David as king several years earlier, David's willingness to wait for the throne proved his submission to

God's authority. Through the years of patiently waiting for God's timing, the Lord prepared David to receive the kingdom in a spirit of grateful dependence on Him.

Still today, God's people are prepared for His service as they put His will and timing above their own desires.

Each of us should pray, *Lord, I am trusting in You. Save me from the shame of defeat; don't let my enemies triumph over me! For those who hope in You will never be put to shame* (Ps. 25:2-3).

Thought for Today: We must seek God's will if we want His blessings.

Christ Revealed: Through Abigail's efforts to make peace between David and Nabal (1 Sam. 25:21-28). God, through Jesus, has reconciled the world to Himself (2 Cor. 5:19).

April 10: Read 1 Samuel 28–31

Verse for Today: *"Then said Saul unto his servants, Seek me a woman that hath a familiar spirit, that I may go to her, and inquire of her"* (1 Sam. 28:7).

God had given Saul the unique position of serving as the first king to reign over His people, but he forfeited this privilege and position because of his continual disobedience. Eventually, Saul did a most despicable thing by turning to a witch for advice. His long ride to Endor during the dark night proved futile for the once-powerful king, who had lived to please himself.

Those who reject the truth of God easily become victims of false prophets, fortune-tellers, astrologers, and the like (Matt. 24:24; 1 John 4:1). To these dupes, God sends *"strong delusion, that they should believe a lie"* (2 Thess. 2:11).

Thinking it is a *fun thing* that will do no harm, many Christians read astrology columns and consult palm readers or fortune-tellers. But God hates these things because He is the source of all wisdom, knowledge, and power. We are to seek Him and His ways alone. Participation in activities that border on dealing with "spirits" is contrary to God's Word, displeases Him, and opens up a person to satanic powers.

"Idolatry, witchcraft . . . seditions, heresies . . . they which do such things shall not inherit the kingdom of God" (Gal. 5:20-21).

Thought for Today: Those who reject the light of God's Word leave themselves open to spiritual deception.

Christ Revealed: Through the Urim (1 Sam. 28:6), which was used to determine God's will. Today, Jesus speaks to us through His Word and Spirit (John 14:6).

 2 SAMUEL

The book of 2 Samuel covers the forty-year period of Israel's history during David's reign. Immediately after the death of King Saul, David inquired of the Lord and was directed to go to Hebron, where he reigned as king over the tribe of Judah (chapters 1–4).

However, the other tribes of Israel, prompted by Abner (leader of Saul's army), chose to make Ishbosheth (Saul's son) their king. It wasn't until Ishbosheth was assassinated that these tribes went to Hebron and anointed David as their leader and shepherd-king (2 Sam. 5:3; 1 Chron. 12:18).

David then captured the city of Jebus, changed its name to Jerusalem, and made it the capital of the united kingdom of Judah and Israel. Although very little emphasis had been placed on the ark of the covenant during Saul's forty-year reign, when David became king, he brought the ark to Jerusalem, and acknowledged Jehovah as the supreme Ruler of the united kingdom (chapters 5–7).

David fought a series of successful wars and conquered Israel's enemies: the Ammonites, Philistines, Syrians, Moabites, Edomites, and Amalekites. His victories extended the borders of the Promised Land from the Mediterranean Sea to the Euphrates River (chapters 8–10).

David's grievous sins (chapters 11–12) occurred in the middle of his reign. They marked the tragic division between his great success (chapters 1–10) and the numerous tragedies that followed him, his family, and the nation (chapters 13–24).

April 11: Read 2 Samuel 1–2

Verse for Today: *"David inquired of the Lord"* (2 Sam. 2:1).

Saul and David possessed many similarities: both were anointed king of Israel; both reigned about forty years; and both had the loyal support of Samuel, the prophet of God. A marked difference between them, however, made Saul a miserable failure and David a successful king.

Saul was a self-willed man, who made decisions without seeking God's direction. David rarely lost sight of his need to pray and wait upon the Lord to fulfill His promises at His appointed time. Even after Saul was dead, David did not make any effort to seize control of the nation. Instead, he *"inquired of the Lord."*

One of David's greatest desires was to worship the Lord in the temple at Jerusalem (Ps. 27:4). Yet even in this, he patiently waited for God's timing.

So often, we tend to get ahead of the Lord in our eagerness to have, or do, something. But there is a peaceful rest for those who patiently trust in the Lord's timing.

"Rest in the Lord, and wait patiently for him. . . . Those that wait upon the Lord, they shall inherit the earth" (Ps. 37:7, 9).

Thought for Today: God always knows the best time, and the best way, to answer prayer.

Christ Revealed: In David's noble poem, which honors Jonathan and even Saul, despite his treatment of David (2 Sam. 1:17-27). David forgot all his injuries and considered only the pleasant aspects. David typifies Jesus, who loves us even when we are in rebellion against God (Rom. 5:8).

April 12: Read 2 Samuel 3–5

Verse for Today: *"So all the elders of Israel came to the king to Hebron . . . and they anointed David king over Israel"* (2 Sam. 5:3).

While David was still a youth, he was anointed king of Israel, although it took years for complete fulfillment. It took the death of King Saul before David was welcomed as king over the tribe of Judah. Another 7½ years passed before the other tribes of Israel acknowledged their need for the Lord's leadership and asked David to be their king.

David faced many hardships and difficulties throughout his life, especially during the years Saul sought to kill him. Once, David cried out in despair, saying, *"I shall now perish one day by the hand of Saul"* (1 Sam. 27:1). Through these seemingly hopeless experiences, God prepared him to be His faithful shepherd-ruler—*"a captain over Israel"* (2 Sam. 5:2). In his trials, David drew closer to the Lord, and learned of the absolute care of the Great Shepherd for His children. David could say about the Lord, *"He is my refuge and my fortress: my God; in him will I trust"* (Ps. 91:2).

Some Christians fail to exhibit any clear image of Christlikeness. Even after a number of years, they still are not living by the principle of dying to self. Few are willing to accept and endure the Lord's discipline because they do not recognize the hand of God in their difficulties. They see only people or problems opposing them. They fail to ask God what He is trying to teach them, and do not cry out for His assistance and wisdom.

We, ourselves, are the greatest obstacle to being used by God. Only when we are willing to die to *self* can we be an expression of the Lord's life.

"For we which live are always delivered unto death for Jesus's sake, that the life also of Jesus might be made manifest in our mortal flesh" (2 Cor. 4:11).

Thought for Today: As we grow spiritually, we lose confidence in self and in our own abilities, and we develop confidence in the Lord's wonderful ability to guide and sustain us.

Christ Portrayed: By David, the anointed king of Israel (2 Sam. 5:3). Christ is God's Anointed. *Christ* means *"Messiah,"* or *"Anointed One"* (Ps. 2:2; John 1:41).

April 13: Read 2 Samuel 6–9

Verse for Today: *"And thine house and thy kingdom shall be established for ever before thee: thy throne shall be established for ever"* (2 Sam. 7:16).

David was the greatest king ever to rule the nation of Israel. However, he was not made great for his own sake, but to fulfill God's covenant promise that *Your kingdom shall be established forever.* God's covenant with David was a guarantee that He would one day send a perfectly righteous king—the Messiah.

This promise was fulfilled in Jesus Christ, the descendant of David (Matt. 1:1). The angel of the Lord appeared to Mary (a descendant of David), saying, *"He shall be great, and shall be called the Son of the Highest: and the Lord God shall give unto him the throne of his father David"* (Luke 1:32).

When a person accepts Christ as Savior and Lord, Christ begins to reign in that life.

Christ is King of kings and Lord of lords (Rev. 19:16). *Those who are with Him are His called, chosen, and faithful followers* (Rev. 17:14).

Thought for Today: The mind cannot imagine all the wonders prepared for those who accept Christ as Lord and Savior.

Christ Revealed: Through David's kindness to Mephibosheth (2 Sam. 9:7). This is a picture of the Lord's kindness and salvation to us. In Jesus, the helpless and needy receive mercy and grace (Rom. 7:14).

April 14: Read 2 Samuel 10–12

Verses for Today: *"At the time when kings go forth to battle . . . David tarried still in Jerusalem. And it came to pass in an eveningtide, that David arose from off his bed, and walked upon the roof of the king's house: and from the roof he saw a woman washing herself"* (2 Sam. 11:1-2).

David was a man of exceptional character—a man after God's own heart (1 Sam. 13:14). On this occasion, though, he sought to gratify the lust of the flesh, instead of turning from temptation. David inquired about the beautiful woman and learned that she was the wife of one of his very best soldiers, who was away in battle. Instead of turning from the lust that was in his heart, he dishonored the God-ordained family relationship of Uriah and Bathsheba and stole his neighbor's wife. Then, in an attempt to cover up that evil, David committed murder.

Perhaps Bathsheba could have prevented this wickedness and all the sorrows that followed if she had resisted and said (as Tamar did), *"Do not force me; for no such thing ought to be done in Israel"* (2 Sam. 13:12).

From the moment David first lusted after Bathsheba until their marriage, there seemed to not be one adverse circumstance to interfere with his plan—except that it *"displeased the Lord"* (2 Sam. 11:27).

When the Lord confronted David through Nathan, the prophet, David humbly confessed his sin, and God forgave him. However, the prophet still foretold that there would be bitter consequences for his sin (suffering, incest, murder, rebellion, and civil war), which would continue throughout David's lifetime (2 Sam. 12:10-12).

David learned firsthand that God does not show partiality. His former reputation as a man after God's heart was greatly marred, and many others fell into sin because of his bad example.

"Then when lust hath conceived, it bringeth forth sin: and sin, when it is finished, bringeth forth death" (James 1:15).

Thought for Today: Sin seldom ends with one act alone—it always takes us further than we want to go.

Christ Revealed: In the prophet's giving Solomon the name Jedidiah, which means *"Beloved of the Lord"* (2 Sam. 12:25). Jesus was greatly loved by the Father (John 17:24).

April 15: Read 2 Samuel 13–14

Verse for Today: *"But Absalom fled. . . . And David mourned for his son every day"* (2 Sam. 13:37).

When David's great sin became publicly known, not only was he filled with remorse, but it appears he was filled with shame, as well. He was no longer seen in public; his palace became his hiding place.

Sin always produces side effects—often with sad and evil consequences, which go far beyond all calculation or expectation. Our sin not only affects us, but it also affects others. Up until that time, David had lived a godly life, but his older sons did not follow his good example. Instead, they followed his sinful ways.

His oldest son, Amnon, cruelly raped his half sister Tamar, but David did not punish his son as the law required. Absalom, motivated by selfish ambition to become king, and hatred toward Amnon for raping his sister, welcomed the opportunity to carry out justice. Eventually, he murdered his half brother Amnon, who was heir to the throne. The crimes of David's two sons must have caused him to recall memories of the sins he committed—adultery and murder.

The consequences of sin cannot be avoided, postponed, or ignored by anyone—whether king or peasant. Sin brings with it suffering and sorrow.

Encourage one another day after day, while there is still time, so that none of you will be hardened by sin's deceiving ways (Heb. 3:13).

Thought for Today: All who compromise their Christian convictions for self-satisfaction leave themselves open to Satan's attacks.

Christ Revealed: Through David's restoration of Absalom (2 Sam. 14:33). If an earthly father's compassion reconciles him to his estranged son, how much more will our loving heavenly Father reconcile us to Himself when we confess our sin (Luke 15:11-32).

April 16: Read 2 Samuel 15–16

Verses for Today: *"And there came a messenger to David, saying, The hearts of the men of Israel are after Absalom. And David said unto all his servants that were with him at Jerusalem, Arise, and let us flee; for we shall not else escape from Absalom: make speed to depart, lest he . . . smite the city with the edge of the sword"* (2 Sam. 15:13-14).

One of the most pitiful passages in the Bible reveals King David trying to escape from his son Absalom. Heartbroken, the aged king is described as barefoot, running across the rough hills leading to the Mount of Olives. Shimei, one of Saul's relatives, followed David as he fled from Jerusalem, cursing him and throwing stones at him. He accused David of being responsible for Saul's death and *"all the blood of the house of Saul"* (2 Sam. 16:8).

This accusation was not true, and Abishai asked David for permission to kill Shimei. David refused, saying, *"Let him curse, because the Lord hath said unto him, Curse David"* (2 Sam. 16:10). Because David had lost the throne due to his sin, he felt he deserved the humiliation and insults from Saul's relative.

Too often, we retaliate, fight back, or seek revenge, and do not see the hand of God in our sufferings. However, once we know the Lord is in everything, and we yield to Him, we discover His perfect will. Our highest privilege is for Him to work His highest good in and through us. May the Lord teach us the precious privilege of accepting and loving His ways, for then we will receive His blessings in due time.

"For as the heavens are higher than the earth, so are my ways higher than your ways, and my thoughts than your thoughts" (Isa. 55:9).

Thought for Today: God is our strength in times of trouble.

Christ Revealed: Through David as he rebuked his people when they wanted to execute his enemies (1 Sam. 26:8-9; 2 Sam. 16:10-11). Jesus declared, *"I say unto you, Love your enemies"* (Matt. 5:44-45; Luke 9:54-56).

April 17: Read 2 Samuel 17–18

Verse for Today: *"O my son Absalom, my son, my son Absalom! Would God I had died for thee, O Absalom, my son, my son!"* (2 Sam. 18:33).

The majority of Israel's leaders and people joined Absalom in attempting to overthrow King David. Absalom was then declared king and entered Jerusalem without resistance. Up to this point, all Absalom's plans had been successful. Now he was determined to pursue and execute his father, David. In the ensuing battle, Absalom was defeated, and twenty thousand men died (2 Sam. 18:7). Many had supported and stayed by Absalom; but when his hair became caught in the limbs of an oak tree, he didn't have a friend to help him escape. Everyone rushed past, intent on saving his own life. God permitted an insignificant branch of a tree to hold Absalom by his hair until he was killed by Joab.

Absalom's rebellion against David and his own subsequent downfall are typical of those who *take their stand against the Lord and against His Anointed One* (Ps. 2:2). The wicked are successful only until God's purposes have been fulfilled. Many people die an untimely death after taking an open stand against one of God's leaders.

We are not to take matters into our own hands. Instead, we are to submit to, and pray for, those in authority, and pray for wisdom in handling difficult situations.

Do not be wise in your own eyes, but fear the LORD, and depart from evil (Prov. 3:7).

Thought for Today: No one can defeat God's purposes.

Christ Revealed: Through Mahanaim, a city of refuge, where David went when he fled from Absalom (2 Sam. 17:27). Jesus is our refuge (Heb. 6:18).

April 18: Read 2 Samuel 19–20

Verse for Today: *"So every man of Israel went up from after David, and followed Sheba the son of Bichri: but the men of Judah clave unto their king, from Jordan even to Jerusalem"* (2 Sam. 20:2).

The general discontent of Israel gave Sheba, an ambitious leader, the opportunity to start a civil war. The years of suffering, rebellion, murder, and civil war during David's reign were directly related to his sin with Bathsheba. Little could David realize, when he held the beautiful Bathsheba for one night of enjoyment, how much suffering his sin would bring.

Although the Lord forgave David's sin (2 Sam. 12:13), its consequences continued to plague him throughout his reign. Year after year—with each tragedy—he must have cried out, "Why did I do it? How could I have done it?" These are some of the most pathetic questions men and women can ask themselves.

The pleasures of sin always come at a price much higher than expected.

Lord, help us willingly relinquish all things and count them as worthless compared with the priceless privilege of knowing You (Phil. 3:8).

Thought for Today: Satan finds it easy to influence the life that is unguarded by daily prayer and reading God's Word.

Christ Portrayed: By David, who wished to be invited back as king (2 Sam. 19:11). Our Lord Jesus wants to be invited into the hearts of all mankind. He won't force His will on us; He comes only by invitation (Acts 2:21; Rom. 10:13). *"Behold, I stand at the door, and knock: if any man hear my voice, and open the door, I will come in to him, and will sup with him, and he with me"* (Rev. 3:20).

April 19: Read 2 Samuel 21–22

Verse for Today: *"Then there was a famine in the days of David three years"* (2 Sam. 21:1).

David prayed and asked God why there was a famine in the land. God told him it was because Saul had broken the covenant Joshua had made with the Gibeonites more than four hundred years earlier (Josh. 9:16-27). This incident shows how sacred God considers a vow, even though it was made to an unbelieving Canaanite nation.

God has clearly stated, *"When thou shalt vow a vow unto the Lord thy God, thou shalt not slack to pay it: for the Lord thy God will surely require it of thee"*

(Deut. 23:21; Num. 30:2). The three years of famine that resulted from a broken vow reveal the seriousness of keeping one's word.

God is faithful to His Word, and He expects us to be faithful to our word. Can people depend upon what you say, or are your words meaningless? Do you say only what others want to hear? Or do you keep your promises? Far too many Christians have good intentions, but allow circumstances to sway their convictions, words, and actions; consequently, their word is unreliable.

"That which is gone out of thy lips thou shalt keep and perform" (Deut. 23:23).

Thought for Today: God is faithful to us and always keeps His Word and promises.

Christ Revealed: As the One we call upon for salvation (2 Sam. 22:4). *There is salvation in no one except Jesus; for there is no other name under heaven that has been given among men, by which we can be saved* (Acts 4:12).

April 20: Read 2 Samuel 23–24

Verse for Today: *"And David's heart smote him after that he had numbered the people. And David said unto the Lord, I have sinned greatly in that I have done"* (2 Sam. 24:10).

Satan, who is the author of pride, prompted David to take a census to determine how many men were available for his army (1 Chron. 21:1). Although the counting of the people may have seemed quite harmless, *"the anger of the Lord was kindled against Israel"* (2 Sam. 24:1). Even Joab recognized that David's purpose in taking the census was to enhance his own prestige (1 Chron. 21:3).

There was never to be a numbering of the people or a census taken without making an atonement offering. The atonement offering was necessary to protect the Israelites against a plague (Ex. 30:12), and remind the people not to become a victim of their own success and lose their dependence upon God and His mercy.

You are worthy, our Lord and our God, to receive glory, honor, and power. For You created all things; and, by Your will, they were given existence and life (Rev. 4:11).

Thought for Today: When the Lord says, *I will send you,* we can rest assured He will provide everything necessary for the appointed task.

Christ Revealed: Through the altar that David built and the sacrifices that he offered on it. Because they were acceptable to God, the plague stopped (2 Sam. 24:25). Jesus, our worthy sacrifice, offered Himself up to God, so that we are saved from God's judgment. In Jesus, we are forgiven, accepted, and made holy (Heb. 10:10).

1 KINGS

The book of 1 Kings is a continuation of Israel's history from the book of 2 Samuel and covers about 120 years. It confirms again how the rise of the nation, or the decline, was in direct relation to whether or not the leader and the people followed God.

Chapters 1–2 relate David's death and the crowning of Solomon.

Chapters 3–11 are devoted to the forty-year reign of Solomon. Under his reign, Israel enjoyed her most prominent years of fame. Kings from all over the world heard about his wisdom and came to speak with him and ask him questions (1 Kings 4:34). At the beginning of his reign, King Solomon expressed a desire to honor God. He was chosen by God to build the magnificent temple, and God appeared to him at least twice and spoke in an unmistakable way (1 Kings 3:5-14; 9:2-9; 11:9-13).

But Solomon's numerous foreign wives, wealth, and great fame all influenced him away from God. Although he had inherited a powerful united kingdom that was growing in wealth and world superiority, he brought about its division, as pronounced by the Lord: *Because you have not observed My covenant but have disobeyed My commands, I will surely take the kingdom away from you* (1 Kings 11:11). Still, there were no signs of repentance.

The nation continued to decline spiritually, and the people became bitter under the heavy burden of paying the excessive taxes that were necessary to maintain Solomon's government and luxurious lifestyle.

Chapters 12–16 cover the division of the once glorious kingdom. After Solomon's death the united kingdom split into Israel, the Northern Kingdom, and Judah, the Southern Kingdom.

The Northern Kingdom established their capital in Samaria. They immediately rejected Solomon's son, Rehoboam, and appointed Jeroboam as king. (Jeroboam is remembered as the king who led Israel into the sin of worshiping the golden calves. The account is related in 1 Kings 22:52 and 2 Kings 10:29.)

Judah, the Southern Kingdom, consisted of the tribes of Judah and Benjamin, and the majority of the Levites. Their capital was Jerusalem.

Chapters 17–22 concentrate primarily on the prophet Elijah and his ministry and miracles, and also Israel's most wicked king, Ahab.

The book of 1 Kings reminds us that the health and well-being of the Israelite nation was the result of whether or not the people chose to listen to and obey God.

April 21: Read 1 Kings 1–2

Verse for Today: *"And keep the charge of the Lord thy God, to walk in his ways, to keep his statutes, and his commandments . . . that thou mayest prosper"* (1 Kings 2:3).

David's last words to Solomon revealed his greatest desire for his son—that he would live to please the Lord. David said nothing to Solomon about gaining fame or enlarging his kingdom. Rather, he stressed the importance of keeping God's commandments and pleasing God. David's concern was not that Solomon gain material wealth, but that he prosper spiritually by living in harmony with God's Word.

Material blessings are incidental. Those who *prosper* in the eyes of the Lord may, or may not, have wealth. In the New Testament, Stephen and Paul did not prosper in the eyes of the world, but their true prosperity cannot be measured.

The truly "blessed" man is protected against a fruitless life of failure because *he delights in the law of the Lord, meditating on the Word of God day and night. He prospers in whatever he does* (Ps. 1:2-3). Truly the Scriptures are one of our greatest gifts that has been bestowed upon mankind. They enable us to discover God's unique revelation and live out His will. What a privilege we have to prayerfully read the Bible each day!

Whoever accepts My commandments and obeys them is the one who loves Me. And whoever loves Me will be loved by My Father, and I will love him and will make Myself real to him (John 14:21).

Thought for Today: Our daily happiness should not be dependent upon material possessions or worldly gain.

Christ Portrayed: By Solomon, whose life was threatened by those who feared he would be king (1 Kings 1:11-12). When Jesus was a baby, King Herod heard about Christ and the prophecies surrounding Him. Fearing Jesus would be king, Herod ordered all the male babies in Bethlehem and its vicinity (two years old and younger) to be killed (Matt. 2:13-18).

April 22: Read 1 Kings 3–4

Verses for Today: *"And Solomon made affinity with Pharaoh king of Egypt, and took Pharaoh's daughter. . . . And Solomon loved the Lord . . . only he sacrificed and burnt incense in high places"* (1 Kings 3:1, 3).

At the beginning of his reign, Solomon loved the Lord and followed the teachings of his father, David. But it soon became evident that Solomon did not take seriously his sacred responsibility to obey God's laws (1 Kings 2:3).

Solomon made an alliance with Pharaoh, instead of seeking help from the Lord. This was the first association between Israel and Egypt since the time of the exodus from Egyptian slavery 480 years earlier (1 Kings 6:1).

In addition, he married Pharaoh's daughter. These actions may have been politically motivated to prevent future wars with Egypt, and to increase his prestige among the neighboring nations (1 Kings 9:16).

But Solomon's association with Egypt led to other alliances and actions, which eventually separated him from God's blessings. Instead of loving the Lord with all his heart (Deut. 6:5), he offered sacrifices and burned incense on the high places, which constituted idol worship.

Solomon's thousand burnt offerings to the Lord (1 Kings 3:4) could not compensate for his compromises. His worldly associations and powerlessness were inseparably linked.

We must not team up with unbelievers; for what common interest is there between righteousness and unrighteousness or between light and darkness? What accord is there between Christ and Satan, between a believer and an unbeliever? (2 Cor. 6:14-15).

Thought for Today: It is impossible to obtain God's best while trying to live for both worlds.

Christ Portrayed: By Solomon who had great wisdom and treasure (1 Kings 3:12). In Christ are *hidden all the treasures of wisdom and knowledge* (Col. 2:3) and the *fullness of God* (Col. 2:9-10).

April 23: Read 1 Kings 5–7

Verses for Today: *"And it came to pass in the four hundred and eightieth year after the children of Israel were come out of the land of Egypt, in the fourth year of Solomon's reign over Israel . . . he began to build the house of the Lord. . . . And in the eleventh year . . . was the house finished"* (1 Kings 6:1, 38).

No other building in the world compared with Solomon's temple. The most costly materials and treasures were lavished upon it. But the world observed only the external beauty of the temple because its true glory was inside. The *Shekinah glory*—the presence of God—dwelled within the holy of holies.

The Israelites and people from other nations could only *hear* about this glory. This was because only the priest was allowed to enter this holy sanctuary and experience God, and this, on an extremely limited basis.

What magnificent truth we should ponder as Christians. When we receive the Lord and His salvation, we are not only reconciled to God, but we are invited and instructed to come boldly into His presence with our requests at any time, with every need (Heb. 4:16). And there's more. As believers, each of us is a temple where God and His glory dwell within us!

The miracle of the new birth and the indwelling Holy Spirit mark a great difference between Christians and the unsaved, who are unable to experience God's magnificent presence. However, as we live our lives, those we encounter should experience a bit of God's glory through us, and be able to hear about His marvelous invitation.

Through union with Him, we are continuously being built into a dwelling place for "God through the Spirit" (Eph. 2:22).

Thought for Today: Truly, we must let our light shine for the Lord (Matt. 5:16).

Christ Revealed: Through the temple (1 Kings 6). Jesus is the true temple, whom God prepared (John 2:21; Heb. 10:5); and it is through Jesus that we have access to God (Eph. 2:18).

April 24: Read 1 Kings 8

Verses for Today: *"What prayer and supplication soever be made by any man. . . . Then hear . . . and forgive . . . and give to every man according to his ways, whose heart thou knowest"* (1 Kings 8:38-39).

At the dedication of the temple, King Solomon knelt before God, stretching his hands toward heaven, and prayed one of the longest prayers recorded in the Bible. He proclaimed, *"Lord God of Israel, there is no God like thee, in heaven above, or on earth beneath"* (1 Kings 8:23). Solomon acknowledged God as the one true God. He reaffirmed before the people that receiving God's blessings was dependent upon their returning to the Lord *"with all their heart"* (1 Kings 8:48).

And yet, *"Solomon did evil . . . and went not fully after the Lord"* (1 Kings 11:6). Solomon's pride, and his love for power, luxury, and physical satisfaction brought God's judgment upon himself (1 Kings 11:1, 3, 9, 11). What a difference the outcome would have been if Solomon had lived the truths he expressed in prayer!

The Lord knows whether our prayers are mere passing emotion, or if they are an expression of a true desire to please Him. The emphasis we place on the things of this world—wealth, fame, and other physical attractions—will eventually reveal the depth of our sincerity and loyalty to God.

"For all that is in the world, the lust of the flesh, and the lust of the eyes, and the pride of life, is not of the Father, but is of the world" (1 John 2:16).

Thought for Today: A person who knows the truth, but does not live it, deceives himself.

Christ Revealed: In Solomon's dedicatory prayer, as a type of Christ's high-priestly prayer of dedication for His disciples (1 Kings 8:22-54; John 17).

April 25: Read 1 Kings 9–11

Verses for Today: *"And he said to Jeroboam, Take thee ten pieces: for thus saith the Lord, the God of Israel, Behold, I will rend the kingdom out of the hand of Solomon, and will give ten tribes to thee. . . . Because . . . they have forsaken me, and have worshipped Ashtoreth"* (1 Kings 11:31, 33).

The discontent of the Ephraimites continued to grow as Solomon's popularity diminished. Jeroboam, who at one time was highly honored in Solomon's administration, became a spokesman for his tribe, the Ephraimites, and instigated a rebellion (1 Kings 11:26).

The prophet Ahijah had announced to Jeroboam that he would rule over ten tribes of Israel. In addition, God had promised Joseph while he was in Egypt that kings would proceed from him (Gen. 49; Deut. 33), and this was remarkably fulfilled when Jeroboam, an Ephraimite, became king.

Solomon was unsuccessful in his attempt to kill Jeroboam. Rehoboam later declared war against Jeroboam's new kingdom and also made every effort to prevent the fulfillment of God's Word to Jeroboam. But the great God of Truth always keeps His Word.

"Heaven and earth shall pass away: but my words shall not pass away" (Luke 21:33).

Thought for Today: God is able to fulfill what He has promised, regardless of adverse circumstances.

Christ Portrayed: By King Solomon, who became greater than all the kings of the earth (1 Kings 10:23-25). Christ will reign as *"KING OF KINGS AND LORD OF LORDS"* (Rev. 19:16).

April 26: Read 1 Kings 12–13

Verse for Today: *"And when the prophet that brought him back from the way heard thereof, he said, It is the man of God, who was disobedient unto the word of the Lord: therefore the Lord hath delivered him unto the lion, which hath torn him, and slain him, according to the word of the Lord, which he spake unto him"* (1 Kings 13:26).

Jeroboam successfully led a revolt that gained the support of the ten northern tribes and divided the kingdom. The tribes of Judah, and Benjamin, and most of the Levites, remained faithful to the worship of God in Jerusalem and became the Southern Kingdom. Jeroboam feared that if the people from the ten tribes continued to worship in Jerusalem, they might desire to reunite the kingdom; therefore, he set up two worship centers—one in Dan and the other in Bethel.

A number of tragedies are revealed in these events. First, King Jeroboam was more concerned about his control of a nation than he was about God's control over himself and the nation.

Second, although the old prophet knew the will of God, he lied. He influenced the young prophet not to complete what the Lord had called him to do. The third tragedy was the young prophet's untimely death. He had God's message and the courage to preach it, and he had refused all the king's bribes. He had stood fearlessly in the center of a crowd, proclaiming the Lord's judgment upon disobedience. Neither the pleasures of a luxurious meal nor the prospect of comfortable lodging after the fatigue of a long journey could persuade him to turn away from doing what God had commanded.

But when the young prophet accepted the aged, backslidden prophet and his warm reception, it resulted in death. This judgment seems severe, but it was necessary because he, too, disobeyed God.

It is not difficult to recognize obvious sins—such as theft, murder, and adultery—and reject them. But Christians often miss God's best by becoming involved in something that doesn't necessarily seem sinful. We must beware of the suggestions or activities of "friends" who would keep us from accomplishing God's purposes.

It is of the utmost importance that we guard against loving things or people more than loving the Lord.

We must not love the world, or anything the world has to offer, including possessions, power, or privilege. Loving the world or any of these things does not come from the Father, but comes from the world (1 John 2:15).

Thought for Today: Those who please God are obedient to His Word.

Christ Revealed: Through the *"man of God,"* who spoke the Word of God (1 Kings 13:1-5). He typified Jesus, who is God and is the Word of God (John 1:1, 14; Rev. 19:13).

April 27: Read 1 Kings 14–15

Verses for Today: *"Shishak king of Egypt came up against Jerusalem: And he took away the treasures of the house of the Lord . . . and he took away all the shields of gold"* (1 Kings 14:25-26).

God Himself was the strength of Jerusalem, but He withdrew His presence when idol worship continued to be practiced. Therefore, the kingdom of Judah was easily overrun by Shishak, king of Egypt. When Rehoboam's kingship was established, and he had become strong, he and all his people abandoned the law of the Lord (2 Chron. 12:1). Consequently, God permitted Shishak to invade Jerusalem and carry away immense wealth, including the golden shields—the symbol of the Lord's protection.

Not wanting to be embarrassed by the absence of the golden shields, Rehoboam made shields of brass (bronze) and continued his ceremonies as though nothing had happened. He substituted cheap metal for gold. They were similar in appearance, but the cheap shields themselves symbolized the absence of God's precious presence and power to protect them.

Pity the poor soul that gives the appearance of living a "good life" and even attends church services, but does not worship God from the heart, truly following His ways. All of his outward actions are worthless.

Jesus said, *Not everyone who calls Me "Lord, Lord," will enter the kingdom of heaven—only those who are obedient to My Father, who is in heaven* (Matt. 7:21).

Thought for Today: The Lord is our strength and our shield. May we actively seek to know and follow Him through reading His Word and prayer.

Christ Revealed: In Asa's ridding the land of idols and sodomites (1 Kings 15:11-14). Jesus cleansed the temple (Matt. 21:12-13; John 2:13-16). Every believer is a temple of God (1 Cor. 6:19-20; 2 Cor. 6:16-17) and to be cleansed by Him.

April 28: Read 1 Kings 16–18

Verse for Today: *"And Elijah . . . said unto Ahab, As the Lord God of Israel liveth, before whom I stand, there shall not be dew nor rain these years, but according to my word"* (1 Kings 17:1).

The prophet Elijah prophesied there would be a drought in the land because of the nation's sin. When it came, Elijah suffered, along with the rest of the nation, but he trusted God for his daily existence.

We should follow Elijah's example of praying and trusting the Lord for our needs. The New Testament holds up Elijah to us as an example of praying. *The prayers of the righteous have a powerful effect. Elijah was only a man like ourselves, but he prayed earnestly that there would be no rain, and no rain fell* (James 5:16-18).

God's Word encourages us to pray earnestly—and keep on praying, not trusting in ourselves, but in the grace and promises of God. It is not enough merely to say a prayer—our thoughts and requests much be in harmony with His Word, and our desires must be from the heart.

"*And he spake a parable unto them to this end, that men ought always to pray, and not to faint*" (Luke 18:1).

Thought for Today: We are to encourage ourselves—and one another—in the Lord, so that we don't give up.

Christ Portrayed: By Elijah, who provided flour and oil for the widow at Zarephath (1 Kings 17:13). Jesus is our Provider, the One who supplies all our needs according to His riches in glory (Phil. 4:19).

April 29: Read 1 Kings 19–20

Verse for Today: "*He requested for himself that he might die; and said, It is enough; now, O Lord, take away my life*" (1 Kings 19:4).

That day on Mount Carmel, the great purpose for which Elijah lived seemed to have been accomplished. False worship was exposed, Baal's prophets were slain, and Jehovah was exalted through a mighty miracle!

Elijah fully expected this great victory to instill the fear of the Lord into the heart of the queen and encourage the king to bring about religious reform. Jezebel, though, swore revenge and demanded that the prophet be put to death. In despair, Elijah cried: "*It is enough; now, O Lord, take away my life.*"

God, however, did not give him his request. Nor did God punish or even rebuke Elijah for making it. Instead of answering Elijah's prayer for death, God gave him rest and food.

All of us have times of disappointment and moments of hopelessness when it seems that our highest expectations are met with ridicule. But we must look beyond appearances and remain faithful to the "*still, small voice*" (1 Kings 19:11-13), and seek His renewing strength (Isa. 40:28-31).

Elijah's greatest success was not in the display of fire on Mount Carmel, but in the strength he imparted to seven thousand people who confessed, "*The Lord, he is the God*" (1 Kings 18:39).

"*Let us not be weary in well doing: for in due season we shall reap, if we faint not*" (Gal. 6:9).

Thought for Today: God, our wise and loving Father, comes in our moments of weakness to restore and strengthen us.

Christ Portrayed: By the prophet who came to King Hezekiah and pronounced healing (2 Kings 20:1-7). In Jesus, we are healed, forgiven, and loved (John 3:16; Rom. 8:38-39).

April 30: Read 1 Kings 21–22

Verses for Today: *"And Micaiah said, Behold . . . thou shalt go into an inner chamber to hide thyself. And the king of Israel said. . . . Put this fellow in the prison"* (1 Kings 22:25-27).

Jehoshaphat, king of Judah, agreed to join Ahab, king of Israel, in attacking Syria. But Jehoshaphat was uneasy about making the attack, so he told Ahab, *Let us first seek counsel from the Lord* (1 Kings 22:5).

Ahab called four hundred of his prophets, and they unanimously assured him of great success. But Jehoshaphat was still hesitant. Reluctantly, Ahab called in Micaiah, a godly prophet, who had been imprisoned because of his faithfulness to God.

The messengers tried to persuade Micaiah to agree with Ahab's four hundred prophets and thus gain the favor of the king. But Micaiah would not be intimidated. There were four hundred "yes" votes to Micaiah's one "no" vote—a miserable minority. But the truth is not dependent upon the majority's vote.

When he foretold that Ahab would be killed, Micaiah was slapped and dragged back to prison. Micaiah knew that God's presence—even in a dungeon—was worth far more than popular acceptance.

For it is pleasing in the sight of God if, from a sense of duty to God, a man endures wrong, even suffering unjustly (1 Pet. 2:19).

Thought for Today: God imparts His strength to those who remain faithful to Him.

Christ Portrayed: By Micaiah, who would say only what God instructed him to say (1 Kings 22:14). Jesus faithfully told others everything God told Him to say (John 8:28).

May

 2 KINGS

In 1 and 2 Kings, all the kings of Judah and Israel are recorded (except for Saul, whose story is recorded in 1 Samuel). After the death of Solomon, the kingdom began to further deteriorate. Ten of the tribes revolted against Solomon's son Rehoboam and formed the Northern Kingdom, called Israel (sometimes referred to as Ephraim or Samaria). The rebellion was led by Jeroboam, who immediately established golden-calf worship centers at Dan and Bethel to keep the northern tribes from worshiping in Jerusalem and reuniting with the other tribes.

Prophets were prominent throughout the history of the kings. They exposed the nation's corruption, foretold God's judgment, and appealed to the people to return to God. The prophets were often in conflict with the kings. The most prominent prophet of 1 Kings is Elijah; in 2 Kings it is Elisha. Both performed miracles.

Second Kings, chapters 1–17, recounts the divided kingdom. Nineteen kings ruled Israel, the Northern Kingdom, during its 210-year history as a divided kingdom, but not one was a faithful worshiper of God. The tribes of Reuben and Gad and half the tribe of Manasseh had chosen to occupy the territory on the eastern side of the Jordan River outside the Promised Land, and consequently, they were the first to be defeated by the Assyrians (1 Chron. 5:25-26). In the ninth year of Hoshea (the last king of the northern tribes), Shalmaneser, king of Assyria, conquered Samaria. Most of the people were transported to various parts of the Assyrian Empire, and all ten tribes lost their identity (2 Kings 17). The few remaining Israelites intermarried with other captives from foreign lands and became known as Samaritans. They were despised by the Jews (John 4:9).

Chapters 18–25 cover the smaller Southern Kingdom of Judah, which was made up of the tribes of Judah and Benjamin, as well as the Levites. These tribes remained faithful to the God-appointed temple worship in Jerusalem (1 Kings 12:20-21).

The Southern Kingdom also had nineteen kings. This does not include the usurper, Queen Athaliah, or Gedaliah, who was appointed governor for two months (2 Kings 11:1-16; 25:22-25). Rehoboam (Solomon's son) was the first king. The Southern Kingdom continued as a nation for approximately 136 years after Israel's destruction, because several kings were godly, particularly Hezekiah and Josiah. Most of the kings were godless and did evil, while a few were a mixture of good and evil.

Eventually, Judah, too, came under God's judgment. Nebuchadnezzar, king of Babylon, destroyed both Solomon's temple and Jerusalem (2 Kings 25:3-13; Jer. 52:12-17). The majority of the population was deported to Babylon. Those who were allowed to remain fled to Egypt, taking Jeremiah with them as a hostage.

A powerful truth revealed in 2 Kings is given to us by Bible teacher and author Leslie M. Grant. He highlights how even the reign of godly kings (such as Hezekiah and Josiah) ended in human failure. This makes plain that the true place of man is one of subjection, rather than of prominence and authority, which in every case proved beyond the capacity of men – even godly men. All of this cries out for the coming of the one true and faithful King, the Lord of glory![9]

9   The above statement, which has been slightly adapted, is from: Leslie M. Grant, *The Bible: Its 66 Books in Brief.* Believers Bookshelf, Inc.; BBUSA.org.; 2006. Grant's book can also be found at https://biblecentre.org/content.php?mode=7&item=1337.

May 1: Read 2 Kings 1–3

Verse for Today: *"And Ahaziah fell down through a lattice in his upper chamber that was in Samaria, and was sick: and he sent messengers, and said unto them, Go, inquire of Baalzebub the god of Ekron whether I shall recover of this disease"* (2 Kings 1:2).

Ahaziah, the king of Israel, was on the rooftop patio of his palace when he accidentally fell through a lattice opening to the marble floor below. The king sent messengers to the idol Baalzebub to ask whether he would recover. However, on their way, the messengers met Elijah, who told them that the king would soon die. Ahaziah's servants returned to tell the king what Elijah said. Instead of turning to the Lord, Ahaziah expressed hatred for the prophet as his mother, Jezebel, had done. He sent fifty solders to arrest Elijah and bring him into custody.

Ahaziah's unfaithfulness to the Lord hardened his heart, and he failed to recognize that the hand of God was in all that occurred—first in the death of his father, Ahab; then in the prophecy of his mother Jezebel's violent death; and now his "accident." Because there was no repentance, Ahaziah died (2 Kings 1:17).

Whether our circumstances occur from our own choices and actions, or from no fault of our own, we are still responsible for the way we react to the events. We can become angry with everything and everyone, including God, or we can seek the Lord, who uses our troubles and trials to draw us to Himself, reveal Himself, and transform us into the likeness of Christ.

"For they verily for a few days chastened us after their own pleasure; but he for our profit, that we might be partakers of his holiness" (Heb. 12:10).

Thought for Today: The Lord's presence, power, and grace are sufficient to meet every need we have.

Christ Revealed: In Elijah being taken up in the whirlwind and dropping his mantle (2 Kings 2:8-15). Being taken up in the whirlwind is a type of the Lord's ascension (Luke 24:50-51; Acts 1:1-11). The dropping of the mantle symbolizes the imparting of God's Spirit and power upon His faithful servants and the giving of His command to evangelize the world (Luke 24; Acts 1–2).

May 2: Read 2 Kings 4–5

Verse for Today: *"And it came to pass, when the king of Israel had read the letter, that he rent his clothes, and said, Am I God, to kill and to make alive, that this man doth send unto me to recover a man of his leprosy? wherefore consider, I pray you, and see how he seeketh a quarrel against me"* (2 Kings 5:7).

When Jehoram (Joram), king of Israel, read the letter from the king of Syria (Aram)—requesting that he heal Naaman of his leprosy—King Jehoram jumped to the wrong conclusion. He assumed that Naaman, the powerful captain of the Syrian army, was seeking an excuse to declare war.

Like his brother, Ahaziah, Jehoram failed to recognize God's hand in his circumstances. However, he did not consult Baalzebub, as his brother did (2 Kings 1:2); neither did he attempt to destroy the prophet of God, as his mother, Jezebel, did (1 Kings 19:1-2). Nevertheless, the king of Israel did not turn to God—even after Naaman was miraculously healed.

Pity the poor unbelievers who, like Jehoram, with all their fears and frustrations, believe that the conflicts in their lives are merely the arrangements of men who threaten to destroy them. How different are the "Elishas." They know the living God and that He has allowed our conflicts, adversities, and distresses according to His own will (Eph. 1:11).

God's purpose is to bring us into close fellowship with Himself by developing our trust in His guidance. In this way, He is able to perfect His plan for our lives.

"For consider him that endured such contradiction of sinners against himself, lest ye be wearied and faint in your minds" (Heb. 12:3).

Thought for Today: Our trials should cause us to seek and know the Lord more intimately.

Christ Revealed: In the meal that took the poison out of the pot (2 Kings 4:40-41). The meal made of crushed corn speaks of Jesus, who *"was wounded [pierced] for our transgressions, he was bruised for our iniquities: the chastisement of our peace was upon him; and with his stripes we are healed"* (Isa. 53:5; 1 Pet. 2:24).

May 3: Read 2 Kings 6–8

Verse for Today: *"Then Elisha said, Hear ye the word of the Lord; Thus saith the Lord, To morrow about this time shall a measure of fine flour be sold for a shekel . . . in the gate of Samaria"* (2 Kings 7:1).

Benhadad's powerful Syrian army had surrounded Samaria, the luxurious fortress city, for so long that the Israelites' food supply had been depleted. To keep from starving to death, they resorted to eating the most repulsive, defiling food (2 Kings 6:25). They even went so far as to eat human flesh (2 Kings 6:29).

The Bible doesn't hesitate to reveal life's painful and sordid realities when God is not a part of our lives. Because the Israelites had rejected His Word, they were helpless before the Syrians. But the Lord in mercy once again intervened, and the prophet Elisha confidently prophesied that food would be plentiful the next day. Since nothing can prevent the fulfillment of God's prophecies, indeed, *"a measure of fine flour was sold for a shekel, and two measures of barley for a shekel, according to the word of the Lord"* (2 Kings 7:16).

The Lord is able to supply our every need as we follow Him. He desires to provide us with both physical food and spiritual nourishment.

"Man shall not live by bread alone, but by every word that proceedeth out of the mouth of God" (Matt. 4:4).

Thought for Today: God often postpones answers to our prayers until we recognize the futility of our own efforts.

Christ Portrayed: By Elisha, who wept when he realized what Hazael would do to Israel and its people (2 Kings 8:11-12). We are reminded that Jesus wept over Jerusalem (Matt. 23:37-38).

May 4: Read 2 Kings 9–10

Verses for Today: *"Thus saith the Lord God of Israel, I have anointed thee king over the people of the Lord, even over Israel. And thou shalt smite the house of Ahab thy master, that I may avenge the blood of my servants the prophets. . . . For the whole house of Ahab shall perish"* (2 Kings 9:6-8).

After Ahab's death, his son Ahaziah reigned over Israel for two years, followed by the twelve-year reign of Ahaziah's brother, Jehoram. All three of these kings of the Northern Kingdom so zealously promoted idolatry in Israel that it spread into Judah and seriously weakened the true worship of Jehovah in Jerusalem.

During this serious spiritual decline, the Lord was preparing Jehu, the powerful captain-commander of the Northern Kingdom armies, as His instrument of judgment. God had revealed to Elijah that Jehu would become king over Israel (1 Kings 19:16). Perhaps as many as twenty years passed before God ordered Elisha to send a young prophet to anoint Jehu as Israel's king and the executioner of Jehoram (Joram) and all the descendants of Ahab. What appeared to be a coincidence when Jehu met Jehoram in the field of Naboth was actually the fulfillment of God's Word against Ahab, as foretold by Elijah (1 Kings 21:19-23; 2 Kings 9:21-26).

The violent and untimely deaths of Jezebel, King Ahab, and King Jehoram affirm the limitation of earthly power and the infallibility of God's Word.

"The word of our God shall stand for ever" (Isa. 40:8).

Thought for Today: Many people die untimely deaths because of disobedience to the Lord.

Christ Revealed: Through Jehu's destruction of Baal worship (2 Kings 10:25-28). Christ will one day destroy the false religions of the world (Rev. 14:10; 20:10).

May 5: Read 2 Kings 11–13

Verse for Today: *"And when Athaliah the mother of Ahaziah saw that her son was dead, she arose and destroyed all the seed royal"* (2 Kings 11:1).

About eight years after the godly reign of Jehoshaphat, Athaliah seized control of the Southern Kingdom and reigned in Jerusalem, the city of David. Athaliah's wicked, six-year reign was the result of a compromise that Jehoshaphat made years earlier when he arranged for his son, Jehoram, to marry Athaliah, daughter of the wicked, idol-worshiping Ahab and Jezebel.

Jehoshaphat had failed to foresee that the "unequal yoke" of his son's marriage to Athaliah would one day destroy all the influence for godliness that he had spent his life building. The eventual destruction of Jerusalem and captivity of the chosen nation of Judah are easily traced back to the fact that the people adopted the ways of unbelievers.

Many Christians are deceived, and their usefulness to God is destroyed, because of close friendship with those who resist and oppose the Lord. We must be careful about the friends we choose.

"Be ye not unequally yoked together with unbelievers: for what fellowship hath righteousness with unrighteousness? and what communion hath light with darkness?" (2 Cor. 6:14).

Thought for Today: Like Jehoshaphat, some Christians today discover too late the danger of being unequally yoked with an unbeliever.

Christ Portrayed: By Joash, who had to be hidden from those who wanted to kill him (2 Kings 11:1-3). Mary and Joseph took Jesus to Egypt to protect Him from those who wanted to kill Him (Matt. 2:13).

May 6: Read 2 Kings 14–15

Verse for Today: *"He restored the coast of Israel from the entering of Hamath unto the sea of the plain, according to the word of the Lord God of Israel, which he spake by the hand of his servant Jonah, the son of Amittai, the prophet"* (2 Kings 14:25).

King Jeroboam II (son of Jehoash of Israel and not Joash of Judah) was very successful in all his battles and brought great prosperity to the nation, but this recognition did not lead him to worship God. Instead, he practiced all the sins of Jeroboam I.

During his reign, Amos, Hosea, Joel, and Jonah all prophesied, but not one of them was successful in turning him toward God. Instead, *"he did that which was evil in the sight of the Lord"* (2 Kings 14:24). Finally, God commanded Amos to go to Bethel to prophesy the destruction of the kingdom (Amos 7:9).

The Israelites seemed to believe that because they prospered, God approved of their idol worship. More and more, they placed their confidence in the supremacy of Baal worship, rather than in God.

How tragic that many people today are like Jeroboam. Many boast of their material success, even though it was achieved at the cost of spiritual neglect. Parents themselves should be more concerned about emphasizing the real spiritual wealth of the Word of God, rather than striving so hard to leave their children material things.

A Christian's greatest tests of loyalty and humility before God often come during times of material blessing. While we are enjoying prosperity, we are usually less concerned about prayerfully seeking the Lord's guidance and will for our lives.

"For what is a man profited, if he shall gain the whole world, and lose his own soul?" (Matt. 16:26).

Thought for Today: We forfeit God's best when we fail to keep His commandments.

Christ Revealed: When the Lord struck the king with leprosy and thrust him out from being king (2 Kings 15:5-7). This incident depicts the time when Christ will cast out the unprofitable servant (Matt. 25:30).

May 7: Read 2 Kings 16–17

Verses for Today: *"In the ninth year of Hoshea the king of Assyria took Samaria [capital of the Northern Kingdom], and carried Israel away into Assyria. . . . They feared the Lord, and served their own gods"* (2 Kings 17:6, 33).

Hoshea paid tribute to the king of Assyria and pretended to be loyal to him. However, he made a secret agreement with the king of Egypt, hoping to receive help from the Egyptians and thus free his nation from Assyrian control.

Hoshea's double-dealing schemes and double-mindedness reveal that his trust was not in God, but in himself. This kind of "clever" plan only temporarily seems to be successful. When the king of Assyria learned about Hoshea's agreement, he led the battle that brought about the end of the Northern Kingdom, and Egypt made no attempt to help Hoshea.

Many today are making the same mistake Hoshea made, who attempted to serve two masters. They believe in Jehovah, the true God, but they also worship the gods of the heathens. They have a certain amount of fear of God, judgment, and death, and consequently try to be religious and go to church. They call themselves Christians, but it is in name only. What a warning against double-mindedness with God!

"This people draweth nigh unto me with their mouth, and honoreth me with their lips; but their heart is far from me" (Matt. 15:8). *Whoever is a friend of the world is an enemy of God* (James 4:4).

Thought for Today: Double-mindedness and compromise have no place in the life of a person who is fully committed to the Lord.

Christ Revealed: Through the initial brazen (bronze) altar (2 Kings 16:10-15). The brazen altar is a picture of the cross where Christ offered Himself as a whole burnt offering to God as our substitute (Heb. 9:11-15).

May 8: **Read 2 Kings 18–20**

Verses for Today: *"Hezekiah . . . trusted in the Lord God of Israel; so that after him was none like him among all the kings of Judah, nor any that were before him. . . . And the Lord was with him"* (2 Kings 18:1, 5, 7).

The Northern Kingdom had already been conquered by the Assyrians, and most of the people were deported as slaves. Sennacherib, the Assyrian king, was then determined to conquer Judah, the Southern Kingdom, and he surrounded Jerusalem with his seemingly invincible army.

The chances for escape for the Southern Kingdom looked impossible; and to all human appearances, there was no hope. But King Hezekiah bypassed all his advisers and went immediately to the temple and prayed. He sent messengers to the prophet Isaiah. After that prayer, the angel of God destroyed 185,000 Assyrian soldiers. Furthermore, when Sennacherib returned to his palace in Nineveh, two of his own sons assassinated him (2 Kings 19:37; Isa. 37:38).

We should not be fearful about our future, but pray and commit our needs to God. No matter how hopeless our situation may appear, remember that when Hezekiah prayed, *"the Lord was with him."* God will be with us, too.

"Ask, and it shall be given you; seek, and ye shall find; knock, and it shall be opened unto you: For every one that asketh receiveth; and he that seeketh findeth; and to him that knocketh it shall be opened" (Matt. 7:7-8).

Thought for Today: There is no substitute for seeking God's help in prayer.

Christ Portrayed: By Hezekiah, who was leading Judah back to God (2 Kings 19). Here we are reminded of Jesus's call: *Come to Me, and I will give you rest* (Matt. 11:28).

May 9: **Read 2 Kings 21–22**

Verses for Today: *"I have found the book of the law in the house of the Lord.... So Hilkiah the priest ... went unto Huldah the prophetess.... And she said unto them, Thus saith the Lord God of Israel"* (2 Kings 22:8, 14-15).

In the midst of this season of apostasy, the discovery of this book is once again confirmation of the indestructibility of God's divine written Word. Huldah, the prophetess, acknowledged the authority of the book found in the house of the Lord and announced that punishment would be imposed because Judah had abandoned Jehovah and turned to other gods.

Though little is known about Huldah, sufficient evidence indicates she had great influence in Jerusalem. The high priest and the king recognized her remarkable prophetic gift and sought spiritual guidance from her.

Just two other prophetesses are mentioned in the Old Testament—Miriam (Ex. 15:20) and Deborah (Judg. 4:4)—but neither one of them seems to have reached the same stature as Huldah achieved. Miriam and Deborah led the people in singing sacred songs of praise and rejoicing after great victories, but they did not prophesy as Huldah did with *"Thus saith the Lord."*

God is no respecter of persons in the distribution of His precious gifts. However, His Word can only be interpreted by those who are led by His Spirit. Just as the physician should be most competent to diagnose physical conditions, so the spiritual man or woman should be qualified to explain spiritual truth. Scripture declares, *Study and show thyself approved unto God, a worker who does not need to be ashamed and who correctly handles the word of truth* (2 Tim. 2:15).

As Christians, we should search for opportunities to serve the Lord and use our gifts. If someone comes to us, instead of viewing it as an intrusion and hoping the person will soon depart, we should consider it a possible opportunity from the Lord to share His Word and grace.

"And he gave some, apostles; and some, prophets; and some, evangelists; and some, pastors and teachers; for the perfecting of the saints, for the work of the ministry, for the edifying of the body of Christ" (Eph. 4:11-12).

Thought for Today: Christ is all-sufficient to supply every need so that we are able to accomplish His will.

Christ Revealed: Through the prophets (2 Kings 21:10). *Long ago, God spoke through His prophets ... in these last days, He speaks to us through His Son* (Heb. 1:1-2).

May 10: Read 2 Kings 23–25

Verse for Today: *"And the king of Babylon smote them, and slew them at Riblah in the land of Hamath. So Judah was carried away out of their land"* (2 Kings 25:21).

Just twenty-three years after the death of godly Josiah, the Southern Kingdom of Judah surrendered to the control of Egypt. Because of the people's unfaithfulness and repeated disobedience to God's Word, the nation was reduced to ruin.

The last four kings were merely puppet kings, appointed and controlled by Egypt and Babylon. Throughout their reigns, the nation experienced a series of conquests and deportations. How pathetic the fall of Judah was, especially since the Northern Kingdom had already fallen about 135 years earlier! Judah and the Northern Kingdom together had once been Israel, one of the most powerful nations on earth. From a very small beginning, Israel reached a height of such imperial greatness that it commanded the admiration of the mightiest nations of its day. But, because of Solomon's idolatry, the nation became divided.

Later, in the midst of Judah's decline, God raised up Jeremiah the prophet. If the people had followed his counsel, the outcome would have been much different. Jehoiachin, like Hezekiah, could have defied the invading forces. Sadly, though, the nation lost its power and the privilege of God's protection.

With an immense army, Nebuchadnezzar swept down upon the northern part of the country and surrounded Jerusalem. Eventually, the city was reduced to starvation. Zedekiah—with his wives, children, and guards—fled through an opening in the wall (Ezek. 12:12), but they were captured in the plains of Jericho. Zedekiah was forced to witness the slaughter of his own family; then his eyes were put out, and he was carried in chains to Babylon. His agonizing ordeal fulfilled two prophecies that appeared to contradict each other: that Zedekiah would come to Babylon, but that he would not see it (Jer. 32:5; 34:21; Ezek. 12:3; 17:20-21).[10]

The destruction of the kingdom of Judah teaches us that the greatest nation on earth cannot survive if its people continually reject God and His righteousness. Wealth, vast armies, and nuclear protection are false security when a nation turns from God.

Some nations boast about their great military programs, but those who continually look to God and remain faithful to Him will be victorious (Ps. 20:7-9).

---

10 Prophecy is a vital component of Scripture, and given, in part, for proof and evidence. Appendix A provides further insight on this topic.

Thought for Today: A nation's true success is dependent upon its faithfulness to the Lord.

Christ Revealed: Through the Passover (2 Kings 23:21-23). The Passover represents Christ, who is our Savior and Redeemer (John 1:29; 1 Cor. 5:6-7; 1 Pet. 1:18-19).

 # 1 AND 2 CHRONICLES

The first twelve books of the Bible (Genesis through the two books of Kings) relate a succession of historical events from the creation of Adam to the time of Judah's captivity. The last four of these twelve books (1 and 2 Samuel, plus 1 and 2 Kings) provide the moral and political history of Israel and Judah.

In 1 and 2 Chronicles, we are given a *religious review* of Judah.

First Chronicles, chapters 1–9, opens with the largest genealogical list of names in the Bible and covers about 3,500 years of history. The genealogies are devoted to the families through whom God would carry out His plan of redemption. Beginning with Adam, they confirm the genealogy of Christ as recorded in the gospels of Matthew and Luke. Many names are omitted, but those related to the prophecies of the promised Savior are recorded, including Zerubbabel, leader of the returning exiles (1 Chron. 3:19).

Chapter 10 records Saul's last battle and his death.

Chapters 11–29 span the reign of David and reveal a government that honors God. The book of 1 Chronicles ends with the death of David and the extension of the kingdom under Solomon.

Second Chronicles continues the history of David's line. It begins with the reign of Solomon, which was the golden age of Israel, and then recounts the kingdom's fall and division under Rehoboam. It includes the history of the Southern Kingdom of Judah until the exile of the people to Babylon. The last verses contain the proclamation of Cyrus, which allowed the Jews to return to Jerusalem.

Chapters 1–9 of Second Chronicles tell of Solomon's reign and the construction of the temple in Jerusalem on Mt. Moriah. The temple was built after the pattern of the tabernacle (chapters 3–4), and completed in the eleventh year of Solomon's reign (chapter 5; and 1 Kings 6:38). The temple was consecrated to God in one of the great prayers of the Scriptures (chapter 6).

The remainder of 2 Chronicles (chapters 10–36) describes the kings of Judah, and the moral and spiritual decline of the nation. It ends with the fall of Jerusalem and the final destruction of the temple.

This historical account emphasizes God's love for His people, and points out that when kings and people honored God, there was prosperity. When they were unfaithful to the Lord, however, He withdrew His presence and defeat was inevitable. This truth is detailed in a key verse from 2 Chronicles:

For the eyes of the LORD run to and fro throughout the whole earth, for He will show Himself strong on the behalf of them whose heart is committed to Him (2 Chron. 16:9).

May 11: Read 1 Chronicles 1–2

Verses for Today: *"Adam, Sheth, Enosh . . . Noah, Shem, Ham, and Japheth. . . . And the sons of Javan; Elishah, and Tarshish, Kittim, and Dodanim"* (1 Chron. 1:1, 4, 7).

To the casual observer, the long list of genealogies in the book of 1 Chronicles may seem dry and uninteresting. In reality, though, they reveal the well-planned design of God down through the centuries, naming the descendants from Adam—the first man—to Christ—the second Adam.

Just as God decided who would be included in the genealogy of Christ, He is personally involved in the lives of those who follow Him, engineering every detail. Things that happen to believers are not "accidents"; our Father, the master engineer, has allowed them. Although we don't understand many of the things God brings into our lives, we can rest assured that He has a purpose for them. He uses them so that we might seek Him, know Him, and become more like Christ, as well as to reveal His grace and truth to others.

Trust in the Lord with all your heart; don't depend on your own understanding. Look to Him in everything you do, and He will guide you (Prov. 3:5-6).

Thought for Today: Through everything that happens in our lives, may we know God more and draw closer to Him.

Christ Portrayed: By the first Adam (1 Chron. 1:1). Jesus is the last Adam (1 Cor. 15:45).

May 12: Read 1 Chronicles 3–5

Verses for Today: *"And Jabez was more honourable than his brethren. . . . And Jabez called on the God of Israel, saying, Oh that thou wouldest bless me indeed, and enlarge my coast, and that thine hand might be with me, and that thou wouldest keep me from evil. . . . And God granted him that which he requested"* (1 Chron. 4:9-10).

We know very little about Jabez, except that he prayed for something besides worldly fame. He was *"more honourable than his brethren. . . . And God granted him that which he requested"* (1 Chron. 4:9-10).

Jabez experienced the joy that comes as one gives himself to God, and seeks Him for His blessings, and for protection from evil of every kind. The only important thing is what we are in the eyes of God. Accomplishments that achieve eternal results are those God enables us to accomplish. Anything the Lord wants us to do, He will help us do as we yield our lives to Him. As we serve Christ, we won't complain or be jealous of others. We will simply desire to please the Lord and do our best with what we have (Phil. 4:11).

God is a rewarder of those who diligently seek Him (Heb. 11:6).

Thought for Today: Those who entrust their all to God receive His best.

Christ Revealed: Through the genealogy of David (1 Chron. 3:1-24). Jesus, the Son of God, was descended from the line of David (Luke 3:23-31).

May 13: Read 1 Chronicles 6–7

Verse for Today: *"And the number throughout the genealogy . . . was twenty and six thousand men"* (1 Chron. 7:40).

The name of every individual, along with the family and tribe to which he belonged, was carefully registered. A striking difference exists in the character of the men mentioned in these chapters. Some were devoted to their God-given responsibilities; others profaned their holy calling.

Aaron was a devoted priest, but his sons were hypocrites. Samuel was a godly judge, but his sons were evil. Abiathar was a high priest for years, but he later became a traitor to King David (1 Kings 1:5-7; 2:26-27). What a strange mixture of devout saints and sinful, undisciplined men! Many begin with heaven-born beginnings but forfeit their opportunities.

The long, "uninteresting" list of names shows that God does not look on mankind as a crowd of human beings who populate the world. He is so concerned about us that even the hairs of our heads are numbered (Matt. 10:30). He knows each of us by name, and either our names are written in the Lamb's Book of Life, or we will face the great-white-throne of judgment.

"And I saw the dead, small and great, stand before God; and the books were opened: and another book was opened, which is the book of life: and the dead were judged out of those things which were written in the books, according to their works" (Rev. 20:12).

Thought for Today: Your name is recorded in the Book of Life when you receive Christ as your Savior.

Christ Revealed: In the cities of refuge (1 Chron. 6:57, 67). For a person to have protection from the avenger of blood, he had to flee to a city of refuge.

God provided His only begotten Son, Jesus Christ, to be our refuge from His judgment against sin (John 3:14-18; 10:24-30; Gal. 2:16; 3:1-13; Heb. 10:1-17; 1 John 2:2; Rev. 1:5), and every travail in life.

May 14: Read 1 Chronicles 8–10

Verse for Today: *"So Saul died for his transgression which he committed against the Lord, even against the word of the Lord, which he kept not, and also for asking counsel of one that had a familiar spirit, to inquire of it"* (1 Chron. 10:13).

In 1 Samuel, God commanded Saul to *"utterly destroy"* the Amalekites and their possessions. Saul did attack the Amalekites and destroy all the people and the animals that were undesirable, but Saul spared King Agag and took home the choicest animals (1 Sam. 15:3, 9). In his partial obedience Saul was deceived, for he proudly announced to Samuel, *"Blessed be thou of the Lord: I have performed the commandment of the Lord"* (1 Sam. 15:13). He obeyed God only to the point that it pleased himself and the people.

Saul knew, and even sought, the Lord's will at times, but he always rejected it. As the years passed, his rejection of God became more apparent—he even ordered the execution of eighty-five *"priests of the Lord"* (1 Sam. 22:17-18).

The night before his last battle with the Philistines on Mt. Gilboa, Saul once again hastily prayed (1 Sam. 28:6), but he neither repented, nor waited for God to answer. Tied to these transgressions was the time Saul rushed through the night to the village of Endor to seek counsel from a spiritualist medium concerning the outcome of the battle. Saul was disloyal to God, who had chosen him as His representative to the people and to enforce His Word: *"There shall not be found among you any one . . . that useth divination, or an observer of times, or an enchanter, or a witch, or a charmer, or a consulter with familiar spirits, or a wizard, or a necromancer [communicating with the dead]. For all that do these things are an abomination unto the Lord"* (Deut. 18:10-12).

Like Saul, many today have missed God's best for their lives, and created problems for themselves by patronizing those who practice sorcery—such as palm readers, fortune-tellers, spiritualists, astrologers—and other deceptive, evil advisers. We are warned, *"But the fearful, and unbelieving, and the abominable, and murderers, and whoremongers, and sorcerers, and idolaters, and all liars, shall have their part in the lake which burneth with fire and brimstone: which is the second death"* (Rev. 21:8).

We are to seek the Lord and His wisdom, and honor Him alone.

Worship the Lord your God, and serve Him only (Matt. 4:10).

Thought for Today: Faith, wisdom, and spiritual success come to those who seek and follow God and His ways.

Christ Revealed: By Jerusalem, which means *"foundation of peace"* (1 Chron. 9:3). Jesus is the foundation of peace between man and God (2 Cor. 5:18; Eph. 2:14).

May 15: Read 1 Chronicles 11–13

Verse for Today: *"And moreover in time past, even when Saul was king, thou wast he that leddest out and broughtest in Israel: and the Lord thy God said unto thee, Thou shalt feed my people Israel, and thou shalt be ruler over my people Israel"* (1 Chron. 11:2).

While Saul was still king, God anointed David to reign over His people. However, David faced many years of waiting and trials before he began his promised reign. Even after Saul's death, when David was named king over the tribe of Judah at Hebron (2 Sam. 2:4), the ten tribes of the Northern Kingdom did not accept him as king. It wasn't until after the death of Abner and Ishbosheth, Saul's son, a puppet king whom Abner controlled, that they asked David to be their king (2 Sam. 3:7-11).

David had learned early in life that the Lord cares for His people, and that human plans are worthless without His blessing. Once we recognize God's authority over our lives, we will patiently look to God for His direction, assistance, and timing.

"But they that wait upon the Lord shall renew their strength" (Isa. 40:31).

Thought for Today: As we grow in patience and contentment, our peace and joy with God will increase.

Christ Portrayed: By David, the anointed king (1 Chron. 11:3). Christ is the Anointed One, who will reign as "KING OF KINGS, AND LORD OF LORDS" (Rev. 19:16).

May 16: Read 1 Chronicles 14–16

Verse for Today: *"And the fame of David went out into all lands; and the Lord brought the fear of him upon all nations"* (1 Chron. 14:17).

David conquered the Jebusites, whom up until that time, the Israelites had never conquered. David then established his capital in Jerusalem. The Philistines, fearing David's growing power, *"spread themselves in the valley"* near Bethlehem to prepare for an attack on Jerusalem (1 Chron. 14:9). David immediately *"inquired of God"* (14:10). He would not take his men into battle until he knew the will of God. Then they experienced a great victory.

The defeated Philistines renewed their force with a second attack. However, notice that although the first battle was successful, David did not assume to know God's will concerning the second attack. He *"inquired again of God"* (1 Chron. 14:14). This time, God directed them in an altogether different way, and David gained another great victory. The often-recorded phrase, *"David inquired of the Lord,"* was the key to his greatness (1 Sam. 23:2, 4; 30:8; 2 Sam. 2:1; 5:19, 23; 21:1).

Prayer should be the most important part of our day. We must guard against Satan, who seeks to disrupt our prayers by any method he can. He will make us think we are "too tired," or "too busy with important matters" to pray. If these don't work, he will bring unexpected interruptions during our quiet time.

"Praying always with all prayer and supplication in the Spirit, and watching thereunto with all perseverance" (Eph. 6:18).

Thought for Today: The fervent, persevering prayers of Christians can put the enemy to flight.

Christ Revealed: Through David's fame and exaltation (1 Chron. 14:17). God has highly glorified Jesus, our Redeemer, and given Him a name above every name (Phil. 2:9).

May 17: Read 1 Chronicles 17–20

Verses for Today: *"David said to Nathan the prophet, Lo, I dwell in an house of cedars, but the ark of the covenant of the Lord remaineth under curtains. Then Nathan said unto David, Do all that is in thine heart; for God is with thee"* (1 Chron. 17:1-2).

David brought the ark to Jerusalem and established true worship. However, he felt ashamed of the contrast between his luxurious house made of cedar and the old tent tabernacle of the Lord. Therefore, he decided to build a temple for worship. This was his personal desire, but the Lord revealed His will and plan: *"Thou shalt not build me an house"* (1 Chron. 17:4). Upon hearing the will and wisdom of God, David, in deep humility, exclaimed, *"Who am I . . . that thou hast brought me hitherto? . . . O Lord, there is none like thee"* (1 Chron. 17:16, 20).

Like David, those who please the Lord have learned that God is the only One who can say what is pleasing to Himself. To grumble about one's circumstances is to question *"the exceeding greatness of his power to us-ward who believe"* (Eph. 1:19).

"O Lord, I know that the way of man is not in himself: it is not in man that walketh to direct his steps" (Jer. 10:23).

Thought for Today: What a privilege it is to trust God for guidance!

Christ Portrayed: By David, the shepherd-king (1 Chron. 17:7). Jesus, our Great Shepherd, said, *"I am the good shepherd: the good shepherd giveth his life for the sheep"* (John 10:11). He is also the *King of kings* (John 12:15; 1 Tim. 6:15; Rev. 17:14).

May 18: Read 1 Chronicles 21–23

Verses for Today: *"And Satan stood up against Israel, and provoked David to number Israel. . . . And God was displeased with this thing; therefore he smote Israel"* (1 Chron. 21:1, 7).

We could ask why it was a sin to number the people. The Lord had commanded a census be taken in the wilderness (Num. 1:1-2). In addition, census-taking was customary with other kings that they might know what size army they would have in case of a war. But, despite human reasoning, the Bible reveals that this decision was not God's will. It was instigated by a supernatural enemy. Satan, the adversary, was permitted in some way to influence David to authorize the census. However, because sin is man's own act, a righteous God administers judgment upon man's wrongdoing.

Israel was God's people to number—not David's. We do not know David's reasons for taking the census. Perhaps David momentarily lost sight of his real source of strength. Maybe he wanted to ascertain and boast of his military strength. Thoughts of pride and the praise of others could have become the means for Satan to provoke David's act of treason against the Lord. David's sin likely had the same root as the sin of Nebuchadnezzar, whom Jehovah taught by a crushing experience to *"honour the King of heaven, all whose works are truth, and his ways judgment: and those that walk in pride he is able to abase"* (Dan. 4:37).

Like David, we are often not conscious that Satan is so near or powerful in prompting sin. Be assured that wherever a ministry is being offered to the Lord, Satan's strategy is to disrupt and destroy it. This was true when Satan tempted the Lord in the wilderness. But Jesus stood against him by speaking the truth of God's Word, and *"the devil left him"* (Matt. 4:3-11).

Scripture reveals that Satan prowls around like a roaring lion, seeking whom he may devour and destroy (John 10:10; 1 Pet. 5:8). Our Lord described our adversary as the *"prince of this world,"* a *"murderer,"* and the *"father of lies,"* who *"abode not in the truth"* (John 8:44; 14:30). He is revealed as possessing the skill of a mastermind, directing—with executive ability—his work *"in the children of disobedience"* (Eph. 2:2). But Scripture also reveals our tactics for warfare.

Finally, my brothers and sisters, be strong in the Lord, and in the power of His might. Put on the whole armour of God, that you may be able to stand against the wiles of the devil. Stand firm; put on God's truth and righteousness; and be ready with the gospel of peace. Take up the shield of faith to extinguish all the flaming arrows of the evil one. Keep on the helmet of salvation, and use the sword of the Spirit, which is the Word of God. And pray in the Spirit on all occasions with all kinds of prayers and requests. Be alert and persevere as you keep on praying for all the Lord's people (Eph. 6:10-18).

Thought for Today: Satan will try to cause us to sin, but God's grace and power enable us to resist Satan and not sin.

Christ Revealed: Through the altar David built, and the sacrifices he made to receive forgiveness for sin (1 Chron. 21:18, 26, 27).[11] When we have sinned, the safest thing to do is to turn to Christ. Only through Him can the joy of our salvation be restored (Ps. 51:12; James 5:16; 1 John 1:5-10).

May 19: Read 1 Chronicles 24–26

Verse for Today: *"God blessed him [Obed-edom]"* (1 Chron. 26:5).

The Lord greatly blessed Obed-edom during the time the ark of the covenant was in his home.

Three months earlier, King David had planned to take the ark to Jerusalem and make Jerusalem the religious center of Israel. The ark was placed on an ox cart driven by Uzzah and Ahio, who were to transport it from Kirjath-jearim to Jerusalem. Along the way, the ox stumbled. Uzzah reached out to grab the ark and was struck dead for touching it. David, fearing God's judgment upon Uzzah, did not continue taking the ark to Jerusalem. It was taken, instead, to the home of Obed-edom (2 Sam. 6:1-11; 1 Chron. 13:7-11). After three months, David was directed to have the ark transported to Jerusalem and this time, he made sure to follow God's instructions (1 Chron. 15:2-3; Num. 4:15; 7:9).[12]

The ark was prominent in leading the Israelites through the wilderness (Num. 10:33-36). Because the ark contained the Ten Commandments, which

---

11 A brief and informative article regarding altars can be found at https://www.gotquestions.org/what-is-an-altar.html.

12 To read more on the ark and this event, following are three short articles: 1) https://www.gotquestions.org/ark-of-the-covenant.html; 2) https://www.gotquestions.org/ark-of-the-testimony.html; 3) https://www.gotquestions.org/Uzzah.html.

God had given to Moses on Mt. Sinai, it represented God's presence, authority, and power. It must be handled in the correct manner.

When Obed-edom accepted the ark, he received more than God's Word; he received the very presence of God (1 Sam. 4:4; 2 Sam. 6:2). Just as the ark brought God's blessing to the home of Obed-edom, God will bless all who allow Christ, the Son of God, to rule their lives (John 1:12).

Before ascending into heaven, Jesus declared, *All power has been given unto Me in heaven and in earth. Go and teach all nations . . . to obey everything I have commanded* (Matt. 28:18-20).

Thought for Today: The more our thoughts are occupied with Christ and His Word, the more we will recognize His presence.

Christ Revealed: Through the temple treasure (1 Chron. 26:20-28). In Christ are the treasures of wisdom, knowledge, and riches to supply the believer's every need (Phil. 4:19).

May 20: Read 1 Chronicles 27–29

Verse for Today: *"Wherefore David blessed the Lord before all the congregation: and David said, Blessed be thou, Lord God of Israel our father, for ever and ever"* (1 Chron. 29:10).

David had grown old and knew his reign was nearing an end. The nearer he came to the world of everlasting worship, the more he spoke the praise language of that world. His last recorded message to his kingdom was one of the greatest outbursts of worship found in the Old Testament. David proclaimed, in adoration of the Lord and His unspeakable grandeur, *"Thine, O Lord, is the greatness, and the power, and the glory, and the victory, and the majesty"* (1 Chron. 29:11).

Worship is not merely rituals, singing, praying, or preaching. People experience true worship in their hearts. We honor God for His greatness. We adore and enjoy Him for His truth and ways, which are good. We are thankful for His grace and salvation in Christ, as well as His comfort and guidance that He provides as we come to Him.

"To the praise of the glory of his grace, wherein he hath made us accepted in the beloved" (Eph. 1:6).

Thought for Today: Let us freely and continuously offer praise and thanks to the Lord.

Christ Revealed: In the gold David offered God (1 Chron. 29:2-5). Gold represents the warmth, preciousness, and great worth of Jesus (Isa. 28:16; Matt. 13:44-46; John 1:14; 6:68; Eph. 3:8; Col. 1:19; 1 Pet. 1:19; 2:4-6; 2 Pet. 1:4).

May 21: **Read 2 Chronicles 1–3**

Verse for Today: *"So Solomon, and all the congregation with him, went to the high place that was at Gibeon; for there was the tabernacle of the congregation of God, which Moses the servant of the Lord had made in the wilderness"* (2 Chron. 1:3).

Solomon, the last king of a united Israel, began his reign in humble submission, saying that he was but a "little child" compared with the Lord's greatness. The young king and all the congregation offered sacrifices and worshiped God.

That night, the Lord appeared to Solomon in a dream, saying, *"Ask what I shall give thee"* (2 Chron. 1:7). When Solomon asked for wisdom, the Lord assured him that He was pleased with this request and would grant it. This was also an answer to David's prayer for his son Solomon (1 Chron. 22:11-12).

All wisdom is to be found in God and *"in Christ Jesus, who of God is made unto us wisdom"* (1 Cor. 1:30). Self-sufficient people do not have any need or capacity to pray for God's wisdom. However, the Lord gives wisdom to those who ask, and who seek His ways.

If any of you lacks wisdom, let him ask of God, that giveth to all men liberally, and without reproach, and it will be given to him (James 1:5).

Thought for Today: The Lord is willing to give us His wisdom when we humbly seek it.

Christ Revealed: By the thousand burnt offerings of Solomon (2 Chron. 1:6). We can be thankful that the one offering of Jesus has done away with the need for endless offerings (Rom. 6:10; Heb. 10:10-14).

May 22: **Read 2 Chronicles 4–6**

Verses for Today: *"Thus all the work that Solomon made for the house of the Lord was finished. . . . There was nothing in the ark save the two tables which Moses put therein at Horeb"* (2 Chron. 5:1, 10).

Eleven months were needed to prepare for the dedication of the temple, which included moving the ark to its final resting place within the holy of holies. For the first time in more than four hundred years, the priests were permitted to lift the ancient lid and see the contents of the ark.

The priests, the king, and the people all sang praises to God, and the temple was filled with His presence in the form of a cloud as the Lord came to guide His people. The Israelites were so grateful that they *"were as one . . . in praising and thanking the Lord"* (2 Chron. 5:13).

Jesus gave the assurance that, after His resurrection, *"the Spirit of truth . . . will guide you"* (John 16:13). How much more we, His redeemed people, should praise God for His indwelling presence!

"Giving thanks always for all things unto God and the Father in the name of our Lord Jesus Christ" (Eph. 5:20).

Thought for Today: Are we so busy expecting recognition and praise from others that we fail to praise Him?

Christ Revealed: Through the ark, which is a type of Christ and contained God's presence (2 Chron. 5). A Christian's body likewise is the *temple for God's Holy Spirit* (1 Cor. 6:19).

May 23: Read 2 Chronicles 7–9

Verse for Today: *"And when the queen of Sheba heard of the fame of Solomon, she came to prove Solomon with hard questions at Jerusalem"* (2 Chron. 9:1).

Solomon attracted the attention of world leaders, including the queen of Sheba, who came to him with *"hard questions."* The Scriptures do not tell us what questions she may have asked Solomon. They most likely included asking about the Lord he worshiped and the way she could receive His blessing. Solomon's profound wisdom caused her to exclaim, *"The one half of the greatness of thy wisdom was not told me"* (2 Chron. 9:6).

When someone comes to the King of all kings—the Lord Jesus Christ—that person comes to One with riches and wisdom far beyond anything Solomon had. The wonders of His grace are beyond compare.

"Let the word of Christ dwell in you richly in all wisdom" (Col. 3:16).

Thought for Today: Those who come to Christ will never be disappointed.

Christ Revealed: Through the glory of Solomon's kingdom (2 Chron. 9:1-28). Even though Solomon had a rich and glorious kingdom, it cannot compare to the coming kingdom of Jesus (Rev. 11:15-17).

May 24: Read 2 Chronicles 10–13

Verse for Today: *"And king Rehoboam took counsel with the old men that had stood before Solomon his father while he yet lived, saying, What counsel give ye me to return answer to this people?"* (2 Chron. 10:6).

When Rehoboam became king, the united kingdom still held its great influence in the world. However, there is no mention of Rehoboam's starting his reign with prayer for divine wisdom, or altar sacrifices, nor do we read that Rehoboam was anointed of the Lord. As a result, it is not surprising to read that *"he prepared not his heart to seek the Lord"* (2 Chron. 12:14). Where was the spiritual influence that had existed forty years earlier when Solomon began to reign? Nowhere do we find Solomon admonishing his son to remain true to God, as David, his father, had done for him. Where were the Nathans or priests who were prominent in David's reign?

It is evident that the guidance of godly prophets and spiritual advisers was no longer wanted. How empty to read that Rehoboam, the shepherd of God's people, *"took counsel with . . . men . . . saying, What counsel give ye me?"*

"Except the Lord build the house, they labour in vain that build it: except the Lord keep the city, the watchman waketh but in vain" (Ps. 127:1).

Thought for Today: Without God, the most clever strategy of the wisest counselors is worthless.

Christ Revealed: Through the gold candlestick [lampstand] (2 Chron. 13:11). Jesus is *"the Light of the World"* (John 9:5).

May 25: Read 2 Chronicles 14–17

Verse for Today: *"The Lord is with you, while ye be with him . . . but if ye forsake him, he will forsake you"* (2 Chron. 15:2).

Having learned that the Lord would be with him, Asa led the nation in a great revival. His faith was put to the test when he was confronted with an invading army almost twice as large as his army. Asa stayed faithful and prayed, *"Help us, O Lord . . . for we rest on thee, and in thy name we go against this multitude"* (2 Chron. 14:11). The Lord gave him an overwhelming victory.

While Asa's wealth and power increased, his dependence on God decreased. When the small army of Israelites invaded Judah, he hired Ben-hadad to fight the battle for him, instead of praying. No longer could he say to the Lord, *"We rest on thee."*

Temptation to rely on our own clever manipulations is as real today as it was for Asa.

"Thou hast left thy first love. . . . Repent" (Rev. 2:4-5).

Thought for Today: Unless our confidence is in God, we are powerless against the attacks of Satan.

Christ Revealed: Through the rest that God gave Judah (2 Chron. 14:7). Those who have the peace of Jesus have rest indeed (Matt. 11:28-30).

May 26: Read 2 Chronicles 18–20

Verse for Today: *"O our God, wilt thou not judge them? for we have no might against this great company that cometh against us; neither know we what to do: but our eyes are upon thee"* (2 Chron. 20:12).

Surrounded by the vast combined armies of Moab, Ammon, and Mount Seir, Jehoshaphat called for a nationwide prayer meeting and proclaimed a fast throughout Judah. The king stood in the midst of a great congregation in Jerusalem and began to pray. He confessed, *"We have no might against this great company that cometh against us; neither know we what to do: but our eyes are upon thee."* God responded to their prayer: *"Ye shall not need to fight in this battle"* (2 Chron. 20:17). Even before the battle was won, Jehoshaphat began praising the Lord for the victory (2 Chron. 20:21).

Jehoshaphat did not close his eyes to the impending disaster, nor did he seek help from other nations. He trusted in God's wisdom.

Likewise, if we commit ourselves in prayer to God's care, He will use everything that comes into our lives for our eternal good. We can be sure that every unfair treatment, every unkind word, and every thoughtless deed that come our way are ultimately for our good.

"In every thing give thanks: for this is the will of God in Christ Jesus concerning you" (1 Thess. 5:18).

Thought for Today: We can praise God; the victory is His.

Christ Portrayed: By Micaiah, who told the truth even though it was unpopular with his listeners (2 Chron. 18:12-27). We are reminded of Jesus, when He spoke unpopular truth to the Pharisees (Matt. 12:1-14).

May 27: Read 2 Chronicles 21–24

Verse for Today: *"And Jehoiada made a covenant between him, and between all the people, and between the king, that they should be the Lord's people"* (2 Chron. 23:16).

The wife of Jehoiada, the priest, hid baby Joash, the only surviving descendant in the royal line of David, thus protecting him from being murdered by Athaliah. In the seventh year of Athaliah's reign, Jehoiada, the priest, anointed Joash king and had Athaliah executed. During Joash's adolescent years, Jehoiada was really the leader of the nation. As high priest, he restored the nation to the laws of God, repaired the temple, and destroyed Baal worship.

With the exception of Samuel, history records no priest equal to Jehoiada. Under his influence, the people strictly obeyed God's Law, and the nation once again prospered. Following Jehoiada's death, however, Joash soon drifted away from *"the house of the Lord . . . and wrath came upon Judah and Jerusalem"* (2 Chron. 24:18).

Neglecting God's Word can cause the truth by which we once lived to become blurred or forgotten, so that we gradually cease doing God's will. Spiritual stability and strength are achieved by those who are willing to sacrifice everything necessary to remain faithful to His Word and His will.

"I count all things but loss for the excellency of the knowledge of Christ Jesus my Lord. . . . That I may know him, and the power of his resurrection, and the fellowship of his sufferings, being made conformable unto his death" (Phil. 3:8, 10).

Thought for Today: Ignoring the Bible has caused many to lose their sense of spiritual direction.

Christ Portrayed: By Joash, who had to be saved from death (2 Chron. 22:10-12). Jesus was hidden from Herod, who wanted to kill Him (Matt. 2:13-14).

May 28: **Read 2 Chronicles 25–27**

Verses for Today: *"Wherefore the anger of the Lord was kindled against Amaziah, and he sent unto him a prophet, which said unto him, Why hast thou sought after the gods of the people, which could not deliver their own people out of thine hand? . . . I know that God hath determined to destroy thee, because thou hast done this, and hast not hearkened unto my counsel"* (2 Chron. 25:15-16).

Following the murder of his father, Joash, Amaziah became king over Judah (2 Kings 12:21), *"and he did that which was right in the sight of the Lord, but not with a perfect heart"* (2 Chron. 25:2). The mixed motives in his life eventually destroyed him.

Amaziah worshiped the Lord, and yet he permitted the people to offer *"sacrifice and burnt incense on the high places"* (2 Kings 14:4). When he went to war against Edom, he hired a hundred thousand men from Israel to help him. These actions revealed his "imperfect heart" and that he did not fully trust in the Lord, who alone *"hath power to help, and to cast down"* (2 Chron. 25:8). Warned by a man of God, Amaziah dismissed the Israelites and conquered Edom, but again his "imperfect heart" was revealed when he brought back the gods of the Edomites and bowed down to them.

There were good things about Amaziah, and he did many things that were *"right in the sight of the Lord, but not with a perfect heart."* Consequently, the mixtures in his life brought the Lord's judgment.

In Revelation, our Lord said regarding the church at Thyatira: *"I know thy works, and charity [compassionate love], and service, and faith, and thy patience, and thy works . . . [but] I have a few things against thee, because thou sufferest that woman Jezebel . . . to teach and to seduce my servants"* (Rev. 2:18-20). The works of this good church were enumerated and praised—but there was a mixture, including an attitude of tolerance toward those with deceptive beliefs that led to impurity and false worship.

The Lord added, *"He that hath an ear, let him hear what the Spirit saith unto the churches"* (Rev. 2:29).

Thought for Today: We should serve the Lord with a *"perfect heart"*—not one mixed with worldly interests.

Christ Revealed: Through the hundred talents of silver (2 Chron. 27:5). Silver is symbolic of redemption. We gain a glimpse of this fact in the sockets of the tabernacle, which were made from the redemption money of the Israelites (Ex. 38:27). *Christ is our redemption. He redeemed us from the curse of the law* (Gal. 3:13).

May 29: Read 2 Chronicles 28–30

Verse for Today: *"Now it is in mine heart to make a covenant with the Lord God of Israel, that his fierce wrath may turn away from us"* (2 Chron. 29:10).

During the first month of Hezekiah's reign, he began the greatest religious reforms in Judah's history and did *"that which was good and right and truth before the Lord his God"* (2 Chron. 31:20). He restored worship in the temple, removed idolatry, and proclaimed a national Passover, which exceeded all Passover observances since the time of Solomon. He even sent special letters to the Northern Kingdom of Israel, inviting the people to keep this Passover. He feared neither the reaction of King Hoshea of Israel nor the Assyrian kingdom that dominated them.

Many Israelites from the Northern Kingdom scoffed, but some of them participated in that great Passover feast. This is the only record in 210 years of all ten tribes returning to Jerusalem to worship God.

The importance we place on Jesus—our Passover Lamb (1 Cor. 5:7)—determines what we do with our time and effort. Christ's command is clear that *"as my Father hath sent me, even so send I you"* (John 20:21). We must go into nations, homes, and places of work to seek and save the lost, so they, too, may be saved, come to worship, and celebrate Him.

"Go ye therefore, and teach all nations . . . to observe all things whatsoever I have commanded you" (Matt. 28:19-20).

Thought for Today: Ask the Lord to help you tell others about the great things He has done for you.

Christ Revealed: In the Passover (2 Chron. 30:1-5, 15). Jesus is God's Passover Lamb (1 Cor. 5:7), who takes away our sin when we trust Him (John 1:29, 34, 36).

May 30: Read 2 Chronicles 31–33

Verse for Today: *"And when he was in affliction, he besought the Lord his God, and humbled himself greatly before the God of his fathers"* (2 Chron. 33:12).

Much of King Manasseh's life was spent doing away with the spiritual reformation that his father, Hezekiah, had brought about. Manasseh became a fanatical idolater, thus bringing his country to ruin. Because of his actions, God allowed the king of Assyria to defeat Manasseh and take him bound to Babylon.

During his captivity, Manasseh repented; and, for the first time, it is recorded that Manasseh prayed (2 Chron. 33:12-13). God heard his prayer, forgave his sin, and restored him to his throne in Jerusalem. In his remaining years, he attempted to make amends for his evil ways and turn the nation back to God.

When Manasseh, a very wicked king, repented of his sins, he became an amazing example of God's forgiving love. Scripture can encourage even the most discouraged, defeated Christian. We have assurance that God shows great mercy to all who humbly turn to Him.

"Let us cleanse ourselves from all filthiness of the flesh and spirit, perfecting holiness in the fear of God" (2 Cor. 7:1).

Thought for Today: God, in His mercy, has provided a way for even the most rebellious, or vile, sinner to be saved.

Christ Revealed: In the tithe of oxen and sheep (2 Chron. 31:6). The ox typifies Jesus as the patient and enduring Servant (1 Cor. 9:9-10; Heb. 12:2-3). Sheep represent Christ as the gentle, sacrificial Lamb, who surrendered to death on the cross (Isa. 53:7; Acts 8:32-35).

May 31: Read 2 Chronicles 34–36

Verses for Today: *"Forbear thee from meddling with God, who is with me, that he destroy thee not. Nevertheless Josiah would not turn his face from him. . . . And the archers shot at king Josiah . . . and he died"* (2 Chron. 35:21-24).

The highest honor ever given to a king was given to Josiah: *"Like unto him was there no king before him, that turned to the Lord with all his heart"* (2 Kings 23:25).

During the reign of Josiah, Pharaoh Neco of Egypt wanted to pass through Palestine with his armies to join the Assyrians in a war against Nebuchadnezzar, king of Babylon. The Egyptian king urged Josiah not to interfere: *"Forbear thee from meddling with God, who is with me, that he destroy thee not"* (2 Chron. 35:21).

On this occasion, there is no record that Josiah sought counsel from the Lord or requested advice from the godly prophet Jeremiah. Instead, he tried to keep the Egyptian king from passing through his country. As a result, he was fatally wounded. Just three months after his death, the kingdom of Judah lost its political independence.

Had someone failed to pray for the godly, thirty-nine-year-old king? How vital it is to pray for those in authority and for those who are ministering for God. Pause now to pray for your pastor, spiritual leaders, and our nation's leaders, that God will protect and guide them (Gal. 6:10). Ask the Lord to raise up workers, laborers, and great leaders.

"I exhort therefore, that, first of all, supplications, prayers, intercessions, and giving of thanks, be made for all men; for kings, and for all that are in authority" (1 Tim. 2:1-2).

Thought for Today: Do you pray for yourself as well as others?

Christ Revealed: Through the messengers of God, whom the people rejected (2 Chron. 36:15-16). It was prophesied that Jesus would come, suffer, and be rejected by His own people (Isa. 53:3; Matt. 8:34; Mark 9:12; Luke 4:28-29; 17:25).

June

 EZRA

In the book of Ezra, God, once again, lovingly brings His people back from captivity, and faithfully keeps His promises. Many years before, when the Israelites had sinned, Jeremiah foretold: *This whole land will be left in ruins, and its people will serve the king of Babylon seventy years. . . . For thus saith the Lord, After you*

have been captives for seventy years, I will visit you and keep My promise to bring you back home (Jer. 25:11; 29:10; 2 Chron. 36:22-23; Ezra 1:1-3).

In fulfillment of the first portion of the prophecy, Nebuchadnezzar conquered Judah and began deporting the people to Babylon. Twenty years later, when Jerusalem was defeated and the temple was destroyed, most of the remaining Israelites were taken to Babylon. Eventually, the Medes and Persians, in a joint effort, conquered Babylon and made it part of the Persian Empire. In amazing fulfillment of the second half of the prophecy and another prophecy, King Cyrus of Persia encouraged the Jews to *"build the house of the Lord God of Israel"* (Ezra 1:3).

The book of Ezra tells of these devout exiles, who courageously returned to Jerusalem. Chapters 1–2 cover the first expedition, which consisted of 42,360 Jews and 7,337 servants (Ezra 2:64-65), and was led by Zerubbabel, the grandson of King Jeconiah [Jehoiachin] (1 Chron. 3:17-19). Upon their arrival in Jerusalem, they built an altar and observed the Feast of Booths (Tabernacles). They started work on the temple but, after two years, had completed only the foundation due to fierce opposition (chapters 3–4). Eventually, the Samaritans succeeded in obtaining a decree to halt the work (Ezra 4:21).

Chapters 5–6 explain how, fourteen years later—through the preaching of God's Word—they once again *"began to build the house of God"* (Ezra 5:1-2) and finished it in four years, despite intense opposition. (In between the sixth and seventh chapters, there was an interval of about sixty years. During this time, the events in the book of Esther happened, along with the deaths of Zerubbabel and Haggai, and possibly that of Zechariah. The books of Haggai and Zechariah record some of these same events, as well.)

Chapters 7–8 cover how Ezra led about eighteen hundred Jewish men (plus women and children, for a total of about five thousand people) from the Persian capital to Jerusalem. This occurred approximately eighty years after Zerubbabel's expedition. When Ezra arrived, he discovered that the law of God was being neglected and that many of the Israelites had intermarried with people from heathen nations. Ezra immediately set about to correct these evils and proceeded to lead the people to a renewal of true worship and fellowship with God (chapters 9–10).

Restoration is the theme of Ezra. In this book, the people *return* to God, *restore* God's rightful place in their hearts, *rebuild* the place of worship, and *reform* their lives according to His Word. The *"Word of the Lord"* appears eleven times in Ezra. Five times we are told how God's hand of blessing was with them (Ezra 7:6, 9, 28; 8:18, 22). One of the great intercessory prayers in the Bible is in Ezra 9:5-15. It is a wonderful example of how to confess sins within a community of people and seek God's forgiveness.

June 1: Read Ezra 1–2

Verses for Today: *"Thus saith Cyrus king of Persia, The Lord God of heaven . . . hath charged me to build him an house at Jerusalem, which is in Judah. Who is there among you of all his people? his God be with him, and let him go up to Jerusalem"* (Ezra 1:2-3).

The Lord *"stirred up the spirit"* of the famous Persian king, Cyrus, and caused him to make a decree allowing the Israelites to return to Jerusalem and rebuild the temple (Ezra 1:1-3).

Most of the new generation of Israelites had no desire to leave Babylon—symbolic of the world and all it offers—nor any vision to rebuild the temple in the old, ruined city of Jerusalem more than five hundred miles away. In fact, they were enjoying the luxuries, freedom, and prosperity of the new Persian Empire. Only a few whose hearts God had moved (Ezra 1:5) were willing to hazard the long and difficult four-month journey on foot, sacrifice all the social and material pleasures in Babylon, and return with Zerubbabel to the place where they could truly worship the Lord.

The majority of Christians today, likewise, are caught up in seeking worldly possessions and pleasures. Only a few desire to serve and please the Lord above all else. Just as the Israelites could not fulfill God's will while remaining in Babylon, Christians cannot please the Lord, or experience true satisfaction, until they turn their back on the world, and desire above all else to know Christ, and allow Him to guide their lives.

It is God who, in His kindness, works in you, making you willing and able to do His will (Phil. 2:13).

Thought for Today: Christ left all the pleasures and privileges of heaven to save you. What are you willing to give up in order to know Him and serve Him?

Christ Portrayed: By Sheshbazzar, the prince (governor) of Judah (Ezra 1:8). Jesus is both the Prince of Peace (Isa. 9:6) and the Lion of the tribe of Judah (Rev. 5:5).

June 2: Read Ezra 3–5

Verses for Today: *"And all the people shouted with a great shout, when they praised the Lord, because the foundation of the house of the Lord was laid. But many of the priests . . . who were ancient men, that had seen the first house . . . wept with a loud voice"* (Ezra 3:11-12).

When Zerubbabel and the returning Jews left the pleasures and prosperity of Persia for the hardships of Jerusalem, they could have assumed that the first thing to do was build their own homes. But, instead, they *built an altar to the God of Israel and offered burnt offerings on it, as written in the law of Moses* (Ezra 3:2). These spiritual offerings and sacrifices were not mere empty religious rituals. No, these Jews had sacrificed everything in Persia to restore fellowship with God and put Him first, and this was just the beginning. Then came the slow, day-by-day, difficult task of laying the foundation of the temple, which brought opposition and trouble.

Simply deciding to serve the Lord and do His work does not guarantee a life of ease and freedom from problems. To the contrary! Once Satan knows that we have set our hearts on pleasing the Lord, he will use everything and everyone he can to keep us from our task. In addition, he will seek to divert our attention from the Word of God and prayer—the Christian's very weapons of spiritual warfare against his attacks.

We must strengthen ourselves in the Lord and purpose in our hearts to finish the work that He has given us to do. He has not called anyone else to do it for us.

"No man, having put his hand to the plough, and looking back, is fit for the kingdom of God" (Luke 9:62).

Thought for Today: Each of us is individually responsible for accomplishing what God has planned for us to do.

Christ Revealed: Through the huge stones used for the temple of God (Ezra 5:8). Jesus is the Stone the builders rejected; He is God's chief Cornerstone (Ps. 118:22; Matt. 21:42).

June 3: Read Ezra 6–7

Verse for Today: *"And this house was finished on the third day of the month Adar"* (Ezra 6:15).

The building of the temple was at a standstill for fourteen years, but, once God's Word was made known, the people *"began to build the house of God"* (Ezra 5:2). What caused this revival? Their circumstances had not changed, and the enemy still determined to stop the work (Ezra 4).

This time, they were strengthened by the power of God's Word, and the enemy *"could not cause them to cease"* (Ezra 5). The key to the people overcoming the opposition and gaining power to complete the temple is clearly stated: *"They prospered through the prophesying of Haggai the prophet and Zechariah"* (Ezra 6:14).

The Lord's work can be sustained and strengthened only through His Word.

This is to be the foundation of our Christian lives. It is the power by which God's children cannot be defeated and the power that Satan cannot overcome.

Many of God's people make little or no spiritual progress year after year because they neglect, and consequently disobey, the Word of God.

"Desire the sincere milk of the word, that ye may grow thereby" (1 Pet. 2:2).

Thought for Today: Obedience and confident faith are characteristics of a life of faith.

Christ Revealed: Through the Feast of Unleavened Bread (Ezra 6:22). Jesus said, *"I am the Bread of Life"* (John 6:35).

June 4: Read Ezra 8–9

Verses for Today: *"I am ashamed . . . for we have forsaken thy commandments"* (Ezra 9:6, 10).

Ezra, the priest, not only prepared his own heart to seek the law of God, but he wanted all God's people to know God's will, as well. His purpose for going to Jerusalem was *"to teach in Israel statutes and judgments"* (Ezra 7:10).

Four months after leaving Babylon, Ezra and his thousands of followers completed the more than five-hundred-mile journey and arrived in the Holy City.

When Ezra arrived, he was heartbroken at the low moral and spiritual condition that prevailed among the inhabitants of Jerusalem. Fifty-seven years earlier, Haggai and Zechariah inspired the nation *"to seek the Lord God of Israel"* (Ezra 6:21) but, since that time, there had been no prophets to teach God's commandments to the new generation. However, when he read and taught the Scriptures to them, a great sweeping revival took place (Ezra 10:12-44).

The Holy Spirit dwells within every believer today. May we ask Him to restore us, guide us *"into all truth"* (John 16:13), and fill us with His power and strength!

"Thy word is a lamp unto my feet, and a light unto my path" (Ps. 119:105).

Thought for Today: Only the humble will yield to the Holy Spirit and follow His leading.

Christ Revealed: Through the burnt offerings (Ezra 8:35). The burnt offering typifies Jesus as He offered Himself completely to God, delighting to do His Father's will (Heb. 10:10-12).

June 5: Read Ezra 10

Verse for Today: *"And Ezra the priest stood up, and said unto them, Ye have transgressed, and have taken strange wives, to increase the trespass of Israel"* (Ezra 10:10).

When Ezra and his followers arrived in Jerusalem, he was grief-stricken at the low moral and spiritual condition that had developed in a relatively short period. It had been only about sixty years since Haggai and Zechariah had preached God's Word and inspired the nation to rebuild the house of God (Ezra 6:14-16). But now, even some of the priests and rulers of the people had intermarried with the idol-worshiping Canaanites, which previously led to their captivity (Deut. 7:3-4).

Ezra's great sorrow over their sins drove him to intense prayer, *"weeping and casting himself down"* (Ezra 10:1). As Ezra read from God's Word, the Lord brought conviction to the hearts of the people. They had to put away their heathen, idol-worshiping wives, so *"the fierce wrath"* of God would be turned from them (Ezra 10:14).

What heartbreak and tears are brought about because of disobedience to God! The price of sin is high—much higher than anyone suspects! It does not matter if our actions come from willful disobedience to Him, or from simply not knowing His Word and commandments.

Those who sow wheat, reap wheat; and those who sow tares, never reap wheat. It is the law of nature. Those who sow to the flesh walk *"after the flesh"* (Rom. 8:4). They have their hearts set on *"earthly things"* and make themselves available as *"instruments of unrighteousness"* (Rom. 6:13; Phil. 3:19).

If we want God to bless us, then our actions and motives need to be in harmony with His Word. If we acknowledge our sins to God, He is ready and willing to forgive us. He can strengthen us, through His Word, to live to please Him.

"Be not deceived; God is not mocked: for whatsoever a man soweth, that shall he also reap" (Gal. 6:7).

Thought for Today: When we go against God's will, we displease Him and cheat ourselves.

Christ Revealed: Through the ram (male sheep) offered for the offenses of the sons of the priests (Ezra 10:19). Jesus offered Himself for the sins and offenses of mankind (Heb. 7:27).

 # NEHEMIAH

About fourteen years had passed since Ezra led close to five thousand people to Jerusalem. (There were eighteen hundred Jewish men, plus women and children.) Nehemiah, a Jew, held the honored position of cupbearer to Artaxerxes (the king of the powerful Persian Empire), when he received a report of the spiritual and physical poverty that existed there.

Heartbroken, Nehemiah mourned for several days with fasting and praying (Neh. 1:4). The result was that the Persian king granted him a leave of absence, appointed him governor of Jerusalem, and gave him permission to rebuild the walls surrounding the city (chapters 1–2).

For more than one hundred years (since Nebuchadnezzar had invaded and destroyed the city), it had seemed impossible to restore the walls of Jerusalem (2 Kings 25:8-11). Once Nehemiah arrived, he gathered the willing workers. Many of the leading citizens refused to cooperate with them, and there was intense opposition from the enemies surrounding Jerusalem (Neh. 2:19; 3:5; 4:1-11). But with continued prayer and faith in God, Nehemiah led the people to complete the walls in just fifty-two days (chapters 3–7)!

After the walls were finished, Ezra *"opened the book"* (Neh. 8:5) and read the Scriptures from early morning until noon. The leaders returned to Ezra the next day for additional insight, which led to the celebration of the Feast of Tabernacles (Booths). *Daily, Ezra continued to read from the book of the law of God, from the first day to the last day. And they celebrated the feast for seven days* (Neh. 8:18). These events resulted in much prayer, confession, fasting, and a renewed covenant with God (chapters 8–11). The restored walls were dedicated by Ezra and Nehemiah (chapter 12).

Nehemiah continued as governor of Jerusalem and implemented reforms in several areas. Then Nehemiah returned to the Persian court for possibly twelve years. During Nehemiah's absence from Jerusalem, a number of evils once again gained acceptance, such as Eliashib's alliance with Tobiah, the people's failure to support the Levites, breaking the Sabbath, and intermarriage with the heathen. However, when Nehemiah returned, he once again turned the nation from these evils and reestablished true worship (chapter 13).

June 6: Read Nehemiah 1–3

Verses for Today: *"When Sanballat the Horonite, and Tobiah the servant, the Ammonite, heard of it, it grieved them exceedingly that there was come a man to seek the welfare of the children of Israel. . . . They laughed us to scorn, and despised us, and said, What is this thing that ye do? will ye rebel against the king? Then answered I them . . . The God of heaven, he will prosper us; therefore we his servants will arise and build: but ye have no portion, nor right, nor memorial, in Jerusalem"* (Neh. 2:10, 19-20).

Expressing mockery, Sanballat and his followers inquired, *"What is this thing that ye do?"* The persecution turned to slander: *"Will ye rebel against the king?"* Scoffing and implying evil motives have always been favorite tools of Satan to hinder the Lord's work.

Any ministry initiated of God will suffer satanic opposition. Ahab accused Elijah of troubling Israel (1 Kings 18). Daniel was accused of disobedience and was consigned to the lion's den (Dan. 6). Christ was accused and executed as a malefactor (John 18). Our Lord declared, *"It is enough for the disciple that he be as his master, and the servant as his lord. If they have called the master of the house Beelzebub, how much more shall they call them of his household?"* (Matt. 10:25). It is not surprising to hear rumors of scandal and vicious ridicule against an individual, ministry, or church that is effectively being used by God.

Just as the building of Jerusalem had many enemies, so the ministry of the gospel has seemingly numerous formidable enemies. But deliverance comes from God!

"Commit thy way unto the Lord; trust also in him; and he shall bring it to pass" (Ps. 37:5).

Thought for Today: Be an expression of God's love, peace, and joy even when you face opposition.

Christ Revealed: Through Nehemiah's prayer for his people (Neh. 1:4-11). Jesus also prayed for His own (John 17).

June 7: Read Nehemiah 4–6

Verse for Today: *"Our God shall fight for us"* (Neh. 4:20).

Sanballat did all he could to disrupt the work. He used ridicule, trickery, and flattery. Then he resorted to openly accusing the Jews of rebelling against Persia. All the while, he made every effort to distract Nehemiah, frequently requesting an opportunity to discuss the situation. Realizing that Sanballat's intentions were solely to do evil, Nehemiah replied: *"I am doing a great work, so that I cannot come down: why should the work cease, whilst I leave it, and come down to you?"* (Neh. 6:3).

It had seemed impossible to restore the walls for more than a hundred years, but Nehemiah and his few organized workers rebuilt them in just fifty-two days. This fact seems incredible, compared with the highly skilled laborers David used in building the first walls. Surely, this should reinforce our faith and remind us of God's great promise: *What seems impossible with men is possible with God* (Matt. 19:26).

Nehemiah did not depend on human strategy, power, or ability. His eyes were upon the Lord as he said, *"The God of heaven, he will prosper us"* (Neh. 2:20). *"So the wall was finished"* (Neh. 6:15).

True obedience and power flow from continuous fellowship with God. Jesus's fellowship with the Father is so complete and real that Christ lived in full dependence upon the Father, saying, *"The Son can do nothing of himself"* (John 5:19). Nehemiah proclaimed this truth: *"Our God shall fight for us."*

We can do all things through Christ, who strengthens us (Phil. 4:13).

Thought for Today: When our strength seems weak, we are to ask the Lord to supply us with His all-sufficient strength.

Christ Portrayed: By Nehemiah, who bought back the Jews who had been sold to the heathens as slaves (Neh. 5:8). Jesus redeemed us when we were enslaved by sin (Rom. 7:14; 1 Pet. 1:18-19).

June 8: Read Nehemiah 7–8

Verses for Today: *"For all the people wept, when they heard the words of the law. Then he said unto them . . . neither be ye sorry; for the joy of the Lord is your strength"* (Neh. 8:9-10).

Under the leadership of Zerubbabel, Ezra, and Nehemiah, the people had the privilege of restoring the altar, the temple, and finally the gates and walls of Jerusalem. It appeared that everything had been complete. But God's ultimate purpose for His people was more than the restoration of city walls and buildings.

These things were meaningless unless the people fellowshipped with God and obeyed His Word. The law of God had not been read to them since their return from Babylon. Without God's direction through His Word, further actions would be in vain. Previous failures were a testimony to this. When Ezra read from the book of the law, explaining the Scriptures day after day, a marvelous revival took place accompanied with great joy (Neh. 8:1-12).

Once sin is confessed, God forgives and cleanses us from all unrighteousness. This is why Ezra told the people not to grieve any longer over their past sins, saying that *"the joy of the Lord is your strength."* Because the Lord has accepted us, we can fellowship with Him, and we can accept ourselves, as well as others. This guilt-free conscience is one of the greatest blessings a Christian can possess—physically, mentally, emotionally, and spiritually.

"If we confess our sins, he is faithful and just to forgive us our sins, and to cleanse us from all unrighteousness" (1 John 1:9).

Thought for Today: Confession of sin has no value unless we are willing to forsake the sin.

Christ Revealed: Through the register of names required for priestly service (Neh. 7:63-64). We must be certain our names are written in the Lamb's Book of Life, and make every effort to ensure that our loved ones and friends are included, as well (Luke 10:17-20; Rev. 20:12, 15).

June 9: Read Nehemiah 9–10

Verse for Today: *"Thou gavest also thy good spirit to instruct them, and withheldest not thy manna from their mouth, and gavest them water for their thirst"* (Neh. 9:20).

Listening carefully as Ezra read to the people from the book of the law, the Israelites realized they had not been living according to God's commandments. Humbly, the children of Israel *"assembled with fasting"* (Neh. 9:1), resulting in a spontaneous outpouring of confession, praise, and worship.

In reviewing the history of God's dealings with the Israelites in the wilderness, the priests revealed that the Lord had provided His *"good spirit"* to instruct His people. This is a remarkable statement in the Old Testament, revealing the Holy Spirit teaching His people. (A similar example is found in Isa. 63:10.) In the wilderness on the way to the Promised Land, God's people could *see* the manna and *drink* of the miraculous flow of water in the desert, but they didn't fully understand that God's Holy Spirit was being poured out upon them.

One of the greatest needs in the Christian world today is for God's people to take a fresh look at the importance of having a *right* relationship with Him. This is a must if the Holy Spirit is to teach and guide us. Let us seek to have God reveal our sins to us, cleanse us from them, and desire to be led in His paths of righteousness (Ps. 23:3). Let us earnestly plead for a strong outpouring of His Spirit upon ourselves and our nation so that personally, and collectively, our land and nation might be cleansed and healed (2 Chron. 7:14).

Repent, and be baptized, every one of you, in the name of Jesus Christ for the forgiveness of your sins; and you will receive the gift of the Holy Spirit (Acts 2:38).

Thought for Today: Only to the extent that we seek to know the Lord and truly desire to please Him will the Holy Spirit reveal His will.

Christ Revealed: As the Creator (Neh. 9:6). *For by Him all things were created* (Col. 1:16).

June 10: Read Nehemiah 11–12

Verse for Today: *"And the people blessed all the men, that willingly offered themselves to dwell at Jerusalem"* (Neh. 11:2).

Jerusalem is the city the Lord selected as the center of sacrifice and worship. It is known as the City of God, the Holy City. For a time, the buildings of Jerusalem were in ruins and the city was filled with rubbish—a testimony to Israel's disobedience to God's Word.

The completion and dedication of the walls surrounding this sacred place were made possible because the exiles returned and offered themselves for service to God. Ordinary people denied personal interests, left Babylon, and journeyed to Jerusalem. Even though they were not skilled in building walls, they willingly went to work and did their best.

After the walls were finished, just a few *"offered themselves"* to dwell inside the walls of Jerusalem. They willingly sacrificed personal interests to strengthen the City of God. Even today, only a few do not put a limit on the personal benefits they are willing to give up to serve the Lord.

And whatsoever you do, do it heartily, as to the Lord, and not unto men; it is the Lord who will reward you and give you an inheritance; you are serving the Lord Christ (Col. 3:23-24).

Thought for Today: No one who has willingly given up personal pleasures to do God's will has ever been cheated out of life's best.

Christ Revealed: Through the people as they blessed the men who volunteered to live in Jerusalem (Neh. 11:2). We are blessed when we abide in Jesus and His words abide in us (John 15:7).

June 11: Read Nehemiah 13

Verse for Today: *"Now it came to pass, when they had heard the law, that they separated from Israel all the mixed multitude"* (Neh. 13:3).

Over the years, the Israelites had become slack in reading God's Word and obeying His commandments. Changes needed to be made in everyone's lives.

When Nehemiah returned to Jerusalem, he was shocked at the low moral and spiritual condition that existed in the nation. This was evident in the fact that the people allowed Tobiah—the same man who tried to hinder the work a number of years earlier—to live in the house of God! Nehemiah immediately threw Tobiah's belongings out of the house of the Lord and ordered him to leave. As God's ordained leader, Nehemiah promptly set about to clean up God's house and restore the Levites to the priesthood. No one could discourage him from doing what was right because he knew where he stood with God and didn't care what anyone else thought.

Christians who are truly concerned about getting the job done for Christ are often not very popular with the world. However, many Christians seem to believe that they can live like the world, act like the world, and talk like the world and still be a godly witness for Jesus.

The Lord is not interested in mixed multitudes or a lukewarm attitude (Rev.

3:15-16). He cannot bless us as long as there is a mixture in our lives. If we are to be used as vessels to dispense His Word to the world, our lives must be clean—*"holy, acceptable unto God"* (Rom. 12:1).

"Every man that hath this hope in him purifieth himself, even as he is pure" (1 John 3:3).

Thought for Today: Fear of ridicule and loss of popularity keep many people from doing God's will.

Christ Revealed: Through Nehemiah's discovery that the Levites were not receiving the tithes due them and, instead, had to work in the fields (Neh. 13:10). We are reminded of the words of Jesus when He commissioned seventy of His followers: *Stay in that house, eating and drinking what they give you, because the laborer is worthy of his wages* (Luke 10:7).

 # ESTHER

The book of Esther is the last of the historical books in the Old Testament. It covers approximately twelve years and concerns an edict to kill the Jews who were in Persia following the seventy years of captivity. The events of this book probably occurred a number of years after the temple was reconstructed, but before the walls of Jerusalem were rebuilt. Esther may have made it possible for Nehemiah to accomplish his work in Jerusalem.

Most of these Jews had been born in captivity and therefore held no loyalty to Jerusalem. They may not have realized the importance of the prophetic destiny of the Jewish race when a decree came to have them all executed.

The book of Esther reveals the overruling power of the unseen God and His willingness to protect His people in answer to prayer. The events in this book did not happen by accident because we discover in Esther 4:16 that fasting—which would include prayer—had a part in bringing about God's plan of deliverance. God desires to save many, but He also calls on us to pray for salvation.

June 12: Read Esther 1–3

Verse for Today: *"And the letters were sent by posts into all the king's provinces, to destroy, to kill, and to cause to perish, all Jews, both young and old, little children and women, in one day, even upon the thirteenth day of the twelfth month, which is the month Adar, and to take the spoil of them for a prey"* (Esther 3:13).

When the Persians defeated King Nebuchadnezzar and the Babylonian Empire, all the Jews were urged to return to Jerusalem. They had lived in Babylon for fifty years, so most of them had never seen Jerusalem because they were descendants of those who had been taken captive. Since they were now free from Babylonian slavery, most of them preferred to remain in the friendly, prosperous atmosphere of the Persian kingdom, rather than leave Babylon and return to Jerusalem as God said they should. Perhaps another fifty years passed before Haman decreed that all Jews were to be destroyed.

It is no surprise that the book of Esther does not directly mention God, prayer, or the Scriptures. When we refuse to obey God's Word, our prayers and Bible reading become mere ritual, or nonexistent, and God seems far removed from our daily experiences.

"Come out of her, my people, that ye be not partakers of her sins. . . . Standing afar off for the fear of her torment, saying, Alas, alas that great city Babylon . . . for in one hour is thy judgment come" (Rev. 18:4, 10).

Thought for Today: When we are obedient to God's Word, our Bible reading becomes a sweet time of fellowship with Him.

Christ Revealed: Through Esther's name, which means *"star."* Jesus is called *"the bright and morning star"* (Rev. 22:16).

June 13: **Read Esther 4–7**

Verse for Today: *"And so will I go in unto the king, which is not according to the law: and if I perish, I perish"* (Esther 4:16).

Haman issued a decree to have all Jews executed (Esther 3:9-13). When this was made known, Mordecai and Queen Esther (both Jews) prayed and fasted. Mordecai told Esther that she must go to the king and ask him to spare her people.

Esther understood that to do this meant risking her life because the king had a law that declared no one could enter his presence unless he called for that individual. To make Esther's situation more serious, she had not been called to see the king for thirty days. If the king had lost interest in Esther, how could she hope to influence him for the condemned Jewish race?

With the words, *"If I perish, I perish,"* Queen Esther stood in the inner court of the palace, waiting to learn from the king who ruled the Persian Empire whether she would live or die. She was willing to give up everything—even her own life, if necessary—for what she knew to be the will of God for her people.

Not only did the king accept her, but he also offered her *"half of the kingdom"* (Esther 5:3, 6; 7:2). Esther could have clutched her prize, considering it far too precious to risk losing by mentioning her request to the king. But saving the lives of her people meant more to her than riches did.

The attitude of most people is to firmly hold on to their rights and possessions. However, the way to gain the most for our lives, our time, and our possessions is to commit everything to the Lord. The same is true with our children, spouses, loved ones, and friends—we can commit them to God.

"For whosoever will save his life shall lose it; but whosoever shall lose his life for my sake and the gospel's, the same shall save it" (Mark 8:35).

Thought for Today: God never asks us to do anything He doesn't supply the strength to accomplish.

Christ Revealed: In the honor shown to Mordecai as he was led through the streets (Esther 6:10-11). Jesus was greatly honored during His triumphal entry into Jerusalem (Matt. 21:8-9).

June 14: Read Esther 8–10

Verses for Today: *"Because Haman . . . the enemy of all the Jews, had devised against the Jews to destroy them, and had cast Pur, that is, the lot, to consume them, and to destroy them. . . . Wherefore they called these days Purim after the name of Pur"* (Esther 9:24, 26).

Haman appeared to be invincible, and his decree to execute all the Jews seemed final. The law had been established, and the Persian king had approved the decree. Under the law of the Medes and Persians, a decree could not be changed.

Haman's astrologers *"had cast Pur"* (cast lots) to determine the most favorable time for the execution. Haman's "lucky day" fell on the thirteenth day of the last month. The divine principle Haman did not realize was that *"the lot is cast into the lap; but the whole disposing thereof is of the Lord"* (Prov. 16:33).

The determined day of execution, known as Purim, was turned from death to deliverance for God's people. Since that time, the Jews have celebrated it every year for centuries.

How tragic that years later, when Christ, their Messiah, came to bring a far greater deliverance, the Jews failed to recognize Him. The judgment of death has been decreed upon all men because all have sinned. However, we are saved and granted eternal life with Jesus when we accept Him as our Savior. We should rejoice and celebrate in our great deliverance!

"For God so loved the world, that he gave his only begotten Son . . . that the world through him might be saved" (John 3:16-17).

Thought for Today: No sin works more deceitfully than does the sin of pride. *The Lord resists the proud, but gives grace to the humble* (James 4:6; 1 Pet. 5:5).

Christ Revealed: By Mordecai's exaltation from servant to a position of honor and glory (Esther 8:2, 15). Jesus came to earth as a servant, and is exalted at the right hand of God (Mark 16:19; Phil. 2:7-9).

 # JOB

This book opens with a brief history about a godly and very prosperous man called Job. He was *the greatest man among all the people of the East . . . blameless and upright* (Job 1:3; 2:3). (The name 'Job' rhymes with 'robe.')

In chapters 1–2, we find a startling exchange between God and Satan. Not only do we read about Satan's accusations against Job, and Satan's challenge to God, but we find that God allowed Job to experience this ordeal. Surely, the cosmic battle between God and the Evil One is greater than we can comprehend, and we desperately need God's wisdom and strength for this spiritual war.

Through the book of Job, we observe the reasonings of God, Satan, Job, his wife, and four friends. We are to consider the differences between the wisdom of Job and the well-meaning, but inaccurate, arguments of his friends (chapters 3–37).

God highly complimented Job for having spoken the truth, but was greatly displeased with what Job's friends said (Job 1:1, 8; 42:7). The speeches of Job's friends show the fallacy of human reasoning without the guidance of Scripture.

In the final chapters (38–42), God reveals His wisdom and once again acknowledges Job's righteousness. Through the fierce trials and sufferings of Job, his faith, love, and relationship to God were tested, and yet also strengthened. He was brought into a deeper relationship with God and gained a greater understanding of His wisdom. The book reveals that it is not necessary for us to know *why* we suffer, but it is vital that we maintain trust in God. To stay steadfast in suffering, we must have an accurate understanding of God's nature, goodness, purposes, and plan, which are all revealed in His Word.

June 15: Read Job 1–4

Verse for Today: *"Again there was a day when the sons of God came to present themselves before the Lord, and Satan came also among them to present himself before the Lord"* (Job 2:1).

We are startled to find Satan in the presence of the Lord (Job 1:6-12; 2:1-7). He was there to slander and accuse *"a perfect and an upright man, one that feareth God, and escheweth evil"* (Job 1:1, 8; 2:3). God's Word is true when it describes Satan as *"the accuser of our brethren"* (Rev. 12:10). Satan not only accused Job (through Job's friends), but also belittled him, and did all he could to discourage and defeat him.

Who can understand the heartache and sorrow of Job—the servant of the Lord—who was stripped of loved ones, possessions, and health? In addition, he was unfairly attacked and criticized by his "friends."

Job's suffering was not misfortune or bad luck; nor was it punishment from God, as Job's friends supposed. All Job's sufferings were the attacks of Satan. God did allow Satan to try Job, but God brought good out of the events. God not only brought Job into a closer relationship with Himself, but He used Job's experience and faith to strengthen great numbers of believers through the centuries.

Spiritual victories do not simply happen. They are dependent upon one's faith in God, and on a right understanding of Him, His ways, and His attributes. For this, we require His Word, which is able to impart truth to us, and give us strength.

"Wherefore take unto you the whole armour of God, that ye may be able to withstand in the evil day . . . and the sword of the Spirit, which is the word of God" (Eph. 6:13, 17).

Thought for Today: To remain faithful in the midst of trials, we must develop a love for God and His Word. We must seek the Lord in quiet times of prayer.

Christ Revealed: In the conversation between Satan and the Lord (Job 1:8-12). We are reminded of Christ's statement to Peter: *"Satan hath desired to have you, that he may sift you as wheat: But I have prayed for thee, that thy faith fail not: and when thou art converted, strengthen thy brethren"* (Luke 22:31-32).

June 16: Read Job 5–8

Verses for Today: *"But Job answered and said, Oh that my grief were throughly weighed, and my calamity laid in the balances together! . . . For the arrows of the Almighty are within me, the poison whereof drinketh up my spirit: the terrors of God do set themselves in array against me"* (Job 6:1-2, 4).

After one full week of silent contemplation about Job's suffering, Eliphaz, the eldest of his four friends, was the first to speak. His many years of observation led him to believe that all suffering was the result of sin. Therefore, he said to Job, *"I have seen, they that plow iniquity, and sow wickedness, reap the same"* (Job 4:8). Eliphaz tried to convince Job that he should confess his sin. Bildad and Zophar agreed with Eliphaz's opinion.

Ignoring the insinuation of being a hypocrite, Job appealed for a more complete assessment of his character, saying, *"Oh that my grief were throughly weighed.*" Job felt the bitter sting of condemnation from Eliphaz; but even worse, it seemed that he had been struck down by *"the arrows of the Almighty."*

Job's experiences teach us to examine our lives and hearts, cry out to God, and remain faithful in our trials. God is in control and can bring good from every situation. Let every trouble we experience draw us closer to God.

"Beloved, think it not strange concerning the fiery trial which is to try you, as though some strange thing happened unto you: But rejoice, inasmuch as ye are partakers of Christ's sufferings" (1 Pet. 4:12-13).

Thought for Today: God never forsakes one of His children.

Christ Revealed: Through Job's sorrowful condition (Job 7:1-6). Jesus is known as *"a man of sorrows, and acquainted with grief"* (Isa. 53:3).

June 17: Read Job 9–12

Verses for Today: *"Then answered Zophar the Naamathite, and said . . . Should thy lies make men hold their peace? and when thou mockest, shall no man make thee ashamed? For thou hast said, My doctrine is pure, and I am clean in thine eyes. But oh that God would speak, and open his lips against thee"* (Job 11:1, 3-5).

Zophar was misled by the same false opinion expressed by his companions that severe sufferings prove gross sins. As is often the case, this legalistic religious "comforter" became a critic. He proceeded to reprove and denounce Job as a vain and lying, self-righteous pretender.

Zophar went on to say, *"Oh that God would speak, and open his lips against thee!"* God did open His lips and speak, but it was against these critics. God declared, *"My wrath is kindled against thee . . . for ye have not spoken of me the thing that is right"* (Job 42:7). The words of this man and his friends were merely human reasoning and not from God. We need to recognize God's estimate of these three men and their viewpoints.

Those who express unkind criticism of others do Satan's work. Religious, judgmental critics of Christians often misunderstand God's method of dealing with His disciples. As believers, we are to offer comfort and help to those who are facing trials and loss. We are not to stand in judgment of others and add more suffering on them. We are to show them grace, pray for them, and pray for wisdom.

If we have been offended by the actions and words of others, we must do as Job did, and pray for them. Nothing shows our character, and to whom we belong, more than the way we react to critics who misjudge us.

"But I say unto you, Love your enemies, bless them that curse you, do good to them that hate you, and pray for them which despitefully use you, and persecute you" (Matt. 5:44).

Thought for Today: Be careful with how you react to those who are unkind to you.

Christ Portrayed: Through the *'daysman'* [mediator] (Job 9:32-33). Jesus is the *"one mediator between God and men"* (1 Tim. 2:5).

June 18: Read Job 13–16

Verses for Today: *"Though he slay me, yet will I trust in him: but I will maintain mine own ways before him. . . . How many are mine iniquities and sins? make me to know my transgression and my sin"* (Job 13:15, 23).

Zophar, a highly opinionated man, was convinced (by mere outward circumstances) that Job was guilty of great sin since tragedy struck in every area of Job's life. His conclusions led him to ask, *"Should thy lies make men hold their peace? . . . Know therefore that God exacteth of thee less than thine iniquity deserveth"* (Job 11:3, 6). This criticism, along with that of the other men and Job's wife, were all instigated by Satan, to substantiate his destructive accusation that Job would curse God if he were put to the test of death—that he would give up everything, even his faith in God, to save his own life. But each accusation only deepened Job's faith and love for God until he could say, *"Though he slay me, yet will I trust in him."* This was the turning point in Job's testing.

To truly trust God means that we fully depend on Him in good times and bad. To be conformed to Christ's death (Gal. 2:20; Phil. 1:20-21, 3:10; Heb. 2:10), we must be willing to give up everything dear—even life itself, if necessary—for the privilege of pleasing Him.

"For I reckon that the sufferings of this present time are not worthy to be compared with the glory which shall be revealed in us" (Rom. 8:18).

Thought for Today: When our heart does not condemn us, we have confidence that God will hear and answer our prayers.

Christ Revealed: In the striking of Job from those who looked upon him with contempt (Job 16:10). Jesus was struck and afflicted by those who despised and ridiculed Him (Ps. 22:7; 109:25; Isa. 53; Matt. 27:29-44).

June 19: Read Job 17–20

Verse for Today: *"For I know that my redeemer liveth, and that he shall stand at the latter day upon the earth"* (Job 19:25).

Bildad's second speech was the most critical of all. He said that Job's sufferings exposed him as a sinful hypocrite, who was trapped by his own evils (Job 18:8).

He concluded by saying about Job, *"Surely such are the dwellings of the wicked, and this is the place of him that knoweth not God"* (Job 18:21). These staggering accusations from Job's friends must have been a bitter blow.

And yet, Job's suffering and continuous harassment drove him closer to his Lord. He could look beyond his suffering and say, *"I know that my redeemer liveth."* Job uttered this magnificent revelation when it seemed no one cared, and God seemed distant or nonexistent. However, Job trusted that *God is good and did care.* Job could bear the intense suffering and unjust reproaches because he was living in the expectation of the glorious appearing of his Redeemer.

We, too, can endure trials and be victorious as we look to Jesus, our living Redeemer. He is always faithful.

"I know whom I have believed, and am persuaded that he is able to keep that which I have committed unto him" (2 Tim. 1:12).

Thought for Today: May we live in such close communion with God, our heavenly Father, that we are aware of His faithful presence.

Christ Revealed: As the Redeemer (Job 19:25). Jesus, our Redeemer, bought us with His own blood shed on the cross (Rev. 5:9).

June 20: Read Job 21–24

Verses for Today: *"My foot hath held his steps, his way have I kept, and not declined. Neither have I gone back from the commandment of his lips; I have esteemed the words of his mouth more than my necessary food"* (Job 23:11-12).

In a final attempt to convince Job that he was a hypocrite, Eliphaz remarked, *"Acquaint now thyself with him, and be at peace"* (Job 22:21). Eliphaz figured that wicked men are miserable and, since Job was very miserable, he must be an extremely wicked man.

Job said that God's Word was more precious to him than his *"necessary food."* Because of this, he knew that God is faithful to His Word and would, therefore, be faithful to Job.

In every generation, faithful Christians are satisfied with nothing less than reading God's Word and seeking to know, understand, and do His will. In the midst of confusion, pain, and suffering, His great promises are a believer's source of strength.

"It is written, Man shall not live by bread alone, but by every word that proceedeth out of the mouth of God" (Matt. 4:4).

Thought for Today: As we receive strength from God's Word on a day-to-day basis, we can be faithful to Him in times of testing.

Christ Revealed: By Job's faithfulness to God through his suffering (Job 23:10). *"Christ also suffered for us, leaving us an example"* (1 Pet. 2:21).

June 21: Read Job 25–29

Verses for Today: *"But where shall wisdom be found? and where is the place of understanding? . . . Behold, the fear of the Lord, that is wisdom; and to depart from evil is understanding"* (Job 28:12, 28).

In the midst of all the false accusations, Job's faith in the Lord was the source of his strength. His critics' opinions did not sway his spiritual insight. Job wasn't as concerned about knowing the "reason" for his suffering as he was in having a right relationship with God, who knows all things.

Human knowledge about our ever-changing world is very limited and continuously revised, enlarged, and discarded. Apart from God, man does not have any knowledge or ultimate answers to life's problems, God's ways, or eternity. In fact, Scripture declares, *"The world by wisdom knew not God"* (1 Cor. 1:21).[13]

Spiritual truth and wisdom can only be understood by those who have been born again in Christ and who have received His Spirit and truth (Luke 24:45; 2 Cor. 3:16; 1 John 5:20). Not only is spiritual understanding granted to the believer, but the Lord promises us that if we need more wisdom, we are to ask for it (James 1:5). Finally, as strange as it may seem to a skeptical world, we discover God's wisdom only as we obey His Word—*"a good understanding have all they that do his commandments"* (Ps. 111:10).

When we meet the Lord in person, the mystery of suffering will be more fully understood. We will see that God in wisdom had some eternal purposes for allowing it.

In Him are hidden all the treasures of wisdom and knowledge (Col. 2:3).

Thought for Today: The depth of our faith is revealed by the way we react to our sorrows and sufferings.

Christ Revealed: Through Job's compassion for others (Job 29:15-16). Scripture tells us, and shows us, that Jesus had compassion for the multitudes—even giving His life, so that we might be saved (Matt. 14:14; 15:30-39).

---

13 A thought-provoking and enjoyable commentary on this verse of God's wisdom versus man's can be found under "Barnes' Notes on the Bible" at https://biblehub.com/commentaries/1_corinthians/1-21.htm.

June 22: Read Job 30–33

Verses for Today: *"They abhor me . . . and spare not to spit in my face. . . . I cry unto thee, and thou dost not hear me"* (Job 30:10, 20).

There appeared to be no end to the anguish that Job suffered, even contempt from those who spit in his face as he cried out in prayer. Furthermore, as much as he could determine, God was not hearing his prayers—*"Thou regardest me not"* (Job 30:20).

One of the greatest struggles for a Christian is to pray, and continue praying, even when there is no apparent sign that God has heard. The effectiveness of our prayers cannot be judged by immediate results, though. There are various reasons for delay and seemingly unanswered prayer.

At times, God does not grant the thing we specifically ask for, but He gives us something better. There are times He withholds material benefits to impart spiritual enlightenment and understanding. The very fact that our requests are sometimes granted and sometimes denied may be difficult to understand, but it is further proof that we are cared for by a God of love, whose ways are governed by wisdom and always for our best.

And Jesus told His disciples parables to show them that they should always pray and not give up (Luke 18:1-8).

Thought for Today: We are to draw near to our Lord with confidence, praying for mercy, grace, and help in times of need (Heb. 4:16).

Christ Revealed: Through the ridicule and affliction that Job suffered (Job 30:10-11). Jesus was afflicted and spit upon (Isa. 50:6; 53:2-5; Matt. 27:26; Mark 15:15-20; John 19:1-5).

June 23: Read Job 34–37

Verses for Today: *"My desire is that Job may be tried unto the end. . . . For he addeth rebellion unto his sin. . . . Therefore doth Job open his mouth in vain; he multiplieth words without knowledge"* (Job 34:36-37; 35:16).

The youngest man, Elihu, did not speak until the other friends had ended their complaints, criticism, and condemnation of Job. Elihu was angry with the others since they had accused Job, yet were unable to answer him. He was also angry at Job because he thought Job was a self-righteous sinner (Job 34:7-8). Elihu believed that he alone could act as God's priest to intercede on Job's behalf.

We are frequently prone to criticize and condemn another's actions when we simply do not know what God is doing, or how He is working in the heart of someone with different circumstances and experiences from our own. We must not judge others, for this is a serious sin (James 3:1). In addition, it robs us of joy, and instills a root of bitterness in our hearts.

"Who art thou that judgest another man's servant? to his own master he standeth or falleth. Yea, he shall be holden up: for God is able to make him stand" (Rom. 14:4).

Thought for Today: Enjoying fellowship with the Lord is dependent upon one's attitude toward others (Prov. 21:13; Matt. 5:7; 7:1-2).

Christ Revealed: As the One whose *"eyes are upon the ways of man"* (Job 34:21). *"For the eyes of the Lord are over the righteous, and his ears are open unto their prayers"* (1 Pet. 3:12).

June 24: Read Job 38–40

Verse for Today: *"Canst thou bind the sweet influences of Pleiades, or loose the bands of Orion?"* (Job 38:31).

God finally spoke to Job. He challenged Job to consider the limitations of his own wisdom, compared with the wisdom of God, who created the vast constellations and planets that are spread throughout the heavens. Neither the wisest astronomer nor the most spiritual person can explain or change one star in the marvelous array of the stars of Pleiades—one of the most beautiful clusters of stars visible to the naked eye. The only true explanation of the arrangement of the world is that which is recorded in the first chapters of Genesis.

God's questions to Job reveal that man is totally inadequate to comprehend the Lord's glorious wisdom. This mighty God, who created the universe, is our Lord. He cares for us, listens to our prayers, and helps us! Surely, we should bow before Him in adoration and praise.

"Ah Lord God! behold, thou hast made the heaven and the earth by thy great power and stretched out arm, and there is nothing too hard for thee" (Jer. 32:17).

Thought for Today: The vastness of the universe reveals God's unlimited resources, matchless wisdom, and His glory.

Christ Revealed: As the One who *"laid the foundations of the earth"* (Job 38:4). By Christ, God *"made the worlds"* (John 1:1-4; Col. 1:15-20; Heb. 1:1-2).

June 25: Read Job 41–42

Verse for Today: *"So the Lord blessed the latter end of Job more than his beginning"* (Job 42:12).

From all outward appearances, it seemed that Job's four friends were enjoying God's favor and that God was displeased only with Job. His friends fully expected God's approval of their efforts to convince Job how wrong he was. The men must have been astounded to hear the voice from heaven say to Eliphaz, *I am angry with you and your two friends because you did not speak of Me what is right, the way My servant Job did* (Job: 42:7).

On the other hand, Job must have been equally surprised to hear that God was pleased with him because immediately preceding the voice from heaven, Job had said, *I am ashamed of myself for what I have said, and I repent in dust and ashes* (Job 42:6). Job was not only humble in recognizing his inadequacies, but he had a sincere desire to please the Lord.

Job could have become proud when he realized that God was coming to his defense. Instead, however, he prayed for his friends, who had so greatly misjudged him. Because of Job's gentle, submissive spirit, God granted him even greater blessings and possessions than he had enjoyed before his trials and sufferings.

As we review this account, we discover that God lovingly answered all of Job's prayers! Job asked God to stop frightening him; he asked for God to talk to him, answer him, and reveal his sins; and he requested that his own words be recorded in a book. All that Job asked for, God granted (Job 13:20-23; 19:23).

Truly, our Lord is able to do much more than we can ever imagine (Eph. 3:20) for *everything under heaven belongs to Him* (Job 41:11).

Thought for Today: God declares that we are not to judge those who are suffering, but we are to love, comfort, and help them (1 Thess. 5:14; Titus 3:2).

Christ Revealed: Through Job's prayers for his friends, who hurt him (Job 42:10). We are reminded of Christ's command to *pray for those who mistreat you* (Luke 6:28), and of Jesus interceding for us in prayer (Rom. 8:34).

 # PSALMS

The book of Psalms is composed of 150 poems, prayers, praises, and songs to God. The Hebrew word for psalms means "praises," which is a term that reflects much of the book's content. In addition, this book helps teach us how to pray, admit our fears, confess our sins, think on God, and express gratitude and praise to God. Psalms is the second book, in a grouping of five, which are writings on wisdom and poetry. The five are Job, Psalms, Proverbs, Ecclesiastes, and Song of Songs.

The ultimate author of the Psalms is the Holy Spirit, who moved many writers to compose them. King David wrote more than seventy. Other writers include Moses, Solomon, Asaph, Ethan, and the sons of Korah. The writers of about fifty psalms are not identified.

The psalmists' thoughts often wander from feelings of utter failure to ones of delight, but conclude by expressing adoration, thankfulness, and trust in God. In these passages, we can learn the right way to be honest with our struggles and our emotions and bring our complaints to God. Our trials can either cause us to complain (thus revealing a lack of faith in the Lord and His promises), or they can lead us to Him. When we admit our needs, fears, and frustrations to the Lord, and acknowledge His power and goodness, we are able to rest in His care, peace, and truth.

Understanding a bit about the different types or categories of Psalms can enable us to receive greater comfort and truth from them. A brief categorizing of the Psalms would include historical; messianic; songs of praise, as well as trust and confidence in God; songs used for coming into God's presence for worship; royal psalms; psalms declaring the beauty of God's wisdom and law (especially Ps. 119); songs of ascent, and songs for our pilgrimage to Zion. In addition, there are psalms and prayers of lament. These include expressions of grief, as well as complaints during times of tribulation. Penitent or penitential psalms include confession of sin and asking for forgiveness, along with seeking God's help in circumstances that are ultimately caused by the problem of sin. There are also imprecatory psalms, in which the psalmist cries out in pain, while calling for God's judgment on sin and the evildoer.

The Psalms make a clear distinction between sin and righteousness. They reveal what sin really is—rebellion against God. The words *righteous* and *righteousness* are used more than 130 times, while *sin*, *iniquity*, and *evil* occur more than ninety times. When the psalms speak of judgment on evildoers, they are not referring to personal revenge. Rather, the Spirit of God is revealing God's judgment and the ultimate outcome upon those who do evil. (The writers of these Psalms have identified themselves with the Lord in hating wrongdoing.) All injustice and sin will inevitably be punished. The same truth is revealed in the New Testament—*"Be not deceived; God is not mocked: for whatsoever a man soweth, that shall he also reap"* (Gal. 6:7).

Some of the psalms, such as Psalm 51, teach us how to confess sin and humbly seek God's forgiveness. Others, like Psalm 23, instruct us to be aware of, and content in, the Lord's personal care for us.

Many psalms reveal prophecies regarding the Messiah. Details are declared about His birth, life, betrayal, crucifixion, resurrection, and ascension. Jesus revealed that the Psalms spoke of Him: *"All things must be fulfilled, which were written in the law of Moses, and in the prophets, and in the psalms, concerning me"* (Luke 24:44). Those who read only the New Testament limit their knowledge of

Jesus, since the Holy Spirit speaks of our Savior throughout the Old Testament (John 5:39).

The Psalms are quoted or referred to about a hundred times in the New Testament—more than any other book of the Old Testament, with the possible exception of Isaiah. The New Testament encourages us and teaches us to sing the psalms (Col. 3:16) and speak *"to yourselves in psalms and hymns and spiritual songs, singing and making melody in your heart to the Lord"* (Eph. 5:19).

June 26: Read Psalms 1–9

Verse for Today: *"Blessed is the man that walketh not in the counsel of the ungodly"* (Ps. 1:1).

A blessed person is one who possesses happiness produced by experiencing God's favor. Such an individual is content with God's love and guidance, regardless of outward circumstances.

The secret to having a blessed life is to refuse to walk *"in the counsel of the ungodly."* More than simple worldly goodness, the Psalms teach us that we are to *delight in the law of the Lord* (Ps. 1:2).

What a contrast this joy is to the superficial, empty happiness the world offers! As we meditate day and night upon God's Word for the purpose of doing His will, our lives take on new meaning.

"This book of the law shall not depart out of thy mouth; but thou shalt meditate therein day and night . . . for then thou shalt make thy way prosperous, and then thou shalt have good success" (Josh. 1:8).

Thought for Today: Only to the extent that we love God will we enjoy obeying His Word.

Christ Revealed: As the Son of God (Ps. 2:7). *"For God so loved the world, that he gave his only begotten Son, that whosoever believeth in him should not perish, but have everlasting life"* (John 3:16; Acts 13:33; Heb. 1:5).

June 27: Read Psalms 10–17

Verse for Today: *"In the Lord put I my trust: how say ye to my soul, Flee as a bird to your mountain?"* (Ps. 11:1).

David's friends advised him to flee to the mountainous parts of Judah to avoid the danger that threatened him. But he refused to retreat from the scene of conflict, nor would he resort to taking revenge against Saul. God seemed to have deserted David, yet he did not allow his circumstances to weaken his faith. Even though he was a victim in great personal danger, his faith was unshaken. He stood his ground and trusted in the Lord.

While God's people may expect to be tested, there is absolute assurance that, in due time, the faithful Christian will triumph (Ps. 11:7). We must reject the advice of those who want us to *flee as a bird to the mountains* and retreat or withdraw from our convictions due to opposition. The voice of logic may ask what is safe and easy, but God's child will inquire what is right and pleasing to Him.

"And fear not them which kill the body, but are not able to kill the soul: but rather fear him which is able to destroy both soul and body in hell" (Matt. 10:28).

Thought for Today: Knowing God's Word and that He is in control enables us to face our difficulties.

Christ Revealed: In the prophecy, *"For thou wilt not leave my soul in hell; neither wilt thou suffer thine Holy One to see corruption"* (Ps. 16:10). This declaration foretells the resurrection of our Lord Jesus Christ (Acts 2:25-27; 13:35-39).

June 28: Read Psalms 18–22

Verses for Today: *"Now know I that the Lord saveth his anointed; he will hear him from his holy heaven with the saving strength of his right hand. Some trust in chariots, and some in horses: but we will remember the name of the Lord our God. They are brought down and fallen: but we are risen, and stand upright"* (Ps. 20:6-8).

Prayer has always turned apparent defeat into victory for God's obedient servants. The "armies" of those who trust in "chariots and horses" and rely on vast resources often seem secure and invincible. We discover, however, that the people of God who pray and trust in His unseen presence will always rise up triumphantly, while the unbeliever will be brought down. Prayer will deliver; pride will defeat.

If David could pray and testify how the Lord delivered him from Saul and his armies, how much more can we pray and trust God to answer our prayers because we know that Jesus is our Savior and our intercessor! Jesus's repeated reminder to pray proves that He knows our hearts. He knows how natural and easy it is to doubt God, and how we are inclined to repeat our prayers without expecting an answer. Instead, we must know God's Word, abide in it, continue to pray, and not give up (John 14:13-14; 15:7; 16:23-24; 1 John 3:21-22; 5:14-15).

Let us be like Jehoshaphat who, before he entered into battle against the vast armies of the Moabites and Ammonites, prayed and appointed singers to praise the Lord for the answer! He obtained an easy victory (2 Chron. 20:20-22).

"Ask, and it shall be given you; seek, and ye shall find; knock, and it shall be opened unto you: For every one that asketh receiveth; and he that seeketh findeth; and to him that knocketh it shall be opened" (Matt. 7:7-8).

Thought for Today: Have you remembered to praise and thank the Lord for the victories in your life?

Christ Revealed: As the One who was forsaken by God for our benefit (Ps. 22:1). On the cross, Jesus cried out, *"My God, my God, why hast thou forsaken me?"* (Matt. 27:46; Mark 15:34).

June 29: Read Psalms 23–30

Verses for Today: *"The Lord is my shepherd; I shall not want. . . . He restoreth my soul: he leadeth me in the paths of righteousness for his name's sake"* (Ps. 23:1, 3).

David, the shepherd-king, considered himself as nothing more than a sheep that had to be led by the Great Shepherd in the paths of righteousness.

No other type of livestock requires so much attention as do sheep. A sheep can become so engrossed in following its own eating path that it is separated from the flock and lost. Without a shepherd, sheep follow the same trails until those trails are ruts, and there is no good pasture.

We—by nature—are like sheep, blindly and habitually following the same paths, even when we have seen those same paths ruin the lives of others. We become so wrapped up in our own affairs that we lose our way. There is something sad and terrifying about the destructive, self-willed determination of those who are not willing to be led *"in the paths of righteousness."* They continue going their own way, knowing it ends with calamity.

How many times have we prayed, "Lord, lead me in paths of righteousness," while, in our day-by-day conduct, we still refuse to deny ourselves—to give up our "rights," and yield our interests to God? How many times do we refuse to yield to others? If we truly want God's will and blessings, we will follow the Great Shepherd.

"Then said Jesus unto his disciples, If any man will come after me, let him deny himself, and take up his cross, and follow me" (Matt. 16:24).

Thought for Today: The tender voice of our Good Shepherd is still calling, *"Come unto me."*

Christ Revealed: As our Shepherd (Ps. 23). Jesus is the Good Shepherd, who *"giveth his life for the sheep"* (John 10:11).

June 30: Read Psalms 31–35

Verse for Today: *"I acknowledged my sin unto thee, and mine iniquity have I not hid. I said, I will confess my transgressions unto the Lord; and thou forgavest the iniquity of my sin"* (Ps. 32:5).

When Nathan, the prophet, confronted David with his iniquity, David confessed his sin and his need for mercy and forgiveness. The Lord then forgave David—not only for his sins, but also for the iniquity of his sin.

"Iniquity" means more than rejecting God's Word—more than mere failure or weakness. It means turning aside from what we know is right by twisting the truth to satisfy our personal desire. The inevitable results of iniquity are always misery and unhappiness. There can be no lasting peace and joy until sin is sincerely confessed and forsaken.

"Be not deceived; God is not mocked: for whatsoever a man soweth, that shall he also reap" (Gal. 6:7).

Thought for Today: To continue in sin is to choose a life of misery and emptiness.

Christ Revealed: In the prophecy, *"He keepeth all his bones: not one of them is broken"* (Ps. 34:20). Not a bone of His was broken when Christ was crucified (John 19:36).

July

July 1: Read Psalms 36–39

Verses for Today: *"For with thee is the fountain of life: in thy light shall we see light. O continue thy lovingkindness unto them"* (Ps. 36:9-10).

Our Heavenly Father's loving-kindness is manifested through the gift He has given the world—the gift of *"his only begotten Son"* (John 3:16). Jesus reveals God's marvelous loving-kindness.

Through Jesus, God has given the light of the knowledge of His glory (2 Cor. 4:6; Eph. 1:17). Jesus is the Source of life and light to all who accept Him as their Savior. Just as our earthly existence is dependent upon the *sun* to maintain physical life, we are dependent upon the *Son* of God to maintain spiritual life.

The "light" of human wisdom or effort can never produce assurance that one is saved and at peace with God. We are totally dependent upon the light of God's Word to receive His loving-kindness, for *"thy words giveth light; it giveth understanding unto the simple"* (Ps. 119:130). When a person neglects God's Word, he rejects the Source of life and light—Christ—the Light of the World (John 1:1-14).

"Then spake Jesus again unto them, saying, I am the light of the world: he that followeth me shall not walk in darkness, but . . . if ye believe not that I am he, ye shall die in your sins" (John 8:12, 24).

Thought for Today: When we read God's Word, it provides light for life's pathway.

Christ Revealed: As the Fountain of life, and Light (Ps. 36:9). *Jesus is the Fountain of Life, the Source of the river of Living Water* (John 4:10, 14; Rev. 22:1). *He is the Light of the World* (John 8:12).

July 2: Read Psalms 40–45

Verses for Today: *"My tears have been my meat day and night, while they continually say unto me, Where is thy God? . . . I shall yet praise him for the help of his countenance"* (Ps. 42:3, 5).

Because of King Saul's jealousy, David was forced to leave Jerusalem—the City of God—and stay in hiding for years. The Lord allowed David to face difficult and trying events, which David did not understand. From all outward appearances, it seemed that his life was being wasted—that God did not care.

But David's suffering was God's way of deepening his spiritual life. The Lord allowed his circumstances to develop the characteristics that made David a man after God's own heart (Acts 13:22), and a wise and godly leader.

To become frustrated with our circumstances is a natural tendency. However, whether our apparent dilemmas are caused by our own shortcomings or by Satan, God is able to use them all for good purposes if we let Him. We don't have to understand *why* we are having struggles. God wants us to accept our trials, and in this way, He can develop our faith.

Always rejoice in the Lord, pray for everything, and give thanks in all circumstances since this is God's will for you in Christ Jesus (1 Thess. 5:16-18).

Thought for Today: God's grace and power are sufficient to sustain us in every situation—regardless of its severity or duration.

Christ Revealed: As the One who loves to do God's will (Ps. 40:6-8; John 4:34; Heb. 10:7, 9). As the One who will one day reign as Lord in righteousness and justice (Ps. 33:5; 45:6-7; Isa. 9:6-7; Heb. 1:8-9).

July 3: Read Psalms 46–51

Verses for Today: *"Have mercy upon me, O God, according to thy lovingkindness: according unto the multitude of thy tender mercies blot out my transgressions. . . . For I acknowledge my transgressions: and my sin is ever before me. . . . Create in me a clean heart, O God; and renew a right spirit within me"* (Ps. 51:1, 3, 10).

David was capable of the highest spiritual triumphs as noted in the psalms he wrote. However, in the midst of all his victories, he selfishly took for himself Bathsheba, the beautiful wife of Uriah. David was guilty before God, and especially as Jehovah's anointed shepherd-king, he could not evade the judgment of God.

The fearless prophet Nathan went to the king and denounced his selfish act. David was convicted of his sin, filled with remorse, and prayed for mercy and grace: *"Create in me a clean heart, O God; and renew a right spirit."*

Oh, the destructive power of even one sin! No child of God should look upon sin as merely a mistake or failure to obey God. "Sin" is far more than "missing the mark" of God's high calling; it is cooperating with Satan—the supreme enemy of the God of righteousness and the destroyer of all that is good.

"It is a fearful thing to fall into the hands of the living God" (Heb. 10:31).

Thought for Today: The Lord does not overlook our sins because of our position or the good that we have done.

Christ Revealed: As the One who redeemed us from sin with His own precious blood (Ps. 49:8-9, 15; 1 Pet. 1:18-19).

July 4: Read Psalms 52–59

Verse for Today: *"Consume them in wrath, consume them, that they may not be: and let them know that God ruleth in Jacob unto the ends of the earth"* (Ps. 59:13).

Some of the Psalms express anger against enemies and evildoers. This may seem hard to understand, but they reveal the judgment of God against all who do evil. These inspired words of God express His abhorrence of sin.

This authoritative reaction against sin, which is found in the Psalms of judgment, is also in the New Testament. Paul declared, *"Alexander the coppersmith did me much evil: the Lord reward him according to his works"* (2 Tim. 4:14).

The psalmist's motive, along with that of the apostle Paul, had nothing to do with personal jealousy, spite, or hatred. Both men were anointed of God to express His hatred against sin.

A Christian's attitude toward sin must be in harmony with God's Word. We are to recognize every transgression as the Lord does and speak with truth and grace. When we are mistreated, we should pray for those who oppose us, and trust the Lord to mete out justice. He alone is worthy and able (Rom. 12:19; Heb. 10:30).

Bless those who persecute you; bless, and do not curse . . . . Do not repay anyone evil for evil. Be careful to do what is right. As much as you are able, live at peace with everyone. Do not take revenge, but leave room for God's judgment and wrath. In fact, if your enemy is hungry, feed him; if he is thirsty, then give him something to drink (Rom. 12:14, 17-20).

Thought for Today: Rebellion against God is *"exceeding sinful"* (Rom. 7:13).

Christ Revealed: As the One who saves those who call upon Him (Ps. 55:16-17). *"For whosoever shall call upon the name of the Lord shall be saved"* (Rom. 10:13).

July 5: Read Psalms 60–66

Verses for Today: *"Hear my cry, O God; attend unto my prayer. From the end of the earth will I cry unto thee, when my heart is overwhelmed: lead me to the rock that is higher than I"* (Ps. 61:1-2).

King Saul forced David to retreat to the area east of the Jordan River, which was not part of the Promised Land. The psalmist felt exiled from God's presence in the foreign country. Although the desolate location seemed like *"the end of the earth,"* he prayed and, in the midst of his dilemma, could state with confidence, *"So will I sing praise unto thy name"* (Ps. 61:8).

Every person has burdens, and each one frequently thinks his are the heaviest. The Lord never promised to take away our burdens, but He did promise, *"My grace is sufficient"* (2 Cor. 12:9). When our burdens seem too heavy to bear, we should remember that the Lord is working to bring good from them. He uses every problem to draw us closer to Him, and to refine our character to be like Christ. In addition, it's His intent that in the midst of life's dark moments, His glory and goodness will shine through us to others, and they will encounter Him and know Him. God's children are not to fear but, rather, we are to walk in His promises and draw closer to Him.

All things work together for good to those who love God for they are called according to his purpose (Rom. 8:28).

Thought for Today: As we daily read God's Word, seeking to know Him, our confidence in the Lord's power and protection will increase.

Christ Revealed: As *the Rock*—the unmovable, eternal, unchanging Savior (Ps. 61:2; 62:2, 6-7). Jesus is the Rock of our salvation (1 Cor. 10:4).

July 6: Read Psalms 67–71

Verse for Today: *"God setteth the solitary in families: he bringeth out those which are bound with chains: but the rebellious dwell in a dry land"* (Ps. 68:6).

The unbelieving world often misunderstands Christianity, believing it to be a gloomy, uninteresting existence. However, exactly the opposite is true—those who rebel against God *"dwell in a dry land."* The brightest prospects of sinful enjoyment eventually leave their victims empty and wretched.

Those who trust in the Lord, though, *"shall be abundantly satisfied"* (Ps. 36:8). Our future is secure and our present is blessed because Christ is our Savior, and our ever-present helper and friend (John 15:15). Even the trying experiences of life are blessings in disguise as God brings good from them. Finally, no matter what our day-to-day circumstances may bring, a Christian's ultimate future is radiant, beautiful, and inviting. We are to joyfully ponder meeting our Savior, Jesus Christ, and anticipate the glories of His kingdom.

"Let us therefore come boldly unto the throne of grace, that we may obtain mercy, and find grace to help in time of need" (Heb. 4:16).

Thought for Today: Our life is like a raging sea until we turn to the Lord, who is able to bring peace.

Christ Revealed: As the One who "led captivity captive" (Ps. 68:18). Jesus's death and resurrection broke the captive power of sin, Satan, and death (Gal. 5:1).

July 7: Read Psalms 72–77

Verses for Today: *"Give the king thy judgments, O God, and thy righteousness unto the king's son. . . . He shall redeem their soul from deceit and violence: and precious shall their blood be in his sight"* (Ps. 72:1, 14).

This Psalm is a prayer that the king might rule with justice and righteousness just as God would govern. How wonderful it would be to have a just government that values the rights of all—even the widows, aged, orphans, and handicapped. Achieving equality, justice, safety, and prosperity for all people has never existed, however. It seems more difficult than ever in our modern, complex world. Not only that, but the Lord has foretold that, as time goes on, *"evil men and seducers shall wax worse and worse"* (2 Tim. 3:13).

A day is coming, though, when the King of kings shall reign in perfect wisdom and righteousness for all. As God's children, we are to wait expectantly and confidently for Jesus and that joyful day.

"And I heard a great voice out of heaven saying, Behold, the tabernacle of God is with men, and he will dwell with them, and they shall be his people, and God himself shall be with them, and be their God. And God shall wipe away all tears from their eyes; and there shall be no more death, neither sorrow, nor crying, neither shall there be any more pain: for the former things are passed away. And he that sat upon the throne said, Behold, I make all things new" (Rev. 21:3-5).

Thought for Today: Do not set your hope on the things of this world but, rather, on the solid and precious promises of God.

Christ Revealed: As the righteous Judge: *"He shall . . . break in pieces the oppressor"* (Ps. 72:4). Those who refuse to accept the freely offered salvation of Jesus, the Lamb of God (John 1:29-36), will face the judgment and *"wrath of the Lamb"* (Rev. 6:15-17).

July 8: Read Psalms 78–80

Verses for Today: *"For he established . . . a law in Israel, which he commanded our fathers, that they should . . . declare them to their children: That they might set their hope in God, and not forget the works of God, but keep his commandments"* (Ps. 78:5-7).

The responsibility of teaching God's Word to children rests upon the parents, but this is a weakness in many Christian families. Some parents even go so far as to say, "I do not intend to interfere with my children's religion. When they become old enough, I want them to choose their own religion." Yet, the same parent does everything possible to encourage the child to eat the right food to maintain good health, and to choose a career that best ensures financial security. It seems strange that in eternal matters, parents refuse to give direction.

Far too many parents plan and work to prepare their children for the few short years of life, while their relationship with Christ is ignored. As followers of Christ, though, we have a *valuable and incredible gift of truth and salvation,* and it is vital that we share it with our children.

Let us ask God to help us understand His Word more, and enable us to talk about spiritual matters in natural ways as we go about our day (Deut. 6:7; 11:19). May the Lord grant us spiritual understanding, timely words, and courage and grace to share His wonderful truth with our children and grandchildren!

"And that from a child thou hast known the holy scriptures, which are able to make thee wise unto salvation through faith which is in Christ Jesus" (2 Tim. 3:15).

Thought for Today: Daily Bible reading and prayer in the home will bless and strengthen your family.

Christ Revealed: As the true Shepherd (Ps. 80:1). Jesus Christ is the Good Shepherd, and the Door of the sheepfold. He alone is the way to heaven. *"I am the door. . . . I am the good shepherd. . . . I am the way, the truth, and the life: no man cometh unto the Father, but by me"* (John 10:7, 11; 14:6).

July 9: Read Psalms 81–87

Verses for Today: *"For a day in thy courts is better than a thousand. . . . No good thing will he withhold from them that walk uprightly"* (Ps. 84:10-11).

David was greatly aware of God's presence. Nothing—not the rebellion of his sons, the betrayal by his best friend, or the disloyalty of the people—could separate him from the presence of the Lord. David could say with confidence, *"No good thing will he withhold."* He knew that God would not permit him to miss out on, or be deprived of, any good thing.

Oh, that more of God's children would enjoy the presence and assurance of God! A day in the Lord's presence is better than a thousand days spent elsewhere.

Most of us want to tell God what we think is best for us, instead of being content to let Him lead us one day at a time. Waiting patiently on the Lord not only tests our faith, but additionally strengthens it. If we think about it, most of our mistakes are the result of impatience and the failure to recognize His presence.

Do you doubt God's day-by-day guidance for the future? If you do, think back over the years. No child of God's can do so without a feeling of grateful praise and thankfulness for His mercies. He has been with you.

"Commit thy way unto the Lord; trust also in him; and he shall bring it to pass" (Ps. 37:5).

Thought for Today: God's grace is available for you today. Rest in His love.

Christ Revealed: In the cry for God to arise and judge the earth (Ps. 82:8). This foretells the coming of Christ (Rev. 22:20), who will judge the earth (John 5:22).

July 10: Read Psalms 88–91

Verses for Today: *"He that dwelleth in the secret place of the Most High shall abide under the shadow of the Almighty. I will say of the Lord, He is my refuge and my fortress: my God; in him will I trust"* (Ps. 91:1-2).

David's life was filled with dangers, but he regarded God as a *"refuge"* and a *"fortress."* The godly recognize the need for a refuge during times of struggles, sorrows, mental perplexities, and bodily pain.

The very nature of trials and testings involves the idea of possible failure. Bodily pain can result in bitterness; mental perplexities can lead to unbelief; and trials may end in defeat. Truly, we need a *"refuge and fortress."*

Other troubles threaten us, as well. Our adversary, the devil, goes about *"as a roaring lion . . . seeking whom he may devour"* (1 Pet. 5:8). Powerful forces and deceptive influences bear upon us, aiming to lead us astray. The spirit and principles of the world system—many of its practices, amusements, literature, and media—are opposed to God and to the interests and lifestyle of Christians. Followers of Christ are often hated by the world. Additionally, we have *fleshly lusts, which war against our own soul* (1 Pet. 2:11).

However, Christians who are victorious have *"no confidence in the flesh"* (Phil. 3:3), but *dwell in the secret place*—in prayer and meditation on God's Word. We are to reflect on His promises and rely upon *"the Most High"* for wisdom and strength. Those who trust in *"the Most High"* have no need to fear.

"The Lord knoweth how to deliver the godly out of temptations, and to reserve the unjust unto the day of judgment to be punished" (2 Pet. 2:9).

Thought for Today: Think back on your life and recognize how the Lord has cared for you along the way.

Christ Revealed: God will appoint His firstborn as the most exalted King of the earth (Ps. 89:27). *For unto us a child will be given who will be ruler, and called Wonderful, Counselor, Mighty God, Everlasting Father, Prince of Peace* (Isa. 9:6-7). *"And the angel said unto them, Fear not: for, behold, I bring you good tidings of great joy, which shall be to all people. For unto you is born this day in the City of David a Saviour, which is Christ the Lord"* (Luke 2:10-11).

July 11: Read Psalms 92–100

Verses for Today: *"O come, let us sing unto the Lord: let us make a joyful noise to the rock of our salvation. Let us come before his presence with thanksgiving. . . . O come, let us worship and bow down: let us kneel before the Lord our maker. For he is our God; and we are the people of his pasture, and the sheep of his hand. To day if ye will hear his voice, harden not your heart"* (Ps. 95:1-2, 6-8).

One of the reasons many Christians make such a little impression on the world is their melancholy attitude. Their general mood is the reflection of a funeral, rather than a celebration of Christ, our risen Lord.

God intends for us to know and experience His greatness and goodness, and have a singing, joyful attitude. The Lord wants us to know all that He has done for us, and all that He abundantly and freely provides for us. He is *"the Lord our maker,"* and desires that we *"come before his presence with thanksgiving."*

Consider the insult of our conduct when we are critical, dull, or unhappy.

The psalmist calls, *"O come, let us worship and bow down."* The biblical word *"worship"* does not mean an emotionless, mindless bowing down. Our worship is to include knowing our low, humble state; enjoying God; and praising Him for His greatness and His loving-kindness toward us.

We are to rejoice in God's many attributes and gifts. He forgives our sins, heals our diseases, redeems our lives from the pit, crowns us with love and compassion, satisfies us with good things, renews us, strengthens us, guides us, and makes known His great deeds and truth to us (Ps. 103:2-8). The Lord desires that our enjoyment of Him is real, and overflows back to Him and to others (1 Chron. 16:23-31; Ps. 71:14-24; Jer. 20:13).

You have shown me the path of life, and you fill me with joy in your presence (Ps. 16:11).

Thought for Today: Is your attitude today a reflection of God's love toward you?

Christ Revealed: As the Creator—*"It is he that hath made us"* (Ps. 100:3). As the wonderful Creator of all things, the Lord is worthy to receive glory and honor (John 1:3; Col. 1:16; Rev. 4:11).

July 12: Read Psalms 101–105

Verses for Today: *"Moreover he called for a famine upon the land. . . . He sent a man before them, even Joseph, who was sold for a servant: Whose feet they hurt with fetters: he was laid in iron . . . the word of the Lord tried him"* (Ps. 105:16-19).

During Jacob's life, a famine forced Jacob to send his sons to Egypt to buy food (Ps. 105:6-16). There they discovered that Joseph, whom they had sold as a slave years earlier, had become a great ruler in Egypt. Although their treatment of Joseph had been evil, God *"meant it unto good"* for the saving of many lives (Gen. 50:20).

For years, Joseph may not have understood his circumstances as *"the word of the Lord tried him,"* but he held on to God's promises. Joseph's life is evidence of God's blessings that come when we continue to faithfully trust the Lord, even when we do not know the reasons for our troubles (Prov. 3:5-6). God often withholds the understanding of His will to develop our faith and trust in Him.

"For all the promises of God in him are yea, and in him Amen, unto the glory of God by us" (2 Cor. 1:20).

Thought for Today: Sometimes the Lord overrules our wishes and plans to accomplish His good purposes.

Christ Revealed: Through Jesus, we receive the numerous blessings described in Psalm 103. He is the one who *"forgiveth all thine iniquities; who healeth all thy diseases"* (Ps. 103:3). *He delivers the captives, gives sight to the blind, and liberates those who come to Him* (Luke 4:18-19).

July 13: Read Psalms 106–107

Verses for Today: *"He sent his word, and healed them, and delivered them from their destructions. Oh that men would praise the Lord for his goodness, and for his wonderful works to the children of men!"* (Ps. 107:20-21).

The psalmist could have said, "the Lord delivered them" but, instead, he specifically said, *"He sent his word, and healed them."* God's Word is an endless fountain of supply for all our needs. It is the only reliable source of counsel for our inner turmoil, struggles, and emotions.

Scripture teaches the absolute necessity of relying on God's Word for every problem and situation—without exception. *The Word by which the heavens were made* (Ps. 33:6; Gen. 1) is the same Word by which the Lord *"is able to do exceeding abundantly above all that we ask or think, according to the power that worketh in us"* (Eph. 3:20; Ps. 33:6). Through daily Bible reading, we obtain power and faith to trust God to fulfill His promises.

"For the word of God is quick, and powerful, and sharper than any twoedged sword, piercing even to the dividing asunder of soul and spirit, and of the joints and marrow, and is a discerner of the thoughts and intents of the heart" (Heb. 4:12).

Take up the sword of the Spirit, which is the word of God (Eph. 6:17).

Thought for Today: How much of the Word do you make available for the Lord to use in your life?

Christ Revealed: As the One who *"maketh the storm a calm"* and gives peace in the midst of it (Ps. 107:29). When Jesus calmed the storm, His disciples exclaimed: *"What manner of man is this, that even the winds and the sea obey him!"* (Matt. 8:27; John 14:27).

July 14: Read Psalms 108–118

Verse for Today: *"Praise ye the Lord. Blessed is the man that feareth the Lord, that delighteth greatly in his commandments"* (Ps. 112:1).

Godly fear means we are to have reverence, respect, and obedience for God and His ways. We are to be aware of our humble state before the Lord, even as we know His great love for us. When we have a reverential fear of God and love Him in return, as a child with a parent, we can delight in Him, His ways, and His commandments, which are good.

A reverent *'fear of God'* characterizes the prophets of the Old Testament, and is the foundation for *the more abundant life* that Jesus speaks about in the New Testament (John 10:10). It is one of the great promises foretold by the prophet Jeremiah: *"And I will make an everlasting covenant with them . . . but I will put my fear in their hearts, that they shall not depart from me"* (Jer. 32:40). The New Testament shares this truth about the early followers of Christ after His ascension: *"Then had the churches rest . . . and were edified; and walking in the fear of the Lord, and in the comfort of the Holy Ghost, were multiplied"* (Acts 9:31).

When we walk in the truth (Ps. 86:11), we have a true comprehension of both aspects of God's nature. Recognizing God's hatred and eventual judgment against sin gives us an appropriate fear of the Lord, and understanding Jesus's sacrifice for us helps us recognize His loving-kindness. To reconcile these two aspects of God's character (His justice and love) isn't easy—it takes the work of Christ! Reverence for God is an essential part of the life of every Christian who pleases Him.

"Let us have grace, whereby we may serve God acceptably with reverence and godly fear" (Heb. 12:28).

Thought for Today: Fears about our circumstances, or judgment, are removed as we trust in Jesus's love and saving grace.

Christ Revealed: *"The stone which the builders refused"* refers to Jesus (Ps. 118:22). Our Lord quoted this Scripture to the chief priests and Pharisees when they rejected Him (Matt. 21:42-45).

July 15: Read Psalm 119

Verses for Today: *"With my whole heart have I sought thee. . . . Righteous art thou, O Lord. . . . Thy testimonies . . . are righteous and very faithful"* (Ps. 119:10, 137-138).

In Psalm 119, preeminence is given to *"the Scriptures."* God's Word is referenced with terms such as "law," "lamp," and "testimonies" more than 170 times in Psalm 119. Because Christ and the testimony of Scriptures are one and the same (John 1:1), the *"Righteous . . . Lord"* is also central in this passage. Jeremiah foretold: *"He shall be called,* THE LORD OUR RIGHTEOUSNESS" (Jer. 23:6). Everything else is incidental to the Lord and His Word.

Our concern for understanding all Scripture will be in direct relationship to our love for Jesus. We cannot expect the Lord to impart further revelation of Himself or His will until we delight with our *"whole heart"* to know and live what He has already made clear to us in His Word. The more we treasure His Word, the more light and understanding we receive from it (Ps. 119:130).

The psalmist declared how precious God's Word was to him by saying it is *"better unto me than thousands of gold and silver"* (Ps. 119:72). This verse reflects the Lord's parable of the merchant, *"Who, when he had found one pearl of great price, went and sold all that he had, and bought it"* (Matt. 13:46).

"Blessed are they which do hunger and thirst after righteousness" (Matt. 5:6).

Thought for Today: Are you reading His Word to draw close to Him, know His grace, and do His will?

Christ Portrayed: By the psalmist, who delighted in God's commandments (Ps. 119:47). Jesus said, *"For I came down from heaven, not to do mine own will, but the will of him that sent me"* (John 6:38).

July 16: Read Psalms 120–131

Verses for Today: *"I wait for the Lord, my soul doth wait, and in his word do I hope. My soul waiteth for the Lord more than they that watch for the morning: I say, more than they that watch for the morning"* (Ps. 130:5-6).

There is an unusual emphasis in the repetition, *"I say, more than they that watch for the morning."* This statement illustrates the importance of waiting upon the Lord and looking to Him to supply our every need. The watchmen on Jerusalem's walls were required to stay awake, watch for danger and alert the people, and be on the lookout for messengers bringing good news.

It is a natural tendency to depend upon one's own strength, or the strength of others, as the Israelites did when they sought aid from Egypt. But those who value the Lord's blessing live in confidence that He will fulfill His Word. The psalmist urged the Israelites to be as vigilant as a watchman, and place their full confidence and trust in God. They were to seek His help and expectantly watch for Him to act on their behalf. Every believer is to be a watchman—looking for, and waiting for the Lord (Ps. 130:7).

Blessed are those servants, whom the Lord finds watching when he comes (Luke 12:37).

Thought for Today: Happy Christians are those who trust that He can choose for us better than we can choose for ourselves.

Christ Revealed: As our Protector—the One who *"shall preserve thy going out and thy coming in"* (Ps. 121:8). *"By me if any man enter in, he shall be saved, and shall go in and out, and find pasture"* (John 10:9).

July 17: Read Psalms 132–138

Verse for Today: *"Behold, how good and how pleasant it is for brethren to dwell together in unity!"* (Ps. 133:1).

When the Israelites went to Jerusalem at least three times a year to worship, they sang this psalm along the way. There were many types of people on the road to Jerusalem, but they all had one thing in common—they were on their way to the City of God to worship Him.

Members of God's family, who love the Lord, ought to live together in peace with one another. All believers—regardless of their nationality, education, or wealth—are redeemed by the same Savior, love the same Master, and anticipate living together with Jesus in the same Eternal City. Because all Christians are forgiven and loved by Christ, and since all Christians experience trials, temptations, and sorrows, we ought to love and encourage one another.

We should seek the unity for which our Lord prayed: *Holy Father, protect them by the power of your name, which you gave me, so that they may be one as we are one* (John 17:11).

"Keep the unity of the Spirit in the bond of peace" (Eph. 4:3).

Thought for Today: The unity of believers may be compared with a great orchestra—many varied instruments, and yet beautiful harmony.

Christ Revealed: As the descendant of David, who will sit upon the throne (Ps. 132:11). *"He shall be great, and shall be called the Son of the Highest: and the Lord God shall give unto him the throne of his father David: And he shall reign over the house of Jacob for ever; and of his kingdom there shall be no end"* (Luke 1:32-33; Acts 2:30).

July 18: Read Psalms 139–143

Verses for Today: *"O Lord, thou hast searched me, and known me. Thou knowest my downsitting and mine uprising, thou understandest my thought afar off"* (Ps. 139:1-2).

The psalmist knew that everything in his life was an open book to God. Loneliness lost its power, and fears had little control over him, for he knew that God was with him, loved him, and cared for him.

The same is true for you and me. God is so concerned about you that nothing in your life is too insignificant for His attention. Morning, noon, and night, He knows your thoughts, desires, beliefs, feelings, and needs. And yet, it is true that He tells us, and requires us, to pray and bring our requests to Him.

The more we pray and know His presence in our quiet times, the more we can experience His presence throughout each day. Then, during times of unexpected temptations, we will also be aware of His presence, which will enable us to control our attitudes, words, and actions, and make us amenable to being changed by His Holy Spirit into the image of Christ.

"Being confident of this very thing, that he which hath begun a good work in you will perform it until the day of Jesus Christ" (Phil. 1:6).

Thought for Today: God is as near as prayer.

Christ Revealed: As our Deliverer (Ps. 143:11). *"The Lord knoweth how to deliver the godly out of temptations"* (2 Pet. 2:9).

July 19: Read Psalms 144–150

Verses for Today: *"Put not your trust in princes, nor in the son of man, in whom there is no help. . . . Happy is he that hath the God of Jacob for his help, whose hope is in the Lord his God"* (Ps. 146:3, 5).

In situations that baffle us, we are prone to place our faith and confidence in ourselves (our wisdom, strength, or abilities), or in other people. But even our closest friends may fail us at times.

When *our hope is in the Lord,* we will begin our day by seeking Him and experiencing fellowship with Him through prayer and Bible reading. Then, because our hope is in the Lord, and not in others, there will be no need for disappointment, no matter how God directs the events.

We should not put any confidence in the flesh or anything in the world. This means in our careers, we must not allow our human nature to seek advancement by catering to influential people who we think can promote us. The psalmist declares that no one, regardless of how powerful, is able to advance us to a desired position unless it is God's will. Let us humbly seek to please the Lord, who will *exalt us in due time* (1 Pet. 5:6). Scripture proclaims, *"Cursed be the man that trusteth in man"* (Jer. 17:5).

We are to turn from the flesh, and the things of the world, and seek God wholeheartedly through His Word and prayer. Then our faith will be strengthened, and He will meet our needs and fulfill His good purposes for us. Lasting blessings and value are found only in *"the God of Jacob."*

"And again, The Lord knoweth the thoughts of the wise, that they are vain. Therefore let no man glory in men" (1 Cor. 3:20-21).

Thought for Today: Trusting in the Lord's unsearchable ways is better than hoping in man's ways.

Christ Revealed: As the One who gives sight to the blind (Ps. 146:8). Christ gave sight to the man who was born blind (John 9:1-41).

 # PROVERBS

A *"proverb"* is a succinct, pithy nugget of truth, which is easy to remember, think on, and talk about. The book of Proverbs is filled with these moral and spiritual teachings. Nearly every topic is touched on, including families, relationships, business dealings, morality, common sense, good manners, and more.

The words *"wisdom"* and *"wise"* occur over a hundred times in Proverbs. Other terms—like fear of the Lord, guidance, knowledge, understanding, instruction, truth, righteousness, and *"the way"*—are found throughout its passages, as well.

This book of practical wisdom divides mankind into two classes—wise and foolish—and exposes a series of pitfalls that defeat many people on life's pathway. The word *"wisdom"* is a term describing the godly person; the ungodly are referred to as *"fools."* The truly wise person recognizes that *"the fear of the Lord is the beginning of knowledge"* (Prov. 1:7). Many warnings are presented against subtle evils and foolishness.

Several key themes include that we are to choose our friends wisely and be careful of our thoughts, attitudes, and our words. We are to work diligently. And what we sow, we will eventually reap.

In contrast to the book of Proverbs, the word *"wisdom"* in the book of Ecclesiastes primarily speaks of human learning or worldly knowledge, which is considered vanity and, ultimately, meaningless (Eccl. 2:12-15). King Solomon wrote most of the Proverbs, along with the next two books, Ecclesiastes and Song of Solomon. (It's interesting to note that King David, Solomon's father, composed many of the Psalms.)

Proverbs, chapters 1–9, are a discourse regarding true wisdom for all aspects of life, and the outcome of pursuing foolish ways. Wisdom is depicted as a person calling to us. The entire book points to *Christ, who is our wisdom from God and our righteousness* (1 Cor. 1:30; Col. 2:3). Chapters 10–30 are a compilation of moral and spiritual sayings. Chapter 31, the last chapter, depicts a godly wife—one who is of noble character, virtuous, and therefore, beautiful.

Following are two key passages from Proverbs:

• *Trust in the Lord with all our heart; do not lean on your own under-standing, but in all your ways submit to Him, and He will direct your paths. Do not be wise in your own eyes; have reverence and fear for the LORD, and shun evil* (Prov. 3:5-7).

• *Blessed is the one who finds wisdom, and the one who gains understand-ing* (Prov. 3:13).

July 20: Read Proverbs 1–3

Verses for Today: *"Wisdom crieth without; she uttereth her voice in the streets. . . . Because I have called, and ye refused; I have stretched out my hand, and no man regarded; but ye have set at nought all my counsel, and would none of my reproof: I also will laugh at your calamity; I will mock when your fear cometh; when your fear cometh as desolation, and your destruction cometh as a whirlwind; when distress and anguish cometh upon you. Then shall they call upon me, but I will not answer; they shall seek me early, but they shall not find me: For that they hated knowledge, and did not choose the fear of the Lord"* (Prov. 1:20, 24-29).

Do not misunderstand. This Scripture is not saying that God Himself will laugh but, rather, His words of wisdom will haunt you. If you choose to ignore God and His truth, a day will come when His words of wisdom will mock your mis-ery. Our Lord made this clear: *"He that rejecteth me, and receiveth not my words, hath one that judgeth him: the word that I have spoken, the same shall judge him in the last day"* (John 12:48).

What could be worse for a person than to remember throughout eternity that he refused to read and heed the Word of God? How terrifying to think of the lost, who will cry out in hell, forever remembering that the Lord was *"not willing that any should perish, but that all should come to repentance"* (2 Pet. 3:9). The lost shall remember it was because *"they hated knowledge, and did not choose the fear of the Lord"* (Prov. 1:29).

However, the Lord is gracious and merciful. He invites everyone, *"Come. And let him that heareth say, Come. And let him that is athirst come. And whosoever will, let him take the water of life freely"* (Rev. 22:17). Now is the time. His invi-tation is open to receive His mercy, grace, new life, and blessings! We are invited to become a part of His family!

"For God so loved the world, that he gave his only begotten Son, that whosoever believeth in him should not perish, but have everlasting life" (John 3:16).

Thought for Today: Read God's Word with a willingness and desire to accept His wisdom and reproof.

Christ Revealed: As the wisdom of God (Prov. 1:20). Jesus *"is made unto us wisdom"* (1 Cor. 1:30).

July 21: Read Proverbs 4–7

Verses for Today: *"These six things doth the Lord hate: yea, seven are an abomination unto him: a proud look, a lying tongue, and hands that shed innocent blood, an heart that deviseth wicked imaginations, feet that be swift in running to mischief, a false witness that speaketh lies, and he that soweth discord among brethren"* (Prov. 6:16-19).

The first of these seven most hated sins is a proud look. It was pride that caused Eve to believe Satan and eat the forbidden fruit (Gen. 3:5-6). Pride precedes the six other sins that are abominable to God. Then we find three, perhaps four of these sins, are directly caused by an evil tongue.

Both pride and an undisciplined tongue are sins that everyone struggles with, even Christians. In fact, the tongue seriously hinders the effectiveness of many Christians. Instead of showing the love and the truth of Christ, careless talk can destroy a believer's witness.

The blessed Christian is a peacemaker, whose words are an overflow of the Spirit-filled life.

"A good man out of the good treasure of the heart bringeth forth good things: and an evil man out of the evil treasure bringeth forth evil things. . . . and by thy words thou shalt be condemned" (Matt. 12:35, 37).

Thought for Today: Our speech exposes our hidden thoughts and attitudes.

Christ Portrayed: By the teacher of wisdom (Prov. 4:7, 11). Jesus is the Teacher *"in whom are hid all the treasures of wisdom and knowledge"* (Col. 2:3).

July 22: Read Proverbs 8–11

Verse for Today: *"The liberal soul shall be made fat: and he that watereth shall be watered also himself"* (Prov. 11:25).

One of our greatest privileges as Christians is to cooperate with God. Some people say, "I believe God can do much," but they make no effort to participate with Him in fulfilling His will. Scripture warns us that *"faith without works is dead"* (James 2:26).

When we use our time and money to share God's truth with others, He sees to it that we gain much—*"The liberal soul shall be made fat."*

These great promises of God can only become a reality when we give in the right spirit. Whether we give money, kind words, or pray, everything depends upon our motive.

If we give expecting thanks, that is vanity.

If we give to be seen, that is vainglory.

If we give expecting to receive as much in return, that is exchange.

If we give in order to receive more, that is covetousness.

If we give with ulterior motives, it is bribery.

When we give from a heart of compassion, it is love.

Those who give with the right motive are always receiving and always have more to give.

"Freely ye have received, freely give" (Matt. 10:8).

Thought for Today: What motivates you to give?

Christ Revealed: As being with the Father *"when he prepared the heavens"* (Prov. 8:27-31). *"Thou, Lord, in the beginning hast laid the foundation of the earth; and the heavens are the works of thine hands"* (Heb. 1:10; Col. 1:15-20).

July 23: Read Proverbs 12–15

Verse for Today: *"Lying lips are abomination to the Lord: but they that deal truly are his delight"* (Prov. 12:22).

Jesus exposed the fact that all lies originate with Satan (John 8:44). It was Satan who first lied to Eve and brought sin and death into the world (Gen. 3). Satan is still lying today. He lies to each of us, and he loves to use people to spread lies, which bring hurt and destruction.

Lies can strip individuals of their good names and destroy their character. Even one conversation can do irreparable damage. Although *"a lying tongue is but for a moment"* (Prov. 12:19), its effects can last a lifetime and sometimes for generations.

The judgment day of Christ may reveal that the damage done by loose talk exceeds that done in any other way. Once words have escaped the lips, they cannot be recovered. They go on and on—from mouth to ear, and ear to mouth—spreading damage as they go. One can repent and be forgiven, but no one can retrieve what has been unleashed. The careless words of the tongue release a seemingly endless destructive force.

May the Lord show us where we twist and change things for our purposes. And may He forgive us, heal us, and change us, so that our words, attitudes, and actions bring healing, instead of harm.

"Not that which goeth into the mouth defileth a man; but that which cometh out of the mouth, this defileth a man" (Matt. 15:11). *"For he that will love life, and see good days, let him refrain his tongue from evil, and his lips that they speak no guile"* (1 Pet. 3:10).

Thought for Today: Let us always be alert, and separate ourselves from associations that would involve us in careless talk, lest we jeopardize our usefulness to the Lord.

Christ Revealed: As One who hates lying (Prov. 12:22). *"All liars, shall have their part in the lake which burneth with fire and brimstone"* (Rev. 21:8).

July 24: Read Proverbs 16–19

Verses for Today: *"The preparations of the heart in man, and the answer of the tongue, is from the Lord. . . . By mercy and truth iniquity is purged: and by the fear of the Lord men depart from evil"* (Prov. 16:1, 6).

When the earth was *"without form, and void; and darkness was upon the face of the deep"* (Gen. 1:2), the earth was not "prepared" to receive seed. Preparation was necessary before it was fit to produce *"herb yielding seed after his kind"* (Gen. 1:12).

Man's heart, in its fallen condition, needs preparation from the Lord, just as the earth did when the *"Spirit of God moved upon the face of the waters"* (Gen. 1:2). Our hearts need to be cleansed and transformed; then, *"the answer of the tongue, is from the Lord."* When *"by mercy and truth iniquity is purged,"* our words become sincere, kind, and thoughtful.

As we yield ourselves to the Lord and His Word, we are able to speak peace, healing, and comfort to others. We can soothe the afflicted, subdue anger, and heal divisions. We can offer hope and eternal life to the lost and dying. The tongue that the Holy Spirit controls becomes an instrument of good—imparting His grace and truth to others.

Life and death are in the power of the tongue (Prov. 18:21).

Thought for Today: Let us ask God to put a guard over our mouths so we do not speak words displeasing to Him and hurtful to others. Let us speak words of life, grace, and truth.

Christ Revealed: As the One who punishes the proud (Prov. 16:5). *"For whosoever exalteth himself shall be abased; and he that humbleth himself shall be exalted"* (Luke 14:11).

And in the Scripture, *"there is a friend that sticketh closer than a brother"* (Prov.

18:24). Jesus is our true Friend (John 15:14-15), who will never leave us or forsake us (Heb. 13:5).

July 25: Read Proverbs 20–22

Verse for Today: *"Train up a child in the way he should go: and when he is old, he will not depart from it"* (Prov. 22:6).

Obedience to God means that we *listen* to Him and *follow* Him. Obedience is the key to pleasing Him.

Ideally, this begins with parents, for it is their responsibility to teach their children to be obedient. Some parents do not correct their children when they do wrong. How deceptive is the philosophy of many parents who say they love their children too much to discipline them! Failing to discipline a child is a cruel injustice.

Scripture admonishes us: *"Correct thy son, and he shall give thee rest; yea, he shall give delight unto thy soul"* (Prov. 29:17). And, *"He that spareth his rod hateth his son"* (Prov. 13:24). To love is to correct. Parents' failure to discipline their children shows a lack of concern for their ultimate destiny.

Discipline should be firm, but still manifest the gracious love of Christ. Discipline (for both earthly children and God's children) far exceeds the pain, as expressed by the psalmist: *"Before I was afflicted I went astray: but now have I kept thy word"* (Ps. 119:67).

"Blessed is the man whom thou chastenest, O Lord, and teachest him out of thy law" (Ps. 94:12).

Thought for Today: With the same love our heavenly Father disciplines us, we must discipline our children.

Christ Revealed: As the One who can say, *I am clean and without sin* (Prov. 20:9). Jesus is without sin (Heb. 4:15).

July 26: Read Proverbs 23–26

Verses for Today: *"I went by the field of the slothful, and. . . . it was all grown over with thorns"* (Prov. 24:30-31).

A slothful person is a lazy person. This can be evident in a number of different ways. Some people are slack to provide for their family, or to fulfill tasks and responsibilities. Slothfulness destroys character and discourages others who have to assume responsibilities the slothful person shirks. Proverbs considers an indolent person to be a great waster (Prov. 18:9). Idlers are admonished to observe the ant and watch how it works, storing up food for the long winter months (Prov. 6:6).

Christians are not to be lax in working for the Lord. We are not to be neglectful of our gifts and bury them, or we risk losing what we thought we possessed (Luke 8:18). We are to discover and utilize our spiritual gifts, build up the church, and respond to opportunities to serve the Lord.

We are to *make the most of every opportunity* (Eph. 5:16). Let us use our time, talent, and resources, for we have no assurance of being able to serve our Lord tomorrow. Let us take advantage of every opportunity, so that one day we will hear the Lord say those wonderful words, *"Well done, thou good and faithful servant"* (Matt. 25:21).

"We commanded you, that if any would not work, neither should he eat" (2 Thess. 3:10).

Thought for Today: A slothful person forfeits the privilege of being the person God wants him to be.

Christ Revealed: As the One who will reward those who repay evil with good (Prov. 25:21-22). *If our enemy is hungry, we are to feed him; if he is thirsty, we should give him a drink* (Rom. 12:20). Jesus said, *"Love your enemies . . . and pray for them which . . . persecute you"* (Matt. 5:44; Luke 6:27, 35).

July 27: Read Proverbs 27–31

Verses for Today: *"There be . . . things which are too wonderful for me . . . which I know not: The way of an eagle in the air"* (Prov. 30:18-19).

If we could ask the eagle if it is afraid of the law of gravity, it would reply, "I have never heard of gravity and know nothing of its law. I fly because it is my nature to fly." The eagle possesses the power of flight and the ability to overcome the law of gravity. Yet gravity remains. Once life is gone from the eagle, we are reminded again of the law of gravity. While the eagle lives, it overcomes gravity by the very nature of its life.

The unconverted are sinners in rebellion against God because it is their nature to be so. Sinners are children of Adam in that they are like him—inwardly sinful. However, the saved are children of the "second Adam" in that they possess Christ's nature (1 Cor. 15:45-49). *"For as by one man's disobedience many were made sinners, so by the obedience of one shall many be made righteous"* (Rom. 5:19; 1 Cor. 15:22, 45).

What a miracle conversion is! The Lord is able to transform us, so that we become Christ-focused! We begin to read and meditate upon God's Word. We desire to know and do all that He says. We become conscious of sin and want to overcome it. We desire to bring others to a saving knowledge of His love. These are the natural, joyous impulses in the heart of a child of God.

"For the law of the Spirit of life in Christ Jesus hath made me free from the law of sin and death" (Rom. 8:2).

Thought for Today: Christ is not just the world's Savior in the sweet by and by, but here and now.

Christ Revealed: As the Son of God (Prov. 30:4). *"This is my beloved Son, in whom I am well pleased"* (Matt. 3:17).

 ## ECCLESIASTES

When reading and studying the Bible, it's important to understand the purpose and literary style of each book. This is especially true with the book of Ecclesiastes. Some passages of Ecclesiastes seem contrary to God's Word, but this is because the author is trying to point out the folly of human reasoning apart from God and the emptiness of life without Him.

Solomon, the author of the book, had great money and resources, which enabled him to pursue anything he wanted in life, whether power, pleasures, possessions, riches, or great work projects (Eccl. 1:16; 2:3, 8). But the more he searched, the harder he tried, and the more he pursued pleasure, the more he concluded that—without God—everything in life is meaningless and empty. When Solomon's worldly pursuits left him empty, he wrote this pessimistic confession and concluded that we need the Lord to know life's purpose and to have joy (Eccl. 2:24-26; 3:12-13; 5:18-20; 7:14; 8:15; 9:7).

Because of its truth and beautiful poetic style, Ecclesiastes is a book that is often quoted or referred to in secular writings.[14]

Ecclesiastes tells us:

God has put eternity in the hearts of mankind (Eccl. 3:11).

The end of the matter is this: "Fear God, and keep his commandments," knowing that the Lord will bring every deed into judgment, including every secret thing, whether good or evil (Eccl. 12:13-14).

---

14 *"Turn! Turn! Turn! (To Everything There Is a Season)"* is a song written by Pete Seeger. The lyrics, except for the final two lines, are the words of Ecclesiastes 3:1-8. The song became an international hit in 1965 when it was adapted by the American folk rock group the Byrds. Numerous other artists also recorded it. https://en.wikipedia.org/wiki/Turn!_Turn!_Turn!

July 28: Read Ecclesiastes 1–4

Verses for Today: *"And I gave my heart to seek and search out by wisdom concerning all things that are done under heaven. . . . behold, all is vanity and vexation of spirit"* (Eccl. 1:13-14).

King Solomon spoke with inexcusable discontent when he said, *"I gave my heart to seek and search out . . . all things."* He concluded that he knew all that was to be known, but he chose to ignore the Word of God. Solomon was given the remarkable privilege of having the Lord appear to him and say, *"If thou wilt walk before me . . . in integrity of heart . . . I will establish . . . thy kingdom upon Israel for ever"* (1 Kings 9:4-5). But the "wisest" man on earth tried to substitute his knowledge for God's wisdom (1 Kings 11:9-10).

The pleasure-seeking Solomon began life with high hopes, but later became cynical and pessimistic, saying, *"Therefore I hated life . . . for all is vanity and vexation of spirit"* (Eccl. 2:17). Solomon is a testimony to the fact that no one can be satisfied with mere worldly knowledge. Even with all his wisdom and resources, he was unable to escape the reality that God has instilled within each person a hunger that can only be satisfied by Christ—the Bread of Life.

"I am the Bread of Life: he that cometh to me shall never hunger; and he that believeth on me shall never thirst" (John 6:35).

Thought for Today: Worldly possessions and pleasures are no substitute for knowing the Lord, for in Him are found life, truth, purpose, blessings, and joy.

Christ Revealed: Through the words spoken in Ecclesiastes: *"Then I looked on all the works that my hands had wrought, and on the labour that I had laboured to do: and, behold, all was vanity and vexation of spirit, and there was no profit under the sun"* (Eccl. 2:11). We are reminded of Jesus's words: *"For what is a man profited, if he shall gain the whole world, and lose his own soul? or what shall a man give in exchange for his soul?"* (Matt. 16:26).

July 29: Read Ecclesiastes 5–8

Verses for Today: *"And so I saw the wicked buried, who had come and gone from the place of the holy, and they were forgotten in the city where they had so done: this is also vanity. Because sentence against an evil work is not executed speedily, therefore the heart of the sons of men is fully set in them to do evil"* (Eccl. 8:10-11).

It often seems as if God does not hear the groanings of the innocent, or see the hypocrisy of those who do evil and attend the sanctuary of God, *"the place of the holy."* It frequently appears that divine justice has been suspended as we observe the chaotic condition of world affairs. Evil continues, and God does not immediately interfere to bring judgment upon those involved. We are staggered by the delay of divine justice upon the wicked, and their prosperity, along with the ongoing oppression of the defenseless.

Not only during life, but often after they die, the wicked are praised and buried with recognition and popularity. Yet, with all their seeming advantages, external trappings, and appearances, they fail to deceive God. When the course of a sinner's life seems to run smoothly, people begin to imagine that God is indifferent to human conduct, and He can be ignored, with no ill consequences. However, the judgment that God's law attaches to sin is certain and comes with eternal consequences.

"For if the word spoken by angels was stedfast, and every transgression and disobedience received a just recompence of reward; How shall we escape, if we neglect so great salvation?" (Heb. 2:2-3).

Thought for Today: Do not envy the prosperity of evildoers—it is only temporary.

Christ Revealed: As the One who expects us to keep our vows (Eccl. 5:4). Christ said, *"But let your communication be, Yea, yea; Nay, nay: for whatsoever is more than these cometh of evil"* (Matt. 5:37).

July 30: Read Ecclesiastes 9–12

Verses for Today: *"Let us hear the conclusion of the whole matter: Fear God, and keep his commandments: for this is the whole duty of man. For God shall bring every work into judgment, with every secret thing, whether it be good, or whether it be evil"* (Eccl. 12:13-14).

King Solomon lived to please himself, and sought to satisfy his every whim and desire. He forfeited his opportunities to exalt the great name of Jehovah, which caused him to miserably confess that *life was meaningless* (Eccl. 2:17). Solomon's life ended in regret. He knew he must face the Lord, who *"shall bring every work into judgment."* Although Solomon knew that God was angry with him because he *"did evil in the sight of the Lord,"* we have no record that he repented or asked God to forgive him for leading the nation of Israel into idolatry (1 Kings 11:4-11).

King Solomon is an example of those who have great abilities and have achieved great things, but whose desire for pleasure robs them of the joy of fulfilling God's will for their lives. There are many things we can do that are good and worthwhile and are not, in themselves, sinful. Like Solomon, though, we can become so focused on these pursuits that our hearts are turned from the Lord and the things of His kingdom.

Let us not become so engrossed in good activities that we miss out on knowing God and His will for our lives. Let us not miss out on His best and lose eternal rewards because we squander opportunities that He gives us to do good.

"And that which fell among thorns are they, which, when they have heard, go forth, and are choked with cares and riches and pleasures of this life, and bring no fruit to perfection" (Luke 8:14).

Thought for Today: To please the Lord Jesus should be the primary desire of our hearts.

Christ Revealed: In the statement, *"For God shall bring every work into judgment"* (Eccl. 12:14). Scripture declares that *God has fixed a day when he will judge the world with justice and equity by the Man He has chosen, and He has given proof and assurance of this to everyone by raising him from the dead* (Acts 17:31). *"True and righteous are his judgments"* (Rev. 19:2).

SONG OF SOLOMON (ALSO CALLED SONG OF SONGS)

This book, Song of Solomon, is also called Song of Songs, and its great theme is love. Song of Songs presents a picture of love in marriage, and also the love between God and His people.

This book reveals God's intended beauty, joy, and sacredness of a married-love relationship, which He created and ordained (Gen. 2:20-25). The Lord desires to bless the faithful union between a man and a woman, a husband and wife, with much joy and pleasure.

Song of Songs additionally expresses the great love between God and His chosen people. The Jews recognized that the king represents God, and the bride represents the people of Israel. This is reflected in many Old Testament passages that proclaim, *"As the bridegroom rejoiceth over the bride, so shall thy God rejoice over thee"* (Isa. 62:5; see also Hos. 2:19-20).

Christians understand this book is symbolic of the great love between Jesus and His people. The king represents Jesus, and the bride represents His church. Throughout the New Testament, the church (and believers) are called the bride of Christ (Eph. 5:23-33; Rev. 19:7-9).

This is the story of the King of kings leaving His throne in glory, coming to earth, and demonstrating His love for undeserving sinners lost in darkness. We are His beloved! No matter how poverty-stricken a Christian may feel, the believer is rich and can say, *"I am my beloved's, and his desire is toward me"* (Song 7:10).

Believers are like the one who longed to be with her beloved: *"The voice of my beloved! behold, he cometh"* (Song 2:8). Our desire should be for the One we love, our king, *"chiefest among ten thousand"* (Song 5:10). Just as the shepherdess-maid yearned for her beloved, every believer is expectantly waiting for the return of our dear Savior.

July 31: Read Song of Solomon 1–8

Verse for Today: *"Rise up, my love, my fair one, and come away"* (Song 2:10).

King Solomon owned a vineyard in the area of Ephraim (Song 8:11). His tenant family had a daughter, whose brothers seemingly despised her. They made her work long, hard hours, taking care of the family vineyard, as well as their sheep. She worked in the hot sun all day and became very dark, causing her to say, *"Mine own vineyard have I not kept"* (Song 1:6).

One day, as she was caring for the flock, she looked up and saw a stranger-shepherd. Embarrassed, she said, *"Look not upon me, because I am black, because the sun hath looked upon me"* (Song 1:6). But to him, she was altogether lovely: *"Behold, thou art fair, my love"* (Song 1:15).

Little by little, the friendship grew into love, and finally this shepherd won the heart of the despised and forsaken daughter. When she asked him where he fed his flock, he was evasive (Song 1:7). Before her beloved went away, though, he told her that he would return and said, *"Rise up, my love, my fair one, and come away"* (Song 2:10). She trusted that someday he would come back for her.

After he went away, she thought of that day when she would be his bride. Sometimes she dreamed of him, but awakened only to find that he was not there (Song 3:1).

One day, a long procession of the king's *"valiant men,"* led by Solomon himself, stopped at the vineyard (Song 3:7). To the amazement of the Shulamite daughter, the royal guard announced that the king had arrived for her! As she approached and looked into his face, she was surprised to learn that he was the stranger-shepherd who had won her heart. She exclaimed, *"I am my beloved's, and his desire is toward me"* (Song 7:10).

From Genesis to Revelation, we have the story of the Shepherd-King, who came from heaven's highest glory down into this dark world that He might win a bride for Himself. Then He went away, but said, *"I will come again, and receive you unto myself"* (John 14:3). So, His bride is expectantly waiting for the royal announcement: *"Behold, the bridegroom cometh"* (Matt. 25:6).

Thought for Today: Are you ready for the Lord's return?

Christ Revealed: As *"the chiefest among ten thousand"* (Song 5:10). Jesus is the *"KING OF KINGS, AND LORD OF LORDS"* (Rev. 19:16).

August

 ## ISAIAH

Isaiah is the first book of five Major Prophets. These books are followed by the last twelve books of the Old Testament, which are considered the Minor Prophets. The designation major and minor has to do with the length and scope of the prophet's message (not any kind of ranking). They are all God-inspired.

The book of Isaiah is written by the prophet Isaiah. His name means *"salvation comes from the Lord"* (or *"the Lord saves"*), and this is the theme of the book.

Isaiah lived in Jerusalem, the capital of Judah, and ministered for fifty to sixty years through the reigns of four, and possibly five, kings. He served during an age of prosperity, and only a few people in the kingdom of Judah remained faithful to Jehovah. The sister kingdom of Israel (under Jeroboam II) also enjoyed prosperity, but it was even more corrupt than Judah was—socially, politically, and morally.

In the beginning of Isaiah's ministry, Assyria dominated the world. During the lifetime of Isaiah, Assyria attacked Samaria, capital of the Northern Kingdom, and defeated the ten-tribed kingdom of Israel, as Isaiah had prophesied (Isa. 9:8–10:4). The Israelites were taken as captives to Assyrian territories because the nation had forsaken *all the commandments of the Lord their God, and made themselves two golden images cast in the shape of two calves.* It was because of this, the prophet foretold they would be destroyed (2 Kings 17:16, 18).

Isaiah's burden was to keep the small kingdom of Judah from a similar destruction by turning the people back to the Lord.

The first chapter in Isaiah is a summary of his entire message. It exposes the sinfulness of Judah and Jerusalem (Isa. 1:3-8), expresses the Lord's loving appeals for them to repent (1:16-19), and points out the certainty of coming judgment (Isa. 1:24-25, 29-31). Isaiah appealed to them to walk in the light of God's Word (Isa. 2:5), but the nation of Judah was indifferent and continued in mere formality of worship, thus despising their covenant relationship with God. The phrase *"the Holy One of Israel"* (Isa. 1:4) is used thirty times in this book, but the people rejected this "Holy One."

Isaiah foretold that, because of its sins, the nation of Judah would be destroyed by the Babylonians. But he also gave messages of comfort and hope for those who would remain faithful.

Many of the prophecies of salvation reach beyond the kingdom of Judah to all mankind. The invitation to accept this salvation is extended to everyone in chapter 55.

Though Isaiah wrote the book about seven hundred years before Christ was born, he foretells of the coming Messiah with specific prophecies. Chapters 49-55 reveal many details concerning God's anointed, Suffering Servant. A few of the prophecies about Jesus include that He would be born to a virgin (Isa. 7:14); descend from David's line (Isa. 11:1-2); suffer for our transgressions (Isa. 53:4-12); and rule the world eternally with righteousness and truth (Isa. 9:6-7).

The New Testament quotes more prophecies from Isaiah than from any other Old Testament book. The following is one of its beautiful promises regarding Jesus: *"For unto us a child is born, unto us a son is given: and the government shall be upon his shoulder: and his name shall be called Wonderful, Counsellor, The mighty God, The everlasting Father, The Prince of Peace"* (Isa. 9:6).

At the very start of His ministry, Jesus read a prophecy from Isaiah and declared it was fulfilled in Him: *"The Spirit of the Lord is upon me, because he hath anointed me to preach the gospel to the poor; he hath sent me to heal the brokenhearted, to preach deliverance to the captives, and recovering of sight to the blind, to set at liberty them that are bruised, to preach the acceptable year of the Lord"* (Isa. 61:1-2; Luke 4:18-19).

Isaiah provides believers with powerful promises, such as this one: *"They that wait upon the Lord shall renew their strength; they shall mount up with wings as eagles; they shall run, and not be weary; and they shall walk, and not faint"* (Isa. 40:31).

August 1: Read Isaiah 1–4

Verse for Today: *"The ox knoweth his owner, and the ass his master's crib: but Israel doth not know, my people doth not consider"* (Isa. 1:3).

During Isaiah's ministry, the ten-tribed nation of Israel was defeated by Assyria. The people had *"provoked the Holy One of Israel unto anger"* by placing their faith in false gods (Isa. 1:4). Isaiah's burden was to call the remaining small nation of Judah back to the Lord: *"Make you clean, put away the evil of your doings from before mine eyes; cease to do evil"* (Isa. 1:16); *"O house of Jacob, come ye, and let us walk in the light of the Lord"* (Isa. 2:5).

Even though God had chosen the Israelites to be His people, delivered them from Egyptian slavery, guided them through the wilderness journey, and given them the Promised Land, they did not remain faithful to Him. However, the prophet Isaiah looked far beyond their sins and God's imminent judgment to a glorious future when God's people would be established in peace.

We, too, look forward to that day when the King of kings shall reign and *"the Lord alone shall be exalted"* (Isa. 2:17). What peace and fellowship we will experience!

"Having therefore these promises, dearly beloved, let us cleanse ourselves from all filthiness of the flesh and spirit, perfecting holiness in the fear of God" (2 Cor. 7:1).

Thought for Today: Continued disobedience blinds people and hardens their hearts to the will of the Lord.

Christ Revealed: As the One who will judge the nations (Isa. 2:2-4; Mic. 4:1-3). Our Lord is a righteous Judge, who will reward those who obey His Word and look for His return (Rom. 6:17-18; 2 Tim. 4:1-8). Also as *"The branch of the Lord"* (Isa. 4:2), which refers to Christ as the descendant of David.

August 2: Read Isaiah 5–9

Verses for Today: *"In the year that king Uzziah died I saw also the Lord sitting upon a throne. . . . Holy, holy, holy, is the Lord of hosts: the whole earth is full of his glory"* (Isa. 6:1, 3).

During the reign of King Uzziah (also called Azariah), the nation of Judah reached its greatest power and prosperity since the death of Solomon. At the height of King Uzziah's popularity, he ignored the priests, entered the temple to worship God, and burned incense (symbolic of prayer) on the altar—a ceremony that only priests were allowed to perform. God said that Uzziah's *"heart was lifted up to his destruction: for he transgressed against the Lord his God."* Therefore, the Lord struck him with leprosy (2 Chron. 26:16-21). Although he was a king, he did not have the right to ignore the fact that sinful man can only worship a holy God through an intercessor and in the right manner.

After Uzziah's death, Isaiah beheld another priest and King, *"high and lifted up"* (Isa. 6:1). He *"shall be called Wonderful, Counsellor, The mighty God, The everlasting Father, The Prince of Peace"* (Isa. 9:6).

This King is our Savior and intercessor. Jesus alone is able to reconcile sinful man to God (2 Cor. 5:18-21; Eph. 2:13; 1 Pet. 3:18). No matter how good and important we may think we are, we are unworthy to approach a holy God—except through our High Priest, the Lord Jesus Christ, who *"ever liveth to make intercession"* for us (Heb. 7:25).

"It is Christ that died, yea rather, that is risen again, who is even at the right hand of God, who also maketh intercession for us" (Rom. 8:34).

Thought for Today: Self-righteous people assume they are "good enough" without the Savior.

Christ Revealed: Following are a few of Isaiah's many prophecies about Christ with the New Testament references:

He will be born of a virgin; a Son will be born; and He shall be called Immanuel, which means "God with us" (Isa. 7:14; Matt. 1:18-25).

"For unto us a child is born . . . and his name shall be called Wonderful, Counsellor, The mighty God, The everlasting Father, The Prince of Peace" (Isa. 9:6; John 14:27; Rom. 5:1; Eph. 2:14; Col. 1:25-23; 3:15; 1 Tim. 3:16).

Jesus is an uncut stone, the Rock, the chief cornerstone (Isa. 8:14; Isa. 28:16; Matt. 21:42; Acts 4:11).

He will be a great light to people who walk in darkness and death (Isa. 9:2; Matt. 4:13-16).

The government (all authority) shall be upon His shoulder, and His reign shall be without end (Isa. 9:7: Luke 1:32-33).

August 3: Read Isaiah 10–14

Verses for Today: *"Behold, God is my salvation. . . . Therefore with joy shall ye draw water out of the wells of salvation. . . . Praise the Lord, call upon his name, declare his doings among the people"* (Isa. 12:2-4).

Salvation, which includes abundant blessings and fellowship with God, is the great theme of the Bible. All the wells of salvation and the abundant life are found in Christ. Every believer may receive the priceless, satisfying *water* found only in Jesus as revealed in God's Word (John 3:3-5; 7:37-38; 15:3). All who trust in the Lord— the Living Water of salvation—are able to experience satisfaction beyond compare.

Followers are then able to discover another added joy—that of leading others to Christ and His wellspring of eternal life. The Lord calls us to *go into all the world and proclaim this glorious, life-giving gospel to others* (Mark 16:15). *Whatever spiritual gift the Lord has given you, use it to serve others as good stewards of God's varied grace* (1 Pet. 4:10).

"And the Spirit and the bride say, Come. And let him that heareth say, Come. And let him that is athirst come. And whosoever will, let him take the water of life freely" (Rev. 22:17).

Thought for Today: Our Lord's life-giving water is overflowing and inexhaustible.

Christ Revealed: As the descendant of Jesse, King David's father, and in Christ's earthly rule of righteousness (Isa. 11:1; and Isa. 11; Matt. 25:31-46; Rev. 20–21).

August 4: Read Isaiah 15–21

Verses for Today: "*He calleth to me out of Seir [Edom], Watchman, what of the night? Watchman, what of the night? The watchman said, The morning cometh, and also the night*" (Isa. 21:11-12).

Edom's watchman delivered an unfavorable report. There was nothing to look forward to, except a long, dark *night* of Babylonian captivity because of sin. The Edomites, who were descendants of Abraham and Isaac, were treated as brethren by Israel at the time they came out of Egypt. But the Edomites returned evil for good (Num. 20:14-21), and consequently lost all hope of God's future blessings. Scripture declares the inevitable result: "*Whoso rewardeth evil for good, evil shall not depart from his house*" (Prov. 17:13).

As Christians, we are surrounded by a *night* of sin and unbelief. It is a moral and spiritual *night*. "*Men loved darkness rather than light*" (John 3:19). We may be discouraged about many things defiling our society—wickedness, violence, and cruelty, along with materialism exalted by leaders and the media. However, we are able to look beyond the current chaos and strife, as we read in God's Word of a new day with the coming of the King of kings. We know that this new *morning* will soon arrive.

Christians are to let the light of the Lord shine through them in this dark world, and be watchmen who proclaim the advent (arrival) of the new *morning* that is soon to come.

"*And, behold, I come quickly; and my reward is with me*" (Rev. 22:12).

Thought for Today: Be prepared and vigilant for the return of Jesus Christ.

Christ Revealed: As the One who will sit on the throne of David (Isa. 16:5; Luke 1:32-33), and as the Savior (Isa. 19:20).

August 5: Read Isaiah 22–26

Verse for Today: "*O Lord our God, other lords beside thee have had dominion over us: but by thee only will we make mention of thy name*" (Isa. 26:13).

Because of the sins of God's chosen people, they were defeated again and again. Not only did the people themselves sin, but the evil, idolatrous kings led them into sin, and nations that ruled over them attempted to force the faithful minority to accept their pagan worship.

God's people in every generation face enemies of His, who seek to force them to accept ungodly ways. Evil influences, motivated by Satan, are constantly trying to corrupt those who are loyal to Christ.

The true worshiper of God can say with Isaiah, *"Other lords beside thee have had dominion over us: but by thee only will we make mention of thy name."* Christ is to be Lord of our lives. It is never acceptable to God for us to compromise our loyalty to Him.

"Neither yield ye your members as instruments of unrighteousness unto sin: but yield yourselves unto God, as those that are alive from the dead, and your members as instruments of righteousness unto God. For sin shall not have dominion over you: For ye are not under the law, but under grace" (Rom. 6:13-14).

Thought for Today: Trials have helped many people come to know God's will for their lives.

Christ Revealed: As the One who holds *"the key of the house of David"* (Isa. 22:22). Jesus is holy and true and *"hath the key of David."* It is He *"that openeth, and no man shutteth; and shutteth, and no man openeth"* (Rev. 3:7).

August 6: Read Isaiah 27–31

Verse for Today: *"For the Egyptians shall help in vain, and to no purpose: therefore have I cried concerning this, Their strength is to sit still"* (Isa. 30:7).

The Israelites were under the special guardianship of God. He had miraculously delivered them many times. Yet, when the Assyrians threatened to invade their nation, they turned to Egypt—the very people who had once so cruelly oppressed their forefathers. To ensure Egyptian alliance, they even sent Egypt a large sum of money.

Through the prophet, God rebuked their lack of faith and declared to them to *"sit still."* They were not to fear, but were to rely on God and His help. Today, the believer in Christ is often tempted to sin in a very similar way.

To *"sit still"* means that we are to fully depend on God and not our own wisdom or plans. We must pray and wait for Him to lead us.

"It is good that a man should both hope and quietly wait for the salvation of the Lord" (Lam. 3:26).

Thought for Today: When it seems there is no hope, is it because we are relying on human strength and wisdom, instead of God's strength and wisdom? Have we asked Him what He would have us do and waited to hear His response in our spirit?

Christ Revealed: As *"a tried stone, a precious corner stone, a sure foundation"* (Isa. 28:16). Jesus Himself is the chief cornerstone (Matt. 21:42-46; Acts 4:10-12; Rom. 9:29-33; Eph. 2:8-22; 1 Pet. 2:6-8).

August 7: Read Isaiah 32–37

Verses for Today: *"Now it came to pass in the fourteenth year of king Hezekiah, that Sennacherib king of Assyria came up against all the defenced cities of Judah, and took them. . . . Thus saith the king [of Assyria], Let not Hezekiah deceive you. . . . Neither let Hezekiah make you trust in the Lord, saying, The Lord will surely deliver us: this city shall not be delivered into the hand of the king of Assyria"* (Isa. 36:1, 14-15).

Just eight years after he invaded and destroyed the Northern Kingdom, Sennacherib, king of Assyria, attacked Judah, the Southern Kingdom (2 Kings 18:13-17; 2 Chron. 32:1-8). When Hezekiah read the letter that the Assyrian ambassador brought from Sennacherib, he *"went up into the house of the Lord, and spread it before the Lord. And Hezekiah prayed"* (2 Kings 19:14-15). After Hezekiah prayed, he sought to lead his people to trust in God as their only hope of survival against Assyria. He trusted in God and was able to tell his nation, *"With us is the Lord our God"* (2 Chron. 32:8).

The prayer was short, but sincere, and the angel of the Lord destroyed 185,000 soldiers in Sennacherib's army. If we truly live in fellowship with God, we will look to Him in prayer. Not merely when we are in trouble, but we will seek to commune with Him in prayer about everything.

"In every thing by prayer and supplication with thanksgiving let your requests be made known unto God" (Phil. 4:6).

Thought for Today: You can depend on God's promises—they will not fail.

Christ Revealed: As the unmovable Rock (Isa. 32:2). Jesus provides security and rest to all who put their trust in Him. *"The Lord is my rock, and my fortress"* (Ps. 18:2). And He is the *King* who will bring judgment upon the earth (Isa. 33:17; 34:4-5). One day, Jesus will come as King, with power and great glory, and the lost will face His fiery judgment (Matt. 24:30; 2 Pet. 3:10).

August 8: Read Isaiah 38–42

Verses for Today: *"Comfort ye, comfort ye my people, saith your God. . . . The voice of him that crieth in the wilderness, Prepare ye the way of the Lord, make straight in the desert a highway for our God. . . . The grass withereth, the flower fadeth: but the word of our God shall stand for ever"* (Isa. 40:1, 3, 8).

Although there does not seem to be any comfort in the words, *"All flesh is grass, and . . . the grass withereth, the flower fadeth"* (Isa. 40:6-7), they illustrate a basic principle. Until we see our utter helplessness, we will never turn to Christ for salvation. If we think we are good enough, we will never seek the Savior. Pride and self-righteousness loom like a mountain and are in opposition to God and His salvation, mercy, and grace.

A sense of total desolation is needed to bring us to dependence upon Him. We can never know Him as Savior until we come to the end of our own resources. Then we are able to repent of our sins, and trust in His love.

"And they said, Believe on the Lord Jesus Christ, and thou shalt be saved, and thy house" (Acts 16:31).

Thought for Today: Don't be deceived by trusting in anything or anyone but the Lord Jesus Christ for your eternal salvation.

Christ Revealed: A few references from Isaiah's chapter readings: As the Creator (Isa. 40:28; John 1:1-3); as our Shepherd (Isa. 40:11; John 10:11); and as our Redeemer (Isa. 41:14; John 3:16; Gal. 3:13-14).

And in the words, *"The voice of him that crieth in the wilderness, Prepare ye the way of the Lord, make straight in the desert a highway for our God"* (Isa. 40:3). John the Baptist spoke these words when he introduced Jesus as the Messiah (John 1:23).

August 9: Read Isaiah 43–46

Verses for Today: *"Thus saith the Lord . . . I am the Lord . . . that saith to Jerusalem, Thou shalt be inhabited; and to the cities of Judah, Ye shall be built, and I will raise up the decayed places thereof . . . that saith of Cyrus, He is my shepherd, and shall perform all my pleasure"* (Isa. 44:24-28).

Only the Spirit of God could have given Isaiah such amazing details about a man named Cyrus 130 years before Cyrus was even born.

When Isaiah foretold, *"I [God] will raise up the decayed places thereof,"* there were no *"decayed places"* to be raised up. The temple was still standing; the walls were in perfect condition; and the nation was still enjoying freedom. Furthermore, it did not seem likely that a world conqueror would release the Jews and then urge them to return to Jerusalem to rebuild the temple for *"the God of heaven"* (Neh. 1:4). No prophecy seemed more unlikely to be fulfilled. Yet, all these things happened exactly as Isaiah foretold.

The prophet's message reveals our lack of knowledge to foresee the future, and our need to trust the Lord for whatever lies ahead. We dare not doubt God's loving concern, or His almighty power to keep His promises. We can have confidence in Him and His Word.

"Heaven and earth shall pass away, but my words shall not pass away" (Matt. 24:35).

Thought for Today: God is not limited; He will keep His Word—in His timing.

Christ Revealed: As the Redeemer (Isa. 43:1; 44:22-24). Through His death on the cross, Jesus has redeemed all who will trust Him as Savior (1 Cor. 6:20; 1 Pet. 1:18-19).

August 10: Read Isaiah 47–51

Verse for Today: *"Who is among you that feareth the Lord, that obeyeth the voice of his servant, that walketh in darkness, and hath no light? let him trust in the name of the Lord, and stay upon his God"* (Isa. 50:10).

We naturally expect judgment upon the ungodly and even the backslider. However, we think it is strange when seemingly bad things happen to the most sincere Christians—those *"that feareth the Lord, that obeyeth the voice of his servant."* But many servants of God have their times of being afflicted and overwhelmed with calamities (Isa. 49:14).

When we find that hope after hope is shattered, plan after plan is crushed, and a succession of trials takes place—each darker and more painful than before—we can agree with Jeremiah, *"I am the [one who] hath seen affliction by the rod of his wrath. He hath led me, and brought me into darkness, but not into light"* (Lam. 3:1-2).

Yet even as Jeremiah continued to face darkness, and answers to his prayers seemed to be withheld, he was confident that there was but one safe decision: *"It is good that a man should both hope and quietly wait for the salvation of the Lord"* (Lam. 3:1-2, 26).

We are to wait upon the Lord with earnest, fervent, persevering prayer. When the way is dark, keep praying just as the man did in our Lord's parable, who was hungry and didn't have a loaf of bread in his house. He went to his friend at midnight and kept knocking and pleading until his friend got up and gave him some bread (Luke 11:5-8). God tells us to come to Him and ask, seek, and knock. We are not to seek our own remedy, or remain passively idle. Keep asking, seeking, and trusting God to provide an answer.

All servants of God know what it is to feel that the light they expected has turned to darkness. Our Lord felt it when He uttered the cry, *"My God, my God, why hast thou forsaken me?"* (Matt. 27:46). But the cry of the forsaken

Savior was followed by the words, *"Father, into thy hands I commend my spirit"* (Luke 23:46).

For God, who commanded light to shine in darkness, has made His light shine in our hearts. We have Christ within us, in these jars of clay [our feeble bodies], showing that this all-surpassing power and glory are from God and not from us. We are hard-pressed from every direction, but we are not crushed. We are perplexed, but we are not in despair; we are persecuted, but we are not abandoned; we are struck down, but we are not destroyed. We carry around in our body the death of Jesus, so that the life of Christ may also be revealed in our body. His light and life shine forth through us (2 Cor. 4:6-11).

Thought for Today: Remember that God never forsakes His children. He is with us always (Matt. 28:20).

Christ Revealed: As the "light" of the nations (Isa. 49:6). Jesus has brought the light of God's salvation to all the nations of the earth (Luke 2:32; Acts 13:47).

August 11: Read Isaiah 52–57

Verse for Today: *"All we like sheep have gone astray; we have turned every one to his own way; and the Lord hath laid on him the iniquity of us all"* (Isa. 53:6).

Sheep wandering without a shepherd are easy prey to wild predators. Furthermore, wandering sheep are likely to perish for lack of pasture. They are unable to provide for themselves, or find their way back when they have strayed.

"All we . . . have gone astray." All of us are guilty; all need the Savior Shepherd. Surely Jesus Christ deserves the name of the Good Shepherd, who freely laid down His life to restore His sheep. Praise the Good Shepherd for His tender mercy.

Jesus Christ is the *"man of sorrows, and acquainted with grief,"* and *"the Lord hath laid on him the iniquity of us all."* The full meaning of His crucifixion is indescribable. No one can fully express the suffering and sorrows that Jesus Christ endured for our sins (Isa. 53:3-6).

God's judgment on sin was expressed in the garden of Eden: *"In the day that thou eatest thereof thou shalt surely die"* (Gen. 2:17). Christ felt that punishment as He *yielded His life unto the Father* (Matt. 27:50).

Think of the astounding mass of sin that must have been laid on Christ (John 1:29; 1 John 2:2)—all the sins against God—open sins, hidden sins of the heart, sins against the Father, sins against the Son, sins against the Holy Spirit, and sins against all the revealed Word of God. The sins of all mankind were laid upon Him!

Oh, why are so few affected by God's redeeming love?

"That in the ages to come he might shew the exceeding riches of his grace in his kindness toward us through Christ Jesus" (Eph. 2:7).

Thought for Today: How slow we are to express gratefulness for the amazing love of our Lord.

Christ Revealed: Isaiah contains many prophetic revelations. These are just a few from chapter 53, which has approximately eighteen. Jesus was the One rejected by His own people (Isa. 53:3; Luke 23:18; John 1:11). He remained silent when He was falsely accused (Isa. 53:7; Mark 15:4-5). He was buried with the rich (Isa. 53:9; Matt. 27:57-60), and was crucified with sinners (Isa. 53:12; Mark 15:27-28). Jesus's sacrifice brought us forgiveness for our sins, peace with God, and healing [including spiritual, physical, and emotional] (Isa 53:5; Rom. 4:25; Col. 1:19-20; 1 Pet. 2:24).

August 12: Read Isaiah 58–63

Verse for Today: *"But they rebelled, and vexed his holy Spirit: therefore he was turned to be their enemy, and he fought against them"* (Isa. 63:10).

Isaiah urged the people to remember the nation's past history and failure. When the Israelites grumbled on the way to the Promised Land, they rebelled against God and *"vexed his holy Spirit."* They complained ten times against God and Moses *and did not hearken to His voice* (Num. 14:22). Consequently, their unbelief resulted in thirty-eight wasted years of wandering in the wilderness.

Even with their miraculous history with God, the kingdom of Judah failed to relate His miraculous provisions in the past to their present needs. The great kingdom, so richly blessed of God, was as guilty of unbelief as were the children of Israel in the desert since *"they rebelled, and vexed his holy Spirit."*

Interruption in personal plans causes many to complain because they believe they deserve better. Far too often, we fail to realize the seriousness of discontent. Not only are we actually questioning the wisdom and ability of our loving heavenly Father to guide us, but Satan can easily gain the victory. Grumbling about our circumstances does *vex God's Spirit,* and we forfeit the victories and blessings that He wants to give to us. The Lord is more than able to bring good from every circumstance (Rom. 8:28). Let us draw close to Him and seek His peace, good purposes, and blessings.

"And grieve not the holy Spirit of God" (Eph. 4:30).

Thought for Today: In all things, seek God's assistance and wisdom, and praise Him.

Christ Revealed: As the One anointed *"to preach good tidings"* (Isa. 61:1-2). Jesus preached this passage to the rulers of the synagogue (Luke 4:16-22), stopping midsentence, to reveal that He fulfilled the first part, but the second part (the day of judgment) was yet to be fulfilled. In addition, Christ is the One who heals the brokenhearted (Isa. 61:1; Ps. 147:3), and frees us by His truth (John 8:32-36).

August 13: Read Isaiah 64–66

Verses for Today: *"Oh that thou wouldest rend the heavens, that thou wouldest come down, that the mountains might flow down at thy presence. . . . For since the beginning of the world men have not heard, nor perceived by the ear, neither hath the eye seen, O God, beside thee, what he hath prepared for him that waiteth for him"* (Isa. 64:1, 4).

It may seem that our relationship with the Lord is hindered by what appear to be huge, insurmountable problems. Some of these "mountains" are the result of active opposition from Satan and can be overcome *because greater is he that is in us, than he that is in the world* (1 John 4:4).

Then, there are mountains of sin and self-interest that sever connection with divine power. These must be broken down to enjoy God's presence.

Other mountains of hindrance actually arise from our lack of faithfulness in praying. We cannot be effective in our Christian life unless we are effective in prayer. When we *"do those things that are pleasing in his sight"* (1 John 3:22), we can pray and trust God to remove the mountain and difficulty, or give us the grace and strength we need for them.

"Eye hath not seen, nor ear heard, neither have entered into the heart of man, the things which God hath prepared for them that love him" (1 Cor. 2:9).

Thought for Today: Self-seeking and sin break our communion with the Lord and prevent us from receiving His wisdom, peace, and joy.

Christ Revealed: As the Creator of new heavens and a new earth (Isa. 65:17; 66:22; 2 Pet. 3:13), and the One whose glory will be declared among the nations (Isa. 66:18-19; Rev. 5:12-13).

 # JEREMIAH

There is an interval of about seventy years between the books of Isaiah and Jeremiah. During Isaiah's time, Assyria destroyed the ten-tribed nation of Israel. But, as the years passed, Assyria's empire weakened considerably, and Babylon gradually gained supremacy.

Jeremiah, who was born about seventy-five years after the Assyrians had defeated the Northern Kingdom of Israel, prophesied during the last part of the kingdom of Judah's history and through the reigns of five kings. During this time, the Babylonians defeated two great empires—Assyria and Egypt.

The prophet Jeremiah pleaded with the nation of Judah to repent of its sins and serve the Lord, but the people refused. Eventually, Nebuchadnezzar—the Babylonian king—attacked Jerusalem, as foretold by the prophet. Following a siege of about eighteen months, the city was defeated; the walls and temple were destroyed; and many people were taken captive to Babylon. Nebuchadnezzar left Jeremiah and the poor people in Jerusalem and appointed Gedaliah as the Jewish puppet governor of Jerusalem. Two months later, however, Gedaliah was assassinated. Fearing Nebuchadnezzar's retaliation, the few people who remained in Judah fled to Egypt, taking Jeremiah as a hostage. According to the last record we have of the aged prophet Jeremiah, he was preaching against the Jewish women worshiping *"the queen of heaven"* (Jer. 44:15-30).

Although Jeremiah lived to witness his prophecy against Jerusalem come true, he additionally foretold that Babylon would sink to rise no more (Jer. 51:64), the people of Judah would return, and the nation would be restored.

Jeremiah's message of judgment was unwelcome. He never came to like his task, his message, or having to stand alone against the people to deliver it, but he stayed faithful to the Lord.

August 14: Read Jeremiah 1–3

Verses for Today: *"My people have changed their glory for that which doth not profit. Be astonished, O ye heavens, at this. . . . For my people have committed two evils; they have forsaken me the fountain of living waters, and hewed them out cisterns, broken cisterns, that can hold no water"* (Jer. 2:11-13).

In the desert climate of Palestine, water was the key necessity for life. Men fought and died over wells. No man in his right mind would exchange an artesian well—with a great supply of fresh water—for some man-made, broken cistern, and hope for water to sustain his life. We would consider such an individual foolish indeed.

However, the Israelites were even more foolish. They were the only people in the world who had received a revelation of the one true God and His will—the only source of the water of life. Yet, they deserted Him for man-made, lifeless gods—broken cisterns that cannot support life. What foolishness and ingratitude!

This action is symbolic of those who reject the Bible as the Fountain of Living Water. In place of the Scriptures, many turn to substitutes written by men. Compared with the Word of God, they are little more than *"cisterns . . .*

that can hold no water." While secular writings from others can sometimes be helpful, none are to replace the Bible and be used as a substitute for knowing the Lord.

"Whosoever drinketh of the water that I shall give him shall never thirst; but the water that I shall give him shall be in him a well of water springing up into everlasting life" (John 4:14).

Thought for Today: God's Word and Spirit reveal the difference between truth and error.

Christ Revealed: As the Fountain of Living Waters (Jer. 2:13). Jesus is the only Fountain that can satisfy the thirsty soul (John 4:1-26).

August 15: Read Jeremiah 4–6

Verses for Today: *"The prophets prophesy falsely, and the priests bear rule by their means; and my people love to have it so. . . . Behold, the word of the Lord is unto them a reproach; they have no delight in it"* (Jer. 5:31; 6:10).

It is deplorable and unthinkable that the kingdom of Judah had *"no delight"* in the *"word of the Lord."*

When those who call themselves Christians live day after day without reading the Word of God—year after year without ever reading the Bible through—it is quite apparent that they also *"have no delight in it."*

Turning away from God's message leads to apostasy (total abandonment of faith and spiritual truth). But reading and upholding every word of God as pure, true, and vital for our well-being are marks of sonship. A true Christian delights in His Word: *"More to be desired are they than gold"* (Ps. 19:10).

The trend in our secular society is a moving away from the *"word of the Lord."* This is a sign that we are drawing nearer to the *"day of the Lord"* and end times (Joel 2:1; Acts 2:20). Scripture teaches us that the day of the Lord will come after there is a falling away (literally, "the apostasy"), and the man of sin is revealed (2 Thess. 2:1-3). Many who call themselves Christians will forsake the Lord as Demas did (2 Tim. 4:10). Jude warns us with these words: *"For there are certain men crept in unawares, who were before of old ordained to this condemnation, ungodly men, turning the grace of our God into lasciviousness, and denying the only Lord God, and our Lord Jesus Christ"* (Jude 1:4).

We must know God's truth and pray for deliverance and protection, so that we will not follow a wrong path and be swept away with the ungodly.

"Blessed is the man that walketh not in the counsel of the ungodly, nor standeth in the way of sinners, nor sitteth in the seat of the scornful. But his delight is in the law

of the Lord; and in his law doth he meditate day and night" (Ps. 1:1-2).

Thought for Today: As we spend more time reading God's Word, His thoughts become our thoughts, and His ways become our ways.

Christ Revealed: God would have pardoned Jerusalem for one righteous person (Jer. 5:1); He is very willing to forgive those who come to Him with repentant hearts (1 John 1:9).

August 16: Read Jeremiah 7–10

Verse for Today: *"Is this house, which is called by my name, become a den of robbers in your eyes? Behold, even I have seen it, saith the Lord"* (Jer. 7:11).

Jehoiakim, Josiah's son, was an evil ruler (2 Kings 23:36-37). He despised Jeremiah's prophecies against his cruel oppression of the people—especially the prophecies against perverted temple worship. Jeremiah had accused the king of making the temple of God *"a den of robbers."*

Our Lord used this Scripture hundreds of years later, when He entered the courts of the temple with a whip made of small cords and drove out the money changers, saying, *"My house shall be called the house of prayer; but ye have made it a den of thieves"* (Matt. 21:13; see also Isa. 56:7).

God's people had a mixture of beliefs and actions that were offensive to Him. Although they offered sacrifices to the Lord, they treated His house as a marketplace for their own benefit. In addition, they did not give honor to Him for their harvest (Jer. 5:23-25); they were greedy for unjust gain (Jer. 8:10); they worshiped other gods; and they did not administer care and justice to the orphans, widows, downtrodden, and needy. Through Jeremiah, God had made it clear that no amount of sacrifice could replace obedience, stating, *Obey My Word* (Jer. 7:23).

Many individuals overlook the importance of cleansing themselves *from all that pollutes the flesh and spirit* (2 Cor. 7:1). They fail to see that there is no substitute for desiring to please the Lord (2 Cor. 7:11).

Pursue righteousness, faith, love, and peace, together with those whose prayers go up to the Lord from a clean heart (2 Tim. 2:22).

Thought for Today: Religious activity is never a substitute for godly living.

Christ Revealed: As the One who demanded a cleansed temple and undefiled worshipers (Jer. 7:1-11). Jesus spoke these words when He cleansed the temple with a whip and drove out the money changers (Matt. 21:13; Mark 11:17).

August 17: Read Jeremiah 11–14

Verse for Today: *"This evil people, which refuse to hear my words, which walk in the imagination of their heart, and walk after other gods, to serve them, and to worship them, shall even be as this girdle, which is good for nothing"* (Jer. 13:10).

It seems strange indeed that God would lead His chosen prophet to travel nearly 250 miles to the Euphrates River, bury a girdle there until it was rotten, and wear the worthless garment back to Jerusalem to tell Judah about its national condition and its spiritual value before the Lord. But because God passionately loved His people, He continued to pursue them, go to great lengths to capture their attention, and save them.

These people had access to the one true God above all other nations. To them were committed the Scriptures, the only Guide for true worship. Yet they did not listen, or follow the Lord. It had to be written of them, *"good for nothing."*

Jeremiah's journey may have seemed a waste of time and effort, but his unquestioned obedience was evidence of his willingness to fulfill God's will. God's commandments are often, according to human reasoning, not essential. His instructions frequently involve much effort and inconvenience that we would prefer to avoid.

Many would have asked: "Why go to the Euphrates?" "Why wear a rotten girdle?" "What will people think?" "Why me, Lord?" But those who desire to obey God willingly surrender all of self to please Him. They are not burdened with the responsibility of life's decisions because they understand that their lives belong to the Lord.

"And he that sent me is with me: the Father hath not left me alone; for I do always those things that please him" (John 8:29).

Thought for Today: Are you willingly serving the Lord?

Christ Revealed: As the Hope and Savior of His people (Jer. 14:8-9). Neither Jews, nor gentiles, will have peace until they accept Christ, the King of peace, as Savior (Rom. 1:16).

August 18: Read Jeremiah 15–18

Verses for Today: *"Then I went down to the potter's house. . . . And the vessel that he made of clay was marred in the hand of the potter: so he made it again another vessel, as seemed good to the potter to make it. . . . O house of Israel, cannot I do with you as this potter?"* (Jer. 18:3-4, 6).

The potter was not satisfied with the first vessel he made—perhaps because the clay was not the right texture to make the shape he had in mind—so he reshaped it.

This is the story of God's chosen people. God is the Potter; Israel is the clay. History is the wheel, slowly turning as God, the Master Potter, changes and shapes His chosen vessel. As a nation, Israel resisted God's will and was marred miserably by sin. Therefore, the clay vessel (this time, the remnant of Judah) was broken by Babylon, and the people were taken into captivity. After the people had spent seventy years in exile, God made yet another vessel of the clay as He brought the Jews back to Jerusalem to rebuild the temple.

God wants our will to be as submissive to His will as clay is in the potter's hands—*"as seemed good to the potter to make it."* We are like earthen vessels, and the Lord—the Master Potter—has a plan for each of our lives as a vessel to honor Him.

"For it is God which worketh in you both to will and to do of his good pleasure" (Phil. 2:13).

Thought for Today: It is for God's glory that we were created.

Christ Revealed: In Jeremiah's words, *"Thy word [O Lord] was unto me the joy and rejoicing of mine heart"* (Jer. 15:16). Jesus said, *"The words that I speak unto you, they are spirit, and they are life"* (John 6:63).

As the One who searches the heart of man and rewards him accordingly (Jer. 17:10; Ps. 139:23-24; Rev. 2:23).

August 19: **Read Jeremiah 19–22**

Verse for Today: *"Inquire, I pray thee, of the Lord for us; for Nebuchadnezzar king of Babylon maketh war against us"* (Jer. 21:2).

King Zedekiah was afraid the Babylonians would soon destroy the small nation of Judah. As a result, he sent Zephaniah and Pashur to ask Jeremiah to pray, hoping perhaps the Lord would bless them *"according to all his wondrous works"* (Jer. 21:2). (This is not the same Pashur who had beaten the prophet Jeremiah and put him in stocks, which is mentioned in Jeremiah 20:1-2; 21:1.)

The king's inquiry sounded spiritual, but there was no indication that he desired to worship God as the true King of Israel. Jeremiah directed the messengers to tell Zedekiah that the Lord would not fight for him, but would fight against him. Furthermore, he said that Nebuchadnezzar would defeat King Zedekiah and his people and take them as slaves.

Many would-be believers today are making the same mistake as King Zedekiah did. They have gone to the right source for information, and have called upon the right God, but they are not truly seeking the Lord's will. They merely want God to agree with them and give them words of comfort.

"Your faith should not stand in the wisdom of men, but in the power of God" (1 Cor. 2:5).

Thought for Today: When praying for God to bless your plans, be willing to pray, *Not my will, but Yours, be done* (Matt. 26:39).

Christ Revealed: As the One who speaks judgment upon evildoers and all those who do not obey His Word (Jer. 19:15). Jesus declared, *"Every one that heareth these sayings of mine, and doeth them not, shall be likened unto a foolish man, which built his house upon the sand: And the rain descended, and the floods came, and the winds blew, and beat upon that house; and it fell: and great was the fall of it"* (Matt. 7:26-27).

August 20: Read Jeremiah 23–25

Verses for Today: *"Behold, the days come, saith the Lord, that I will raise unto David a righteous Branch, and a King shall reign and prosper, and shall execute judgment and justice in the earth. . . . and this is his name whereby he shall be called, THE LORD OUR RIGHTEOUSNESS"* (Jer. 23:5-6).

The Israelites, God's chosen people, had once been a powerful nation among the kingdoms of the earth. But due to their disregard for God's commandments, the prophet Jeremiah announced the terrifying news that the nation of Judah would soon face God's judgment. However, he gave them a ray of hope beyond the judgment when he foretold of the coming Messiah—a *"righteous Branch,"* the King of righteousness, the Savior—who would deliver God's people from bondage.

In man, there is no righteousness, for *"all have sinned"* (Rom. 3:23). However, Christ is *"The Lord Our Righteousness."* When we accept Him as our Savior and Lord, His life—His righteousness—flows through us. Therefore, we stand justified before God—not upon our own merits, but on the righteousness of Christ. As God looks upon us, He sees Jesus's righteousness in us, and we become acceptable to Him.

Many Christians are weak and worldly because they do not understand this fact. They believe that it took Christ, the Righteous One, to save them, but they do not recognize that His indwelling Holy Spirit can empower them to live holy, righteous lives through the Word of God.

"I count all things but loss . . . that I may win Christ, and be found in him, not

having mine own righteousness, which is of the law, but that which is through the faith of Christ, the righteousness which is of God by faith" (Phil. 3:8-9).

Thought for Today: Our righteousness is Christ in us— *"The Lord Our Righteousness."*

Christ Revealed: As *"THE LORD OUR RIGHTEOUSNESS"* (Jer. 23:6; 1 Cor. 1:30; 2 Cor. 5:21).

August 21: Read Jeremiah 26–28

Verse for Today: *"Then spake the priests and the prophets unto the princes and to all the people, saying, This man is worthy to die; for he hath prophesied against this city, as ye have heard with your ears"* (Jer. 26:11).

For more than nine years, all Jeremiah's fervent appeals for King Zedekiah to heed God's Word had been in vain. Urijah also *"prophesied against this city . . . according to all the words of Jeremiah"* (Jer. 26:20). These prophecies so infuriated the king, he sought the death of both men.

The prophet Urijah escaped into Egypt, but was captured, brought before King Jehoiakim, and executed. However, Jeremiah did not flee; he persisted in pleading with the king: *"Why will ye die, thou and thy people, by the sword, by the famine, and by the pestilence, as the Lord hath spoken against the nation?"* (Jer. 27:13).

Jeremiah would rather have died than be silent about the Lord's judgment upon His nation. What became of Jeremiah was wholly unimportant, compared with his hope that the people of Judah would repent and turn to the Lord.

This same Spirit led the apostle Paul to say, *"I am ready not to be bound only, but also to die at Jerusalem. . . . I could wish that myself were accursed from Christ for my brethren"* (Acts 21:13; Rom. 9:3). This same self-sacrificing Spirit enables Christians to willingly reject self-interests that interfere with what we know would please Him.

As followers of God's Word, we are to gently instruct those who oppose His truth in the hope that God will bring them to repentance and lead them to saving knowledge of the truth (2 Tim. 2:25).

Thought for Today: Your boldness to speak out for Jesus helps others escape secular deceptions, false religions, sin, and death.

Christ Portrayed: By Jeremiah, whom the priests and false prophets falsely accused (Jer. 26:8-9). Our Lord was threatened and unjustly accused on many occasions because His teachings did not agree with the teachings of the religious rulers of His day (John 8:48, 59).

August 22: Read Jeremiah 29–31

Verse for Today: *"For I am with thee, saith the Lord, to save thee: though I make a full end of all nations whither I have scattered thee, yet will I not make a full end of thee: but I will correct thee in measure, and will not leave thee altogether unpunished"* (Jer. 30:11).

The prophets repeatedly foretold that the Jews would be scattered throughout the world, yet would not be totally destroyed by their conquerors. They would remain a distinct people. On the other hand, God declared that He would destroy their conquerors.

This unusual prophetic truth has been fulfilled. The mighty world kingdoms of Babylon and Assyria have vanished. Nothing remains except for ruins—evidence of their once-magnificent grandeur.

Although the small Jewish nation was also destroyed and her people taken as slaves and scattered throughout the world, they have continued to exist as a distinct people for centuries. In our generation, the Jews have fulfilled a portion of still another prophecy by returning to Jerusalem and once again becoming a nation (Isa. 11:11-16; Jer. 16:14-15; Ezek. 36:24; 37:11-12, 14, 21).[15]

We can rest assured, dear Christian friends, that our faith is founded upon the powerful, eternal, and unchanging Word of God. His promises will prevail.

The word of prophecy has been confirmed. We will do well to pay attention to it because it is like a lamp, shining in a gloomy place until the day dawns, and the light of the morning star shines in our hearts (2 Pet. 1:19).

Thought for Today: Every sincere reader of the Bible can see clearly that it is the inspired Word of God.

Christ Revealed: As the One who forgives sin (Jer. 31:34). *"But that ye may know that the Son of man hath power on earth to forgive sins, (then saith he to the sick of the palsy,) Arise, take up thy bed, and go unto thine house"* (Matt. 9:6).

---

15 Through the years and centuries, Israel has often been under attack and involved in wars and skirmishes. Unrest plagues the Middle East. Still, the fulfillment of this prophecy began May 14, 1948, when Israel declared itself a sovereign state. The United States recognized Israel as such that same day. Nearly a year later, the United Nations approved its application as the fifty-ninth member. On June 28, 1968, Israel declared Jerusalem unified and announced free access to holy sites of all religions. Jerusalem and Israel have continued to gain strength and be recognized as a nation by other countries.

August 23: Read Jeremiah 32–33

Verses for Today: *"Ah Lord God! behold. . . . Thou shewest lovingkindness unto thousands, and recompensest the iniquity . . . to give every one according to his ways, and according to the fruit of his doings"* (Jer. 32:17-19).

Jeremiah stated truth similar to David's when he wrote, *"How excellent is thy loving-kindness, O God! therefore the children of men put their trust under the shadow of thy wings"* (Ps. 36:7). Even in the midst of suffering and final defeat, the prophet Jeremiah proclaimed that the Lord, in loving-kindness, was waiting to bless the nation of Judah if the people would turn from their sins, but they would not heed his warning.

Whether we are accepted or rejected, we should faithfully remind others how important it is to read all of God's Word and how He bestows His loving and steadfast goodness upon all who put their trust in Him.

As Christians yield themselves to the influence and guidance of the Holy Spirit, there will be no room in our hearts for anger, jealousy, bitterness, or hatred. Every adverse circumstance that confronts us becomes an opportunity to express His mercy and love—a privilege to bless and pray for those who offend us. In the words of the psalmist, we can say, *"It is a good thing . . . to shew forth thy lovingkindness"* (Ps. 92:1-2).

"A new commandment I give unto you, That ye love one another; as I have loved you" (John 13:34).

Thought for Today: All who turn away from God's Word will one day be judged by the very Word they have rejected.

Christ Revealed: As the Branch of David (Jer. 23:5; 33:15). Christ is the Messiah, who is *"made of the seed of David according to the flesh"* (Rom. 1:3).

August 24: Read Jeremiah 34–36

Verses for Today: *"So the king sent Jehudi to fetch the roll. . . . And it came to pass, that when Jehudi had read three or four leaves, he cut it with the penknife, and cast it into the fire"* (Jer. 36:21, 23).

Through the prophet Jeremiah, God foretold that the king of Babylon would again come and destroy the kingdom of Judah, leaving neither man nor beast. When Jehudi read the prophecy to King Jehoiakim, the king should have humbly turned to God. Instead, Jehoiakim destroyed the scroll by cutting it with a penknife and casting it into the fire. Unknowingly, he sealed his own death by willfully rejecting and trying to destroy God's Word (Jer. 36:29-30).

Thousands since Jehoiakim have attempted to demolish the Word of God by burning Bibles and killing Christians. Their names have been forgotten, but God's Word continues to remain the most sought-after book year after year.

"Heaven and earth shall pass away: but my words shall not pass away" (Luke 21:33).

Thought for Today: Those who obtain counsel from the Lord through His Word will not be deceived.

Christ Revealed: As the One who desires liberty for those in bondage (Jer. 34:13-16; Isa. 61:1). Jesus declared, *"The Spirit of the Lord is upon me . . . to set at liberty"* (Luke 4:18; 2 Cor. 3:17).

August 25: Read Jeremiah 37–40

Verse for Today: *"Then Zedekiah the king sent, and took him out: and the king asked him secretly in his house, and said, Is there any word from the Lord? And Jeremiah said, There is: for, said he, thou shalt be delivered into the hand of the king of Babylon"* (Jer. 37:17).

During the last year of Zedekiah's reign, the world-conquering armies of Nebuchadnezzar had surrounded Jerusalem. Fearful of the outcome, Zedekiah secretly removed Jeremiah from prison and asked, *"Is there any word from the Lord?"* He had appealed to the prophet to intercede in prayer once before when the king of Babylon's army first approached, but Zedekiah did not trust the Lord or repent of his sins (Jer. 21). Jeremiah would not pray; instead, he said, *"Thus saith the Lord; Deceive not yourselves"* (Jer. 37:9).

Since Zedekiah was not truly seeking the Lord, his downfall was inevitable. Pitiful as it may seem, Israel's last king, Zedekiah, was captured in Jericho (Jer. 39:5)—the same area where Joshua had won the first victory in entering the Promised Land.

This blinded and imprisoned king (Jer. 39:7) is an example of what happens spiritually to anyone who fails to follow the will of God.

"In whom the god of this world hath blinded the minds of them which believe not" (2 Cor. 4:4).

Thought for Today: A person who rejects the Lord and His Word is working toward his own destruction.

Christ Portrayed: By Jeremiah, who stood as a faithful witness to God's revealed will even when religious leaders hated him and tried to put him to death (Jer. 38:2-9; Matt. 26:59).

August 26: Read Jeremiah 41–44

Verses for Today: *"And all the captains of the forces, took . . . Jeremiah the prophet. . . . So they came into the land of Egypt"* (Jer. 43:5-7).

After Nebuchadnezzar defeated Zedekiah, he made Gedaliah governor over the few who remained in Judah, *"the poor of the land"* (Jer. 40:7). About two months later, because of his loyalty to Babylon, Ishmael assassinated Gedaliah. The Jewish people expected Nebuchadnezzar to retaliate, so they fled to Egypt, forcing the prophet Jeremiah to go with them.

Nothing could have been more distressing to Jeremiah than finally being forced into Egypt as a prisoner. There he watched the people sink further into sin and idolatry. Rejecting the true God, they worshiped the Egyptian false goddess, the queen of heaven (Jer. 44:15-19).

Some would assume that surely the great prophet Jeremiah deserved better treatment for his loyalty to God than to be forced to Egypt. But Jeremiah was not looking for an easy life; he was living to please the Lord.

Like Jeremiah, we will not experience true joy and purpose until we learn to sacrifice our interests to do the Lord's will.

"But what things were gain to me, those I counted loss for Christ" (Phil. 3:7).

Thought for Today: The person who rejects God's Word is walking in darkness that ends in defeat.

Christ Revealed: By the words, *"I sent unto you all my servants the prophets"* (Jer. 44:4). Jesus said, *"For I came down from heaven, not to do mine own will, but the will of him that sent me"* (John 6:38).

August 27: Read Jeremiah 45–48

Verses for Today: *"Thus saith the Lord, the God of Israel, unto thee, O Baruch; Thou didst say, Woe is me now! for the Lord hath added grief to my sorrow; I fainted in my sighing, and I find no rest. . . . And seekest thou great things for thyself? seek them not"* (Jer. 45:2-3, 5).

The greatest moment in Baruch's life came when he wrote *"all the words of the Lord"* (Jer. 36:4) at Jeremiah's dictation.

As national security became more critical, a fast was proclaimed in Jerusalem. At that time, Baruch had the privilege of reading all Jeremiah's prophecies to the multitude assembled at the temple. When King Jehoiakim heard the news, he issued an order for the arrest of both Baruch and Jeremiah, *"but the Lord hid them"* (Jer. 36:26).

Baruch became discouraged in the midst of such strong opposition. Perhaps it was godly sorrow over the rejection of the Word of God. However, when the faithful Christian is hated or slandered, he should remember that the servant can be no greater than the Lord.

Jesus was continuously rejected. There was no room for Him in the inn at His birth; He had no place among the notable people in His life; and He was crucified by those He came to save. A day came, though, when Christ was raised in power to life, victory, and the highest place of honor.

We must remain faithful to Christ. He alone is our help, life, and reward.

"Christ also suffered for us, leaving us an example, that ye should follow his steps" (1 Pet. 2:21).

Thought for Today: It is far better to be poor and despised in this life and have our Lord's approval—than it is to seek great riches, or approval from the world, and be turned away by God.

Christ Revealed: As the One who corrects His people (Jer. 46:28). *"For whom the Lord loveth he chasteneth"* (Heb. 12:6).

August 28: Read Jeremiah 49–50

Verses for Today: *"Therefore thus saith the Lord of hosts, the God of Israel; Behold, I will punish the king of Babylon and his land. . . . And I will bring Israel again to his habitation . . . and his soul shall be satisfied"* (Jer. 50:18-19).

Babylon's defeat was foretold to strengthen the Israelites' faith in God and to re-assure them that He had not forgotten His covenant promise to their forefathers. It was also given to prevent them from participating in Babylon's idol worship and to encourage them to return to Jerusalem.

The Lord was faithful to His Word that He proclaimed through His proph-ets. In this instance, Babylon was brought down, and Israel was brought back to the land that God had promised to Abraham and his descendants.

We are to trust in God's mighty Word. It will not fail. We can trust Him.

If we have strayed from walking with the Lord, let us return to Him with our whole hearts! Let us walk in freedom from the power of sin and enjoy intimate fellowship with God.

"If the Son therefore shall make you free, ye shall be free indeed" (John 8:36).

Thought for Today: God will hear the cry of any repentant sinner.

Christ Revealed: As the Redeemer (Jer. 50:34). *"Blessed be the Lord God of Israel; for he hath visited and redeemed his people"* (Luke 1:68).

August 29: Read Jeremiah 51–52

Verse for Today: *"And thou shalt say, Thus shall Babylon sink, and shall not rise from the evil that I will bring upon her: and they shall be weary"* (Jer. 51:64).

The great Babylon—*"the land of the Chaldeans"* (Jer. 24:5; 25:12)—was enjoying its greatest power when God declared that it would be *like a desert forever*—that the nation would *sink to rise no more* (Jer. 51:62, 64).

Under the rule of Nebuchadnezzar, who ruled much of the known world at that time, Babylon seemed unconquerable (Dan. 2:37-38). However, Babylon's splendor and gigantic world empire did not prevent God from bringing about her defeat at the end of the Israelites' seventy years of Babylonian captivity. The great Babylonian Empire fell the night Belshazzar saw the handwriting on the wall (Dan. 5). To this day, ancient Babylon is uninhabited as the Lord predicted (Jer. 51:61-62).

The world, as we know it, is a system, as well as a planet. Babylon represents the world system with its many attractive things that people see and desire, including riches, power, and glamour (1 John 2:16). These possessions and activities can occupy our time and keep us from accomplishing what we should for the Lord.

Behind the worldly system is a satanic kingdom, which seeks to rule the world, and defeat and destroy God's work. We are living in a world that does not know God and hates Christ (John 15:18; 1 Cor. 1:21). We are warned not to become captivated and controlled by the things of the world.

Do not adopt the customs of this world, but let God transform you inwardly by a complete change of your mind and attitude (Romans 12:2).

Thought for Today: As Christians, we must live in the world, but we are not to live by its standards.

Christ Revealed: As the Creator (Jer. 51:15). *"For by him were all things created"* (Col. 1:16).

 # LAMENTATIONS

The book of Lamentations is a book of lament, or grief. Jeremiah the prophet is the author, and he pours out his grief concerning God's painful judgment on the people because of their sin. Jeremiah, who lived in Jerusalem, saw the prophecies of terrible judgment and destruction fulfilled regarding his beloved city and people.

Through prophets like Jeremiah, God repeatedly warned the people about the consequences for their sins, but they would not listen or believe Him. The Lord called for the people to return to Him and to live righteous, pure lives, and He would bless them. Jeremiah, knowing God is merciful, pleaded with Him in prayer. Still, it wasn't enough to stir the people's hearts back to the Lord to worship Him.

Lamentations declares that the City of God had become as evil as Sodom was (Lam. 4:6; Luke 12:47-48), and therefore, *the Lord made Israel suffer because of its many sins* (Lam. 1:5). Jerusalem was first subjected to the horrors of starvation (Lam. 2:19; 4:10). Then the Babylonian armies marched in, ravaged the Holy City, and destroyed the temple. Outside Jerusalem, Jeremiah wept.

Jeremiah poured out his deep mourning over the destruction of the kingdom and people he tried so hard to save. Through Jeremiah, God expresses His righteousness, and love, and still offers hope.

Lamentations holds important and beautiful promises for believers today, including this one:

"This I recall to my mind, therefore have I hope. It is of the Lord's mercies that we are not consumed, because his compassions fail not. They are new every morning: great is thy faithfulness. The Lord is my portion, saith my soul; therefore will I hope in him. The Lord is good unto them that wait for him, to the soul that seeketh him" (Lam. 3:21-25).

August 30: Read Lamentations 1–2

Verse for Today: *"Her gates are sunk into the ground; he hath destroyed and broken her bars: her king and her princes are among the Gentiles: the law is no more; her prophets also find no vision from the Lord"* (Lam. 2:9).

Jerusalem—that great and glorious City of God—was in ruins. The grief-stricken prophet expressed the pitiful emptiness and anguish that swept over the people due to their terrible loss. The loss of the temple with its holy of holies; the mercy seat; and the ark of the covenant, containing the original law of Moses, is evidence of the awful consequences of sin.

Jeremiah first expressed sorrow over the loss of all the precious material things in the City of God. But his sorrow turned to the still greater calamity—the loss of God's presence and protection. The religious worship had been all empty pretense, and God's presence was withdrawn.

If we give less than our best—only our spare time (possibly one hour on

Sunday or less) and some spare change—it is possible that our worship is empty. Let us examine our spiritual lives. Are we reading His Word and praying to know Him and do His will? Are we spiritually growing in Him, bearing good fruit, and serving Him?

"My people are destroyed for lack of knowledge: because thou hast rejected knowledge, I will also reject thee, that thou shalt be no priest to me: seeing thou hast forgotten the law of thy God, I will also forget thy children" (Hos. 4:6).

Thought for Today: While God provides honest seekers with plenty of evidence to believe His Word, a time comes for each of us when we must simply trust in faith.

Christ Revealed: By Jeremiah's sorrow over Jerusalem at her fall (Lam. 1:12-22). Jesus expressed sorrow that Jerusalem would not come to Him and be saved (Matt. 23:37; Luke 13:34).

August 31: Read Lamentations 3–5

Verses for Today: *"I AM the man that hath seen affliction by the rod of his wrath. He hath led me, and brought me into darkness, but not into light"* (Lam. 3:1-2).

The old prophet Jeremiah had walked with God through one adversity after another: *"He hath led me, and brought me into darkness."* And yet Jeremiah had assurance that the God he represented was able to guide him through the darkness. Although Jeremiah experienced the sad memories of a thankless ministry to which he had given his life, he never regretted his faithfulness.

Even though a Christian may be in *"darkness,"* it need not lead to despair. It should draw him closer to God. There are times that God does not reveal Himself in darkness because He is teaching us to walk by faith—not by sight. He wants us to hunger for Him more. Be prepared for times of darkness when you just can't understand what God is doing in your life. Hold on, persevere, and stay faithful.

"Fear none of those things which thou shalt suffer . . . be thou faithful unto death, and I will give thee a crown of life" (Rev. 2:10).

Thought for Today: God's Word gives assurance that His hand guides us, whether we walk with Him in darkness or in light.

Christ Revealed: As a merciful Savior (Lam. 3:22). *"For I will be merciful to their unrighteousness, and their sins and their iniquities will I remember no more"* (Heb. 8:12).

September

 ## EZEKIEL

Ezekiel was among the second group of captives taken to Babylon. At this time, Nebuchadnezzar returned to Palestine and removed Jehoiachin, puppet king of Judah and appointed Zedekiah (the third son of Josiah) to govern Palestine for him (2 Kings 24:10-17; 1 Chron. 3:15).

About ten years after Zedekiah was appointed, he rebelled against Nebuchadnezzar, who then attacked Jerusalem, broke down its walls, and destroyed the temple (2 Kings 24:18–25:21; 2 Chron. 36:11-21). The prophet Jeremiah was still in Jerusalem, where he had been prophesying for about thirty-five years. Daniel, who had been taken to Babylon about nine years earlier than Ezekiel, now held a prominent position in the Babylonian Empire. Ezekiel mentioned Daniel three times (Ezek. 14:14, 20; 28:3).

Ezekiel's message declared the approaching destruction and judgment because of the people's sin of idolatry. Ezekiel communicated God's message through symbols, allegories, and visions—the same methods used by Daniel and by John in the book of Revelation.

The purpose of his symbolic actions—such as his silent grief over the death of his wife (Ezek. 24:15-24) and his lying on the ground (Ezek. 4:4-6)—was to gain the people's attention. All these revealed a yielded life of obedience to God. Indeed, he was a powerful communicator, who was driven by an overwhelming sense of obligation to warn that Jerusalem would be destroyed unless the people repented. However, the hearts of the people were already hardened in idolatry.

After Jerusalem's fall in 586 B.C., Ezekiel shifted his emphasis to comforting the exiled Hebrews with messages of hope, consolation, and reconstruction. Just as forcefully as he had prophesied God's judgment, he foretold that the Israelites would be restored to their own land—a prophecy thrillingly fulfilled in our generation.[16]

God's purpose in the remarkable fulfillment of prophecy concerning the restoration of the nation of Israel is that all mankind *"shall know that I am the Lord"*—a phrase that occurs more than sixty times in the book of Ezekiel.

---

16 Information regarding fulfillment of this prophecy is provided in the footnote of the August 22 reading.

The book of Ezekiel proclaims the glory of the Lord (Ezek. 3:23). It closes by foretelling the coming of the New Jerusalem and its temple, where God Himself will dwell with His people.

September 1: Read Ezekiel 1–4

Verses for Today: *"I send thee . . . to a rebellious nation. . . . And thou shalt speak my words unto them. . . . Be not thou rebellious like that rebellious house: open thy mouth, and eat that I give thee"* (Ezek. 2:3, 7-8).

God spoke to Ezekiel, saying, *"Speak my words,"* but told him he would not be appreciated, and the people would not accept his message. They were *a rebellious nation.*

The servant of God should not be concerned about success—only *faithfulness.* In serving the Lord, there is so much that is rewarding, even though there are disappointments.

Perhaps we have accepted a task in the name of the Lord only to feel unappreciated. God allows discouragement, so that we might place our faith in Him—and not in ourselves. It is impossible for us to know *"what is the exceeding greatness of his power toward us who believe"* (Eph. 1:19) until we have stood in the midst of the work that the Master has given and have experienced the futility of our own strength.

"Nay, in all these things we are more than conquerors through him that loved us" (Rom. 8:37).

Thought for Today: When our lives are in harmony with His Word, we will recognize that God is working through us to accomplish His eternal purposes.

Christ Revealed: In *"the likeness as the appearance of a man"* who sat upon the throne (Ezek. 1:26-28). The description is that of the pre-incarnate Christ (before He came in the flesh), who alone is worthy to receive glory, honor, and power (Rev. 4:3-11).

September 2: Read Ezekiel 5–9

Verses for Today: *"And the word of the Lord came unto me, saying . . . your altars shall be desolate, and your images shall be broken: and I will cast down your slain men before your idols. . . . Yet will I leave a remnant, that ye may have some that shall escape the sword among the nations, when ye shall be scattered through the countries"* (Ezek. 6:1, 4, 8).

When the Israelites first entered Canaan, God provided an abundance of material blessings. As the people lived in obedience to His Word, the land was fruitful, their flocks multiplied, and no enemy was able to invade the nation. However, the blessings were withdrawn as they ignored God's Word, turned to idols, and lived to please themselves.

But God did not forget His promise to Abraham and his descendants. Ezekiel foretold that after a time of judgment, Jerusalem would be rebuilt and the Israelites would recognize that Jehovah had dealt with them not according to their evil ways, but according to His loving-kindness. They would be restored to their land after they repented of their evil ways.

A remnant of faithful believers has always *"feared the Lord, and . . . thought upon his name"* (Mal. 3:16). Even in a godless society, believers seek opportunities to meet for mutual fellowship to honor His Word.

"Even so then at this present time also there is a remnant according to the election of grace" (Rom. 11:5).

Thought for Today: Restoration is always available to those who repent.

Christ Portrayed: By the man clothed in linen (Ezek. 9:2-11), who represents Jesus as High Priest and Mediator, and the One who will save His people from the flaming sword of vengeance. (Daniel 10 also speaks of this One clothed in linen.) *"For there is one God, and one mediator between God and men, the man Christ Jesus"* (1 Tim. 2:5). Jesus is our Savior (Matt. 1:21; Acts 4:12; 2 Tim. 1:10).

September 3: Read Ezekiel 10–13

Verse for Today: *"Thus saith the Lord . . . I know the things that come into your mind, every one of them"* (Ezek. 11:5).

God exposed the plans of Israel's twenty-five princes, who were national leaders and advisers. Believing their clever strategy would ensure their national security against Nebuchadnezzar, they ignored God's command spoken by the prophet Ezekiel. Instead, they placed their confidence in their secret defense alliance with Egypt. This was in opposition to the will of God and brought about the final destruction of the Holy City, Jerusalem. How foolish to believe that their own thoughts and plans could be successful when they ignored God's Word.

No thought is so small or so clever that God does not take notice, for He knows *the things that come into our minds.* No one can hide anything from Him.

We must not think that foolish or evil thoughts are insignificant, or that they can do no harm, as long as they remain unexpressed. Our thoughts mold our minds and character, *for as a person thinks in his heart, so he is* (Prov. 23:7). Oh, how often we need to pray, *"Cleanse thou me from secret faults"* (Ps. 19:12).

"Casting down imaginations, and every high thing that exalteth itself against the knowledge of God, and bringing into captivity every thought to the obedience of Christ" (2 Cor. 10:5).

Thought for Today: It is impossible to please the Lord if we are thinking wrong thoughts.

Christ Revealed: As the One who gives us a new spirit (Ezek. 11:19). This promise is fulfilled when one accepts Jesus as Savior (Gal. 4:4-7).

September 4: Read Ezekiel 14–16

Verse for Today: *"Thou hast also taken thy fair jewels of my gold and of my silver, which I had given thee, and madest to thyself images of men, and didst commit whoredom with them"* (Ezek. 16:17).

God made the Israelites prosper above all nations. He drew them out of slavery and gave them royal dignity, great power, and wealth. His blessings should have encouraged them to be a holy people, who would teach the world to worship the one true God—but they turned to idols. Disobedience kept them from fulfilling all their purpose as God's chosen people (Isa. 5; Jer. 2:21; Hos. 10; Rev. 14:18).

We, too, are a chosen generation and are *"kings and priests unto God"* (Rev. 1:6). All Christians should desire to *show forth the praises of Him who hath called us out of darkness into His marvelous light* (1 Pet. 2:9). To accomplish our task, we must be diligent students of the Word, not reading into the Bible, not trying to interpret from our backgrounds, but humbly beseeching the Lord to speak to us and guide us in His holy will.

Each one of us needs the Lord for spiritual understanding. We must seek, know, and receive the Author to comprehend His Word and spiritual truth (Luke 24:45; John 3:3-6; 1 Cor. 2:9-16; Col. 1:9, 17-22). If you have never received Jesus into your life, the Bible is a closed Book to you (2 Cor. 3:16; Eph. 4:18; 1 John 5:20).

To know the Author, you must be born again, that is, born from above by believing on Christ. You need a spiritual birth (John 3:3). This is a miracle of the Lord. You cannot achieve it. You cannot obtain it. You can only receive it by faith—by believing on Christ—the Son of the Living God, the One who died in your place, so you might live. You are saved by calling on His name (Joel 2:32; Acts 2:21; Rom. 10:13).

"Thus saith the Lord, Let not the wise man glory in his wisdom, neither let the mighty man glory in his might, let not the rich man glory in his riches: But let him

that glorieth glory in this, that he understandeth and knoweth me, that I am the Lord" (Jer. 9:23-24).

Thought for Today: If our hearts are truly set on doing the Lord's will, we will give much attention to the study of *all* His Word.

Christ Revealed: In the everlasting covenant (Ezek. 16:60-63). Jesus is the same yesterday, today, and forever (Heb. 13:8).

September 5: Read Ezekiel 17–19

Verse for Today: *"Yet saith the house of Israel, The way of the Lord is not equal [fair or just]. O house of Israel, are not my ways equal? are not your ways unequal?"* (Ezek. 18:29).

During the final days of Jerusalem, the people of Judah endured much suffering, and then were taken as slaves to Babylon. Consequently, they were bitter and accused God of being unjust in allowing them to be disgraced and defeated by the Babylonians. Why didn't God keep them from slavery? Surely, they were not as evil as Nebuchadnezzar and his cruel heathen armies. Why would God permit the wicked Babylonians to prosper and control the earth?

Because the Israelites refused to turn from their sins, God could not bless or protect them. Nebuchadnezzar became His instrument for executing judgment upon them, destroying Jerusalem, and taking the people captive. Then, as foretold by Jeremiah, God's judgment fell upon the Babylonians (Jer. 50:1-3).

The ways of the Lord will seem unfair only to those who live in rebellion against what is truly right. His ways are always perfect.

God does not suggest—He demands—that everyone repent and turn from sin (Ezek. 18:30). Just as the idols had to be removed from the temple, sin must not remain in the Christian's life. *"How shall we, that are dead to sin, live any longer therein?"* (Rom. 6:2).

With truth and love, the Lord desires that everyone turn from sin, reflect His glory, and enjoy His protection and provisions.

"The Lord is . . . not willing that any should perish, but that all should come to repentance" (2 Pet. 3:9).

Thought for Today: The highest calling of God in Christ Jesus is that we may know Him (John 17:3) and make Him known to others.

Christ Revealed: As the One whose forgiveness provides life (Ezek. 18:20-22). *God made Jesus—who knew no sin—to be sin for us that we might be made the righteousness of God* (2 Cor. 5:21).

September 6: Read Ezekiel 20–21

Verse for Today: *"But the house of Israel rebelled against me in the wilderness: they walked not in my statutes, and they despised my judgments"* (Ezek. 20:13).

Through the prophet Ezekiel, God declared that the actual reason for the Israelites' failure was that *"they walked not in my statutes, and neither kept my judgments"* (Ezek. 20:11, 18, 21). Morally, they had sunk to the corrupt conduct of the heathen nations around them. Since they disregarded His Word and did as they pleased, God could not bless them. He cannot bless evil.

On three occasions, the elders went to Ezekiel *"to inquire of the Lord,"* presumably to seek God's will (Ezek. 8:1; 14:1; 20:1). On the first occasion, Ezekiel exposed their sins and foretold Jerusalem's doom because of idolatry. At the second meeting, God revealed to Ezekiel that the elders were not sincere and did not have a desire to do His will. The third time, Ezekiel announced that the destruction of Jerusalem and the nation was certain.

To *"inquire of the Lord"* without a sincere desire to please Him and obey His Word is just as foolish for Christians today as it was for the Israelites.

"Blessed is the man that walketh not in the counsel of the ungodly, nor standeth in the way of sinners, nor sitteth in the seat of the scornful. But his delight is in the law of the Lord; and in his law doth he meditate day and night. And he shall be like a tree planted by the rivers of water, that bringeth forth his fruit in his season; his leaf also shall not wither; and whatsoever he doeth shall prosper" (Ps. 1:1-3).

Thought for Today: In loving-kindness, God chastens His people when they sin to bring them back into fellowship with Him.

Christ Revealed: As the One who will gather His people from all nations and *"will purge out"* the false from the true (Ezek. 20:34-38; Matt. 3:12; 25:32).

September 7: Read Ezekiel 22–24

Verses for Today: *"Again in the ninth year, in the tenth month, in the tenth day of the month, the word of the Lord came unto me, saying . . . the king of Babylon set himself against Jerusalem this same day"* (Ezek. 24:1-2).

Ezekiel foretold that Nebuchadnezzar, king of Babylon, would soon destroy Jerusalem. The siege and capture were described as a cauldron (a large iron pot) set over a fire. The cauldron represents the nation, and pieces of flesh inside the cauldron represent its people, who would be consumed.

Despite all the optimistic forecasts made by false prophets, who said that the families already taken into captivity would soon be set free, the time of destruction for the kingdom of Judah had finally come. The people recognized too late that Ezekiel's prophecies were true. The final sentence of destruction was carried out upon the people of Judah because they had turned from God and were worshiping idols.

When people, possessions, or passions keep us from living to please the Lord, these things become our idols.

"He that loveth father or mother more than me is not worthy of me: and he that loveth son or daughter more than me is not worthy of me. And he that taketh not his cross, and followeth after me, is not worthy of me" (Matt. 10:37-38).

Thought for Today: The more we see things from God's point of view, the more we will see how destructive and defiling sin really is (Rom. 7:13).

Christ Revealed: In the denunciation of Israel's false prophets (Ezek. 22:25-28). Compare these denunciations with the words Jesus spoke against the scribes and Pharisees (Matt. 23:13-36).

September 8: Read Ezekiel 25–28

Verses for Today: *"Behold, I am against thee, O Tyrus. . . . I will make thee like the top of a rock . . . thou shalt be built no more"* (Ezek. 26:3, 14).

The island fortress of Tyre, including its coastal territorial possessions, was one of the greatest trading centers of its time. Tyre gained control of world commerce when Jerusalem, its greatest competitor, was destroyed. Surrounded by water and protected by her great fleet of Phoenician ships, Tyre seemed like the most secure place on earth.

Because the nation rejoiced over the fall of God's people, God told Ezekiel to prophesy that Tyre would be completely destroyed, though it seemed an impossible prediction. But the day came when Ezekiel's prophecy was fulfilled.

Alexander the Great besieged Tyre, tore down the walls and other buildings on the mainland, and literally built a rock road to the island fortress, thus fulfilling Ezekiel's amazing prophecy: *"I will make thee like the top of a rock: thou shalt be a place to spread nets upon; thou shalt be built no more"* (Ezek. 26:14).

Why hasn't this great seaport been rebuilt? There are no laws that say it can't be done, except for the One who inspired Ezekiel to prophesy that it shall never be rebuilt. Every hour of every day, ancient Tyre is a testimony to the reliability of the Bible.

Likewise, God wants our lives to be a testimony and witness to His Word and truth.

"Thy word is true from the beginning: and every one of thy righteous judgments endureth for ever" (Ps. 119:160).

Thought for Today: God will keep every promise in His Word.

Christ Revealed: As the One who will execute judgment upon Satan (Ezek. 28:14-17; Rev. 20).

September 9: Read Ezekiel 29–32

Verses for Today: *"And I will make the land of Egypt desolate . . . and her cities among the cities that are laid waste shall be desolate forty years. . . . At the end of forty years will I . . . cause them to return. . . . It shall be the basest of the kingdoms"* (Ezek. 29:12-15).

For centuries, Egypt, a magnificent world power, had been famous for its commerce, art, literature, science, and military might. Observing world politics, it would have been impossible for anyone to foresee that Egypt would be defeated and then rebuilt in forty years. Even more amazing was the added prophecy that Egypt would never regain world superiority, but would remain as one of *"the basest of the kingdoms."* The prediction concerning Egypt's defeat and rebuilding seemed unlikely to be fulfilled, yet it has been.

This prophecy is a striking contrast to the prophecies that Tyre, Assyria, and Babylon would never be rebuilt.

In all the Bible, not one prophecy has ever failed to be fulfilled. God will fulfill all His promises. God's Word is settled in heaven forever (Ps. 119:89). How reassuring it is to read God's promises to Christians and know they will all be kept.

"Heaven and earth shall pass away: but my words shall not pass away" (Luke 21:33).

Thought for Today: During the tests of all the ages, God's Word remains unchanged and sure.

Christ Revealed: Through the prophets, by the *"word of the Lord"* (Ezek. 29:1). *"God, who . . . spake in time past unto the fathers by the prophets, Hath in these last days spoken unto us by his Son"* (Heb. 1:1-2).

September 10: Read Ezekiel 33–36

Verses for Today: *"Woe be to the shepherds of Israel that do feed themselves! should not the shepherds feed the flocks? . . . Therefore will I save my flock. . . . And I will set up one shepherd over them"* (Ezek. 34:2, 22-23).

God expressed anger with Israel's religious leaders because they were more concerned in protecting their own interests than they were in warning the people to turn from their evil ways and worship the Lord. Consequently, the nation was like a shepherdless flock, which eventually the Babylonians took into slavery.

Ezekiel foretold of a Shepherd, who would truly love and care for His sheep—the Messiah and King of kings.

Jesus came and identified Himself as Israel's Shepherd, who would lay down His life for His sheep (John 10:11-15). Our Savior did not give His life as a martyr for truth or moral example of self-sacrifice. Christ died on the cross for our sins, so that we might have eternal life and live with Him. He gave His life freely for lost, sinful people. What amazing love He has for the Father and for us!

Jesus said, *"I am the good shepherd, and know my sheep, and am known of mine. As the Father knoweth me, even so know I the Father: and I lay down my life for the sheep"* (John 10:14-15).

Thought for Today: If the Good Shepherd had not died as our substitute, we could not have eternal life with Him.

Christ Revealed: As the Shepherd (Ezek. 34:23). Jesus said, *"I am the good shepherd, and know my sheep, and am known of mine"* (John 10:14).

September 11: Read Ezekiel 37–39

Verse for Today: *"Then he said unto me, Son of man, these bones are the whole house of Israel: behold, they say, Our bones are dried, and our hope is lost: we are cut off for our parts"* (Ezek. 37:11).

In Ezekiel's vision, he saw a valley full of dry, scattered bones. These bones represent the Israelites, who were in Babylonian captivity and had lost all hope of ever again becoming a nation. They cried out, *"Our bones are dried, and our hope is lost."* Most of the exiled Jews were also dead in the sense that sin had destroyed their faith in God and His promises.

Just as the Lord was the only one who could restore life to the dry bones, He was also the only one who could restore the Israelite nation to life (Ezek. 37:13-14). Israel, as a nation, was made to live again. The people returned to Jerusalem as predicted by Nehemiah.

All mankind is as *spiritually* dead as the dry bones until we are made alive—born again *"of the Spirit"* (John 3:5). It is then that God makes us new, and enables us to be led by His Spirit for glorious purposes. It is not by our own effort or any human wisdom, but by God's Spirit, that we have spiritual insight, accomplish things of eternal significance, and receive His blessings.

"Jesus said unto her, I am the resurrection, and the life: he that believeth in me, though he were dead, yet shall he live" (John 11:25).

Thought for Today: Every believer can be assured that the Lord will transform even the most hopeless situation when we seek Him. His Word gives us promises, as well as answers for every need.

Christ Revealed: As the One who made possible the resurrection from the grave (Ezek. 37:12; John 11:25; 1 Thess. 4:16).

September 12: Read Ezekiel 40–42

Verse for Today: *"Afterward he brought me to the temple"* (Ezek. 41:1).

These three chapters describe a future temple, the priests, and their duties. Once completed, the glory of the Lord will return and truly make this temple magnificent. The glory of the temple is revealed in this statement: *"The Lord is there"* (Ezek. 48:35; 43:5). The presence of God as a brilliant cloud, which was in the holy of holies of the tabernacle, and in Solomon's temple, will once again be in the people's midst.

Ezekiel previously witnessed this same "cloud" linger, then slowly move from the temple to the Mount of Olives, and disappear. Sadly, the people at that time had no true interest in being led of God and missed experiencing God's glorious and comforting presence. Therefore, God withdrew from their midst.

Today, every Christian is a *temple where God's Spirit dwells* (1 Cor. 3:16). We have His glorious presence with us at all times; therefore, He is able to guide us. But we have a choice as to how we will receive direction. One is by human reasoning and our own desires. The other is by God, through His Word and Holy Spirit, who bestows understanding. The natural mind can make decisions only based on limited knowledge in any given situation. But the Holy Spirit may lead in a much different way because all things are known to God. In our decisions, we should pray and seek to know God's will (Luke 22:42). If we are intent on our own ways, we will miss God's leading.

"Trust in the Lord with all thine heart; and lean not unto thine own understanding. In all thy ways acknowledge him, and he shall direct thy paths" (Prov. 3:5-6).

Thought for Today: If you are willing to submit to God, He will take care of the outcome.

Christ Revealed: In the exactness of instruction for the temple (Ezek. 40). Just as our Lord took great care in giving details for the temple, He has provided directions for His people, who are the temple of God (1 Cor. 6:19-20; 2 Cor. 6:16-17).

September 13: Read Ezekiel 43–45

Verses for Today: *"So the spirit took me up . . . and, behold, the glory of the Lord filled the house. And I heard him speaking unto me out of the house; and the man stood by me"* (Ezek. 43:5-6).

At the time Ezekiel prophesied, Israel's worship was not according to God's Word. The people were observing religious rituals, but their hearts were not devoted to God. Consequently, the elders in authority did not desire the presence of the Lord, nor recognize the importance of His Word.

The Spirit of God led Ezekiel to behold *"the glory of the Lord"* and *hear Him speaking.* This is in contrast to the unaided intellect of *"the natural man [which] receiveth not the things of the Spirit of God"* (1 Cor. 2:14).

Nothing so effectually hinders our hearing God's voice as accepting advice from unsaved, worldly minded counselors. Too often, Christians are influenced by the views of people, rather than through the Lord as we daily read His Word. If we are to discern God's will, we must allow the Holy Spirit to speak to us through His Word.

"It is the spirit that quickeneth; the flesh profiteth nothing: the words that I speak unto you, they are spirit, and they are life" (John 6:63).

Thought for Today: We are to love God with all our hearts and seek His ways.

Christ Revealed: As the *"glory of the Lord"* (Ezek. 43:4). Jesus is *"the brightness"* of God's glory (Heb. 1:3).

September 14: Read Ezekiel 46–48

Verses for Today: *"Afterward he brought me again unto the door of the house; and, behold, waters issued out from under the threshold. . . . Then said he unto me, These waters issue out toward the east country, and go down into the desert, and go into the sea: which being brought forth into the sea, the waters shall be healed"* (Ezek. 47:1, 8).

In a vision, Ezekiel saw the waters of life flowing into the Dead Sea, bringing forth life-giving water. Where death and desolation once reigned, great schools of fish could now be seen. The river brought life everywhere it flowed (Ezek. 47:9).

The Lord is a pure river of life to His redeemed ones. All the blessings of life come through Jesus, the source of the Water of Life. It begins with a small stream from Christ, the Fountainhead, and continues to increase in depth and preciousness as we walk after the Spirit in the light of His Word. All who accept Him as Savior shall have *"rivers of living water"* flowing from them (John 7:37-38).

"Whosoever will, let him take the water of life freely" (Rev. 22:17).

Thought for Today: Fellowship with Christ brings a fullness of life that overflows with blessings for others.

Christ Revealed: In the river of living waters (Ezek. 47:1-12) and in the name of the city—*"The Lord is there"* (Ezek. 48:35). Jesus is our Fountain of Living Water (Rev. 22:17); He will reign in the glorious heavenly city (Rev. 21–22).

 DANIEL

Daniel, a God-fearing Jew of royal lineage, was among the first Jews taken captive to Babylon after Nebuchadnezzar seized control of Jerusalem around 605 B.C. (Dan. 1:1-7). At the time, Daniel was probably in his late teens or early twenties. He remained loyal to God and served as an official with distinction in the foreign nations of Babylon and Persia, under four kings. Daniel's ministry covered the entire seventy-year period of Judah's exile in Babylon.

The book of Daniel was written during a time when the Jews were suffering from persecution and oppression. The first section (chapters 1–6) describes Daniel and some of his fellow exiles who, through their faith and obedience to God, triumphed. These chapters contain some of the Bible's well-known and well-loved stories, including Daniel (and his three friends) surviving being thrown in the fiery furnace (Dan. 3:8-25) and Daniel surviving the lions' den (Dan. 6:1-28). Although he was surrounded by wickedness in the great city of Babylon and was far from home, Daniel remained true to the Lord. Daniel is one of the few individuals in Scripture about whom no sin is recorded. Ezekiel compared Daniel's righteous life to the lives of Noah and Job (Ezek. 14:14, 20).

The second section (chapters 7–12) records Daniel's visions. Daniel revealed that the empires of Babylon, Persia, Greece, and Rome would rise and fall. He also foretold the victory of God's people. The book declares the superiority and sovereignty of the Lord over all creation, including world governments, and individuals. God is in control.

Daniel's visions predict the time that the Messiah's work would begin. Christ's kingdom is depicted as a stone *"cut out . . . without hands"* (without human involvement or power), *and a kingdom that shall never be destroyed and will bring to an end all other kingdoms* (Dan. 2:44-45). Jesus is revealed in this book, including as the *fourth man in the fire* (Dan. 3:24-26), and the *"Son of man"* (Dan. 7:13).

The book of Daniel provides vital information about the last days of Israel and the earth. At a time when there seemed little hope, Daniel provided encouragement and strength by revealing God's sovereignty, power, and plans for the future: *The Lord God delivers and rescues; He works signs and wonders in heaven and on earth; and He has delivered Daniel from the power of the lions* (Dan. 6:27).

Jesus quoted frequently from the book of Daniel and called him *"Daniel the prophet,"* meaning *"one through whom divine revelation was given"* (Matt. 24:15; Mark 13:14).

September 15: Read Daniel 1–3

Verse for Today: *"But Daniel purposed in his heart that he would not defile himself with the portion of the king's meat"* (Dan. 1:8).

Daniel was blessed with great faith and wisdom. Soon after Daniel was captured, he and a few Israelite captives were chosen for a special three-year-training course in the language and customs of their new country. Nebuchadnezzar's purpose for this specialized training may have been to weaken their loyalty to the Lord, and use these young leaders to influence other captives to become loyal to the new country.

One of the requirements for these "privileged" men was to eat the same rich, lavish food that the king ate. However, Daniel and his three friends would not eat the "defiled" food. It probably was not prepared according to God's strict Levitical standards. As a result, the Lord honored these men with healthier bodies and clearer minds than any of the others.

God will bless our loyalty and obedience to Him.

Although it may seem difficult at times, God expects His people to remain true to Him in every situation.

"There is therefore now no condemnation to them which are in Christ Jesus, who walk not after the flesh, but after the Spirit" (Rom. 8:1).

Thought for Today: Always remain true to God and His Word—regardless of your circumstances.

Christ Revealed: As the *"stone that smote the image"* (Dan. 2:35). The Stone is Jesus Christ (Acts 4:11; Eph. 2:20; 1 Pet. 2:4-8).

September 16: Read Daniel 4–6

Verse for Today: *"Belshazzar the king made a great feast to a thousand of his lords, and drank wine before the thousand"* (Dan. 5:1).

The seventy years of Jewish exile were nearing an end when Belshazzar was enjoying a great party. In his drunken condition, he ordered his servants to bring him the holy vessels that Nebuchadnezzar had taken from Solomon's temple many years earlier, and to fill the vessels with wine. As his guests drank, they mockingly laughed and *"praised the gods of gold, and of silver"* (Dan. 5:4).

God, though, had no trouble getting the arrogant king's attention through the miraculous handwriting on the wall. In his hour of crisis, the proud king panicked, and his *"knees smote one against another"* (Dan. 5:6). In fear, he cried for his astrologers and soothsayers, but they were unable to interpret the message. Daniel, with God's Spirit, was able to give a message directly from God Himself.

The actions of the God-rejecting Belshazzar find their parallel in the lives of many today who mock God and His Word, disregard attending church, and desecrate the Lord's Day.

Unless our nation heeds the lessons of history, judgment and calamity are knocking at our door. As followers of God, let us draw near to Him and repent of our sins and the sins of our nation. Let us ask the Lord to bring revival and heal our land. May He grant us wisdom, strength, and faithfulness to live for Him in difficult times.

"If my people, which are called by my name, shall humble themselves, and pray, and seek my face, and turn from their wicked ways; then will I hear from heaven, and will forgive their sin, and will heal their land" (2 Chron. 7:14).

Thought for Today: Pride is the root of much sin in our lives. *"God resisteth the proud, and giveth grace to the humble"* (1 Pet. 5:5).

Christ Revealed: Through the sending of an angel to *"shut the lions' mouths"* (Dan. 6:22). The Lord sent an angel to deliver Peter (Acts 12:1-19).

September 17: Read Daniel 7–9

Verses for Today: *"Daniel spake and said, I saw in my vision by night, and, behold, the four winds of the heaven strove upon the great sea. And four great beasts came up from the sea, diverse one from another"* (Daniel 7:2-3).

The great sea, driven by opposing winds, represents the confusion and contention that exist in the world. And from this tempestuous situation arise four savage beasts, depicting the history of the world from the time of Daniel to the kingdom of Christ.

Fifty years prior to Daniel's vision, these same four great kingdoms were revealed to the worldly minded Nebuchadnezzar, but from a slightly different point of view (Dan. 2). Nebuchadnezzar's vision was of a great and glorious giant figure, representing succeeding world empires that would exist until the end of time.

To Daniel, these kingdoms of the world appeared as savage beasts controlled by the impulses of selfish ambition, cruelty, and strife. This is a spiritual vision of humanity when it is degraded by its sinful nature and enslaved by Satan, and rejects Christ. There are many dazzling "giants" in our day—many "good" things to buy and places to go. These "giants" or "beasts" seek to lure us away from God's purpose for our lives. They seek to steal our time and destroy our testimony if we yield to them.

Eternal treasures can be gained only as we desire, more than anything else, to be guided by God's Word and Spirit.

"Love not the world, neither the things that are in the world. If any man love the world, the love of the Father is not in him. For all that is in the world, the lust of the flesh, and the lust of the eyes, and the pride of life, is not of the Father, but is of the world" (1 John 2:15-16).

Thought for Today: To some people, worldly possessions, popularity, and power appear as dazzling, giant prizes to be gained at any price.

Christ Revealed: As the *"Son of man"* (Dan. 7:13-14). Our Lord Jesus Christ confirmed this vision when He spoke about the last days: *"And they shall see the Son of man coming in the clouds of heaven with power and great glory"* (Matt. 24:30).

September 18: Read Daniel 10–12

Verse for Today: *"I ate no pleasant bread, neither came flesh nor wine in my mouth, neither did I anoint myself at all, till three whole weeks were fulfilled"* (Dan. 10:3).

In the first year of his reign, Cyrus, king of Persia, issued a proclamation to encourage the Jews to return to Jerusalem (Ezra 1). Out of many Israelites, only about fifty thousand responded and went with Zerubbabel to help rebuild the temple.

Strong opposition, though, eventually persuaded King Artaxerxes to force the Israelites to stop reconstruction (Ezra 4).

Daniel became distressed when he learned about the difficulties his people were facing. After three weeks of fasting and praying, God revealed to Daniel that evil powers had, for a time, kept his prayer from being answered.

Truly there is constant warfare taking place in the unseen spirit world. It is vital that we comprehend this unseen battle, and that we recognize the power of prayer, and how much God is expecting and depending on us to pray. We must pray for God's laborers, and for His work to be accomplished.

"He that overcometh shall inherit all things; and I will be his God, and he shall be my son" (Rev. 21:7).

Thought for Today: Our faith makes victorious Christian living a reality every day (1 John 5:4-5).

Christ Revealed: As the One *"that liveth for ever"* (Dan. 12:7). Jesus always has been and always will be (Rev. 4:8).

 HOSEA

The book of Hosea begins the last section of the Old Testament. This section contains the twelve books of the Minor Prophets.

The prophet Hosea proclaimed God's message to the Northern Kingdom of Israel. (The prophets Micah, Amos, and Isaiah were in the Southern Kingdom of Judah.) Israel was experiencing great prosperity, but the golden-calf-worship centers, erected many years earlier in the cities of Bethel and Dan, had turned the people far from God. As time passed, the immoral and pagan worship of Baal and Ashtoreth spread throughout their culture (1 Kings 12:28-32; Hos. 10:5-6; 13:2).

Instead of remaining faithful, Israel had broken her covenant relationship with God—just like an unfaithful wife with many lovers (Hos. 2:7-13). But even though Israel was guilty of spiritual adultery due to her idol worship, God still loved the people (Hos. 2:8, 16; 11:8-9; 14:4). The prophet pleaded with Israel to repent, so that God in His mercy could restore His protection and blessings upon them (Hos. 10:12; 12:6; 14:1).

Hosea's message is unique, because God ordained for Hosea to personally experience sorrow and humiliation through his wife's unfaithfulness (Hos. 1:1-3). As Hosea loved and forgave his wife, he vividly expressed God's compassion for people.

The New Testament refers to Hosea several times. (Compare Hos. 6:6 to Matt. 9:13; 12:7; and Hos. 10:8 to Rev. 6:16.)

September 19: Read Hosea 1–6

Verse for Today: *"Hear the word of the Lord, ye children of Israel: for the Lord hath a controversy with the inhabitants of the land, because there is no truth, nor mercy, nor knowledge of God in the land"* (Hos. 4:1).

God called the Israelites to be His chosen people. He compared their relationship to a marriage—they were to Him as a wife; He was to them as a husband (Isa. 54:5). Therefore, Israel's forsaking God and turning to the idols of heathen nations was compared to a woman leaving her faithful husband and living with other men. God charged Israel with rejecting His love (Jer. 2; Mic. 6:2-5).

When Hosea said there was no *"knowledge of God,"* he meant that the people did not fully know God and desire to follow His will. There was no knowledge of the Lord like that which the apostle John wrote about when he said, *"And this is life eternal, that they might know thee the only true God, and Jesus Christ, whom thou hast sent"* (John 17:3).

This kind of knowledge is more than mental; it is spiritual, and must be made real by the Spirit of God. This is the result of hearing His Word, believing it, and acting upon it. As we read His Word and follow Him, God's Spirit gives us greater insight, and greater ability to know Him and hear His voice.

"And why call ye me, Lord, Lord, and do not the things which I say?" (Luke 6:46). *"A good understanding have all they that do his commandments"* (Ps. 111:10).

Thought for Today: An abundant Christian life can be lived only on the basis of obedience to God's revealed Word.

Christ Revealed: Through Hosea's love for his sinful, disloyal, and unworthy wife (Hos. 3:1-5). Our Lord Jesus not only loved us while we were yet in sin, but He died the death of shame for us on Calvary, so that all He had might be ours (Rom. 8:32; 2 Pet. 1:3). When we receive the Lord, His words from Hosea are proved true: *"I will betroth thee unto me for ever"* (Hos. 2:19).

September 20: **Read Hosea 7–14**

Verse for Today: *"I will heal their backsliding, I will love them"* (Hos. 14:4).

The former warnings of judgment changed to a message of love. This does not mean that God had changed His mind; it meant that though a holy God must judge His people, His love was still reaching out to them.

In the past, the Israelites had turned to the powerful nations of Egypt and Assyria for assistance, which had led them to accept the other nations' idols (Hos. 4:17; 8:4; 11:2; 13:2; Isa. 42:17; 44:17). God called for Israel to repent, return to Him, and reject the idols that drew them away, saying, *"O Israel, return unto the Lord thy God; for thou hast fallen by thine iniquity"* (Hos. 14:1). The people needed to seek God for help and put Him first.

God created mankind to love and worship Him. We worship something when we give our affection and devotion to it. If we don't worship God, we will worship something else, such as possessions, financial security, power, social activities, status, ambitions, or even spiritual images or tokens. When anyone does not know (or rejects) Christ as Savior and Lord of one's life, other things or people will take the place of Christ. These objects or people become idols. We are to put Him first.

God declares that we must not seek fulfillment from the things of this world. Instead, we are to honor God and find fulfillment in Him.

"No man can serve two masters: for either he will hate the one, and love the other; or else he will hold to the one, and despise the other. Ye cannot serve God and mammon" (Matt. 6:24).

Thought for Today: What, and whom, do you love greatly?

Christ Revealed: In the Son who was called out of Egypt (Hos. 11:1). This reference is twofold: one is a historical reference pertaining to Israel (Ex. 4:22-23), and the other is prophetic regarding Jesus's time in Egypt as a child (Matt. 2:15).

 JOEL

The prophet Joel's message to the Southern Kingdom of Judah grew out of a national calamity. An invasion of locusts swept through the country, devouring the crops and stripping every leaf from the trees. This brought about a severe famine. The locusts are described in terms of an army—soldiers, horses, and chariots—symbolic of the enemies that God would allow to invade Israel because of sin (Joel 2:4-7). Joel called the people to return to the Lord to avoid further judgment.

Besides judgment, Joel predicted a future day when the Lord would pour out His Spirit *"upon all flesh"* (Joel 2:28). We are living in the *"last days"* that began on the day of Pentecost, when God's Spirit was first poured out on those who received the Lord. God's promise still holds: anyone can receive Christ as Savior and Lord, and be filled with His Spirit (John 7:37-38; Acts 2:38; Eph. 5:18).

Joel prophesied about the coming of the great *"day of the Lord"* (Joel 1:15; 2:1, 11, 31; 3:14), which will bring painful judgment for those not living for God. But he also declared, *"Whosoever shall call on the name of the Lord shall be delivered"* (Joel 2:32). This promise was repeated by Peter at Pentecost (Acts 2:21) and Paul (Rom. 10:13). God gives us the option to choose judgment and death; or Jesus, life, and blessings.

September 21: Read Joel 1–3

Verse for Today: *"And it shall come to pass afterward, that I will pour out my spirit upon all flesh; and your sons and your daughters shall prophesy, your old men shall dream dreams, your young men shall see visions"* (Joel 2:28).

On the day of Pentecost, when the Christians in the Upper Room were filled with the Holy Spirit, the apostle Peter declared, *"This is that which was spoken by the prophet Joel"* (Acts 2:16).

Later, Peter proclaimed, *"Whereby are given unto us exceeding great and precious promises: that by these ye might be partakers of the divine nature, having escaped the corruption that is in the world through lust"* (2 Pet. 1:4). This passage contrasts the two natures of life. We all have a human nature, which we received at birth through Adam. This nature has brought about all *"the corruption that is in the world."*

However, when we accept Jesus as Savior, we receive a second, spiritual nature from God. The contrast between life in Adam, before we were saved, and life in Christ, from the moment we accepted Him as our Savior, is the difference between being children of darkness and children of light. We either have the spirit of this world, which is under Satan's influence, or we have the Spirit of life and truth (God's life), filling us (1 John 4:6).

Let us remember, though, that being born again spiritually is just the beginning of our Christian life. We are to *grow* in Him and *"be filled with the spirit"* (Eph. 5:18). As we abide in Christ and know Him more, we will bear good fruit (John 15:5).

"This I say then, Walk in the Spirit, and ye shall not fulfil the lust of the flesh. For the flesh lusteth against the Spirit, and the Spirit against the flesh: and these are contrary the one to the other" (Gal. 5:16-17).

Thought for Today: The Holy Spirit, through the Word of God, empowers a believer to do the will of God.

Christ Revealed: As the One who will *"pour out"* His Spirit upon all flesh (Joel 2:28). This act began on the day of Pentecost (Acts 2:1-21).

 # AMOS

Amos was a farmer and preacher, who tended sheep and a grove of sycamore-fig trees. Although he lived near the small mountain village of Tekoa, located about twelve miles south of Jerusalem in the kingdom of Judah, God called him to preach to the Northern Kingdom of Israel (Amos 1:1; 3:9; 7:7-15). Uzziah was king of Judah, and Jeroboam II was king of Israel. Both kingdoms were enjoying prosperity (2 Kings 14:25; 2 Chron. 26).

Amos, the country boy, spoke against the religious and social evils of that period (Amos 2:4-8; 3:13–4:5), and foretold the destruction of the Northern Kingdom (Amos 5:1-3).

Nothing looked less likely to be fulfilled than the warnings of this herdsman. Fewer than forty years later, however, Assyrians invaded and destroyed the Northern Kingdom of Israel.

Amos ends with prophecies about the coming of the Messiah, and the restoration of the Israelites to their land (Amos 9:11-15).

Verse for Today: *"They hate him that rebuketh in the gate, and they abhor him that speaketh uprightly"* (Amos 5:10).

The prophecy of Amos seems to have been proclaimed *"in the gate"* at Bethel, about thirty years before the Assyrians defeated Israel. "The gate" was one of the well-known business centers of the Israelites, and where the elders judged the people (Jer. 17:19; 19:2). This place of commerce and justice is where the Lord spoke through Amos, saying, *"For I know . . . your mighty sins."*

The people's sins and evils included complacency, idolatry, and oppression of the poor. God hated their hypocrisy. They claimed to love God, but were living self-indulgent lives and not living for Him. Amos appealed to them to *"seek good, and not evil, that ye may live"* (Amos 5:12, 14). But God's message through Amos was unwelcome and ignored.

Speaking God's truth is not easy. Christians who speak out against sin can expect to be criticized.

"He that rejecteth me, and receiveth not my words, hath one that judgeth him: the word that I have spoken, the same shall judge him in the last day" (John 12:48).

Thought for Today: It is only through the power of God's Word that we will seek good and not evil.

Christ Revealed: As the Creator (Amos 5:8). Jesus was with God in the beginning at creation (John 1:1-4).

 # OBADIAH

The book of Obadiah is the shortest book in the Old Testament, with just twenty-one verses. (It is generally assumed that Obadiah prophesied during the reign of either Jehoram or Zedekiah, the last king of Judah.) Obadiah warns of the certainty of God's *just* judgment on all who oppose Him, and those who oppose His people, while also highlighting the ultimate establishment of God's kingdom.

The prophet Obadiah predicted the final destruction of the Edomites, who were the descendants of Esau and should have shown brotherly concern for Judah. However, they were cruel and aided Nebuchadnezzar in destroying Jerusalem (Obad. 1:10). Within four years after Jerusalem was conquered, the Edomites were defeated, too.

Unlike the prophecy against the Edomites, who were to be destroyed and never again to be a nation, Obadiah foretold that the nation of Judah would recover and *"possess their possessions"* (Obad. 1:15-17).

September 23: Read Amos 6–9 and Obadiah

Verse for Today: *"And the Lord said unto me, Amos, what seest thou? And I said, A plumbline. Then said the Lord, Behold, I will set a plumbline in the midst of my people Israel: I will not again pass by them any more"* (Amos 7:8).

A plumbline is a line with a weight at one end, which masons use as they build walls with stone or brick. A plumbline ensures that a wall is perfectly upright and vertical as stones are laid one upon another.

The Lord stood upon a wall with a plumbline in His hand. His purpose for standing on the wall was not to build it, but to announce its destruction. God had been building up Israel like a wall. They were to be a symbol of the difference and separation between God's kingdom of Israel and the world. God's prophets were the "plumbline"—proclaiming His message of Truth. But the wall had become so hopelessly off-center that destruction was the only solution (Amos 7:7-9).

God's Word is our plumbline. It is to be our guide to make sure our thoughts and ways are upright in God's sight. Just as a mason uses a plumbline to make sure the wall is truly upright, we as Christians must be just as precise in applying Scripture's truth to our lives. Let us seek His help to grow in His righteousness.

"Not every one that saith unto me, Lord, Lord, shall enter into the kingdom of heaven; but he that doeth the will of my Father which is in heaven" (Matt. 7:21).

Thought for Today: God's Word is the only reliable standard for our lives. It reveals God's viewpoint to us.

Christ Revealed: As the Plumbline (Amos 7:7-8). Jesus walks among His people, revealing what is good, right, and true, and exposing what is evil and displeasing to Him (Rev. 2–3).

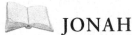 **JONAH**

Jonah, a prominent prophet in Israel, lived during the prosperous, but evil, reign of King Jeroboam II. Jonah had foretold the great military success of King Jeroboam II over the Syrians (2 Kings 14:25).

This book relates the historic account of Jonah and his mission from the Lord to go to the people of Nineveh—Israel's great enemy—and announce its destruction. At first, Jonah ran from God's call and willfully failed to comply with His directive, because he didn't like the idea of ministering to his enemies, and believed that God, with mercy, would forgive them.

After Jonah was swallowed by a whale, and God rescued him, Jonah reluctantly obeyed God's instructions. But when the king and people of Nineveh repented, Jonah was unhappy that his enemies were saved. Once again, God had to deal with wayward Jonah.

This book highlights that God is a God of love and mercy. He will forgive and save even His enemies if they will repent. The Lord does not want to punish and destroy anyone.

Jesus, during His ministry on earth, used this account to teach a number of truths. He contrasted the repentance of the heathen people of Nineveh, who had so little knowledge of God's righteous judgment, with the hard stubbornness of the Israelites, who possessed so much knowledge about God's Word and His ways (Matt. 12:41). The people of Nineveh repented at the preaching of Jonah, but most of the people refused to repent at Jesus's teaching and preaching.

Moreover, Jesus declared that Jonah was a depiction of the Lord's resurrection: *"As Jonah was three days and three nights in the whale's belly; so shall the Son of man be three days and three nights in the heart of the earth"* (Matt. 12:39-41; Luke 11:29-32).

God's judgment is sure—whether we have little or much knowledge of His Word. Everyone who does not receive Christ as Savior and Lord will be eternally lost. As believers today, we have the privilege of knowing God and having His Word available to us, and with that honor comes the great responsibility to share it with others.

September 24: Read Jonah 1–4

Verses for Today: *"Now the word of the Lord came unto Jonah . . . saying, Arise, go to Nineveh, that great city, and cry against it. . . . But Jonah rose up to flee . . . from the presence of the Lord, and went down to Joppa; and he found a ship going to Tarshish: so he paid the fare thereof, and went down into it"* (Jonah 1:1-3).

Jonah was unwilling to be a foreign missionary to Nineveh, that great capital city of the cruel and ruthless Assyrian enemy. He mistakenly thought he could choose his own city in which to serve God, ignore God's revealed will for his life, and bring about a change in the mind of the Lord.

It must have seemed like an answer to prayer when Jonah discovered that a ship was sailing to Tarshish on the exact day he arrived in Joppa. However, while Jonah was discovering such satisfying answers to prayer, a lot of "going down" is recorded: he went *"down to Joppa"*; *"down into the . . . ship"*; and finally, *"down to the bottoms of the mountains"* (Jonah 1:3–2:6).

For a while, circumstances seemed to favor Jonah's plan and gave him such peace of mind that he was soon *"fast asleep"* on the ship (Jonah 1:5). He thought he was leaving his troubles behind, but his "good luck" ended in "deep water." When Jonah *"paid the fare,"* he did not realize the high price he was paying for self-satisfaction.

God, though, loved this unsettled prophet too much to permit him to prosper in his self-centered ways.

Seemingly favorable circumstances, when we are trying to avoid God's will, never lead to a satisfactory end. One may boast of acting for God and talk of having His approval, but, if self is satisfied instead of Christ, the steps will always be down, down, down. We are walking toward our own ruin if we are resisting God's will.

"For whom the Lord loveth he chasteneth, and scourgeth every son whom he receiveth" (Heb. 12:6).

Thought for Today: Ask the Lord to prevent you from doing your will if it conflicts with His will for your life.

Christ Revealed: *"And Jonah was in the belly of the fish three days and three nights"* (Jonah 1:17). Jesus used this as an illustration to proclaim His death, burial, and resurrection when the Pharisees demanded a sign from Him about His identity (Matt. 12:39-40; 1 Cor. 15:4).

 # MICAH

During the time of King Hezekiah's reformation, both Micah and Isaiah prophesied in Judah (Isa. 1:1; Jer. 26:18).

Micah was faithful *"to declare unto Jacob his transgression, and to Israel his sin"* (Mic. 3:8). He charged the people with loving evil and hating good (Mic. 3:2), and sought to bring Israel and Judah to turn back to God and avoid His judgment.

Micah reminds us that God hates sin, but He forgives and rescues those who turn to him and change their hearts and ways. This is repentance. Micah warns of judgment, but he also offers hope. The remedy is to choose God.

"Who is a God like unto thee, that pardoneth iniquity, and passeth by the transgression of the remnant of his heritage? he retaineth not his anger for ever, because he delighteth in mercy. He will turn again, he will have compassion upon us; he will subdue our iniquities; and thou wilt cast all their sins into the depths of the sea" (Mic. 7:18-19).

"He hath shewed thee, O man, what is good; and what doth the Lord require of thee, but to do justly, and to love mercy, and to walk humbly with thy God?" (Mic. 6:8).

September 25: Read Micah 1–7

Verse for Today: *"But thou, Bethlehem Ephratah, though thou be little among the thousands of Judah, yet out of thee shall he come forth unto me that is to be ruler in Israel; whose goings forth have been from of old, from everlasting"* (Mic. 5:2).

Our Savior's birthplace was foretold by Micah seven hundred years before Jesus was born. Micah was the only prophet who specifically stated the location would be Bethlehem.

Nineteen of Judah's twenty kings were born in the royal city of Jerusalem; therefore, it seemed unlikely that the Messiah-King would be born in Bethlehem. In addition, all the circumstances surrounding the birth of Jesus made the prophecy seem unlikely to be fulfilled. Mary, Jesus's mother, and Joseph were living in Nazareth, about ninety miles from Bethlehem. However, Caesar Augustus made an official decree in Rome concerning taxation. Mary could have stayed in Nazareth, but she traveled with Joseph to Bethlehem, where Jesus—the Messiah—was born (Luke 2:1-7). God's promise was fulfilled.

The size of Bethlehem is also significant—*"little among the thousands of Judah."* Bethlehem was an insignificant place until the Lord Jesus was born there. Christ is always "born" among the "little ones." He comes to those with hearts humble enough to confess sin and acknowledge Him as Lord.

Maybe you feel as if your life is insignificant. But when you receive Christ as your Savior and are born of the Spirit, your body becomes a temple of the living God, and that makes you even more important to Him. What makes our lives significant is the One who lives in us and expresses Himself through us.

"What? know ye not that your body is the temple of the Holy Ghost which is in you, which ye have of God, and ye are not your own?" (1 Cor. 6:19).

Thought for Today: True satisfaction can only be found in Jesus.

Christ Revealed: As the coming Ruler from Bethlehem Ephratah (Mic. 5:2; Matt. 2:5-6).

 NAHUM AND HABAKKUK

The prophet **Nahum,** in the book bearing his name, foretold the destruction of Nineveh (the powerful capital of Assyria). But unlike the people of Nineveh in Jonah's day more than one hundred years earlier, there was no sign of repentance. Within fifty years after Nahum's prophecy, the Babylonians conquered the mighty world empire of Assyria—the nation that had destroyed the Northern Kingdom of Israel. As foretold by Nahum, Assyria never again rose to power.

Nahum reminds us that God always fulfills His Word, and that He is God of both justice and love. While judgment for sin is certain, the Lord is loving and good and provides a refuge in Christ to those who trust Him (Nah. 1:7).

Habakkuk prophesied in Judah, probably during the reign of King Jehoiakim, who *"did that which was evil in the sight of the Lord"* (2 Kings 23:37). Although King Jehoiakim's father, Josiah, had been godly, King Jehoiakim did not follow his father's example.

Habakkuk cried out against the moral corruption that prevailed. He foretold that God would use the wicked Babylonians to bring judgment upon His people. Although they were to expect destructive days ahead, God told Habakkuk that the *just shall live by faith* and have confidence that He is doing what is right. Habakkuk, too, had to live by faith.

"The just shall live by faith" has been called the watchword of the Christian church (Hab. 2:4; Rom. 1:17; Heb. 10:38).

Our loving and all-wise God knows what is best, and we must accept every situation with trust in Him. The book of Habakkuk provides encouragement that, ultimately, justice and righteousness will triumph.

September 26: Read Nahum 1–Habakkuk 3

Verse for Today: *"O Lord, how long shall I cry, and thou wilt not hear! even cry out unto thee of violence, and thou wilt not save!"* (Hab. 1:2).

The prophet Habakkuk knew what it was like to live in difficult times. He prayed, Why is it, Lord, that violence, strife, and contention abound; the law is ignored; the righteous are oppressed; the evil man reigns; and I am helpless to stop it?

Then, in the midst of the horrifying Chaldean invasion of their country— the Promised Land—the prophet Habakkuk declared, *"The just shall live by his faith"* (Hab. 2:4).

In difficult times, we may ask, Why is this happening? Though we often don't understand why the Lord allows painful events to occur, we should be encouraged with the assurance that our all-wise and loving heavenly Father cares for His people. In difficult times, we must faithfully hold on to God's promises. When God has not answered your prayers and defeat seems inevitable, declare with the prophet, *"The just shall live by his faith."*

The apostle Paul—who *"suffered the loss of all things"*—proclaimed this same great truth, *"The just shall live by faith"* (Hab. 2:4; Rom. 1:17; Gal. 3:11; Phil. 3:8; Heb. 10:38). Today, all over the world, Christians declare confident trust in a caring, wise, powerful Father—regardless of their circumstances.

"Now the just shall live by faith" (Heb. 10:38).

Thought for Today: There are problems to which no one but God has the answer. We are to take our questions to God. Learning about Him—His attributes, character, purposes, and promises—and calling on Him enable us to experience His peace during difficulties.

Christ Revealed: As the One whom even the sea obeys (Nah. 1:4; Matt. 8:26-27).

ZEPHANIAH

The book of Zephaniah contains warnings of bad news, but also declares good news. Zephaniah affirms that God makes a distinction between the unrighteous, and those who are humble and godly. He proclaims that God will bring a great day of judgment and disaster, but He is mighty to save and rejoices over those who love Him (Zeph. 3:17). The prophecies in this book concern both a time in the past and a time in the future.

Zephaniah, the great-great-grandson of King Hezekiah, was a prophet during the early part of the reign of Josiah. In all probability, he greatly influenced young King Josiah, who was a godly king.

Among the last prophets before the captivity, Zephaniah foretold the fall of Jerusalem about twenty years before it took place (Zeph. 1:4-13). He warned that because of all the people's sin, the Lord would bring judgment on Judah and that a devastating invasion from the north would come in the near future. The people of Judah would be punished for worshiping idols and the surrounding wicked nations would also be punished (Zeph. 1:1—2:15). Zephaniah revealed that, even though Jerusalem was doomed to destruction, in time, the city would be restored (Zeph. 3:1-20).

In addition, Zephaniah prophesied about *the great day of the Lord,* which is referred to at least twenty times in these three chapters. Jesus will return in power and glory. It will be a time of great distress for those who do not live according to God's ways, but those who trust the Lord will be gathered together to live with Him.

HAGGAI AND ZECHARIAH

Both Haggai and Zechariah were probably born in Babylon during the exile, and each one eventually traveled to Jerusalem sometime after King Cyrus pronounced the decree to rebuild the temple.

The work on the temple foundation began immediately after the first exiles arrived in Jerusalem. Although the foundation was laid, the Israelites faced intense opposition from the Samaritans, who convinced the king of Persia to stop the work (Ezra 4:23). About fifteen years later, Haggai and Zechariah began preaching in Jerusalem.

Haggai appealed to those who were selfishly preoccupied with building their own dwelling places, rather than building the Lord's house. Haggai exhorted them to put God first.

Zechariah joined Haggai in encouraging the Jews to rebuild the temple. Zechariah additionally prophesied about the coming of Zion's King, the expected Messiah, and proclaimed about final judgment.

Through preaching the Word of God, both prophets turned the feeble nation from an attitude of indifference to one of zeal for completing the temple (Ezra 6:14).

September 27: Read Zephaniah 1–Haggai 2

Verse for Today: *"Ye have sown much, and bring in little . . . and he that earneth wages earneth wages to put it into a bag with holes"* (Hag. 1:6).

The Israelites went to Jerusalem because of the decree of Cyrus. These returning exiles set up the altar, established daily worship, and rebuilt the foundation of the second temple. But their enthusiasm soon faded, especially due to the persistent opposition by the Samaritans, which caused the construction to cease. Fourteen years passed, and nothing more was accomplished. The Israelites kept hoping for better times and less opposition.

But then, Haggai delivered five messages, urging the people to put God first in their lives. Upon hearing the Word of the Lord, they once again began to build the temple and completed it in just four years.

It's easy to find excuses for not doing the Lord's work. Hearing the Word of God renews our love for God, and our determination to put the Lord first in our lives, and to make the most of every opportunity (Eph. 5:16).

"But seek ye first the kingdom of God, and his righteousness; and all these things shall be added unto you" (Matt. 6:33).

Thought for Today: We can't simply say we believe the Bible without reading it and applying it.

Christ Revealed: As *"the king of Israel, even the Lord"* (Zeph. 3:15; John 18:33-37).

September 28: Read Zechariah 1–7

Verses for Today: *"Then he answered and spake unto me, saying, This is the word of the Lord unto Zerubbabel, saying, Not by might, nor by power, but by my spirit,* *saith the Lord of hosts. Who art thou, O great mountain? before Zerubbabel thou shalt become a plain"* (Zech. 4:6-7).

The foundation of the temple lay desolate for fourteen years. This fact was evidence of the lack of faith among the Israelites, who had returned from Babylonian captivity. God raised up the prophets Haggai and Zechariah (Ezra 5:1) to proclaim His Word and challenge the people to finish rebuilding the temple (Hag. 1:3-11). This time, they ignored the enemies' threats, *"and the elders of the Jews builded, and they prospered through the prophesying of Haggai the prophet and Zechariah"* (Ezra 6:14).

The word *"mountain"* is a symbol of the obstacles, opposition, and evil powers that Christians encounter (Isaiah 40:4; 49:11). Mountain-like problems can be overcome by faith in God and His Word.

Haggai and Zechariah proclaimed God's Word—the source of power through which all work of God is accomplished. It is *"not by might, nor by power,"* but by His Spirit and Word that we are effective workers for our Lord.

Jesus declared, *"It is the spirit that quickeneth; the flesh profiteth nothing: the words that I speak unto you, they are spirit, and they are life"* (John 6:63).

Thought for Today: God's Spirit can perfect His strength in the weakest believer.

Christ Revealed: As *"my servant the Branch"* (Zech. 3:8). Jesus was brought forth into the world in the fullness of time and *"took upon him the form of a servant"* (Phil. 2:7; Gal. 4:4).

September 29: Read Zechariah 8–14

Verse for Today: *"Rejoice greatly, O daughter of Zion; shout, O daughter of Jerusalem: behold, thy King cometh unto thee: he is just, and having salvation; lowly, and riding upon an ass, and upon a colt the foal of an ass"* (Zech. 9:9).

Zechariah's prophetic message was more than words of comfort and encouragement to the returned exiles. It provided hope as it foretold the coming of the King of kings, when *"many nations shall be joined to the Lord"* (Zech. 2:11). This prophecy was fulfilled in part when Jesus entered Jerusalem, *"sitting upon an ass"* (Matt. 21:1-11). This was His formal, but humble, presentation as King.

The cry of "Hosanna," though, soon changed to "Crucify Him!"

However, what Satan meant for evil, God ordained for our good. Jesus died for our sins, was buried, and rose from the grave. After forty days, He was carried *"into heaven itself, now to appear in the presence of God for us"* (Heb. 9:24). Zechariah further predicted a time when the King will return, in honor, power, and glory *"and the Lord shall be king over all the earth"* (Zech. 14:9).

Christians have the wonderful privilege of living after the fulfillment of our Lord's earthly ministry and in the expectation of His soon return as *"king over all the earth."* We are blessed to know forgiveness for our sins, and we have the assurance of being with our king and knowing we will one day reign with Him.

Jesus said, *"If I go and prepare a place for you, I will come again, and receive you unto myself; that where I am, there ye may be also"* (John 14:3).

Thought for Today: If the Lord were to come today, would you rejoice to see Him face-to-face?

Christ Revealed: Following are a few prophecies about Jesus from these chapters: *"Rejoice greatly, O daughter of Zion; shout, O daughter of Jerusalem: behold, thy King cometh unto thee: he is just, and having salvation; lowly, and riding upon an ass, and upon a colt the foal of an ass"* (Zech. 9:9; Mark 11:7-11; John 12:12-19). He was to be sold for thirty pieces of silver (Zech. 11:12; Matt. 26:15); His side, hands, and feet were to be pierced (Zech. 12:10; John 19:34; 20:27). Jesus, the Great Shepherd, was to be smitten, and His disciples scattered (Zech. 13:7; Matt. 26:31, 56).

 # MALACHI

Malachi may have prophesied one hundred years after Zerubbabel led the exiles back to Jerusalem—possibly about the time of Ezra and Nehemiah. His message was to the descendants of the Israelites who returned to Jerusalem from Babylonian captivity.

The Israelites had lost the zeal and dedication to God that existed when the temple was being rebuilt under the preaching of Haggai and Zechariah. They were caught up in greed, worldliness, and lack of concern for God's temple and its offerings. When God did not bless them, they questioned His goodness. Malachi called the people to renew their relationship with God, pointing out that their sins separated them from God's love and blessings.

In addition, the people wrongly thought that God should be pleased with their religious efforts. But everything they did for the Lord was only halfhearted. God is never pleased with leftovers. He wants our "whole heart" and calls us to be attentive to His ways.

Malachi appealed to Israel to return to the Lord, who loved them (chapter 1). He appealed to the priests, pointing out their sins (chapter 2). He foretold a future time, when *"the messenger of the covenant"*—Christ, the Messiah—would appear (Mal. 3:1-3). Malachi also foretold of *"the coming of the great and dreadful day of the Lord"* when *"all that do wickedly"* will be destroyed, and all who have lived to please the Lord will be rewarded (chapter 4). This is still to occur.

September 30: Read Malachi 1–4

Verses for Today: *"And I will come near to you to judgment; and I will be a swift witness against the sorcerers. . . . For I am the Lord, I change not"* (Mal. 3:5-6).

The Israelites who had returned to Jerusalem and rebuilt the city walls and the temple were dead, and their descendants had lost sight of their high calling and the purpose for their existence. Many had developed an attitude of religious formality and indifference toward God, which easily opened the door to toleration of evil, including witchcraft and sorcery. Although God strongly and clearly warned against all forms of sorcery, the people had become insensitive to His Word.

Any attempt to gain guidance or information about the future through occult powers—including fortune-tellers, horoscopes, astrology, communication with the dead, and Ouija boards—is an insult to God, who is the true source of all wisdom, knowledge, and power. (See Lev. 19:26-31; 20:6; Deut. 18:9-14; Isa. 8:16-20; 44:25; Jer. 14:13-16; 27:8-11; Ezek. 13:6-9, 23.) God alone knows the future and is able to guide and direct us.

The Christian's life is a walk of faith—trusting the Holy Spirit to give understanding and guidance from the Word of God, the only reliable source of truth. The Christian should look to God and trust Him for what lies ahead.

"Trust in the Lord with all thine heart; and lean not unto thine own understanding. In all thy ways acknowledge him, and he shall direct thy paths" (Prov. 3:5-6).

Thought for Today: To be led by God's Word is to be led by truth.

Christ Revealed: As *"the messenger of the covenant"* (Mal. 3:1) *Jesus is the mediator of a new covenant* (Heb. 9:11-22).

New Testament

October

MATTHEW

The New Testament begins with four accounts of Jesus's life written by four different authors. These accounts are called "gospels," which is a word that means "good news."[17] The books bear the name of their writers and highlight different important perspectives and facts as they reveal *the good news* of Jesus's life, death, and resurrection, through which we are able to receive salvation and blessings.

A Jew named Matthew wrote this first account. Matthew, who had been a tax collector for the Roman government, became one of the twelve disciples when Jesus called him to leave everything and follow Him.

This gospel is the vital link between the Old and New Testaments. Matthew wrote to the Jewish people, specifically to confirm that Jesus is the fulfillment of all Old Testament prophecies about the Messiah-King. Consequently, Matthew provides wonderful proof and evidence for believing in Jesus and Scripture, because a number of events are highlighted with a phrase, such as, "this is in fulfillment of prophecy." Almost every book in the Old Testament is referenced, with more than sixty quotes. These citations are representative of the entire Old Testament, including the Law, the prophets, and the Psalms.

Jesus is the promised *Messiah,* (or Christ), which means God's Chosen, or Anointed, One.[18] Throughout Scripture, God had promised that His Chosen One would set mankind's captives free. Matthew records twenty-three miracles that Jesus performed, proving His ability to free mankind from sin, sickness, and death—all things that keep a person bound. Jesus forgave sins, healed all kinds of disease, and raised people from the dead. He is the Savior (Matt. 9:1-8).

Jesus is also the King of kings. Because the words of a king are authoritative and of the utmost importance, and because Jesus is the great Teacher, more of what Christ *said* is recorded in Matthew than in the other Gospels. It includes thirty of his instructive parables, and the kingdom of heaven is prominent. This is the only gospel in which the wise men inquire, "*Where is he that is born King of the Jews?*" (Matt. 2:2).

---

17 A brief article on the meaning of the word gospel can be found at https://www.gotquestions
.org/what-is-the-gospel.html.

18 In Scripture, the word "Christ" can be considered both a title and a name. The word "Christ" comes from the Greek word, "Christos," which means "the Anointed One" or "the Chosen One." The Hebrew word for "Christ" is "Messiah." See https://www.bibleinfo.com/en/questions /what-does-christ-mean.

Since the King of the Jews, heir to Israel's throne, was prophesied to be a *"Son of David,"* Matthew traces the genealogy of Jesus from Joseph, the legal (although not the physical) father of Jesus; and through David; and then, all the way back to Abraham. This further confirms that Jesus fulfilled the prophecies of the covenants God made with Abraham and David (Gen. 12:1-3; 2 Sam. 7:8-17).

Matthew establishes to a sincere inquirer, beyond all doubt, that Jesus is God's Chosen One—the Savior and King.

October 1: Read Matthew 1–4

Verses for Today: *"Behold, there came wise men from the east to Jerusalem, saying, Where is he that is born King of the Jews? for we have seen his star in the east, and are come to worship him"* (Matt. 2:1-2).

Guided by a star, wise men from the East (possibly Persia, about eight hundred miles away) made the long journey to worship the promised Messiah-King. Although these respected men weren't Jewish, they were probably familiar with the book of Daniel and other prophecies concerning the Messiah's birth. They sacrificed many weeks of time and money, traveling to Bethlehem to seek and worship Him.

This is in contrast to the chief priests and scribes, Jews living in Jerusalem, who knew the Scriptures concerning the Messiah's birth in Bethlehem just six miles away. But they did not seek Him or present gifts to the newborn King (Mic. 5:2; Matt. 2:4-6).

Many people who hear about Christ are simply curious and, like the chief priests and scribes, satisfied in knowing the historical facts. Others react as Herod did when he *"was troubled"* (Matthew 2:3) about Jesus and the recognition and controversy surrounding Him.

Few are the people who are willing to sacrifice personal pleasure, time, and resources for the privilege of seeking and knowing Christ, and following Him. But "wise men" still seek Jesus.

"For as many as are led by the Spirit of God, they are the sons of God" (Rom. 8:14).

Thought for Today: It takes more than simple human reasoning and mental knowledge to know God. We need His help to know Him.

October 2: Read Matthew 5–6

Verse for Today: *"Blessed are the poor in spirit: for theirs is the kingdom of heaven"* (Matt. 5:3).

Each Beatitude is given in the order in which the Christian life progresses, and each is essential to the next one. *"Blessed are the poor in spirit"* is the first Beatitude and the foundation of all others.

Recognizing one's spiritual poverty is the first step in coming to God. The worldly minded would say, "Blessed are the rich, the wise, the influential, and the great." But those who are *"poor in spirit"* feel their own littleness, and their own sinfulness in the presence of a Most Holy God. They recognize that without Christ, they have nothing, are nothing, and can produce nothing worthwhile. They accept Jesus's words, *You can do nothing without Me* (John 15:5).

"Poor in spirit" has no reference to financial poverty, for there is as much pride and independence among the poor as there is the rich. The majority of people in the world admire an independent, self-sufficient person.

Many books appeal to one's ego and tell how to be "successful," but few teach us that we must renounce our attitudes of self-confidence, self-sufficiency, and self-importance before Christ can fill our lives. Jesus, our perfect example, is gentle and humble. He calls us to *learn from Him* (Matt. 11:29).

The more we recognize our destitute spiritual condition, and His great love and compassion for us, the more we will love Him in return and desire to live for Him.

Let Christ Jesus be your example of humility. He stripped Himself of all His glory and became a servant, humbling Himself and obediently dying on the cross (Phil. 2:5-8).

Thought for Today: The poor in spirit will not be easily offended and are careful not to offend others.

October 3: Read Matthew 7–9

Verse for Today: *"Judge not, that ye be not judged"* (Matt. 7:1).

Judging the motives of others is a serious offense for it invades the office of God Himself—*"Who art thou that judgest another man's servant?"* (Rom. 14:4). One who is quick to look for faults in others is usually not as concerned about his own sins as he should be. In fact, at whatever point a person condemns others, he automatically condemns himself (Rom. 2:1).

Criticizing or judging another is rarely done with justice or fairness; rather, it comes from a spirit of revenge or self-righteousness. The good a person does is usually overlooked, and the attention is placed on a weakness or failure that does not necessarily reveal the true and complete character of the person.

The Bible says, *"Judge not according to the appearance, but judge righteous judgment"* (John 7:24). We must at all times guard against saying or implying anything that puts us in the place of judge and that could harm another's reputation.

You have no excuse when you pass judgment on someone else for at whatever point you judge another, you are condemning yourself because you do these same things (Rom. 2:1).

Thought for Today: As we think on things that are true, honest, just, pure, lovely, and of good report, we will not be as likely to think evil about others or to criticize them.

October 4: Read Matthew 10–11

Verse for Today: *"Learn of me; for I am meek and lowly in heart: and ye shall find rest unto your souls"* (Matt. 11:29).

No one word is capable of fully expressing the meaning of meekness. The meek are humble; yet meekness is more than humility. Gentleness is also a characteristic of the meek: *"I . . . beseech you by the meekness and gentleness of Christ"* (2 Cor. 10:1).

The meek submit themselves to God's Word and yield to His direction. They accept His correction, knowing that *"whom the Lord loveth he chasteneth"* (Heb. 12:6).

True meekness does not mean weakness, compromise, or lack of boldness. It is an expression of the love of Christ, which patiently bears insults and injuries and does not have a harsh, critical spirit, or an attitude of vengeance. We need to express the long-suffering and mercy that the Lord has shown to us—a spirit of gentleness, humility, and patience.

"But the wisdom that is from above is first pure, then peaceable, gentle, and easy to be intreated, full of mercy and good fruits, without partiality, and without hypocrisy" (James 3:17).

Thought for Today: The meek are gentle toward others.

October 5: Read Matthew 12

Verse for Today: *"For as Jonah was three days and three nights in the whale's belly; so shall the Son of man be three days and three nights in the heart of the earth"* (Matt. 12:40).

The ministry of Christ was saturated with the words of the Old Testament. He revealed how *"all the scriptures"* speak of Him (John 5:39), thus removing any doubt as to whether the Old Testament is the Word of God.

Jesus, who knew the truth about all things, quoted from the book of Jonah as the very Word of God and declared unhesitatingly that Jonah had been in the belly of the great fish. The Lord not only acknowledged the validity of Jonah's experience, He also used it as a prophecy of His own death, burial, and resurrection.

The people in Nineveh believed the prophet Jonah, repented, and were consequently saved. The people in Jesus's day, however, did not believe and turn from their sins—even though Jesus is far greater than Jonah.

What do you believe? Do you believe the testimony of God's Word and that Jesus has secured salvation for you? Do you believe that the Lord will judge sin, but that He has provided a way of protection, restoration, and blessing for you? Have you confessed that you are a sinner and turned to Christ for His healing and saving power?

"Beginning at Moses and all the prophets, he expounded unto them in all the scriptures the things concerning himself" (Luke 24:27).

Thought for Today: How foolish are those who question the Scriptures!

October 6: Read Matthew 13–14

Verse for Today: *"But Jesus said unto them, They need not depart; give ye them to eat"* (Matt. 14:16).

Jesus was moved with compassion to feed a *"multitude."* However, the disciples could not see a way to feed so many people, and they said, *"Send the multitude away"* (Matt. 14:13-21).

Jesus did not send them away. Instead, He accepted five loaves and two fishes from a young boy (John 6:9). In the natural realm, this amount seemed ridiculously insignificant, compared with the vast multitude, yet Jesus blessed the boy's gift and instructed the disciples to distribute the food to the people. Even though they could not understand how the multitude could be fed, they obeyed the Lord, and thousands of people ate until they were filled.

Our Lord acts according to the same principle today. He can use anyone who is willing and who obeys His Word. He has given us the privilege of being *"labourers together with God"* (1 Cor. 3:9). Even though we are able to give only a little, God can multiply it to meet many great needs!

Like the disciples, it is possible to be overwhelmed by the pressing physical and spiritual needs that are all around us. However, God has blessed His Word and given us the responsibility to distribute what we can of the *Bread of Life* to the starving multitudes. How thankful we can be that God's blessings are not given according to our strength, but according to our faith in Him and His Word. The Lord always blesses obedience—even when we are weak.

"He that hath my commandments, and keepeth them, he it is that loveth me: and he that loveth me shall be loved of my Father, and I will love him, and will manifest myself to him" (John 14:21).

Thought for Today: Our faith is strengthened as we obey God's Word—the source of faith.

October 7: Read Matthew 15–17

Verses for Today: *"Ye hypocrites . . . This people draweth nigh unto me with their mouth, and honoureth me with their lips; but their heart is far from me. But in vain they do worship me"* (Matt. 15:7-9).

The Pharisees and scribes proclaimed their belief in the Scriptures as the Word of God, and rigidly practiced all the external religious formalities. But the majority would not accept that Jesus is the fulfillment of the Scriptures concerning Christ, the Messiah (John 1:41; 4:25). For a Pharisee or scribe to accept Christ as Savior would mean losing his position of authority, along with the honor and praise he received from the people. He probably would experience the loss of social, political, and economic advantages (John 12:42-43). Therefore, their worship was not truly from the heart. Jesus called them hypocrites, saying their hearts were far from Him.

Like that of the Pharisees, the worship of many is not truly from the heart because of their desire to be popular or to hold some important position. They may believe mentally, but their lives do not reflect following Christ.

True worshipers believe that Christ died for their sins, and they desire for God's Word and His indwelling Holy Spirit to transform their thoughts and actions. They seek to know and follow their Lord.

Be doers of the word, and not hearers only; otherwise, you are deceiving yourselves (James 1:22).

Thought for Today: Our worship is in vain unless we truly desire to obey God's Word.

October 8: Read Matthew 18–20

Verses for Today: *"What good thing shall I do, that I may have eternal life? . . . What lack I yet?"* (Matt. 19:16, 20).

A wealthy religious leader came running to Jesus and knelt before Him, asking the most important question that could ever be asked: *"What shall I do that I may inherit eternal life?"* (Mark 10:17). He greatly desired assurance of salvation. All of his good works and keeping of the commandments left him unsatisfied. He wanted to know, *What else do I need to do?*

Perhaps he thought he was ready to make any sacrifice or do something grand for God. But when Jesus responded, *Go, sell your possessions, give the money to the poor, then come back and follow Me, the young man went away sad because he was very rich* (Matt. 19:21-22). By directing him to sell his possessions, Jesus pointed out that his real problem was covetousness. His wealth was his god, and he needed to face that fact. Sadly, it was money and possessions—maybe even security and admiration—that he truly loved.

Both rich and poor must decide whether their desire to please the Lord is greater than their desire for material satisfactions. Not only will Jesus forgive a repentant sinner of greed for material possessions, defiling lusts, deceitful pride, and self-righteousness, but He is able to create in us a new heart and give us strength to overcome the temptation of these things.

I will give them a heart to know me; I am the Lord. They will be my people, and I will be their God for they will return to me with all their hearts (Jer. 24:7).

Thought for Today: It is better to live for the Lord and enjoy the peace of God than it is to live to please self and end up separated from Him and in hell.

October 9: Read Matthew 21–22

Verses for Today: *"All this was done, that it might be fulfilled which was spoken by the prophet . . . Tell ye the daughter of Sion, Behold, thy King cometh unto thee, meek, and sitting upon an ass, and a colt the foal of an ass"* (Matt. 21:4-5).

More than five hundred years before this event, the prophet Zechariah foretold that the King of kings would one day appear, *"riding upon an ass"* (Zech. 9:9). Nothing could be less pretentious than this memorable event, which fulfilled prophecy. The garments and palm branches that the multitude and the disciples laid out for Jesus could not compare with the extravagant splendor with which other kings would have made their royal entries into Jerusalem!

Christ was humble and meek, as well as gentle and kind, and He has instructed us to learn from Him (Matt. 11:29). The proud and self-willed never recognize that humility and meekness are essential principles of true greatness.

Throughout Scripture, we're told (and shown) that those who exalt themselves will be humbled by God, and those who humble themselves will be exalted by God (Matt. 23:12). True greatness in our Christian lives comes by putting aside our false pride of self-importance and yielding to the Lord. As we grow in humility and meekness, we become willing to go last, to be overlooked, to be misunderstood, and to care for others more than ourselves.

"But the meek shall inherit the earth; and shall delight themselves in the abundance of peace" (Ps. 37:11).

Thought for Today: True humility before God results in a demonstration of humility before men.

October 10: Read Matthew 23–24

Verses for Today: *"Ye blind guides, which strain at a gnat, and swallow a camel. . . . Woe unto you, scribes and Pharisees, hypocrites! for ye are like unto whited sepulchers, which indeed appear beautiful outward, but are within full of dead men's bones, and of all uncleanness"* (Matt. 23:24, 27).

Of the three prominent "denominations" that existed at the time of Christ— the Pharisees, Sadducees, and Essenes—the Pharisees were the largest and most influential. The scribes were a special group of educators whose opinions were accepted concerning the meaning of any doctrine or teaching of the Scriptures. Most of them were members of the Pharisee organization.

The scribes and Pharisees lived in strict obedience to the external demands of the Scriptures, but were equally strict in observing their religious traditions not taught in the Scriptures. They became very indignant and hostile toward anyone who did not accept their rules and regulations. They bitterly opposed Jesus because of His refusal to practice their traditions and because of His claim to be the Messiah (John 9:16, 22).

Do we, like the scribes and Pharisees, tend to put ourselves on a self-righteous pedestal and condemn those who do not accept our standards? Do we seek to understand Scripture, Christ, and God's ways, or do we (like the scribes and Pharisees) want Christ to accept our understanding of spiritual truths and religious ways? Are we teachable, or when we don't understand God, or Scripture, are we quick to throw up our hands and walk away?

The Lord has shown us what is good. What He requires of us is this: to do what is just, to love mercy, and to live in humble fellowship with our God (Mic. 6:8).

Thought for Today: God is more concerned about the inward condition of our hearts than with the outward keeping of rules and regulations.

October 11: Read Matthew 25–26

Verses for Today: *"For the kingdom of heaven is as a man travelling into a far country, who called his own servants, and delivered unto them his goods. And unto one he* *gave five talents, to another two, and to another one; to every man according to his several ability; and straightway took his journey"* (Matt. 25:14-15).

What amazing truth and lessons Jesus communicates through this parable. Scripture reveals to us in many ways that God grants everyone various interests, gifts, and talents, which we are to discover and utilize for Him. This is true of believers as well, to whom He gives *spiritual* gifts.[19] We are to employ our gifts for His service, the good of others, and for His church.

One day, the Lord will ask for an accounting of the gifts, talents, and possessions He has given us, and will reward us accordingly (Matt. 16:24-27; 25:13-46). Let us do all we can, as creatively as we can, to share God's grace, minister to others, and build up the church.

There is even more incredible truth on this topic. Our spiritual gifts are gloriously linked to the Lord's miracles; they confirm His salvation message; and He uses them to bestow His grace on others. We must not bury our gifts and talents!

For this salvation, which was first announced by the Lord . . . has been confirmed with signs, wonders, and various miracles, and by gifts of the Holy Spirit distributed according to His will (Heb. 2:3-4).

Since every believer has received God's gift of grace, minister such to one another as good stewards of the abundant and diversified grace of God. Minister through your gift, whether speaking or serving (1 Pet. 4:10-11).

Thought for Today: Joy and growth increase as we find our God-given purpose, and as we help others know the Lord and grow in Him.

October 12: Read Matthew 27–28

Verse for Today: *"He is not here: for he is risen, as he said. Come, see the place where the Lord lay"* (Matt. 28:6).

Before Mary Magdalene and the others arrived at the tomb, the angel of the Lord had rolled back the stone from the entrance. The triumphant resurrection of Jesus Christ had already taken place when the angel announced to the astounded women, *"He is risen, as he said."* An empty tomb would have been sad

---

19 God's spiritual gifts, which He gives to believers, is a vital and enjoyable topic that warrants study and application. Numerous passages teach on, and illustrate, the importance of knowing and using our God-given gifts and talents. A few beautiful Old Testament verses include Ex. 31:1-11; 35:31; Eccl. 9:10; and Jer. 48:10. Four key New Testament passages are Rom. 12:1-8; 1 Cor. 12; Eph. 4; and 1 Pet. 4:5-11. Following are two great books on the topic: *S.H.A.P.E.: Finding and Fulfilling Your Unique Purpose for Life,* by Erik Rees (Zondervan, 2008); and *Your Spiritual Gifts Can Help Your Church Grow,* by C. Peter Wagner (Chosen Books, 2017).

news indeed if this had been all the women were told, but the exciting news was that Jesus had risen triumphantly from the grave! (Rom. 1:4).

Christians rejoice in the cross of Christ for it was there that He paid the price for our redemption. But we rejoice even more in the resurrection of Jesus because it assures us of God's truth, and of our heavenly home with Him. We have the assurance that *"the dead shall be raised incorruptible, and we shall be changed"* (1 Cor. 15:52). This is the great and glorious hope of every Christian, the comfort at the graveside of a loved one, and the victory that removes the sting of death. We expectantly anticipate one day being with Him.

May we rejoice in all Jesus has done for us (Ps. 103) and seek to live for Him. *"With the Lord there is mercy, and with him is plenteous redemption"* (Ps. 130:7).

Thought for Today: Jesus willingly died for you; are you willing to live for Him?

 # MARK

Mark presents Jesus as a servant, the perfect workman of God, and highlights His life of service to others. No one is concerned about the genealogy of a servant, so the gospel of Mark says nothing about the ancestry of Jesus. In fact, there is no mention of angels announcing His birth, or of wise men seeking Him as King or giving Him costly gifts. Since servants are not recognized for what they say, but for what they do, there is no mention of Jesus's amazing wisdom expressed to the learned doctors of the law when He was only twelve years old. Mark also leaves out the great Sermon on the Mount and most of Jesus's parables.

The urgent mission of Christ as the servant of God is revealed in such words as *"straightway,"* *"immediately,"* *"at once,"* and *"soon"*—which are used more than forty times. In Mark, the hands of Jesus are prominent, revealing the acts and duties of a servant. When the Lord healed Peter's mother-in-law, He *"took her by the hand, and lifted her up"* (Mark 1:31). In healing the deaf-and-dumb man, He put His fingers in the man's ears (Mark 7:33). At Bethany, He took the blind man *"by the hand"* and afterward laid *"his hands upon him"* (Mark 8:23). Christ is shown as a mighty worker.

Mark also portrays Jesus as the Christ, who gave His life and rose from the dead, so that all repentant sinners who receive Him as their personal Savior can inherit eternal life. This is Jesus's ultimate act of service.

As Jesus prepared to leave and return to heaven, He commissioned His followers: *"Go ye into all the world, and preach the gospel to every creature. He that believeth and is baptized shall be saved; but he that believeth not shall be damned"* (Mark 16:15-16). Throughout his ministry, Jesus prepared and instructed His disciples to follow His example, serve others, and preach the gospel. In this way, Jesus continues to serve through His followers.

October 13: Read Mark 1–3

Verse for Today: *"And in the morning, rising up a great while before day, he went out, and departed into a solitary place, and there prayed"* (Mark 1:35).

Our Lord had just endured a long, difficult day and was now facing another equally trying day. After having slept for only a few hours, He arose very early in the morning to pray.

Prayer was an important part of Jesus's life. He habitually devoted the early morning hours to pray to His Father and seek guidance and strength for each day. The many hours in prayer made it possible for Him to say, *I do nothing on My own, but I say exactly what the Father has instructed Me to say* (John 8:28).

Christ's life was much like ours—surrounded by opportunities for service and pressed by great needs. However, unlike Him, most of us give little time to prayer. Too often, we are so busy that we don't take time to pray; we simply hope everything will turn out all right. This is not faith; it is foolishness. When we neglect our time in prayer with the Lord, our efforts will be less effective, and more likely to be hindered by Satan's deceptions.

If we follow our Lord's example, we will spend more time in prayer. Even though we may be surrounded by difficult circumstances or great responsibilities, He enables us to overcome them when we pray. As we spend time with God, He provides wisdom, help, and strength.

"And [Jesus] spake a parable unto them to this end, that men ought always to pray, and not to faint" (Luke 18:1).

Thought for Today: The greater the outward pressures, the more time we must give to unhurried prayer—both seeking and listening.

October 14: Read Mark 4–5

Verse for Today: *"And they come to Jesus, and see him that was possessed with the devil, and had the legion, sitting, and clothed, and in his right mind: and they were afraid"* (Mark 5:15).

Restless, naked, and raging, this demon-possessed man had been dwelling among the tombs, the burial places of the dead. At the sight of Christ, this demon-possessed man ran to Jesus and bowed down before Him, and his life was transformed. He was controlled by Satan until Jesus set him free. Prior to meeting Jesus, he was symbolic of every unsaved person who, in some way, is under the control and mastery of Satan and his evil forces.

When Jesus cast out the demons from this man, Jesus permitted them to enter a herd of pigs. The demons in turn caused the pigs to run violently into the sea and drown. This illustrates how Satan seeks to destroy whomever he can.

People sometimes think that a single individual doesn't count very much, but God and the devil both know that is not true. The devil thought it worthwhile to let a whole legion of demons take possession of one man. Christ considered this man so precious that He was willing to be rejected by an entire city in order to deliver the man from Satan's stronghold. As a result of his encounter with Jesus, the man was changed—*"sitting, and clothed, and in his right mind."* He then became a witness to others. Because of his testimony, many people came to Jesus (Mark 5:20).

As we respond to Christ, we are miraculously transformed!

"Therefore if any man be in Christ, he is a new creature: old things are passed away; behold, all things are become new" (2 Cor. 5:17).

Thought for Today: It is not *what* a person possesses that is important, but *who* possesses him.

October 15: Read Mark 6–7

Verse for Today: *"Howbeit in vain do they worship me, teaching for doctrines the commandments of men"* (Mark 7:7).

Jesus rebuked the Pharisees and the scribes for their hypocrisy. They placed greater importance on their own traditions than they did on the commandments of God. Some of the commandments God gave Moses taught the need for purifying the heart from worldly desires and sinful ambitions. But instead of realizing the importance of their hearts being right with God, the Pharisees substituted many of their own doctrines.

No one today goes by the name of scribe or Pharisee, but many have departed from the revealed Word of God by substituting their own rules. Outwardly they are religious, but inwardly their hearts are not right with God.

"Woe unto you . . . hypocrites! for ye pay tithe . . . and have omitted the weightier matters of the law, judgment, mercy, and faith: these ought ye to have done, and not to leave the other undone" (Matt. 23:23).

Thought for Today: Our daily actions, attitudes, and conversations express the thoughts in our hearts.

October 16: Read Mark 8–9

Verses for Today: *"And he was transfigured before them . . . .And a voice came out of the cloud, saying, This is my beloved Son: hear him"* (Mark 9:2, 7).

Our Lord came into the world and *"took upon him the form of a servant, and was made in the likeness of men"* (Phil. 2:7). But at His transfiguration, Jesus was revealed as the glorious, eternal Son of God.

The Holy Spirit directed Matthew to write, *"His face did shine as the sun"* (Matt. 17:2). Luke was inspired to record that *"the fashion of his countenance was altered, and his raiment was white and glistering"* (Luke 9:29). Our Lord radiated with the glory of His deity!

Moses, who represented the Law, and Elijah, who represented prophets, both foretold the coming Messiah-King (Luke 24:44). Both were great men of God. Jesus, however, is far superior to these great men. All other leaders fade into insignificance when compared with our Lord.

"Seek ye the Lord while he may be found, call ye upon him while he is near" (Isa. 55:6).

Thought for Today: The honor and worship that is due Christ cannot be shared with any man or woman.

October 17: Read Mark 10–11

Verse for Today: *"And when ye stand praying, forgive, if ye have aught against any: that your Father also which is in heaven may forgive you your trespasses"* (Mark 11:25).

The spirit of forgiveness may not seem very important, especially when we feel someone has wronged us. But forgiving others is vital if we desire a right relationship with Christ. An unforgiving spirit not only comes from the Evil One, but it prevents us from receiving God's forgiveness (Matt. 18:32-35). Satan is our real enemy—not others, because they, too, may be struggling against his attacks and need our compassionate love.

When Jesus died on the cross, He paid the price for our sins, secured our forgiveness, and brought us into a restored relationship with God (2 Cor. 5:18-20). Therefore, we are to forgive all who have wronged us. This does not mean merely saying, "I forgive you," and continuing to have ill will toward that person, cutting off all communication, and avoiding all opportunities for reconciliation. On the contrary, we must do all we can to make amends, and to reconcile and restore damaged relationships.

"But if ye do not forgive, neither will your Father which is in heaven forgive your trespasses" (Mark 11:26).

Thought for Today: People become slaves to bitterness and anger when they allow those thoughts to dominate their minds.

October 18: Read Mark 12–13

Verse for Today: *"And Jesus answering said unto them, Render to Caesar the things that are Caesar's, and to God the things that are God's"* (Mark 12:17).

The Pharisees were the strict religious leaders of Israel. They deeply resented the excessive taxes they had to pay to the Roman government. The Herodians, in contrast, were worldly and irreligious, and urged submission to the Roman government.

The gospels of Matthew and Mark tell how these two opposite-thinking groups of people plotted together in an effort to trap Jesus (Matt. 22:15-22; Mark 12:12-17). Luke's gospel, calling them spies, says they were sent to ask Jesus, *Is it lawful to give tribute to Caesar, or not?* (Luke 20:20-26). If He answered yes, the Pharisees would say that He could not be the Messiah of Israel because He taught subjection to a gentile government. If He replied no, the Herodian party would accuse Him of conspiracy against the Roman government.

Our Lord in wisdom told them to give to Caesar what belonged to him, and added in a stinging rebuke of their hypocrisy *to give to God the things that are God's.*

How important it is for Christians to faithfully render to the Lord the things that are His, including reverence, money, and time. As we faithfully give to God, His Word and Christ's love can more effectively be proclaimed throughout the world.

"Give unto the Lord the glory due unto his name; worship the Lord in the beauty of holiness" (Ps. 29:2).

Thought for Today: Have you prayed for your leaders today—the ones you agree with and those you don't? (1 Tim. 2:2).

October 19: Read Mark 14–16

Verse for Today: *"And it was the third hour, and they crucified him"* (Mark 15:25).

Think of these words! The Son of God was crucified! God *"spared not his own Son, but delivered him up for us all"* (Rom. 8:32). Through His death on the cross, Jesus paid the penalty for all who repent of their sins and receive Him as Lord and Savior. Our sins merit death, but our substitute, the Lord Jesus Christ, bore our sins (1 Cor. 15:3).

"But he [Jesus] was wounded for our transgressions, he was bruised for our iniquities: the chastisement of our peace was upon him; and with his stripes we are healed" (Isa. 53:5). Great healing is available to us through Jesus and God's Word. Peter also declared this truth: *He has borne our sins in his own body on the tree; and now, we, being dead to sins, should live unto righteousness: by His stripes you are healed* (1 Pet. 2:24).[20]

Not only did Jesus die for our sins, but He was raised from the dead by the power of God. Through His death and resurrection, our Lord has secured for us wonderful blessings! As Christians, we have the privilege of being identified with the Lord Jesus in both His death and His resurrection. We have the privilege of new life and walking in the promises, healing, and gifts of our Lord.

We are "buried with him by baptism into death: that like as Christ was raised up from the dead by the glory of the Father, even so we also should walk in newness of life" (Rom. 6:4).

Thought for Today: Through Jesus's death on the cross, we receive peace with God, forgiveness of our sins, victory over the power of sin, a great inheritance, and eternal life.

 # LUKE

The gospel of Luke makes it unquestionably clear that Jesus's purpose for leaving heaven and being born in human flesh was *to seek and to save the lost* (Luke 19:10). Jesus's compassionate grace for the needs of mankind has no limits. Truly, this is *good news of great joy* (Luke 2:10).

Luke, a Greek physician, was the only gentile author of the New Testament. He was the missionary companion to the apostle Paul and addressed his book to a gentile man named Theophilus, explaining that because of what he had seen, heard, and investigated, he set out to write an orderly account of the evidence for believing in Jesus as the fulfillment of prophecy (Luke 1:1-4).

Paying special attention to the humanity of the Savior, Luke presents Jesus as the perfect man. He traces Jesus's genealogy back four thousand years to Adam, the first man, and establishes Jesus as the *"Son of Man."* This phrase, used at least

---

20 A mighty promise of Scripture is contained in this verse: *"With his stripes we are healed"* (Isa. 53:5; 1 Pet. 2:24). Great healing and transformative power are available through all that Jesus has done for us and through God's promises. Numerous articles, books, and studies are easily obtained regarding this truth.

twenty-six times, is an important truth. It reveals that Jesus is qualified to take our place in death, and that He understands our weaknesses and has compassion for our needs.

Consequently, more details of the human characteristics of Jesus are given in this gospel than in the others. Chapters 1 and 2 relate details about the birth of Jesus's cousin (John the Baptist), as well as about Jesus's parents, Mary and Joseph, and their journey to Bethlehem—where Jesus was born and placed in a manger.

A number of the most well-known and beloved Bible stories and parables are found only in Luke's gospel. Events not found in the other gospels are the angelic announcement of Christ; Simeon holding baby Jesus in his arms; the genealogy of Jesus through Mary; Jesus's conversation with the teachers in the temple at the age of twelve; His increasing *"in wisdom and stature, and in favour with God and man"* (Luke 2:52); the parables of the good Samaritan (Luke 10) and the prodigal son (Luke 15); the account of the rich man and Lazarus (Luke 16); and events of Christ's final journey to Jerusalem (Luke 22–23).

Throughout Jesus's ministry, His dependence upon the Father in prayer is revealed (Luke 3:21; 5:16; 6:12; 9:29; 10:21; 11:1; 22:17, 19; 23:46). In addition, we see Jesus's compassion for those who are frequently overlooked in society, including children, women, and social outcasts. Jesus disregarded social traditions to minister to those in need.

October 20: Read Luke 1

Verses for Today: *"To give knowledge of salvation unto his people by the remission of their sins, through the tender mercy of our God"* (Luke 1:77-78).

God's plan of salvation springs from His great love and mercy. Five times in the first chapter of Luke, we are reminded of God's mercy in providing a way to redeem mankind from sin (Luke 1:50, 54, 58, 72, 78). God's *"tender mercy"* means more than His willingness to forgive; it means that, with compassion, He accepts us and provides a way for us to have a restored relationship with Him.

Because of the sin of Adam and Eve in the garden of Eden, fellowship between God and man was broken. But our heavenly Father looked down upon mankind—helpless, hopelessly lost, and dead in trespasses and sin—and, in tender mercy, sent His only begotten Son into the world to *"save his people from their sins"* (Matt. 1:21-25). Being saved from sin means being reconciled and restored to God. We are brought back into fellowship with Him.

Oh, how we should rejoice and praise our wonderful heavenly Father! His loving-kindness has made it possible for everyone who will *"call upon the name of the Lord"* to be saved (Rom. 10:13).

"For God so loved the world, that he gave his only begotten Son, that whosoever believeth in him should not perish, but have everlasting life" (John 3:16).

Thought for Today: Because the Lord has given us mercy, we are to show mercy, forgiveness, and kindness to others.

October 21: Read Luke 2–3

Verses for Today: *"And the angel said unto them, Fear not: for, behold, I bring you good tidings of great joy, which shall be to all people. For unto you is born this day in the city of David a Saviour, which is Christ the Lord"* (Luke 2:10-11).

Whether or not the event of Jesus's birth is familiar to us, it is of great importance. It requires our utmost attention.

Thousands of people think of the birth of Christ as merely a delightful Christmas story. They reject the historical accuracy of the Word of God, which declares Jesus is the virgin-born, only begotten Son of God. Yes, the babe in Bethlehem's manger was born of a virgin and is the Son of God. He became a man to lead us to God. He bore our sins in His own body on the cross, thereby making it possible for every repentant sinner to be restored to God and to have eternal life.

Seven hundred years before Jesus was born, Isaiah, the prophet, foretold His birth: *A son is given to us. He will be called Wonderful, Counselor, Mighty God, Eternal Father of everlasting life, Prince of Peace* (Isa. 9:6). That Christ should come to earth, redeem mankind from the curse of sin, reconcile us to God, and grant us new life and blessings—these are indeed *tidings of great joy!*

Thought for Today: The certainty that God's Word is always fulfilled is the foundation of our faith.

October 22: Read Luke 4–5

Verse for Today: *"And when they had brought their ships to land, they forsook all, and followed him"* (Luke 5:11).

In answer to Christ's call, Peter and Andrew immediately *"forsook all"*—a profitable business, valuable property, and friends. They launched out, not knowing how their needs would be met. What wonderful faith—just to trust the Lord Jesus Christ for everything! All else seemed insignificant, compared with Jesus's call to live for Him and reach those who needed a Savior.

God has so arranged His plan of salvation that He works through human beings to carry out His ministry *"to seek and to save"* lost sinners (Luke 19:10). Thus, we become *"workers together with him"* (2 Cor. 6:1). What a privilege and an honor!

When Christ becomes the most important person in our lives, no sacrifice will seem too great to reach those who have not received Him as their Savior. Those to whom we can witness today may be gone tomorrow, and our chance to share His love with them will be gone forever, as well. The call to service is urgent. Every minute of the day, more than a hundred people die and go to a Christless eternity. Whatever we do to reach the unsaved, we must do now!

"The fruit of the righteous is a tree of life; and he that winneth souls is wise" (Prov. 11:30).

Thought for Today: Every Christian has a responsibility to participate in the work of God. May we joyfully look for opportunities to work for the Lord and share His good news with others.

October 23: Read Luke 6–7

Verses for Today: *"And why beholdest thou the mote that is in thy brother's eye, but perceivest not the beam that is in thine own eye? . . . Thou hypocrite, cast out first the beam out of thine own eye, and then shalt thou see clearly to pull out the mote that is in thy brother's eye"* (Luke 6:41-42).

While it is impossible for us to be among people without observing their conduct, this is not what Jesus spoke against. Rather, it is the attitude of judging others' shortcomings, faults, and differences.

Jesus did not say that the mote did not exist; it is quite real. However, because we cannot know another individual's heart and all the facts and circumstances regarding that person, we are commanded not to criticize or judge (John 7:24).

Condemning others comes from a spirit of self-righteousness as we try to build up our self-esteem and tear down another. These are the self-righteous sins that Jesus spoke against when He said that we must *first take the beam out of our own eye*.

Jesus gives an additional serious warning: *For in the same way you judge others, you will be judged; with the measure you use, it will be measured to you* (Matt. 7:2).

Thought for Today: *Let us not speak evil or slander anyone, but be considerate and gentle, showing meekness and courtesy to all* (Titus 3:2).

October 24: Read Luke 8–9

Verses for Today: *"A certain man said unto him, Lord, I will follow thee whithersoever thou goest. And Jesus said unto him, Foxes have holes, and birds of the air have nests; but the Son of man hath not where to lay his head"* (Luke 9:57-58).

The spiritual sincerity of this would-be disciple was put to the test as Jesus pointed out that he would have to face many hardships in order to follow Him. When Jesus said, *"The Son of man hath not where to lay his head,"* He was saying that He was not attached to any earthly possessions. The foxes and the birds had a place of protection, but Jesus's life was exposed to suffering, humiliation, and self-denial.

The cost of discipleship has kept many people from following the Lord for they are not willing to deny themselves the pleasures and interests that conflict with doing God's will. But those who are willing to live for Him know that the rewards for discipleship far exceed earthly pleasures.

"For even Christ pleased not himself; but, as it is written, The reproaches of them that reproached thee fell on me" (Rom. 15:3).

Thought for Today: Worldly ambitions fade into insignificance as we come to know the Lord through His Word and prayer.

October 25: Read Luke 10–11

Verse for Today: *"But a certain Samaritan, as he journeyed, came where he was: and when he saw him, he had compassion on him"* (Luke 10:33).

In reply to the lawyer's question—*"And who is my neighbour?"*—Jesus told a moving parable about a destitute sufferer, who had been beaten, robbed, and left *"half dead"* (Luke 10:29-37). In the parable, a priest and a Levite should have been the first to show compassion to the helpless man. They knew God, and they saw this man in need, but they both avoided him.

Each man may have justified his actions and cruel indifference, believing that because he was on his way to serve God in the temple, he did not have the time, and could not risk becoming defiled. For all they knew, the unconscious man could have been dead! Touching a dead body would have made them ceremonially unclean (Num. 19:11-19).

Yet the priest and Levite knew that the Law taught, *"Thou shalt not see thy brother's ass or his ox fall down by the way, and hide thyself from them: thou shalt surely help him to lift them up again"* (Deut. 22:4).

Christ is the Good Samaritan, who came from heaven and saw lost mankind, lying helpless in the road of this world, stripped of spiritual life, and left dying. Jesus bound up our wounds; poured within us the oil of the Holy Spirit; cleansed our sins by His sacrifice and blood; and lifted us up.

God was lavish with mercy and love—even when we were dead in sins, He forgave us, lifted us up, restored us, gave us new life in Christ, and raised us up to be with Him in heavenly places. God did this, so that for all time, His exceeding riches of His grace might be known and enjoyed (Eph. 2:4-7).

Thought for Today: We serve the Lord best when we show compassion to those who are less fortunate than we are, and to those who are suffering.

October 26: **Read Luke 12–13**

Verses for Today: *"Take no thought for your life, what ye shall eat; neither for the body, what ye shall put on. The life is more than meat, and the body is more than raiment. . . . But rather seek ye the kingdom of God; and all these things shall be added unto you"* (Luke 12:22-23, 31).

Jesus was assuring His people of His care for them. They should not worry about their daily needs because just as He clothes the lilies of the field and cares for the birds (Luke 12:6-7, 24-28), He will supply the needs of those who put Him first in their lives.

Our Lord's message is in contrast to the world's determined effort to accumulate things as a means of security for the future. The Christian is to *seek first the kingdom of God and His righteousness*—then the Lord will take care of the necessities of life (Matt. 6:24-34). This does not mean that we are to sit back and do nothing. It means that we must seek the things of God with all of our hearts. Doing the will of God should be the most important desire of our hearts, even as an outstanding athlete has one desire—to win.

"There is no man that hath left house, or brethren, or sisters, or father, or mother, or wife, or children, or lands, for my sake, and the gospel's, But he shall receive an hundredfold now in this time, houses, and brethren, and sisters, and mothers, and children, and lands, with persecutions; and in the world to come eternal life" (Mark 10:29-30).

Thought for Today: If we are truly concerned with God's interests, He will take care of ours.

October 27: **Read Luke 14–16**

Verses for Today: *"The younger son . . . took his journey into a far country, and there wasted his substance. . . . and he began to be in want. . . . and no man gave unto him. And when he came to himself, he said . . . I perish with hunger! I will arise and go to my father, and will say unto him, Father, I have sinned against heaven, and before thee"* (Luke 15:13-18).

This self-centered son insisted on being free from his father's authority and any responsibility to him. He also wanted the money and inheritance that was due him.

We usually think of the word *"prodigal"* as meaning a wanderer, but it actually means waster. The selfish Prodigal Son *"wasted"* his father's substance. Eventually, the son became destitute. Not only was he hungry and in need, but he also struggled with emptiness, and the shame and regret of a wasted life. Finally, he came to his senses, deciding that he would return to his father, confess his sin, and ask for his father's forgiveness. Then, he would ask to be made like a servant.

This is the story of the human race. It is human nature to be self-willed and self-sufficient. We seek to be independent from God's authority and live to satisfy self.

However, just as the Prodigal Son discovered that his father's compassion and love were far greater than he had realized, every repentant sinner discovers that the heavenly Father—in love and compassion—is waiting to transform the wasted lives of all who come to Him.

We deserved wrath but, because of His great love for us, God, who is rich in mercy, forgave us, paid the penalty for our sins, and raised us up with Christ that He might show the incomparable riches of His grace. For it is by grace that we are saved—through faith—and this is not from ourselves; it is the gift of God, not by works, so that no one can boast (Eph. 2:4-9).

Thought for Today: Do you know how much your heavenly Father loves you and desires to have you draw near to Him?

October 28: Read Luke 17–18

Verse for Today: *"And he spake a parable unto them to this end, that men ought always to pray, and not to faint"* (Luke 18:1).

Jesus shared the story of a judge who would not carry out justice for a poor widow; nevertheless, she went to him day after day, pleading for protection from her adversary (Luke 18:3-5). Because of her persistence, the judge granted her request.

God's Word teaches us that we have an adversary—the devil—who makes every attempt to keep us from receiving answers to prayer. We must continue to trust in God's goodness and faithfulness, praying, and watching for the answers.

This parable is an encouragement to persistently take our requests to God in prayer, even when it seems He does not hear or answer. God is not an unjust judge, for He is very interested in our concerns and in answering our needs. If an unjust judge would respond to the request of a widow he did not know, certainly we can depend upon God—our heavenly Father—to grant the requests of His own children who call upon Him. The Lord is faithful and never fails.

"For every one that asketh receiveth; and he that seeketh findeth; and to him that knocketh it shall be opened" (Matt. 7:8).

Thought for Today: Thank God that He hears and answers our prayers and gives us what is best.

October 29: Read Luke 19–20

Verses for Today: *"And Jesus entered and passed through Jericho. And, behold, there was a man named Zacchaeus. . . . And he sought to see Jesus who he was; and could not for the press, because he was little of stature"* (Luke 19:1-3).

Jericho, located about twenty miles from Jerusalem, was a pleasant, popular place to live, for it was the city of palm trees. It was here that Zaccheus, a Jew, worked as chief tax collector.

Tax collectors were greatly disliked. Not only were they believed to be dishonest, but they were considered disloyal to the Jewish community, because they worked for the Roman government. Consequently, they were unwelcome in the synagogues. Zaccheus *was chief among the publicans and tax collectors and was rich* (Luke 19:2).

However, buried beneath his shrewd, questionable business dealings was a deep dissatisfaction with himself. He desperately longed for something that money could not satisfy. This outcast was a lost sinner, and he knew it.

Though Zaccheus was small in stature and often overlooked, Jesus saw him, loved him, and called to him. When Zaccheus responded to Christ, his life was changed.

It was the love Christ had for a world of outcasts that made Him willing to die on the cross to save us from our sins.

"For the Son of man is come to seek and to save that which was lost" (Luke 19:10).

Thought for Today: Our greatest satisfaction comes through knowing the Lord.

October 30: Read Luke 21–22

Verses for Today: *"And he took bread, and gave thanks, and brake it, and gave unto them, saying, This is my body which is given for you: this do in remembrance of me. Likewise also the cup after supper, saying, This cup is the new testament in my blood, which is shed for you"* (Luke 22:19-20).

The annual Passover is the most sacred feast of the Jewish religious year. It commemorates the Israelites' deliverance from bondage in Egypt. As the sacrifice of the Passover lamb was necessary for the Israelites to have deliverance from

Egyptian bondage and the death angel, so Christ, *"the Lamb of God,"* was sacrificed to *redeem us from the curse of the law, sin, and death* (John 1:29; Gal. 3:13).

When Jesus, the Messiah, gave Himself as the Lamb of God, He fulfilled the true meaning of the Passover. Any observance of the Passover after that time would have been meaningless (Ex. 12:7; 1 Cor. 5:7).

Before the Lord was crucified, He established a new covenant with the words, *"This cup is the new testament in my blood, which is shed for you."* This covenant assures us of God's love and forgiveness, and that our Redeemer will return.

"He is the mediator of a better covenant, which was established upon better promises" (Heb. 8:6).

Thought for Today: Have you been to Jesus for the cleansing power of His blood? Does the power of God's promises make you glad and give you peace?

October 31: Read Luke 23–24

Verses for Today: *"And he said unto Jesus, Lord, remember me when thou comest into thy kingdom. And Jesus said unto him, Verily I say unto thee, To day shalt thou be with me in paradise"* (Luke 23:42-43).

Jesus's cross stood between the crosses of two thieves. Although the arrangement may have appeared to be the outcome of Roman hatred, it was divinely engineered. Jesus came to this world to save sinners and identify Himself with them. He lived among sinners, and it was necessary that He should die among them, thus fulfilling Scripture's prophecy: *"He was numbered with the transgressors"* (Isa. 53:12).

A hardened criminal, who defied and cursed the Savior, was on one cross. The other cross held a man who, at first, blasphemed Christ. But then, in the presence of Jesus, and in the presence of the angry leaders and the jeering, skeptical crowd, he turned to Christ and pleaded for mercy, *"Lord, remember me when thou comest into thy kingdom."* This wicked sinner turned to Jesus and was saved.

The world today consists of two kinds of people: those who continue to reject the Lord and those who accept Him as their Savior. For one, there is the certainty of eternal damnation; for the other, there is the promise of everlasting life (John 5:24; Rom. 6:23).

Like Matthew the publican, Mary Magdalene, and this criminal, God's mercy is sufficient for everyone who is willing to receive it.

"The preaching of the cross is to them that perish foolishness; but unto us which are saved it is the power of God" (1 Cor. 1:18).

Thought for Today: God offers forgiveness and salvation to all who come to Him.

November

 **JOHN**

The gospel of John is both simple and deep. Familiar words (such as light, bread, and shepherd) reveal Jesus and His good news. And yet, John's account is packed with depth and meaning. Someone once described this gospel as if John wrote it sitting underneath a shade tree, contemplating the divine and glorious mysteries.

John opens his book by introducing Jesus as God's Word: *"In the beginning was the Word, and the Word was with God, and the Word was God"* (John 1:1). Jesus and God's Word are one, a fact woven throughout Scripture. In the last book of the Bible, Jesus is again declared to be the Word of God (Rev. 19:13).

Jesus not only reflects God, but He is God, and is everything that God wants to say to mankind. He was with God at the beginning of creation (Gen. 1:26; Col. 1:15-20)! And He stepped out of heaven to become a man, so that we might know God and be restored to fellowship with Him.

John does not present Jesus as the descendant of David the king, as Matthew did, nor does he trace His genealogy back to Adam, as Luke did. John marvelously portrays Jesus in His deity as the Son of God, unveiling *"the glory"* He had with the Father *"before the world was"* (John 17:5). Jesus's equality with God is highlighted a number of ways.

Jesus revealed Himself to be the eternal *"I AM,"* which is the name God called Himself in the Old Testament (Ex. 3:14). Jesus proclaimed to the Jewish leaders, *"Before Abraham was, I am"* (John 8:58), and further revealed Himself with many *"I AM"* statements:

"I am the way, the truth, and the life" (John 14:6). Jesus is our source of all truth and knowledge about God and life. He is our guide. He is the door to God and eternal life. In Him is life.

"I am the light of the world" (John 8:12). Christ illuminates the darkness of sin on earth with the light of God's truth.

"I am the bread of life" (John 6:35, 41, 48, 51). Just as bread sustains life, Jesus gives and sustains physical and spiritual life. Jesus proclaimed this statement after feeding more than five thousand people with a few small fish and loaves of bread. He is forever able to fill and satisfy the hungry soul.

"I am the resurrection, and the life" (John 11:25-26). Jesus—God's sinless Son—died for our sins and rose again. He conquered death, lives again, and offers us His eternal life.

"I am the good shepherd" (John 10:11, 14). Our Lord is the Good Shepherd, who protects, provides for, and cares for His sheep.

"I am the true vine" (John 15:1, 5). As we receive Jesus's life, we are able to truly live, bear good fruit, and glorify God.

The Jews protested against Jesus's claims of deity and wanted to kill Him. In response to their arguments, Jesus revealed seven aspects of His deity (John 5:19-29):

1. In working (5:19);
2. In knowing *"all things"* (5:20);
3. In receiving honor (5:23);
4. In regenerating from *"death unto life"* (5:24-25);
5. In self-existence (5:26);
6. In judging (5:22, 27);
7. In resurrecting *"whom he will"* (5:21, 28-29).

John's gospel is a gospel of love: *"For God so loved the world, that he gave his only begotten Son, that whosoever believeth in him should not perish, but have everlasting life"* (John 3:16). What a glorious promise!

John wrote his account so *"that ye might believe that Jesus is the Christ, the Son of God; and that believing ye might have life through his name"* (John 20:31). To "believe" on the Lord Jesus Christ means that we have prayed to receive Him; we have been baptized in Him, and we are living for Him daily.

November 1: Read John 1–3

Verses for Today: *"And as Moses lifted up the serpent in the wilderness, even so must the Son of man be lifted up: that whosoever believeth in him should not perish, but have eternal life"* (John 3:14-15).

During Israel's wilderness wanderings, the people complained against God and Moses. Because of their sinful rebellion, the Lord sent poisonous snakes and many Israelites were bitten and died (Num. 21:5-6).

When the people confessed their sins, Moses prayed for them. In answer to his prayer, the Lord directed him to make a snake of brass (bronze) and lift it up on a pole. All who obeyed the Lord's command and looked at the brass snake were healed (Num. 21:8-9).

The poisonous snakes in the desert typify the deadly, destructive power of the old serpent—the devil—who tempted Adam and Eve to sin, and their sin brought death. Brass, in the Bible, represents judgment. The brass serpent symbolizes God's judgment on sin and His plan of salvation. This picture of judgment was made real when Christ, the sinless Son of God, came to earth *with a nature and body resembling our sinful nature and body* (Rom. 8:3) and was lifted up on the cross to die for the sins of the world. Such drastic judgment was necessary because all mankind has sinned (Rom. 3:23; 6:23). Christ became sin for us, so that we, through union with Him, might receive the righteousness of God (2 Cor. 5:21).

The bitten Israelites could live only as they trusted in God's provision of the uplifted snake. Likewise, mankind can have eternal life only by obediently looking to the crucified, risen Christ as personal Savior.

Whoever believes the Son is not condemned; but whoever does not believe is already under condemnation (John 3:18). *"For the wages of sin is death; but the gift of God is eternal life through Jesus Christ our Lord"* (Rom. 6:23).

Thought for Today: Only Jesus can forgive sin and restore us to fellowship with our heavenly Father.

November 2: Read John 4–5

Verses for Today: *"Jesus answered and said unto her, Whosoever drinketh of this water shall thirst again: But whosoever drinketh of the water that I shall give him shall never thirst; but the water that I shall give him shall be in him a well of water springing up into everlasting life"* (John 4:13-14).

Weary from His long journey from Judea to Samaria, Christ sat down to rest at Jacob's well, while the disciples went to the village to buy food. While He was there, a woman from Samaria came to draw water from the well. She must have been surprised when Jesus asked her for a drink of water because, ordinarily, a Jew would not even travel through Samaria, much less stop and talk to a Samaritan.

The Samaritan woman reached the turning point in her life when Christ revealed Himself as the fulfillment of her great spiritual need, for she had a thirst that neither religion nor the world could satisfy. She said to Jesus, *"Sir, give me this water, that I thirst not"* (John 4:15).

The person who drinks from the wells of the world will thirst again. However, the living presence of Christ is able to continually satisfy all who turn from their sin and trust Him as Savior.

Thirsty souls are all around us, seeking satisfaction. We can look for opportunities to share with them the One who satisfies. And as we live for Christ with love and joy, people will be drawn to Him. The purpose for our existence is not just that we might know God and His love, but that Jesus Christ might live through us and touch others.

"Blessed are they which do hunger and thirst after righteousness: for they shall be filled" (Matt. 5:6).

Thought for Today: Temporal satisfactions may "quench our thirst" momentarily, but they never truly satisfy.

November 3: Read John 6–8

Verse for Today: *"I am the light of the world: he that followeth me shall not walk in darkness, but shall have the light of life"* (John 8:12).

The unbelieving world is caught in the darkness of sin and spiritual death because *"the god of this world hath blinded the minds of them which believe not"* (2 Cor. 4:4). But all who have accepted Christ as Savior have passed from spiritual death to life. No longer do believers love the *"darkness,"* but they desire God's *"light"*— His instruction, guidance, and direction. To followers of Jesus, the Word of God is *a lamp unto their feet, and a light unto their path* (Ps. 119:105).

Merely knowing that Christ is the Light of the World, or simply believing that the Bible is the inspired Word of God, does not provide enlightenment. A Christian receives light by reading the Bible, praying, and allowing the Holy Spirit to guide one's life with truth and wisdom (John 16:13).

As we live according to what light the Holy Spirit has already given us, we are given more light. Occasionally, this happens in a thrilling way as we read Scripture that we have read a number of times but, this time as we read, we suddenly receive new, enriching insight.

If we say that we have fellowship with God and love Him, and yet we walk in darkness, then we lie, and are not living in the truth; but if we walk in the light, as He is in the light, we fellowship with one another, and the blood of Jesus Christ His Son cleanses us from all sin (1 John 1:6-7).

Thought for Today: To know what is right and not live accordingly is sin.

November 4: Read John 9–10

Verse for Today: *"I am the good shepherd: the good shepherd giveth his life for the sheep"* (John 10:11).

Our Lord is the Great Shepherd of the sheep. He is also *"the Lamb of God,"* who gave His life for His sheep—for everyone who would accept Him as Savior

(John 1:29; Heb. 13:20). Christ did not give His life as a martyr for the truth or as a moral example of self-sacrifice; rather, He died so that we might be saved from judgment and eternal death, and receive a new life and nature.

Our Lord compared this new spirit within us to the nature of a lamb. Sheep are gentle, and Christians should be *gentle, easy to get along with, submissive, and kind* (James 3:17). Lambs are harmless; they do not fight, or bite, or kill. Even children can approach a lamb without fear of being attacked or bitten.

Jesus went even further with this illustration when He instructed the disciples as they went out to minister. He warned them about the opposition they would encounter, likening it to wolves attacking sheep. Regardless of the hostility they encountered, though, the disciples were to be as *"harmless as doves"* (Matt. 10:16). This is still true for Christians today.

Our Lord gives us many lessons to ponder in considering ourselves as sheep. Isaiah declared that all of us, like sheep, have gone astray (Isa. 53:6). It's true that sheep, even old sheep, are prone to wander away from the sheepfold. When placed in a fenced pasture, they find openings and wander out, either straying on their own, or following the others with no thought of where they are going. Scripture teaches us that we are not to walk blindly down a path, or follow "the crowd" but, instead, we must listen for our Shepherd's voice and follow Him. If we are to enjoy "good pasture," we must know His Word and seek His will.

Jesus declared, *"My sheep hear my voice, and I know them, and they follow me"* (John 10:27).

Thought for Today: Christians, like sheep, need to stay close to the Shepherd for protection from the dangers of the world.

November 5: Read John 11–12

Verses for Today: *"Jesus said unto her, I am the resurrection, and the life: he that believeth in me, though he were dead, yet shall he live: and whosoever liveth and believeth in me shall never die"* (John 11:25-26).

Lazarus had been dead four days. When Jesus told the people to remove the stone that sealed the tomb, even Lazarus's sister Martha objected because his body would be decaying in the grave. But Christ commanded, *"Lazarus, come out!"* When Lazarus heard the Lord's voice, he obeyed and walked out of the grave!

Just as Jesus raised Lazarus from the dead, and just as Jesus Himself conquered death and rose again, we are to know this glorious experience of resurrection power and new life. All Christians have within them the indwelling resurrection life of Christ. This is a power over which death and Satan cannot prevail.

Both saint and sinner need to understand clearly that life is not over with death! For the day will come when *"all that are in the graves shall hear his voice, and shall come forth."* The Christian will come forth to eternal life and the unsaved to eternal damnation (John 5:24-29).

This truth, though, is one that we are to realize daily, not just at the end of life. Even though our bodies decline with age, our inner person is to be renewed every day with the Lord (2 Cor. 4:16).

"Verily, verily, I say unto you, He that heareth my word, and believeth on him that sent me, hath everlasting life, and shall not come into condemnation; but is passed from death unto life" (John 5:24).

Thought for Today: We should live in such a way that others can see Jesus living in us.

November 6: Read John 13–16

Verses for Today: *"And when he is come, he will reprove the world of sin, and of righteousness, and of judgment. . . . he will guide you into all truth"* (John 16:8, 13).

Before Jesus returned to the Father, He promised to send the Holy Spirit to be our Comforter, Counselor, and helper. Jesus declared, *"I will send him"* (John 14:16-18; 15:26; 16:7-11).

No matter what the circumstances may be, the Holy Spirit is able to impart peace to the hearts of Christians. He comforts those who are sick, those who have lost loved ones, and those who are experiencing trials. He makes our prayers effective *"for we know not what we should pray for as we ought: but the Spirit itself maketh intercession for us"* (Rom. 8:26).

In addition, the indwelling Holy Spirit imparts spiritual insight into the Word of God, guiding Christians *"into all truth."* The Holy Spirit, however, will only guide us into all truth as we read all His truth—the Bible.

If we diligently read God's Word, and seek Him, He will enable us to see the dangers of *"sin . . . and of judgment,"* and will bring conviction to our hearts. As we yield to His leading, He will continue to work in our hearts the things that are pleasing to the Lord.

"Grieve not the holy Spirit of God, whereby ye are sealed unto the day of redemption" (Eph. 4:30).

Thought for Today: Oh, how we need to become more aware of the ministry of the Holy Spirit!

November 7: Read John 17–18

Verse for Today: *"Holy Father, keep through thine own name those whom thou hast given me, that they may be one, as we are"* (John 17:11).

Our relationship with Jesus unites us with all Christians. While we wait for our Lord's return, let us pray the Master's prayer—that we may be one. Beginning with ourselves, let us determine that His prayer will be answered in our attitude toward other believers. A spirit of unity should be evident in our homes and those we enjoy being with, along with those who may not believe or worship Christ exactly as we do.

God sometimes brings people into our lives who are difficult to love—those who try our patience or are unkind to us—that we might have an opportunity to express His love to them. We should respond to these "difficult" people with an attitude of gentleness, patience, and humility (Eph. 4:2).

Jesus's love enables us to serve one another, share one another's burdens, and love the unlovely. And perhaps when others experience Christ's love through us, they, too, will be transformed.

How wonderful and pleasant it is for God's people to live together in harmony (Ps. 133:1).

Thought for Today: We are to experience peace and love through Jesus, and we must share these gifts with others.

November 8: Read John 19–21

Verse for Today: *"Then said Jesus to them . . . as my Father hath sent me, even so send I you"* (John 20:21).

Jesus linked His disciples with Himself in His great mission when He declared, *"As my Father hath sent me, even so send I you."*

Jesus's supreme purpose for coming into the world is *"that the world through him might be saved"* (John 3:17). In Matthew, the angels announced that Jesus would *"save his people from their sins"* (Matt. 1:21). In Mark, He calls *"sinners to repentance"* (Mark 2:17). And Luke wrote that Christ came into the world *"to seek and to save that which was lost"* (Luke 19:10). Ever since our Lord has ascended to heaven, He depends on and works through us—His disciples—to communicate the message of His redeeming love and truth.

Jesus's words, *"even so send I you,"* reveal that Christians are not to expect the unsaved to look for someone to tell them how to be saved; we must approach them. It is our responsibility to tell others about God's grace and salvation.

"Ye have not chosen me, but I have chosen you, and ordained you, that ye should go and bring forth fruit, and that your fruit should remain" (John 15:16).

Thought for Today: All Christians have a personal "world." We are to be a testimony to Jesus's saving power and tell what He has done for us.

ACTS

The book of Acts is a continuation of Luke's gospel. It was written by Luke, *"the beloved physician"* (Col. 4:14), who traveled with the apostle Paul. Acts chronicles the important time after Jesus ascended to heaven, and relates how the gospel spread and the church grew. Covering about thirty years, it ends with Paul's imprisonment in Rome.

Luke records the disciples' obedience in staying in Jerusalem to wait for the fulfillment of the Father's promise of the Holy Spirit (Acts 1:4), and in being His witnesses to the farthest part of the earth (Acts 1:8). Both the Holy Spirit and God's Word are revealed as vital in God's work of spreading the gospel.

The Holy Spirit and His mighty work and power are mentioned more than thirty times as filling, guiding, and sustaining the Christians. The Spirit's glorious power is the same indwelling force that every Christian is to know and experience.

There are also more than thirty references to *"the Word,"* especially in relation to the early Christians and their witnessing.[21] Jesus—as the *Living Word*—is prominent throughout the book of Acts. Beginning with the first converts, the Word was preached and received, ushered in the Holy Spirit, and brought conviction to the people. It is recorded: *"Many of them which heard the word believed"* (Acts 4:4). *"Then they that gladly received his word were baptized"* (Acts 2:41). *"The Holy Ghost fell on all them which heard the word"* (Acts 10:44).

Chapters 1–12 focus on the apostle Peter and the beginning of the Christian church in Jerusalem. After Stephen was stoned to death, the believers experienced great persecution, which caused them to flee to other places and, consequently, spread the gospel.

Saul of Tarsus was one of the leaders of the persecution, until the Lord miraculously called and converted him (Acts 9). Saul, who became known as the apostle Paul, dedicated his life to worldwide evangelism, and was willing to lay down his life for Christ. He made his headquarters in Antioch, a gentile city,

---

21 Just seeing the list of verses that mention *"the Word"* in Acts is a powerful testimony to its importance: Acts 2:41; 4:4, 29, 31; 6:2, 4, 7; 8:4, 14, 25; 10:36-37, 44; 11:1, 16; 12:24; 13:7, 44, 46, 48-49; 14:25; 15:7, 35-36; 16:6, 32; 17:11, 13; 18:11; 19:10, 20. In Acts 14:3 and 20:32, it is specifically called the *"word of grace."*

which became the center of world evangelism. Antioch was the first place that Christ's followers were called *"Christians"* (Acts 11:26). Paul's three missionary journeys are related in Acts chapters 13–21.

Acts reveals many vital spiritual truths, including principles regarding church growth and Christian success; God's kingdom; Jesus's resurrection and ours; witnessing with our testimony; serving others and the Lord; the church as a community; and worshiping God.

The account makes clear that living for the Lord can bring hardships, confrontation, and persecutions, but it also shows that it is through difficulties God's good purposes are fulfilled, His glory shines brightest, and His grace is extended to many others.

The book of Acts and Romans (the next book) enable us to understand God's plan of salvation through Jesus and the transition from "law" to "grace."

Acts concludes with glorious, victorious proclamations regarding God's church and His Word:

"So mightily grew the word of God and prevailed" (Acts 19:20).

"And now, brethren, I commend you to God, and to the word of his grace, which is able to build you up, and to give you an inheritance" (Acts 20:32).

November 9: Read Acts 1–3

Verse for Today: *"And it shall come to pass, that whosoever shall call on the name of the Lord shall be saved"* (Acts 2:21).

Jesus offers the good news of salvation to everyone. Right before He was taken up into heaven, the Lord commissioned His disciples to carry the salvation message *"unto the uttermost part of the earth"* (Acts 1:8). Because they understood that salvation and eternal life rested in Christ alone, the disciples and early Christians worked together diligently to make this truth known to the rest of the world. *Every day, in the temple courts and in homes, they kept teaching and proclaiming the good news that Jesus is the Messiah* (Acts 5:42).

Since the needs were so great, and the believers desired to be more effective in their ministry, they divided up the tasks. Godly men were appointed to care for the people's physical needs, in order that the spiritual leaders could give themselves *"continually to prayer, and to the ministry of the word"* (Acts 6:4).

Jesus's words are directed to every follower: *"Ye shall be witnesses unto me"* (Acts 1:9). In addition, Scripture warns us *that if we are ashamed to speak of Jesus, He will be ashamed of us when He comes in His glory* (Luke 9:26).

When we know the importance and value of the gift of life that we have been given, and we love the Lord, we will accept our responsibility to be *"doers of the word, and not hearers only"* (James 1:22).

You will be witnesses unto to me . . . unto the ends of the earth (Acts 1:8).

Thought for Today: Everyone can do something to help others come to know the Lord.

November 10: Read Acts 4–6

Verse for Today: *"And now, Lord, behold their threatenings: and grant unto thy servants, that with all boldness they may speak thy word"* (Acts 4:29).

Peter and John had been simple, ordinary fishermen. However, because of Jesus, they became committed to taking the good news of salvation to others. As they witnessed about their faith in Christ, many people were saved.

The officials in Jerusalem, though, were angered and commanded Peter and John to stop preaching about Jesus. But Peter and John did not stop witnessing, nor did they ask God to punish their persecutors. Instead, they met with other Christians and joined together in prayer, asking for courage, boldness, and opportunities to continue proclaiming God's Word (Acts 4).

The book of Acts reveals a number of answers to their prayers. These events should give us encouragement that the Lord hears and answers our prayers. When we are faced with problems, we often do everything but pray. How often we limit God's ability to provide answers because we depend on our own efforts, instead of spending time with Him seeking His help and provisions!

We are to pray about all things, thanking God for everything He brings into our lives; for this is the will of God in Christ Jesus concerning us (1 Thess. 5:17-18).

Thought for Today: Nothing is impossible when we seek and trust God (Gen. 18:14; Jer. 32:17, 27; Matt. 19:26; Mark 9:23; 10:27; Luke 18:27).

November 11: Read Acts 7–8

Verse for Today: *"And Saul was consenting unto his [Stephen's] death. And at that time there was a great persecution against the church which was at Jerusalem; and they were all scattered abroad throughout the regions of Judaea and Samaria, except the apostles"* (Acts 8:1).

The stoning of Stephen marked the beginning of *"great persecution against the church"* and drove the Christians to be *"scattered abroad."* Rather than defeating the churches, it resulted in the first missionary movement and great church growth. Philip, one of the seven deacons in Jerusalem, traveled a short distance north to Samaria, where many people believed and were baptized as a result of his preaching (Acts 8:12).

What had initially seemed a disaster to the early Christians turned out to be a fulfillment of the Lord's words: *"Ye shall be witnesses unto me . . . in Samaria, and unto the uttermost part of the earth"* (Acts 1:8). To see only troubles or Satan in all our misfortunes and suffering is a serious mistake. God often uses persecution and difficulty to bring about the fulfillment of His will.

God is in control. Even though at times Satan deceives us, or it appears someone has kept us from God's best, if we look beyond our circumstances, we will realize that *"all things work together for good to them that love God"* (Rom. 8:28).

"For our light affliction, which is but for a moment, worketh for us a far more exceeding and eternal weight of glory" (2 Cor. 4:17).

Thought for Today: You can never know the Lord's peace until you have encountered some of life's storms.

November 12: **Read Acts 9–10**

Verse for Today: *"And he trembling and astonished said, Lord, what wilt thou have me to do? And the Lord said unto him, Arise, and go into the city, and it shall be told thee what thou must do"* (Acts 9:6).

Saul of Tarsus was born a Roman citizen and received his theological training under one of the greatest rabbinical teachers of the first century—Gamaliel. Saul also had great influence among both Jewish and Roman authorities of his day (Acts 16:37-38; 22:3, 25-29). Because of all this, it is assumed that he was a man of great wealth.

After his miraculous conversion, Saul was passionately convinced that the entire world must hear that Jesus is the Christ, the Messiah-Savior. Saul became known as the apostle Paul—the apostle who wrote, *"I have suffered the loss of all things, and do count them but dung . . . that I may know him, and the power of his resurrection"* (Phil. 3:8, 10). Paul had a steadfast determination to do the will of his Lord—whatever the cost.

Many Christians would like to be greatly used by God, even as Paul was, but few are willing to pay the price—to deny themselves, take up their cross, and follow Jesus (Luke 9:23). All of us must decide whether we will live to please self, or surrender our self-achievements, self-pleasures, and material goals to do God's will. As we yield ourselves to the Lord and His Word, Christ will live His life through us.

"Blessed are ye, when men shall hate you, and when they shall separate you from their company, and shall reproach you, and cast out your name as evil, for the Son of man's sake. Rejoice ye in that day, and leap for joy: for, behold, your reward is great in heaven: for in the like manner did their fathers unto the prophets" (Luke 6:22-23).

Thought for Today: When our desires are in accordance with God's Word, we can be sure of gaining His best.

November 13: Read Acts 11–13

Verses for Today: *"As they ministered to the Lord, and fasted, the Holy Ghost said, Separate me Barnabas and Saul [Paul] for the work whereunto I have called them. . . . They came to Perga in Pamphylia: and John departing from them returned to Jerusalem"* (Acts 13:2, 13).

Paul and Barnabas had chosen John Mark as their minister, or helper (Acts 13:5). Perhaps he worked as Epaphroditus did (Phil. 2:25-30), to assist with financial support, so Paul and Barnabas could devote themselves more fully to preaching the Word of God in countries where the people had never heard that Jesus died for their sins.

But John Mark *"departed from them from Pamphylia, and went not with them to the work"* (Acts 15:38). He quit and returned home before the missionary journey was completed.

Like John Mark, many people give up and go back to an easier way of life. Perhaps they are unwilling to deny themselves personal comforts, not realizing they are cheating themselves of spiritual achievements and God's best blessings. But don't give up on "quitters," because they may change just as John Mark did. Paul later affirmed, *He can be a help to me in the ministry* (2 Tim. 4:11).

Still today, God calls helpers to every ministry. It is often necessary for them to work long, hard hours, usually without receiving recognition for their labors. Many are called to financially support missionary ministries (Rom. 12:6-8). Every part of the ministry, though, is just as important as the work of those who are called to be spiritual leaders.

Even Jesus did not come to earth to be waited on, but to minister to others and to give His life for them (Mark 10:45).

Thought for Today: Every Christian can be a helper in ministering the Word of God to others.

November 14: Read Acts 14–16

Verses for Today: *"Now when they had gone throughout Phrygia and the region of Galatia, and were forbidden of the Holy Ghost to preach the word in Asia, after they were come to Mysia, they assayed to go into Bithynia: but the Spirit suffered them not"* (Acts 16:6-7).

The apostle Paul had planned to preach in the great cities of Asia Minor (now part of western Turkey), but God's Spirit prevented him from carrying out those plans. Paul could have become discouraged, but he recognized that the "forbidding" was done by the Lord, who was instructing and guiding him. (See Acts 8:29; 10:19-20; 11:12; 13:2, 4.)

When our well-laid plans are detoured or shattered, we have a tendency to blame people or circumstances for the hindrances and disappointments, when actually they are God's way of redirecting our lives to accomplish His will.

God frequently works through ordinary, everyday circumstances to reveal what He wants us to do. But it is always in harmony with His Word. As we study Scripture and pray, His Spirit is able to grant us peace and spiritual understanding (1 Cor. 2:9-14; Eph. 1:17; 1 John 2:20).

We have the assurance from Christ that He, the Spirit of truth, will guide us into all truth (John 16:13).

Thought for Today: Failure to be guided into all truth is the result of not reading and seeking all of His truth.

November 15: Read Acts 17–19

Verses for Today: *"After these things Paul departed from Athens, and came to Corinth; and found a certain Jew named Aquila . . . with his wife Priscilla. . . . And because he was of the same craft, he abode with them, and wrought: for by their occupation they were tentmakers"* (Acts 18:1-3).

Although Aquila and Priscilla faced unjust hardship and humiliation when they were forced to leave Rome because of their Jewish nationality, God was directing their lives. They moved to Corinth, where they established their business. Soon they met the apostle Paul, who moved to Corinth after his discouraging meetings in Athens. Through their fellowship with him, they became dedicated Christians.

After some time, Priscilla and Aquila gave up their business in Corinth to assist Paul in his journeys (Acts 18:18). Later, they returned to Rome, where they *"laid down their own necks"*—ready to risk all for Christ—when they opened their house as a place of worship in a hostile country (Rom. 16:3-4).

The ministry of the early church was effective due to ordinary Christians, like Priscilla and Aquila, who believed that evangelism was the most vital aspect of life. They were willing to serve in any capacity to share the good news of the gospel and to assist those who were called to preach and teach His Word.

Priscilla and Aquila could have become resentful when they were forced to leave their home. Instead, as they trusted the Lord during bitter disappointments, they received a deeper revelation of His love. Having passed that test, they could have allowed financial security in Corinth to keep them from full-time service for Christ, but their hearts were set on eternal values.

God always arranges the circumstances in our lives—not only to test the sincerity of our calling, but also to make us more effective for His service.

"For we are labourers together with God" (1 Cor. 3:9).

Thought for Today: In our flesh, we may not always agree with the Lord's way of accomplishing His will through us, but we will find peace as we submit to His will.

November 16: Read Acts 20–22

Verses for Today: *"And the people ran together: and they took Paul, and . . . went about to kill him"* (Acts 21:30-31).

Immediately after he arrived in Jerusalem, the apostle Paul faced serious opposition. His enemies created a riot that resulted in him being brutally beaten by an angry crowd. Throughout Paul's Christian life, he was persecuted, mobbed, and opposed. He was cruelly beaten numerous times. Once, he was stoned and left for dead.

Even many Christians turned against him. In fact, at one time in his ministry, Paul said, *"No man stood with me, but all men forsook me"* (2 Tim. 4:16). However, an even more crushing blow was to hear that some Christians, who had received spiritual insight from the Scriptures under his teaching, were questioning his integrity and his calling from the Lord (2 Cor. 10:10; 11:6, 23, 31; 12:12; 13:3, 6).

Paul faced what seemed to be impossible problems, but he knew he was in the will of God. He was willing to serve the Lord—regardless of loneliness, sorrow, disappointments, suffering, and humiliation. Paul took seriously the Lord's words, *"If any man will come after me, let him deny himself, and take up his cross daily, and follow me"* (Luke 9:23). Bearing a cross does not necessarily mean being a martyr. The cross Jesus spoke about is often one of daily denying ourselves of pleasures, privileges, and even necessities to help others come to know Him—choosing to do His will at any cost.

"For even hereunto were ye called: because Christ also suffered for us, leaving us an example, that ye should follow his steps" (1 Pet. 2:21).

Thought for Today: Our willingness to die daily to self-interests will determine how much we really want to follow in the Master's footsteps.

November 17: Read Acts 23–25

Verse for Today: *"But this I confess unto thee, that after the way which they call heresy, so worship I the God of my fathers, believing all things which are written in the law and in the prophets"* (Acts 24:14).

Paul was tried before three great rulers. As he faithfully testified how Jesus fulfilled all the Scriptures as Messiah, each of his judges had a different reaction. Felix, the governor, trembled. Festus seemed unconcerned. And, for whatever King Agrippa may have meant, he said, *"Almost thou persuadest me to be a Christian"* (Acts 26:28).

But as far as we know, none of them received Christ as Lord and Savior. Little did they realize that it was not Paul who was on trial, but they themselves were on trial before the court of heaven. They were being given a chance to accept or reject the Savior.

It is often said that it doesn't make any difference what a person believes as long as one is sincere. But what a lie and deception that statement is! What a person believes about the Lord has eternal significance.

God has provided only one way for salvation, and it is through the death of His Son on the cross of Calvary: *"Neither is there salvation in any other"* (Acts 4:12). The wrath of God remains on all who refuse to believe that Jesus died for their sins (John 3:36).

Each person must decide either to receive Christ as Lord and Savior, or to reject Him and be eternally lost. The King of kings cannot be ignored.

"Jesus saith unto him, I am the way, the truth, and the life: no man cometh unto the Father, but by me" (John 14:6).

Thought for Today: Christ gave His all for us; let's allow Him to live His life through us.

November 18: Read Acts 26–28

Verses for Today: *"Festus said with a loud voice, Paul, thou art beside thyself; much learning doth make thee mad. . . . Then Agrippa said unto Paul, Almost thou persuadest me to be a Christian"* (Acts 26:24, 28).

When Saul (Paul) of Tarsus threatened believers and had them arrested, his friends thought he was wise. But when Paul confessed his faith in Jesus—the risen Savior—Festus, the Roman governor of Judea, told him he had lost his mind.

Paul's famous and powerful listeners, Felix, Festus, and King Agrippa, all refused Paul's message, but, in reality, they were refusing the Word of Almighty God.

Regardless of whom Paul was speaking to, he faithfully witnessed for Christ, declaring that Jesus is the Messiah who died to save sinners. When King Agrippa heard Paul's message, he could not deny anything Paul had said, but he was not persuaded to become a Christian. His heart was touched and his mind enlightened, but he put off accepting Jesus as Savior and Lord. Whether or not King Agrippa's words were spoken sarcastically, as some people think, is not important; the outcome is still the same—he rejected Christ.

Like King Agrippa and Felix, the former governor to whom Paul was first taken (Acts 23:24—24:27), countless thousands of people have been "almost" persuaded to accept Jesus as their Savior, yet they waited for a more "convenient time" to turn from their sins. Oh, how many have entered a Christless eternity because they hesitated to accept Christ as Savior. They waited until it was too late!

"Behold, now is the accepted time; behold, now is the day of salvation" (2 Cor. 6:2).

Thought for Today: There is no guarantee that you can accept Christ tomorrow—or that you will even have a tomorrow.

 # ROMANS

Twenty-one of the New Testament's twenty-seven books are letters (or epistles) written from the apostles to churches or individuals. At least thirteen of these letters were penned by the apostle Paul. These New Testament letters are similar to modern letters with a greeting, an opening, a body, and a closing.

These letters expound on Jesus's teaching and ministry. They give specific examples of how to apply biblical truth in various circumstances; advise and rebuke; give encouragement and warnings; correct false teachings; and provide hope and promises.

In the book of Romans (the first epistle), salvation is progressively explained, chapter by chapter. A key verse states: *"The gospel . . . is the power of God unto salvation to every one that believeth"* (Rom. 1:16).

Chapters 1–11 reveal the good news of the gospel and show how Jesus reconciles people to God, how the Spirit makes us children of God, and how our salvation glorifies God. The first three chapters particularly establish the truth that all mankind has sinned. Not one person is without sin (Rom. 3:9-10). Neither can someone try to "earn" salvation, for the Word of God declares, *"Therefore by the deeds of the law there shall no flesh be justified in his sight: for by the law is the knowledge of sin"* (Rom. 3:20).

However, our righteous and merciful God has provided a way for any person to be forgiven of all sins—a plan that was fulfilled through the sacrificial death and resurrection of Jesus, the perfect Son of God. To be saved, a person must believe the Word of God and personally receive Jesus Christ as Lord and Savior. Then, His indwelling Holy Spirit enables the Christian to know and live according to the will of God.

Chapters 12–16 present examples of how to live in response to the gospel. A proper attitude of thankfulness will enable us to be transformed and serve the Lord (Rom. 12:1-2). We are to grow in love, be kind to others, and help weaker Christians (Rom. 14). We are to make every effort to maintain harmony with a Christlike spirit (Rom. 15:1-13). As we seek to know our Lord's righteousness, and grow in His likeness, He will be revealed to others through us.

November 19: Read Romans 1–3

Verses for Today: *"For the wrath of God is revealed from heaven against all ungodliness and unrighteousness of men, who hold the truth in unrighteousness. . . . who changed the truth of God into a lie, and worshipped and served the creature more than the Creator. . . . For this cause God gave them up unto vile affections"* (Rom. 1:18, 25-26).

The Lord's judgment is on all sin. No one measures up to God's righteous standards. All of us fall short and struggle in different areas of weakness. The list of sins is long: anger, unforgiveness, resentment, pride, greed, discontentedness, ungratefulness, lustful thoughts, sexual sins, gluttony, laziness, fear, dishonoring parents and authority, lying, coarse talking, stirring up conflict, and more (Ex. 20:2-17; Deut. 5:6-21; Prov. 6:16-19; Eph. 5:1-20).

The judgment of God is on sexual sins, too. The sexual perversion that is accepted today is the same sin that brought God's judgment upon the cities of Sodom and Gomorrah during the time of Abraham and Lot. Because the people of Sodom and Gomorrah participated in perverted sex orgies and the sin of sodomy (homosexuality), God sent fire from heaven and destroyed them (Gen. 19; Jude 1:7).

Our culture tries to claim that individuals should be free to make their own choices and that people of different sexual orientation are "different," or unable to help the way they are. God calls these sexual sins perversion, meaning a corruption of His original plan and command. God created male and female (Gen. 5:2; Matt. 19:4; Mark 10:6), and ordained marriage for a man and a woman. Immoral passions are an expression of our fallen nature, which rejects God and His Word and, instead, determines to fulfill its own desires and lusts of the flesh. When we reject God's plans, we reject God.

Because of God's design and plan, He calls homosexuality a perversion (corruption), shameful, and vile. Scripture even spells it out—men lusting for men, and women lusting for women (Rom. 1:18-32). *Even the women turned against God's natural plan for them and indulged in sex acts with one another. In the same manner, the men gave up natural sexual relations with women and were swept into lustful passion for one another. They did shameful things and, as a result, they brought upon themselves the inevitable punishment of their own perverseness* (Rom. 1:26-27).

There can be no victory over any sin until we understand that it is rebellion against God, our Creator. A day is coming when we will stand before Him and account for our lives, thoughts, words, and actions (Rom. 14:12).

Without God's mercy and salvation, we are all without hope. We all need the Lord and His forgiveness and grace. Those who are willing can be transformed with new life. With His help and grace, we can relinquish sin and be transformed. Through Christ, we can be delivered from sin, judgment, and death, and receive salvation, His Spirit, healing, and spiritual blessings!

"And they that are Christ's have crucified the flesh with the affections and lusts" (Gal. 5:24).

Thought for Today: God's concern has always been that man turn from sin and enjoy His salvation and blessings.

November 20: **Read Romans 4–7**

Verses for Today: *"Likewise reckon ye also yourselves to be dead indeed unto sin. . . . Yield yourselves unto God . . . as instruments of righteousness unto God"* (Rom. 6:11, 13).

As children of God, we are responsible to *"reckon"*—to accept as a fact—that sin is no longer our master and that we are *"dead indeed"* to the old life of sin. This doesn't mean we are not *able* to sin, but that we are able *not* to sin.

God sees the believer as no longer in Adam, but in Christ—the Head of a new creation. *When anyone is in union with Christ, he is a new being* (2 Cor. 5:17). But to *enjoy* this wonderful relationship with Christ, we must yield our will to the indwelling Holy Spirit.

Defeat is always the result of unbelief—a failure to trust in God's Word and act on the fact that the Holy Spirit in us is greater than the power of Satan who seeks to destroy us (1 John 4:4).

God has placed the responsibility on us to yield our lives to Him *to be used for righteous purposes.* We have been brought from death to life, and given His Spirit. Therefore, we are not to trust in our own strength, but in the power of the indwelling Spirit. His life in us makes the difference. The decision is ours!

Our old self has died with Jesus on His cross, so that the power of the sinful nature might be destroyed; therefore, we should no longer be the slaves of sin (Rom. 6:6).

Thought for Today: When we see ourselves for what we really are, we will bow in grateful humility for God's great love to us.

November 21: Read Romans 8–10

Verses for Today: *"That the righteousness of the law might be fulfilled in us, who walk not after the flesh, but after the Spirit. . . . Because the carnal mind is enmity against God"* (Rom. 8:4, 7).

Because of the sin of Adam and Eve in the garden of Eden, every person has inherited a sinful nature and is in rebellion against God (Rom. 5:12-19). But when we receive Christ as personal Savior, we are reconciled to God. We receive the nature and Spirit of God and a desire to live for Him. Because of this, believers must not live any longer according to their old way of life (Rom. 6:4-14).

Someone may imitate a true Christian in a number of ways, such as joining a church, attending worship services, giving generously, or even attempting to keep the Ten Commandments, as the rich young ruler did (Matt. 19:16-22; Luke 18:18-23). But until Christ becomes one's personal Savior, he is still unsaved and at *"enmity against God."*

Scripture teaches that genuine faith in Jesus and repentance are inseparably linked. Repentance means we willingly desire to turn from our sins and we turn to God (Prov. 28:13; 1 John 1:9). Repentance has a prominent place in the teachings of Jesus (Matt. 11:20-21; 12:41; Mark 1:15; Luke 5:32; 10:13; 11:32; 13:3, 5; 15:7, 10; 16:30; 17:3-4; 24:47). Paul summarized this truth by saying: *"Testifying both to the Jews, and also to the Greeks, repentance toward God, and faith toward our Lord Jesus Christ"* (Acts 20:21).

Because sin destroys mankind's relationship to God, sin must be confessed and forsaken. There can be no "secret" sins. God continues working in a believer's heart to bring about remorse, confession, and transformation. Through the convicting and illuminating power of the Holy Spirit, we are led to see our transgressions against the Lord and given a desire to walk with Him in new life.

"Or despisest thou the riches of his goodness and forbearance and longsuffering; not knowing that the goodness of God leadeth thee to repentance?" (Rom. 2:4).

Thought for Today: We need God's illuminating truth, Christ's grace, and the power of the Holy Spirit for salvation *and* transformation.

November 22: Read Romans 11–13

Verse for Today: *"I beseech you therefore, brethren, by the mercies of God, that ye present your bodies a living sacrifice, holy, acceptable unto God, which is your reasonable service"* (Rom. 12:1).

The book of Romans describes the guilty condition of man without Christ—completely corrupt and deserving of eternal death. Then it reveals God's wonderful and perfect salvation through the precious blood of Jesus and His finished work on the cross.

Christianity is a new life—a new beginning. As Jesus lives in and through us, He transforms our lives to be like His.

Because of what Jesus has done for us, it is only "reasonable" that we present our bodies to Him—to accomplish His perfect will. In addition, we should not only strive to do the right things, but our inner desire should be to please Him.

Often, Christians fail to live victoriously, not realizing that His Sprit—the indwelling Living Word—is the source of all spiritual power. As we prayerfully read the Bible with a desire to do His will, His Word becomes our spiritual food—our very life. Just as physical food is assimilated into our bodies to provide physical strength, so the indwelling Spirit strengthens our spiritual lives through His Word. Then, and only then, can we truly accomplish His purposes.

"And be not conformed to this world: but be ye transformed by the renewing of your mind, that ye may prove what is that good, and acceptable, and perfect, will of God" (Rom. 12:2).

Thought for Today: Are we seeking to know and do God's will and to please Him?

November 23: Read Romans 14–16

Verses for Today: *"We then that are strong ought to bear the infirmities of the weak, and not to please ourselves. Let every one of us please his neighbour for his good to edification. For even Christ pleased not himself"* (Rom. 15:1-3).

Even Christ, the Son of God, *"pleased not himself."* It was for the sake of others that He came into the world, lived, prayed, wept, and died, and it is for others that He will come again. How opposite this is to the self-centered philosophy of the world: "Every man for himself!"

Those who allow Jesus to be Lord of their lives will show concern for others, including a weak brother or sister in Christ, and the brokenhearted and fallen.

We are to be a blessing by listening and loving; meeting the needs of others; and praying with those who need comfort and encouragement.

Our desire should be to live for the glory of God and to see souls saved and strengthened with God's Word. We should thank and praise the Lord for the privilege of bearing the burdens of others and helping them learn more about Jesus and His will for their lives!

"Now the God of patience and consolation grant you to be likeminded one toward another according to Christ Jesus: That ye may with one mind and one mouth glorify God, even the Father of our Lord Jesus Christ. Wherefore receive ye one another, as Christ also received us to the glory of God" (Rom. 15:5-7).

Thought for Today: When we are more concerned about giving, rather than getting, we bless others, and receive God's blessings.

 # 1 AND 2 CORINTHIANS

Corinth, the capital of the Roman province of Achaia, was a bustling seaport community, and one of the most prominent cities in Greece, with an estimated population of at least four hundred thousand. Because of its location and size, Corinth's culture was greatly influenced by Greeks, Romans, and Jews, and the pursuit of beauty, pleasure, and immorality.

During one of his extensive missionary journeys, the apostle Paul lived for more than a year and a half in Corinth, where he established a church with the help of Priscilla and Aquila, Silas, and Timothy. A believer named Apollos became a key church leader. (These events are recounted in Acts 18:1-28 and 1 Corinthians 3:5-6.) When Paul left Corinth for additional missionary work, he wrote a number of letters to the church. These books are two of Paul's letters.

Paul wrote **1 Corinthians** to address problems among the members. The church was divided (1 Cor. 1:10–4:21), and some of its members were involved in sins that greatly hindered the spiritual life of the church (1 Cor. 5:1-13). Paul's instruction and encouragement to the believers provided needed guidance for godly living then, as well as today. This letter includes the finest definition of love ever written (1 Cor. chapter 13), and the best explanation of the resurrection of Christ, as well as the believer (1 Cor. chapter 15).

Right after Paul wrote 1 Corinthians, he almost lost his life during the great riot at Ephesus (Acts 19). Paul left Ephesus and went to Macedonia, with plans to return to Corinth. At Macedonia, in the midst of many anxieties and sufferings, he met with Titus, who was returning from Corinth with word that Paul's letter to the Corinthian church had accomplished much good. Paul gave Titus another letter to the Corinthian church and indicated that he himself planned to visit Corinth again soon.

The major theme of the book of **2 Corinthians** is the ministry of reconciliation. Paul commended the church for correcting its moral problems and stressed the necessity of resolving division within the church. He stressed that it is a Christian's responsibility to make every effort to bring about peaceable solutions to family problems and conflicts with others. He instructed the believers about the importance of sharing one's resources with the needy, and encouraged them to contribute a generous offering for the church in Jerusalem.

November 24: Read 1 Corinthians 1–4

Verses for Today: *"Who then is Paul, and who is Apollos, but ministers by whom ye believed, even as the Lord gave to every man? I have planted, Apollos watered; but God gave the increase. . . . Now he that planteth and he that watereth are one"* (1 Cor. 3:5-6, 8).

The church at Corinth was divided about who was the most important spiritual leader. Some preferred Paul; others favored Apollos or Peter; still others said, "I am of Christ" (1 Cor. 1:12).

Paul, Apollos, and Peter were only servants of Jesus, chosen by God, who enabled them to serve His people—no one man possessing all knowledge and abilities. Therefore, all praise is to be given to God, the Giver of all gifts, because He *sets the members every one of them in the body, as it pleases Him* (1 Cor. 12:18).

A Christian should consider himself neither more nor less important than others when it comes to gifts or abilities, which God bestows. It takes every Christian to make up the body of Christ. A body has many parts, with different functions, but each part and each function are necessary for the strength and usefulness of the whole. *"What hast thou that thou didst not receive? now if thou didst receive it, why dost thou glory, as if thou hadst not received it?"* (1 Cor. 4:7).

The true worth of any church or gospel ministry is dependent upon God. Apart from His blessing, the most earnest and well-performed service will be ineffective and fruitless.

Each believer has been given a spiritual gift, which is the manifestation [expression and proof] of the Holy Spirit for the common good (1 Cor. 12:7; 1 Pet. 4:10).

Thought for Today: We should not boast—or complain—about the gifts or abilities that God has bestowed on us or on others. Let us simply enjoy serving our Lord together.

November 25: Read 1 Corinthians 5–9

Verses for Today: *"Be not deceived: neither fornicators, nor idolaters, nor adulterers, nor effeminate, nor abusers of themselves with mankind . . . shall inherit the kingdom of God"* (1 Cor. 6:9-10).

In our culture of individual choice, it is difficult to believe that the Lord will judge sexual sins. However, His Word remains unchanged. The rejection of God's moral standards is what brings about the moral chaos of our day.

The Word of God teaches that the wicked—including adulterers and fornicators—will not *"inherit the kingdom of God."* Many times in Scripture, we are warned about God's judgment upon fornication, adultery, and other sexual sins.[22] The Ten Commandments make it unmistakably clear that *"thou shalt not commit adultery"* (Ex. 20:14).

Jesus warned, in His Sermon on the Mount, that sexual sins start with the eyes and the heart: *Those who look on another with lust commit adultery with that person in their hearts* (Matt. 5:28). One thing is absolutely sure—God's judgment upon sexual sins remains unchanged. Therefore, it is of utmost importance that our conduct concerning sex be based on the inspired, infallible, written Word of God.

God is a God of justice, love, mercy, help, and might. When we recognize our sins, and confess them, He forgives us. As we seek His assistance, He enables us to overcome them and transforms us. Truly, we need His power, grace, and help. Through His Word and Spirit, He enables us to live a victorious and God-honoring life.

"If we confess our sins, he is faithful and just to forgive us our sins, and to cleanse us from all unrighteousness" (1 John 1:9).

Thought for Today: To reject the Bible as the standard for one's life and guidance is to turn away from God Himself.

November 26: Read 1 Corinthians 10–13

Verse for Today: *"And now abideth faith, hope, charity, these three; but the greatest of these is charity"* (1 Cor. 13:13).

---

22 Warnings against sexual sin include Ex. 20:14,17; Lev. 18:20; 20:10-12; 21:9; Deut. 22:13-21; Matt. 5:32; 19:9; Mark 10:11-12; John 8:3-5; Rom. 7:2-3; 13:14; 1 Cor. 5:9-11; 6:9–7:17, 39; Eph. 5:3-6; Col. 3:5-6; 1 Thess. 4:3-7; 1 Tim. 1:9-10; 2 Tim. 2:22; Heb. 13:4; 1 Pet. 2:11; Rev. 21:8; 22:15.

The biblical meaning of the word *charity* is *"love in action."* It is true affection for God, as well as others. This love is the result of a spiritual new birth— *"We know that we have passed from death unto life, because we love the brethren"* (1 John 3:14).

Since God is love, the Bible states that one who hates his brother is as a murderer, in whom eternal life is not found (1 John 4:20). Consequently, love must be characteristic of a Christian. Our love for others is more important to the Lord than are all our talents, knowledge, service, or sacrificial giving (1 Cor. 13:1-3).

Scripture reveals much to us about love, and we are even given a picture of its beauty:

Love does not envy the rich or covet their possessions. It is free from suspicion and evil imagination. Love does not boast or seek recognition. Love does not insist on its own rights; it prompts us to promote the welfare of others (1 Cor. 13). *It forgives the inconsiderate actions of others—even if the offense is repeated seven times in a day* (Luke 17:4). *Love will return good for evil as we remember our indebtedness to God for His love toward us* (1 Cor. 13; Rom. 5:8; 12:20-21).

Don't just say you love someone, but show it by your actions (1 John 3:18). *"By this shall all men know that ye are my disciples, if ye have love one to another"* (John 13:35).

Thought for Today: When you love the Lord with all your heart, love for others will be a natural overflow.

November 27: Read 1 Corinthians 14–16

Verses for Today: *"In a moment, in the twinkling of an eye, at the last trump: for the trumpet shall sound, and the dead shall be raised incorruptible, and we shall be changed. . . . Thanks be to God, which giveth us the victory through our Lord Jesus Christ"* (1 Cor. 15:52, 57).

It is a triumphant fact that Christ rose from the dead! This gives us assurance of the day when *"all that are in the graves shall hear his voice, and shall come forth; they that have done good, unto the resurrection of life; and they that have done evil, unto the resurrection of damnation"* (John 5:28-29).

This victory over death is only for those who believe in, and have received, Jesus as their Lord and Savior. *The one who does not believe in Christ is condemned, but one who does believe in Christ, as the only begotten Son of God, is not condemned* (John 3:18).

The supreme purpose for living is to prepare us for eternity. For the Christian, physical death is a transition into the actual presence of Christ.

"Then said they unto him, What shall we do, that we might work the works of God? Jesus answered and said unto them, This is the work of God, that ye believe on him whom he hath sent" (John 6:28-29).

Thought for Today: Because Christ died and rose again, we can live with Him through eternity. What precious assurance!

November 28: Read 2 Corinthians 1–4

Verse for Today: *"Who comforteth us in all our tribulation, that we may be able to comfort them which are in any trouble, by the comfort wherewith we ourselves are comforted of God"* (2 Cor. 1:4).

Trials and troubles, in one form or another, are a necessary part of every Christian's journey and spiritual growth (Acts 14:22; 1 Pet. 1:6-7; 4:12-13). Christ was always conscious of His purpose for coming to earth—to die on the cross to pay the penalty for the sins of the world. Just as it was necessary for Him to die, we, too, must be willing partakers of His sufferings.

On the basis of forgiveness of sins, Jesus imparts to us His very life, which sustains us in suffering. With faith and prayer, we can bear all suffering and every trial with confident peace that God has privileged us with the opportunity to manifest the characteristics of the resurrected Christ (2 Cor. 4:10).

We can face trials and suffering with the assurance that our Lord has never made a mistake and that He lovingly cares for His people. God provides a comfort that only He can give. This consolation of the Holy Spirit has a twofold effect: our burdens are lifted, and we become qualified to comfort others *"by the comfort wherewith we ourselves are comforted of God."*

"But rejoice, inasmuch as ye are partakers of Christ's sufferings; that, when his glory shall be revealed, ye may be glad also with exceeding joy" (1 Pet. 4:13).

Thought for Today: God's comfort to us enables us to know Him more intimately and to comfort others.

November 29: Read 2 Corinthians 5–8

Verses for Today: *"For the love of Christ constraineth us. . . . God was in Christ, reconciling the world unto himself, not imputing their trespasses unto them; and hath committed unto us the word of reconciliation"* (2 Cor. 5:14, 19).

Reconciliation began with God, who so loved the world *"that he gave his only begotten Son,"* so that sinners could be restored to fellowship with Him (John 3:16).

When a person becomes a Christian, he receives a spiritual nature—God's divine nature. This new nature changes our attitudes from self-interest and hostility toward God and others, especially when things do not go our way, to one of love for others and a desire to please the Lord. Scripture declares: *If we love one another, God lives within us, and His love is made perfect in us* (1 John 4:12).

The ministry of reconciliation is a sacred trust that both *"constraineth us"* and urges us to serve Christ—because of His great love for us. The love of Jesus should so control our lives that our greatest desire will be to accomplish His will. Every decision made in life should be based on what would please Him most.

As we yield to His constraining power, we will have a desire to share the wonderful news of His marvelous love with others, so they, too, can be reconciled to God.

Loving God means doing what He directs us to do (1 John 5:3).

Thought for Today: It is in God that we have worth, and by His grace we can accomplish tasks of eternal value.

November 30: Read 2 Corinthians 9–13

Verses for Today: *"But this I say, He which soweth sparingly shall reap also sparingly; and he which soweth bountifully shall reap also bountifully. Every man according as he purposeth in his heart, so let him give; not grudgingly, or of necessity: for God loveth a cheerful giver"* (2 Cor. 9:6-7).

Scripture commands us to be faithful stewards of all that God has given us. We are promised blessings when we are faithful in our stewardship responsibilities, and warned of the consequences when we shirk our duty (Prov. 3:9-10; Mal. 3:8-12). Christ, too, instructed us to be dependable stewards (Matt. 6:14; Luke 12:42-46).

Stewardship is a part of everyday life with which most of us are familiar. Banks and investment companies are entrusted with money that belongs to other people. Trustees are appointed to take care of the estates of others.

Scripture declares that we are to be good managers of all God's resources. In addition, He has bestowed on everyone various possessions (money, property, belongings, and talents) that we should use wisely for Him. Our time, too, is a resource. Because all that we possess belongs to the Lord, we are to use what we can to help His church and kingdom grow.

Our giving is able to make a difference of eternal life for someone. Have you ever thought about what it means for a person to die without having been saved? The next-door neighbor? A friend? Someone in your own home who is lost and on the way to hell? Surely each person deserves the right to hear, at least once, that *"Christ Jesus came into the world to save sinners"* (1 Tim. 1:15).

We must give monetarily *and* be willing to share *God's good news* with those around us. Assuming that someone else will tell them about Jesus does not relieve us of our privilege and responsibility. God will bless every effort we make to help others know Him, grow in Him, and read His Word.

The Lord gave Himself as an example of the principle of Christian giving: *"Though he was rich, yet for your sakes he became poor, that ye through his poverty might be rich"* (2 Cor. 8:9). We are to give generously and joyfully, not grudgingly or merely from a sense of duty because *"God loveth a cheerful giver."* As we give, we will discover more joy and great blessings.

"It is more blessed to give than to receive" (Acts 20:35).

Thought for Today: Our willingness to give reveals the condition of our hearts.

December

 GALATIANS

The book of Galatians was written to expose the difference between true Christianity and being religious. Doing good works—no matter how good they are—can never make a person right with God (or a Christian).

Galatians reaffirms that we cannot be saved apart from Jesus Christ—even if we were able to keep every commandment—*"for by the works of the law shall no flesh be justified"* (Gal. 2:16). In fact, *all who rely on observing the law are under a curse because it is written that everyone who does not continue to do everything written in the book of the law is cursed* (Gal. 3:10).

It is because of God's great love for us that He has provided a way of salvation. Galatians declares that Jesus has *redeemed us from the curse of the law by taking the curse on Himself* (Gal. 3:13). He is the perfect Son of God, who never once sinned (2 Cor. 5:21); therefore, He is able to take our place as the sinner's substitute. Because no one but Christ can say that his obedience for a lifetime has been perfect, we cannot be saved apart from Him. *Our Lord Jesus Christ gave Himself for our sins that He might deliver us from this present evil world* (Gal. 1:3-4).

Galatians points out that just as Abraham was declared righteous and inherited God's promises by believing God and His promises, those who believe in Christ as their Savior are declared righteous and given a new relationship with God (Gal. 3:6-9).

Not only are we forgiven, but God gives us His indwelling Spirit, who then enables and empowers us to follow His will, keep His commandments, and do good works. As we grow in knowing Him and following Him, we grow in the *fruit of His Spirit—love, joy, peace, patience, kindness, goodness, faithfulness, gentleness, and self-control* (Gal. 5:22-23).

The book of Galatians additionally helps us understand and enjoy the freedom and grace we have in Christ, and to not abuse these gifts. *It is for freedom that Jesus set us free and liberated us; therefore, we are to stand firm in freedom and not let ourselves be subjected to any yoke of slavery* (Gal. 5:1). We are warned not to consider our freedom and grace as a license to sin (Rom. 6).[23] Rather, we are to keep in step with the Spirit, and not the flesh (Gal. 5:13-25; 6:7-8).

Salvation, grace, and freedom—what marvelous gifts God has given us!

December 1: Read Galatians 1–3

Verses for Today: *"Grace be to you and peace from God the Father, and from our Lord Jesus Christ, Who gave himself for our sins, that he might deliver us from this present evil world"* (Gal. 1:3-4).

Although God is a loving God, He is also a holy God. Perfect justice, as well as the law, demands that *all who sin will die* (Ezek. 18:20). Through the sin of Adam and Eve in the garden of Eden, every person has inherited a sinful nature that separates us from God, the Source of life (Isa. 59:2; Rom. 5:12).

But all who believe in Jesus, the Son of God, and receive Him as their Savior, are no longer spiritually dead in their trespasses and sins. We are forgiven and given a new life in Him (John 3:36; Eph. 2:4-7; Col. 2:13).

Not only has *Christ redeemed us from the curse of the law by taking the curse on Himself* (Gal. 3:13), but through Him we are abundantly blessed (Psalm 103:1-6; Eph. 1). Surely we deserve to give Him our lives and serve Him gladly!

The apostle John said it this way: *"Behold, what manner of love the Father hath bestowed upon us, that we should be called the sons of God"* (1 John 3:1).

Thought for Today: How can we help but love Him, who gave Himself for us?

December 2: Read Galatians 4–6

Verses for Today: *"For all the law is fulfilled in one word, even in this; Thou shalt love thy neighbour as thyself. But if ye bite and devour one another, take heed that ye be not consumed one of another"* (Gal. 5:14-15).

---

23 A few other Scriptures regarding our freedom and grace include Rom. 8:1; 2 Cor. 3:17; Gal. 5:13-14; 1 Pet. 2:16.

Love should be the guiding principle for every Christian in every decision. Christians are commanded to love all people.

We are especially to have harmonious love for other Christians (John 13:35) because we are all *members one of another, united together in the body of Christ* (Eph. 4:25). We are as closely knit together with one another as our hands and feet are to our physical bodies. Christ is the Head of this body, and *"we are members of his body"* (Eph. 5:30). No part can be severed from the body without hindering the whole because all the parts are dependent on one another.

We dare not ignore our responsibility to love other Christians *with all our hearts* (1 Pet. 1:22)—even those we feel do not deserve our love. We are to know and experience the love of Christ, express His love to others, and strive to overcome divisions and bitterness. As we endeavor to do these things, we maintain the unity of the Spirit (Eph. 4:1-6) and a right relationship with Christ.

God hates divisions. Whether we are right or have been offended is of little consequence; we are responsible to God for making every attempt to bring the weaker or offended brother or sister back into fellowship. God has left no room for exceptions—not even one.

If someone is caught in any kind of wrongdoing, those of you who are spiritual should make every effort to restore that person to a right relationship with Christ in a spirit of gentleness (Gal. 6:1).

Thought for Today: Perhaps the failure we perceive in another individual's life is a reflection of unseen sin in our own hearts.

 # EPHESIANS

The book of Ephesians reveals the blessings and resources that are available to us *"in Christ."* The phrase *"in Christ"* appears thirty-five times in Ephesians. Although Paul wrote this letter to the Ephesians while he was in prison, he begins by saying: *"Blessed be the God and Father of our Lord Jesus Christ, who hath blessed us with all spiritual blessings in heavenly places in Christ"* (Eph. 1:3).

No matter our circumstances, we are to grow in the blessings we have in Jesus. Ephesians helps us understand the "exceeding greatness" of God's spiritual power and wisdom, which is a part of every Christian's inheritance. This same power that raised Jesus from the dead is available to us.

Chapters 1–3 list many of our heavenly possessions, and our heavenly position, as well. As believers, we are adopted sons and daughters of God. We are citizens of heaven with associated rights, privileges, and responsibilities.

Chapters 4–6 give instructions for living a victorious Christian life, including the weapons that we are to use in spiritual battles.

Ephesians instructs us in numerous places that believers are spiritually united into one body as members together of God's church, and Christ is the Head (Eph. 2:16; 5:23). We are to strive to *"keep the unity of the Spirit in the bond of peace"* (Eph. 4:3).

Christians are empowered by God's Word, through the indwelling Spirit, to be triumphant in each of the four major areas of life:

(1) *in the church*, to maintain unity and help one another (Eph. 1:22-23; 4:13, 16, 32);

(2) *in society*, to practice Christian principles (Eph. 4:22-5:21);

(3) *in the home*, to manifest love and truth (Eph. 5:22-6:4); and

(4) *in the world*, to resist Satan and the powers of darkness (Eph. 6:10-18).

Ephesians is a book of practical Christian living, giving guidance for believers. We not only have the promise of a home in heaven, but we also have a purpose for living—to glorify the Lord and accomplish His purposes for our lives.

December 3: Read Ephesians 1–3

Verse for Today: *"For through him we both have access by one Spirit unto the Father"* (Eph. 2:18).

In Old Testament times, God provided a way, through the high priest, for His people to offer prayer to Him. But only the high priest was allowed to enter into the presence of God in the holy of holies and offer prayer on behalf of the worshipers. He could only do this once a year after much preparation and many sacrifices. The gentiles, before Christ, were excluded from this covenant relationship with God.

But now, through Jesus, salvation and access to God are available to all. When we receive Jesus, we are able to come and freely partake of God's blessings. Jews and gentiles, rich and poor, powerful and lowly, all are invited into a relationship with God. Jews and gentiles alike who have received Christ as Lord and Savior are united in *"one Spirit"* into the family of God.

Because Christ has given us access to God, *we are to come freely and boldly to God in prayer for help at any time* (Heb. 4:16)! In addition to this, Jesus is praying for us! Scripture tells us that *He saves to the uttermost those that come unto God by him, [because] He ever liveth to make intercession for them* (Heb. 7:25). Surely, our blessings overflow!

Satan, though, does not want us to pray and does all he can to keep us from this important task. He strives to make us think we are too busy to pray, and he tries to divert our attention from praying—often just as we start to pray—by interrupting us or reminding us of something we need to do.

We dare not let Satan get the victory in our prayer life. Failure to pray is not merely negligence; it is also sin (1 Sam. 12:23). Prayer is a sacred privilege, a great responsibility, and a wonderful blessing.

"Let us therefore come boldly unto the throne of grace, that we may obtain mercy, and find grace to help in time of need" (Heb. 4:16).

Thought for Today: No one can live for God and make a difference against evil apart from prayer.

December 4: Read Ephesians 4–6

Verses for Today: *"Speaking to yourselves in psalms and hymns and spiritual songs, singing and making melody in your heart to the Lord. . . . submitting yourselves one to another in the fear of God"* (Eph. 5:19, 21).

Because God has made His love known through Jesus Christ, every Christian is to be a representative of His love. In addition, He has given us His indwelling Holy Spirit (Rom. 5:5). As members of our Lord's family, we must reflect His love.

Scripture commands us, *"Beloved, let us love one another: for love is of God; and every one that loveth is born of God, and knoweth God"* (1 John 4:7). Our submission to God will be manifested through our submission *"one to another in the fear of God."*

Since God's love is a healing and unifying power, may we do all that we can to know and experience God's love in greater measure. Let us study His Word, ponder this magnificent truth, and pray to comprehend how much He loves us and forgives us. May we do this not just for ourselves, but that we might love the Lord and others more. The more we recognize and appreciate God's personal kindness and grace for us, the more we will desire to cooperate with Him and with other Christians to win a lost world to Jesus.

"And be ye kind one to another, tenderhearted, forgiving one another, even as God for Christ's sake hath forgiven you" (Eph. 4:32).

Thought for Today: As members of God's family, we are to be joyful and loving!

 ## PHILIPPIANS

When Paul wrote this short letter filled with joy and thankfulness, he was in prison enduring bitter hardships—not because he had committed any crime, but because of his love and loyalty to Christ (Phil. 1:7, 12-16). Whatever the outcome, he knew that his imprisonment encouraged others to be faithful (Phil. 1:14), and it gave him opportunities to share the good news with more people. Paul was extremely bold in sharing the gospel with the guards and those around him. It is no surprise to read that there were Christians even in the emperor's palace (Phil. 4:22).

The apostle Paul viewed every circumstance in his life with the confidence that he belonged to Jesus and was in God's care. Although Paul had been imprisoned for preaching the gospel, he never once mentioned that he was a prisoner of the Roman government; he was a prisoner of Jesus Christ (Eph. 3:1; 4:1; 2 Tim. 1:8; Philem. 1:1, 9).

A spirit of joy permeates the entire book of Philippians because of Christ, who was uppermost in Paul's mind. Christ is mentioned about thirty-eight times in the four chapters of this book, and versions of *"joy"* and *"rejoice"* are shared about seventeen times.

We, too, can have peace and joy in Jesus regardless of our external circumstances. When He is the focus and source of our lives, we can experience contentment and rejoice in every situation. A key thought of Philippians is *"rejoice in the Lord always: and again I say, Rejoice"* (Phil. 4:4).

December 5: Read Philippians 1–4

Verses for Today: *"For it is God which worketh in you both to will and to do of his good pleasure. Do all things without murmurings and disputings"* (Phil. 2:13-14).

Philippians is a triumphant letter from the apostle Paul to the Christians living in Philippi. It is filled with *joy* and *rejoicing,* which are mentioned about seventeen times in these four chapters.

Why all the rejoicing? Did Paul receive an award or special recognition? Were great crowds gathering to hear him preach? No! For quite some time, Paul had been in prison for preaching the gospel. But he praised the Lord because something far more precious than material possessions controlled him—he knew that God was in control and that his present circumstances were for God's great purposes and *"good pleasure."*

It is through difficult experiences that the Christian can exercise faith in God and find pleasure in what pleases Him. This ability, peace, and power come from His Spirit in us, His Word, and prayer (Eph. 3:20; 1 Thess. 2:13). God is working *in* us, just as much as He is working *through* us.

To express discontentment in adverse situations is an insult to our Lord's judgment, since it questions His love, wisdom, promises, and good purposes. Oh, what satisfaction is derived from trusting the Lord in all circumstances—disappointments or delights—knowing that God makes all things work together for good in accomplishing His will (Rom. 8:28-29).

Now there are varieties of gifts, but the same Spirit....And there are varieties of effects, but it is the same God who achieves His purposes through them all (1 Cor. 12:4, 6).

Thought for Today: Christ wants us to be an expression of Himself to those around us.

 # COLOSSIANS

A key thought in the book of Colossians is *that in all things, Christ is to have the preeminence* (Col. 1:18). Colossians declares Jesus's power, glory, and supremacy with a beautiful description:

> *Jesus, God's Son, is the image of the invisible God, the firstborn over all creation. In Him, all things were created: things in heaven and on earth, visible and invisible, including thrones, powers, rulers, and authorities. All things have been created through Him and for Him. He is before all things, and in Him all things hold together. He is the Head of the body, the church; He is the beginning and the firstborn from among the dead, so that in everything He might have the supremacy. God was pleased to have all His fullness dwell in Him, and through Him to reconcile to Himself all things, whether things on earth or things in heaven—by making peace through His blood shed on the cross* (Col. 1:15-20).

Colossians declares that in Christ we have life (in its fullness), and we are complete in Him. "*In him dwelleth all the fulness of the Godhead bodily. And ye are complete in him, which is the head of all principality and power*" (Col. 2:9-10).

The Christian life does not mean resting one's salvation upon obedience to a set of rules; rather, it means trusting Christ and allowing Him to work in and through our lives. Our hope of eternal life is not based on ourselves (or anything we can do or produce); it is based on Christ alone. A personal relationship with Christ produces within the Christian a desire to obey Him, please Him, and live for Him. Christ is our life.

The book of Colossians highlights Christ's supremacy over His people—the church. God's church is compared to a physical body, which is subject to the control of the head. As Christians, we are the body of Christ and are subject to Him, the Head, in all things.

As believers, we have in us *the riches of the glory of this mystery . . . Christ in us, the hope of glory* (Col. 1:27).

Verses for Today: *"For this cause we . . . pray . . . that ye might be filled with the knowledge of his will in* all *wisdom and spiritual understanding . . . strengthened with* all *might, according to his glorious power, unto* all *patience and longsuffering with joyfulness; giving thanks unto the Father"* (Col. 1:9, 11-12).

To grasp the importance of this prayer, notice how many times the word "all" is used: *"all wisdom . . . all might . . . all patience."* There is no limit to God's divine wisdom, strength, and endurance that are available to every Christian.

God desires that we be led by *"the knowledge of his will in all wisdom"* and that we are strengthened with *"his glorious power."* The keys to accomplishing these objectives are through prayer and His Word.

God has given us His Word, so that we might know Him, fellowship with Him, and be blessed. He instructs us *not to be anxious about anything but, in everything with prayer and thanksgiving, to present our requests to Him* (Phil. 4:6). His Word is filled with glorious truth and powerful promises that we must know and claim for ourselves.

Whatsoever we ask, we will receive of him "because we keep his commandments, and do those things that are pleasing in his sight" (1 John 3:22).

Thought for Today: The prayers of the upright are the Lord's delight.

 # 1 AND 2 THESSALONIANS

The Lord led the apostle Paul to Thessalonica, a leading city in Macedonia, on his second missionary journey (Acts 17:1-9). Although he met with violent opposition, some Jews and many Greeks were won to Christ, and a faithful church was established. (Thessalonica, located at the northwest corner of the Aegean Sea, is still a prosperous Greek city.)

The purpose of **1 and 2 Thessalonians** is to prepare us for Christ's return so that our *whole spirit and soul and body will be blameless when our Lord Jesus Christ returns* (1 Thess. 5:23). Christ's return is referred to more than twenty times in the eight chapters of the two short letters.

In **2 Thessalonians,** Paul points out that before Christ returns, evil and wickedness will become more intense under the leadership of a mysterious person, known as the wicked one, who will be in opposition to Christ (2 Thess. 2:3-4).

Through these two letters, Paul prays that God will increase our love for the Lord and others; strengthen and encourage our hearts; give us great hope; strengthen us in good deeds; and enable us to be blameless at His second coming (1 Thess. 3:12-13; 2 Thess. 2:16-17).

Paul refreshes our spirits and reminds us to not become discouraged or afraid when we encounter persecution and see evil increase. We must hold fast to the good and to God's Word of prophecy, and abstain from evil (1 Thess. 5:16-22). We must live in hope and God's love, stand firm, and persevere. We are to keep praying, rejoicing, and giving thanks. We are not to be idle, but to keep doing good as we wait expectantly for Christ. The Lord will reward our faithfulness.

December 7: Read 1 Thessalonians 1–5

Verses for Today: *"And the Lord make you to increase and abound in love one toward another, and toward all men, even as we do toward you: To the end he may stablish your hearts unblameable in holiness before God, even our Father, at the coming of our Lord Jesus Christ with all his saints"* (1 Thess. 3:12-13).

Among the words of comfort to His disciples was the Savior's promise that He would come again and receive them unto Himself (John 14:1-3). This is the confident expectation of every Christian. Christ's return to earth will be the greatest event ever to take place since His ascension when *"a cloud received him out of their sight"* (Acts 1:9).

Christians are to be eagerly awaiting His return, and at work for Him. This means we must not become entangled in worldly activities, which rob us of our spiritual usefulness. We are to faithfully work to serve the Lord, even as we watch and wait for the triumphant return of our Redeemer, *"the author and finisher of our faith"* (Heb. 12:2).

"For the Lord himself shall descend from heaven with a shout, with the voice of the archangel, and with the trump of God: and the dead in Christ shall rise first: then we which are alive and remain shall be caught up together with them in the clouds to meet the Lord in the air: and so shall we ever be with the Lord" (1 Thess. 4:16-17).

Thought for Today: The Lord is returning for those who have prepared themselves (Rev. 19:7).

December 8: Read 2 Thessalonians 1–3

Verse for Today: *"And to you who are troubled rest with us, when the Lord Jesus shall be revealed from heaven with his mighty angels"* (2 Thess. 1:7).

In the New Testament's 260 chapters, Christ's second coming is mentioned 318 times. This theme of Jesus's return fills Thessalonians.

Christ's first coming was sudden, and He surprised the religious leaders of His time; but His second coming will be an even greater surprise to most people. *"The day of the Lord so cometh as a thief in the night"* (1 Thess. 5:2). For those who love Jesus and mourn the chaos and suffering of a world ruined by sin, it will be good news.

Bible-reading Christians are earnestly anticipating the day. As a bride prepares for her bridegroom, so those who sincerely anticipate His return will prepare themselves for this great and wonderful day: *"And every man that hath this hope in him purifieth himself, even as he is pure"* (1 John 3:3).

Although we do not know the exact day or hour of our Lord's return, the time is drawing near *"when he shall come to be glorified in his saints, and to be admired in all them that believe"* (2 Thess. 1:10).

"Watch therefore, for ye know neither the day nor the hour wherein the Son of man cometh" (Matt. 25:13).

Thought for Today: Jesus is coming soon! Are you ready to meet Him?

1 AND 2 TIMOTHY

In these two letters, the apostle Paul, under the inspiration of God, points out the importance of knowing God's Word.

First Timothy (1 Timothy) stresses the necessity of right doctrine in order to worship and live to please the Lord. This is especially vital for churches and their leadership. Elders, deacons, and pastors should meet certain qualifications, which Paul lays out (1 Tim. 3:1-13). Church leaders must live lives consistent with the Word of God and serve as godly leaders.

Paul instructs Timothy (and all believers) to be a good servant of the Lord Jesus Christ (1 Tim. 4:6); remain loyal to Him and His authoritative Word (1 Tim. 6:3-4); and *"fight the good fight of faith"* (1 Tim. 6:12). Paul explains that just as God had entrusted the gospel to him (1 Tim. 1:11), he was being faithful to pass it along (1 Tim. 1:18-19; 6:20).

In **2 Timothy**, Paul highlights the sufficiency of Scriptures—through the indwelling Holy Spirit—to reveal the answers to all of life's problems. We must thoroughly study the entire Bible because *"all scripture is given by inspiration of God, and is profitable for doctrine, for reproof, for correction, for instruction in righteousness: That the man of God may be perfect, thoroughly furnished unto all good works"* (2 Tim. 3:16-17).

These two letters point out that believing God's Word as the ultimate authority is the only effective safeguard against believing false doctrine, and therefore leading a life that is a mixture of truth and error. Think about it! The Bible fully equips and prepares us to accomplish the purposes for which God created us. We must be faithful to read it, know it, and live by it.

December 9: Read 1 Timothy 1–6

Verses for Today: *"I exhort therefore, that, first of all, supplications, prayers, intercessions, and giving of thanks, be made for all men; for kings, and for all that are in authority; that we may lead a quiet and peaceable life in all godliness and honesty"* (1 Tim. 2:1-2).

This world would be a wonderful place to live if all the rulers, kings, and presidents were Christians who were concerned with administering justice for everyone—rich and poor alike. On the contrary, ungodly men rule the majority of the world's people.

Although the Bible does not mention the cruel Roman ruler Nero, it appears that at the time Paul wrote the book of 1 Timothy, Nero was persecuting Christians and having them put to death. Paul emphasized the importance of Christians praying for all those in authority over them.

As we pray for leaders (both good and evil), God hears our prayers. Regardless of how He answers our prayers, He produces in everyone who prays *"a quiet and peaceable life in all godliness"* (1 Tim. 2:2).

Let every Christian submit to the governing authorities. No authority exists without God's permission, and the existing authorities have been put there by God (Rom. 13:1).

Thought for Today: The peace of God can rule our hearts—regardless of our circumstances.

December 10: Read 2 Timothy 1–4

Verse for Today: *"Thou therefore endure hardness, as a good soldier of Jesus Christ"* (2 Tim. 2:3).

The ministry of Paul was marked by much suffering that demanded great endurance (2 Cor. 11:22-28). He was imprisoned in Roman jails many times, but through it all he never considered himself the prisoner of anyone other than Jesus (Philem. 1:1).

Paul knew that the end of his life was near, and he was deeply concerned that Timothy, his "son in the faith," be prepared to carry on the work of the Lord as a good soldier of Jesus Christ. Paul's instructions that he gave to Timothy (and us) reveal Paul's "secrets" of success. *"Study to show thyself approved unto God, a workman that needeth not to be ashamed, rightly dividing the word of truth"* (2 Tim.

2:15). Studying *all* Scripture is necessary to be fully equipped to do the work of God (2 Tim. 3:16-17), and follow Him acceptably.

Paul urges us to *"endure hardness"* (hardships and sufferings). We are to be *"good soldiers of Jesus Christ"* and obey our Lord's orders, while knowing that He is concerned for our welfare and will not leave us alone in any situation. We are to be willing to witness *"in season, out of season"*—when it is easy and agreeable to us, as well as when it is inconvenient and difficult (2 Tim. 4:2).

"But continue thou in the things which thou hast learned and hast been assured of, knowing of whom thou hast learned them; and that from a child thou hast known the holy scriptures, which are able to make thee wise unto salvation through faith which is in Christ Jesus" (2 Tim. 3:14-15).

Thought for Today: The will of God does not lead where the grace of God cannot protect.

# TITUS

Paul wrote this letter to Titus, a fellow worker ministering to the church in the city of Crete. The key thought is that Christ *gave Himself for us that He might redeem us from all sin, and purify unto Himself a special group of people—who live godly lives and are zealous to do good works* (Titus 2:14).

The book of Titus lays out moral and spiritual guidelines for believers and church leaders. Church leaders must be blameless in their personal lives and true to God's Word (Titus 1:6-9). This book warns that *there are many undisciplined people who deceive others with their nonsense. They teach things they should not teach, and all with the shameful motive of making money. They openly claim to know the Lord but, by their actions, they deny Him* (Titus 1:10-11). We must not only evaluate our words *and* actions, but also the words *and* actions of our leaders and those with whom we align ourselves.

The importance of acceptable Christian service is emphasized many times in Titus. Every believer should be *an example of good behavior* (Titus 2:7); *eager to do good* (Titus 2:14); *obedient to those in authority* (Titus 3:1); and *caring for the needs of others* (Titus 3:8, 14).

PHILEMON

Philemon became a convert and believer from Paul's teaching. Philemon was wealthy and owned a slave named Onesimus, who had run away to Rome and met the apostle Paul. The apostle sent Onesimus back to his master with this beautiful letter, urging Philemon to forgive the runaway slave and receive him back—not only as a Christian brother—but as he would receive Paul himself.

We may find it surprising that Paul (and Scripture) urged this runaway slave to return to his owner. There are a number of truths to consider regarding this instruction.

First, while slavery has a very negative connotation today, and is often thought of only in terms of racial injustice, slavery that occurred in Old Testament times was often a matter of economics and survival. People would sell themselves into slavery to pay their debts or be able to provide for their family. Second, it is important to note that stealing someone to sell or traffic that person is condemned in Scripture with a death sentence (Ex. 21:16; 1 Tim. 1:8-10). Finally, the biblical concept of being a slave or bonds-person carries much spiritual meaning, and is worth studying.[24] We are either a slave to sin (and the world), or we are set free in Christ and a servant of His (and His kingdom).

One of Paul's great instructions to all believers is that we are to learn to be content in whatever situation God places us (Phil. 1:1-30; 4:1-13). However, Paul additionally states that if a person could gain freedom from slavery in an honorable way, that person was free to do so (1 Cor. 7:17-24). In this case, Onesimus—who was a believer—needed to restore the relationship with his master-employer in a God-honoring way.

Paul so desired for God's forgiving love and reconciliation to be lived out that he offered to pay any debts that Onesimus owed, just as Christ paid the price for us on the cross. Because Philemon and Onesimus were both believers, and because Jesus has joined every Christian to Himself, both master and slave were to consider themselves as brothers in Christ's family.

December 11: **Read Titus—Philemon**

Verses for Today: *"Put them in mind to be subject to principalities and powers, to obey magistrates, to be ready to every good work, to speak evil of no man, to be no brawlers, but gentle, showing all meekness unto all men"* (Titus 3:1-2).

Under the inspiration of God, the apostle Peter instructs Christians to be law-abiding citizens: *"Submit yourselves to every ordinance of man for the Lord's sake: whether it be to the king, as supreme; or unto governors, as unto them that are sent by him for the punishment of evildoers, and for the praise of them that do well"* (1 Pet. 2:13-14).

---

24 Following are several links to brief articles on the biblical topic of slaves and being a bond servant: 1) https://www.gotquestions.org/Bible-slavery.html; 2) https://www.gotquestions.org/bondservant.html; 3) https://www.gotquestions.org/servant-of-Christ.html; and 4) https://www.gotquestions.org/slave-to-sin.html.

Does this Scripture mean we should submit passively to corrupt governments or be unfaithful to God's Word if evil forces demand it? Of course not!

When religious authorities commanded Peter and the other apostles not to tell others that Jesus was the Messiah-Savior of the world, they reasoned as faithful Christians, saying, *"We ought to obey God rather than men"* (Acts 5:29).

Early Christians knew God's Word and stayed faithful to the Lord. They never reacted with hatred against those who treated them poorly or attempted to silence them. No one is ever justified to respond with force or violence because that is from Satan. Christians must faithfully declare the truth—even if it means imprisonment or death.

"For so is the will of God, that with well doing ye may put to silence the ignorance of foolish men" (1 Pet. 2:15).

Thought for Today: Peace comes to those who joyfully submit to God and His Word.

 # HEBREWS

The book of Hebrews helps us come to know Jesus more fully. Jesus's superiority is its theme. He is presented as far superior to the prophets, the priests, Moses, the Law, and angels. Because Jesus is God's Son and sinless, and because of His sacrifice, He secured a great victory for us; and then, He gives us great gifts. It is no wonder that the words *"better"* and *"superior"* are key words mentioned fifteen times.

For believers to worship God under the old covenant, it was necessary for the blood of many animals to be offered daily. But the new covenant required only one sacrifice—Christ's own blood. Christ's sacrifice cleanses us from our sins (Heb. 10:1-29), and reconciles us to God.

The first covenant of God, which centered upon the Ten Commandments, was written on tablets of stone, but Christ's covenant is written upon our hearts (Heb. 8:10). The old covenant was temporary, but Christ's covenant is eternal (Heb. 13:20).

Now, through Jesus, we are invited and instructed to *"come boldly unto the throne of grace, that we may obtain mercy, and find grace to help in time of need"* (Heb. 4:16). But there's more. Scripture tells us that Jesus is our High Priest and sits at the right hand of God, and ever lives to intercede for us in prayer (Heb. 7:25).

Truly, our Lord is superior to all. Because of Him, we have a *better* hope (7:19), a *better* covenant (8:6), *better* promises (8:6), and a *better* possession (10:34).

Hebrews 11 is often called the faith chapter (or the great hall-of-faith chapter). It urges us to persevere with Christ, as it reminds us of the Old Testament giants of the faith. They lived by faith even if it brought persecution or death.

Some of the believers mentioned had not yet received God's promises, but they knew God would ultimately fulfill His Word. We are to remind ourselves of these faithful believers, while *fixing our eyes on Jesus,* the originator and finisher of our faith, who secured salvation and blessings for us through His sacrifice (Heb. 12:2).

Jesus is the living Word of God and filled with God's wisdom. He *upholds all things by the word of His power* (Heb. 1:3). He is our source of *power* to live the victorious Christian life.

December 12: Read Hebrews 1–4

Verses for Today: *"There remaineth therefore a rest to the people of God. For he that is entered into his rest, he also hath ceased from his own works, as God did from his"* (Heb. 4:9-10).

Believers are to take a day of rest and honor the Lord. But there is even more to this truth. We are to rest in Him and trust Him to empower us and work through us. Even when we "work," we are to have a spirit of rest and peace in Him. As we seek Him to refresh and renew us (Ps. 23:1-3; Isa. 40:31; Jer. 31:25; Col. 1:29), and our thoughts rest in Him, our day-by-day activities are neither frustrating nor boring.

Many have never entered into God's rest. They rely upon their own clever strategies to accomplish their goals and become angry or resentful when their plans fail or when someone opposes them. They have no *"rest"*—no resting from self-effort; therefore, they cheat themselves of enjoying His peace.

We must be careful about our attitudes and thoughts because it will be impossible to experience God's rest if we are angry or critical with others. Even if we are right and can "justify" our opinions, it is a serious offense against God to hold bitterness toward someone. Satan loves to turn our attention from Christ to self, thus destroying the peace of God in our lives.

So then, let us seek those things that make for peace (Rom. 14:19).

Thought for Today: We will either let Christ, the Prince of Peace, rule our hearts, or we will insist on having things our way and suffer frustration and despair.

December 13: Read Hebrews 5–7

Verse for Today: *"And no man taketh this honour unto himself, but he that is called of God, as was Aaron"* (Heb. 5:4).

Every year, on the Day of Atonement, God directed Aaron to offer a sacrifice as atonement (payment) for sins. Aaron made a sacrifice first for his own sins and then for the sins of his family. Only after he had atoned for himself was he qualified to make atonement for the transgressions of the people (Lev. 16:11-16).

By contrast, on the great Day of Atonement, Christ—the Lamb of God—offered Himself once and for all as a sacrifice and was crucified. Because Jesus is the sinless Son of God, there was no need for Him to make a sin offering for Himself as Aaron did. Through His death, He made atonement for the violations of all who would believe in Him.

How assuring it is to know that anytime, day or night, because of Christ's love and sacrifice, we can come to the Lord, confess our sins, and receive gracious mercy through Jesus. He is our sacrifice, our atonement, and our High Priest!

"If we confess our sins, he is faithful and just to forgive us our sins, and to cleanse us from all unrighteousness" (1 John 1:9).

Thought for Today: No sin is so great God's mercy cannot forgive it.

December 14: Read Hebrews 8–10

Verses for Today: *"I will put my laws into their mind, and write them in their hearts: and I will be to them a God, and they shall be to me a people . . . for all shall know me, from the least to the greatest"* (Heb. 8:10-11).

God greatly desires a relationship with us, and to have us experience Him and walk with Him. Fellowship with God became possible in a new way through Jesus's sacrifice and brought many promised blessings. God pledged to put His Spirit in us, and enable us to know Him and live for Him.

All those who turn to Christ as Savior receive a new nature, which makes it possible to *"serve the living God"* (Heb. 9:14). We have the privilege of living in the presence of the Most High every moment of every day, in every circumstance, *"by a new and living way"* (Heb. 10:20).

"And I will give them an heart to know me, that I am the Lord: and they shall be my people, and I will be their God" (Jer. 24:7).

Thought for Today: God created us with hearts so unique that nothing less than fellowship with the Lord can truly satisfy us.

December 15: Read Hebrews 11–13

Verses for Today: *"By faith Abraham, when he was called to go out into a place which he should after receive for an inheritance, obeyed; and he went out, not knowing whither he went. By faith he sojourned in the land of promise, as in a strange* *country, dwelling in tabernacles [tents] . . . for he looked for a city . . . whose builder and maker is God"* (Heb. 11:8-10).

Abraham is the father of the faithful (Rom. 4:11). In obedience to God and His Word, he left family, friends, and the security of his own country to live in a tent as a homeless stranger in the land of promise (Gen. 12:1; Acts 7:2-4).

Abraham *"was called to go out into a place which he should after receive for an inheritance."* Although he encountered numerous disappointments, there is no record he complained that he had been cheated or given less than God's best. Abraham believed God's promise.

Many people feel that it is not possible to give up the security of one's home, country, friends, or family and still be happy and content. However, the example of Abraham illustrates the great secret of faith in God to guide us through the experiences of life—where we should live, what our occupation should be, and even whom we'll have as friends.

God seldom fulfills His promises in ways we expect. We may experience a number of discouragements and disappointments before we recognize that God is leading us to see beyond life's unsatisfying, false, temporary rewards. As our faith in the Lord grows, we will be less concerned about earthly possessions and pleasures, and our thoughts will be more and more occupied with the heavenly city, *"whose builder and maker is God."*

"He is a rewarder of them that diligently seek him" (Heb. 11:6).

Thought for Today: May we each seek to personally know and fulfill God's purposes for us.

 # JAMES

The book of **James** is a guide to Christian living and conduct. It presents a series of practical tests whereby we are to consider the genuineness of our faith. True faith will affect every area of our lives and produce visible works of Christian service in obedience to the Scriptures. James instructs us on various topics, including prayer, patience, our words, wealth and poverty, pride, humility, anger, temptation, sickness, and favoritism. True faith will enable us to endure trials and remain faithful to God and His Word.

In the first and last chapters, James urges Christians to pray (James 1:5-8; 5:13-18). He illustrates the great power of prayer by reminding us of Elijah—just an ordinary person, who believed that God would answer his prayer. Elijah prayed that it wouldn't rain, and it didn't—for 3½ years (1 Kings 17–19; James 5:17). We are to pray with faith as Elijah did.

God and His Word are the source of all true wisdom. When we become aware of this fact, we will read His Word with meekness and pray for understanding, direction, and empowerment. In this way, God is able to work through us and enable us to be *"doers of the word, and not hearers only"* (James 1:22).

December 16: Read James 1–5

Verses for Today: *"Is any among you afflicted? Let him pray. . . . The effectual fervent prayer of a righteous man availeth much"* (James 5:13, 16).

As Christians, it is of utmost importance that we listen to what God says as we read the Bible, for it is through His Word that we learn about His plans for us, along with the wonderful resources available to us.

We are all "afflicted" at times. Afflictions are the distresses, burdens, and problems of life. Every affliction we face presents the opportunity, as well as the responsibility, to pray and trust the Lord for the solution. But too often, we allow people or wrong attitudes to keep us from praying. Furthermore, when we fail to pray, or to wait for God's direction, our efforts become fruitless because we are substituting our own plans for His will. Our prayer lives should express a desire for the Lord to work in us and fulfill His will through us.

Prayer is God's way of releasing His power to accomplish His will. Just as praying Christians release God's power, prayerless Christians are a hindrance to accomplishing His will.

"If ye abide in me, and my words abide in you, ye shall ask what ye will, and it shall be done unto you" (John 15:7).

Thought for Today: It is not only sinful things that blight our lives; even good things can if we allow them to take the place of prayer and Bible reading.

 ## 1 AND 2 PETER

The letters of **1 and 2 Peter** were written by Peter, one of Jesus's twelve disciples.

The purpose of **1 Peter** is to encourage Christians to depend on God to answer prayer, sustain and strengthen us, and meet our needs in the midst of suffering (1 Pet. 5:10). Since the days of the early church, when great persecution forced believers to leave Jerusalem (Acts 8:1), Christians have been subjected to all kinds of affliction. During times of difficulty, the assurance of the Lord's presence and the expectation that He will soon return become even *"more pre-cious"* to us (1 Pet. 1:7).

In **2 Peter**, true knowledge of our Lord is contrasted with false knowledge. The work of false teachers and the immorality that results from such false doctrine are exposed (2 Pet. 3:3-8, 17-18). "Knowledge" and its related words occur at least thirteen times. It's important to note that out of the twenty-seven books in the New Testament, at least twenty of them warn us against deceptive spiritual teaching.

We are to walk in truth and love others, which take discernment and careful reading of Scripture, so that we won't be led astray. To counteract false teaching and contend for the faith, we must know and study God's Word.

The apostle closes 2 Peter by urging us to *"grow in grace, and in the knowledge of our Lord and Saviour Jesus Christ"* (2 Pet. 3:18).

December 17: Read 1 Peter 1–2

Verses for Today: *"Wherefore gird up the loins of your mind . . . not fashioning yourselves according to the former lusts in your ignorance: But as he which hath called you is holy, so be ye holy in all manner of conversation"* (1 Pet. 1:13-15).

In Bible times, girding up the loins meant tucking up one's long garments with a sashlike belt to prepare for physical work. Loose hanging clothing would hinder someone's ability to move and work. Christians, too, are commanded to *"gird up the loins"* of our minds in preparation for service to God. This can only be done by reading His Word and praying for the indwelling Holy Spirit to guide us and strengthen us to live according to His Word.

We are prone to let our minds follow the "fashion" of the world and have an attitude of indifference to the Lord's will and to reaching a lost world unless we set aside a time for prayer and reading through His Word. It is so important that we do what we can to share Christ with others.

At the time we accepted Jesus as our Savior, the Holy Spirit came to live within us and brought about a miraculous change, which we call the new birth or being born again. No longer should we live by the desires we had before we received Christ. As we yield our lives to Christ, and separate ourselves from the defiling things of the world, we will live for Him and please Him.

"Stand therefore, having your loins girt about with truth, and having on the breastplate of righteousness" (Eph. 6:14).

Thought for Today: If the world cannot see a difference between the life of a Christian and that of an unbeliever, the Christian is not fully walking with the Lord and serving Him effectively.

December 18: Read 1 Peter 3–5

Verses for Today: *"But and if ye suffer for righteousness' sake, happy are ye: and be not afraid of their terror, neither be troubled. . . . Forasmuch then as Christ hath suffered for us in the flesh, arm yourselves likewise with the same mind"* (1 Pet. 3:14; 4:1).

It was through His *suffering* that Jesus gained a great victory for us, God, and Himself. Although we don't fully understand it, God has ordained for great good to be wrought from suffering.

It's also true that in the midst of our troubles, our Lord provides strength and spiritual weapons to believers, so that we may be victorious just as He was when He was on earth.

When Jesus told His disciples that *He must go to Jerusalem, suffer much, and be put to death,* Peter did not yet realize that affliction is sometimes God's will. This is why Peter rebuked the Lord, saying, *"Be it far from thee, Lord: this shall not be unto thee"* (Matt. 16:21-22). But through the years, Peter learned that all of us at times may experience humiliation and adversity. We may have to go without certain personal enjoyments because of our stand for Christ. *This is the life to which we have been called, for Christ Himself suffered for us* (1 Pet. 2:21).

Other times we can willingly choose adversity and sacrifice in order to help others. Suffering briefly now in this life, to help others know our Lord and avoid eternal suffering, is a small price to pay, especially as we know that we will soon enter into God's kingdom, peace, and reward.

Our reaction to difficulties depends on our faith in the sovereignty and wisdom of God. When we realize that all things work together for good and that we are actually strengthened through trials and suffering, we will praise the Lord. Our troubles ought not to make us angry, or bitter, or lead us to sin. *When Christ was insulted, He did not retaliate; when He suffered, He made no threats. Instead, He entrusted Himself to God, the righteous Judge* (1 Pet. 2:23).

"But the God of all grace, who hath called us unto his eternal glory by Christ Jesus, after that ye have suffered a while, make you perfect, stablish, strengthen, settle you" (1 Pet. 5:10).

Thought for Today: Jesus always provides the needed strength to those who pray and remain faithful to Him in times of testing.

December 19: Read 2 Peter 1–3

Verses for Today: *"What manner of persons ought ye to be in all holy conversation and godliness, looking for . . . the coming of the day of God?"* (2 Pet. 3:11-12).

As Christians, our greatest desire should be to please Jesus and glorify Him—not only in the way we think, act, and talk, but also in helping others prepare to meet the Lord. There is a real danger in becoming so involved with personal, material, or social demands that our daily lives do not glorify Christ. Even though we may not be committing any particular sin, our time, conduct, and thoughts can be squandered on "good things" that keep us from God's best.

As Christians, we need to avoid the things that are not in harmony with God's eternal purpose and calling. Out of a grateful heart to the Lord for our salvation, we should seek opportunities to serve Him, giving freely of ourselves, so that the same saving gospel may be spread throughout the world.

Let us humbly and diligently walk with God, dedicating our lives to Him, dying to self-exaltation, and avoiding things that waste our time. May we make the most of every opportunity we have to serve Him (Eph. 5:16).

"*Whereby are given unto us exceeding great and precious promises: that by these ye might be partakers of the divine nature, having escaped the corruption that is in the world through lust*" (2 Pet. 1:4).

Thought for Today: Those who continuously yield to worldly influences and activities will stand ashamed before the Lord.

 # 1 JOHN

The book of 1 John encourages Christians to live in loving fellowship with the Lord and with others. The word *"love"* and its various forms appear more than forty times in these five short chapters. We are to deeply know and experience God's great love through Jesus who laid down His life for us. *What great love the Father has lavished on us that we should be called children of God! And that is what we are!* (1 John 3:1, 16).

As we fellowship with God, His love causes a remarkable, twofold change in our lives: a desire to please God, and a love for others—regardless of their attitudes and actions toward us (1 John 3:10-11,14; 4:7,11-12, 19-20). Love is the distinguishing characteristic of a Christian. Love for God and love for others are inseparably linked. If a person says he loves the Lord but hates another person, he is only deceiving himself. Scripture declares that *anyone who keeps on hating his brother is a murderer, and you know that a murderer does not have eternal life in him* (1 John 3:15).

The book of 1 John also includes warnings against following false teaching that would keep us from true fellowship with God and His Son. The closer we draw to the Lord's return, the more religious deception will increase. Because religious falsehood abounds, it is vital that we study the tests John provides to carefully examine our convictions and our lives.

December 20: Read 1 John 1–3

Verses for Today: *"Whosoever doeth not righteousness is not of God, neither he that loveth not his brother. For this is the message that ye heard from the beginning, that we should love one another. Not as Cain, who was of that wicked one, and slew his brother. And wherefore slew he him? Because his own works were evil, and his brother's righteous"* (1 John 3:10-12).

Cain was a religious person—one who built an altar and offered a sacrifice to God. But God declared that his offering was not acceptable. Scripture doesn't tell us all the reasons for God's disapproval, but Cain's faith and attitude toward God were not right. God warned Cain to repent, saying, *If you do what is right, you will be accepted* (Gen. 4:7).

When God corrected him, Cain lacked humility, submission, and contrition. He disregarded the Lord's warning and became jealous because God was pleased with his brother Abel's offering and not his. In his jealousy and unhappiness, he murdered his brother, Abel (Gen. 4).

The Lord knows our hearts. Cain's prideful heart led to further sins of jealousy and murder. To become envious, resentful, or hateful of others is sin. In fact, Scripture equates hatred to murder (1 John 3:15) and calls it one of the *"works of the flesh."*

However, love is a *"fruit of the Spirit"* (Gal. 5:19-26). And every Christian is to grow in love.

We know that we have left death and have come over into life because we love our fellow Christians. Whoever does not love them is still under the power of death (1 John 3:14).

Thought for Today: Those who continue to harbor ill will do more damage to themselves than they do to those they hate.

December 21: Read 1 John 4–5

Verse for Today: *"Beloved, if God so loved us, we ought also to love one another"* (1 John 4:11).

Men have written millions of books about every conceivable subject. In contrast, God has given mankind only one Book, and each word is important—*"All scripture is given by inspiration of God, and is profitable"* (2 Tim. 3:16).

A rule to remember concerning the importance of what God has said is this: When God says something once, it is important, but when He says something more than once—we are to give it utmost consideration. In 1 John 4, love is referred to more than *twenty-five* times. In view of this, let's consider the serious-ness of our responsibility as stewards of God's love.

The very nature of God is love and, if we have received His nature, we are to love others. It is not enough merely to know of God's love; we must manifest His love and long-suffering in our daily encounters with others. Expressing the nature of God's love should be more important to us than insisting on our rights.

"If a man say, I love God, and hateth his brother, he is a liar: for he that loveth not his brother whom he hath seen, how can he love God whom he hath not seen?" (1 John 4:20).

Thought for Today: The very nature of love compels us to give of ourselves for the sake of others.

 # 2 AND 3 JOHN, JUDE

Five books of the Bible are only one chapter in length. The books are Obadiah (in the Old Testament), Philemon, 2 John, 3 John, and Jude.

The book of **2 John** is a letter with just thirteen verses. It focuses on love and truth. The word *"truth"* is used several times in the first four verses. John urges believers to examine their opinions, beliefs, and motives to make sure they are living according to the truth and commands of God's Word (2 John 1:4). God's truth includes knowing that Christ came in the flesh. The book warns against false teachers and urges us to love one another.

The book of **3 John** introduces three people: Demetrius, a pleasant Chris-tian, whom John praises; Gaius, a generous helper in the Lord's work; and Di-otrephes, a proud, demanding man with exceptional abilities, but one who is a hindrance to the ministry of God's Word. These men are given as examples. Are we helping, or hindering, the ministry of Christ?

The book of **Jude** was written by Jude, the brother of James, and half-brother of Jesus.[25] This letter reveals the terrible consequences of believing false doctrines and exposes the nature and conduct of false teachers (Jude 1:3-4). These god-less people are denounced, and their inevitable fate made known—*"Woe unto them! . . . To whom is reserved the blackness of darkness for ever"* (Jude 1:11, 13).

Although Jude speaks of judgment, he carefully points out that the true

---

25 Jude and his brother James were half-brothers to Jesus, but in their letters they do not claim this casual familiarity with Him. Instead, they show reverence for Christ and His divine identi-ty by acknowledging they are servants of His. Incidentally, when Jesus began His ministry, Jude and James did not believe His claims, but later they each received Him as Savior. See https://www.gotquestions.org/Jude-in-the-Bible.html.

believer is *kept in Christ* and will be presented *faultless before His glorious presence* (Jude 1:1, 24).

December 22: Read 2 and 3 John, and Jude

Verse for Today: *"For many deceivers are entered into the world, who confess not that Jesus Christ is come in the flesh. This is a deceiver and an antichrist"* (2 John 1:7).

Scripture warns us in numerous places to beware of false teachers who come as "angels of light" (2 Cor. 11:14). Many people have some Bible truth in their religion, and base their beliefs on part of the Scriptures, but even Satan can quote Scripture (Matt. 4:5-6).

False teachers can be identified by their answer to the question, "Who is Jesus Christ?" Some refuse to accept both His *deity* and *humanity.* They refuse to accept that He died *and* was resurrected, returning to the right hand of God. Others believe that Jesus was a good man and great teacher, but they deny that He came to die for mankind's sins.[26]

There are many religions today that are deceiving multitudes who will be eternally lost. False teachers pose as "angels of light," but they are wolves "in sheep's clothing" (Matt. 7:15). They are motivated by Satan to deceive those who do not know the Scriptures.

We are to pray for and carefully examine the doctrines of preachers and teachers according to God's Word to ascertain if they are actually being led by the Spirit of God (1 John 4:1).

"For there shall arise false Christs, and false prophets, and shall shew great signs and wonders; insomuch that, if it were possible, they shall deceive the very elect" (Matt. 24:24).

Thought for Today: God's Word is able to keep you from being deceived.

 REVELATION

The final book of God's Word is Revelation. The key theme is Christ and His glorious and eternal reign. Revelation is the only New Testament *book* of prophecy. It is filled with more than three hundred symbolic terms or descriptions concerning Jesus, His church, end-times, and the battle between the Lord and the Evil One. It "reveals" what is still to come, and reminds us that all of God's promises will be fulfilled.

---

26 A few other verses regarding false teachers include 1 John 2:1, 22-29; 3:5, 8; 4:1-15; 5:1-15; 2 John 1:7-11.

Many Christians become so involved in trying to understand all the symbols, mysteries, and judgments that they fail to see that the book of Revelation is the unveiling of the Person, Jesus Christ, who is the center of everything. He is revealed as the *"Alpha and Omega, the first and the last"* (Rev. 1:11); *"a Lamb as it had been slain"* (Rev. 5:6); *"the first begotten of the dead"* (Rev. 1:5, 18; 2:8); and the *"KING OF KINGS, AND LORD OF LORDS"* (Rev. 19:16).

Throughout Scripture, starting in Genesis 1, God has revealed Himself to mankind. He has revealed Himself through creation, the prophets, His Word and, ultimately, Jesus. Our Lord came as the Suffering Servant and will soon return to earth, this time, in glory and power. This book is the *revelation* of Christ's final triumph over all evil. It gives assurance that God is ruling behind the scenes and uses all the activities of men and all the calamities of nature to accomplish His purposes.

Chapters 1–3 begin by giving praise and warnings to seven churches that we must heed for ourselves, as well.

Chapters 4–5 include visions that bear upon those in Daniel 7 and Ezekiel 1 and provide glimpses into heaven's throne room.

Chapters 6–20 further unveil the Lamb who was sinless, slain, and overcame death. Therefore, He alone is worthy to open the seals, execute judgment, fulfill what God has written, and sit on the throne. Revelation discloses times of tribulation, the final judgment, and the Lord ruling over all creation.

Revelation 21-22 conclude gloriously with the new heaven and earth, and also a warning, and an invitation.

The book begins with a vital promise: *"Blessed is he that readeth, and they that hear the words of this prophecy, and keep those things which are written therein: for the time is at hand"* (Rev. 1:3).

The book ends with Christ's last words, what our response should be, and a prayer for us: *"He which testifieth these things saith, Surely I come quickly. Amen. Even so, come, Lord Jesus. The grace of our Lord Jesus Christ be with you all. Amen"* (Rev. 22:20-21).

December 23: Read Revelation 1–2

Verses for Today: *"I know thy works, and tribulation, and poverty, (but thou art rich). . . . Be thou faithful unto death, and I will give thee a crown of life"* (Rev. 2:9-10).

The Christians at Smyrna faced great tribulation—not merely small tests of faith, but intense trials because of their faith.

Jesus did not tell the church at Smyrna what we would like to hear—"Be faithful, and I will reward you and show the world how it pays to be a Christian."

Instead, He observed their suffering and said, *"Thou art rich,"* and proceeded to say, *"Be thou faithful unto death."* These Christians were to remain faithful to Christ and *"fear none of those things"* that they were to suffer (Rev. 2:10).

We don't understand all God's reasons for allowing persecution, but we do know that trials enable God's grace and truth to shine forth, and they enable us to become more like Him. His Word tells us, *"All that will live godly in Christ Jesus shall suffer persecution"* (2 Tim. 3:12; 1 Pet. 4:12-19). One day evil will be totally conquered, God will gain great glory, and each person will receive their just reward.

The safeguard against defeat for ourselves is to be strengthened—in the Word and with prayer—daily. In this way, when we face tribulation, we will be able to remain faithful.

"Yet if any man suffer as a Christian, let him not be ashamed; but let him glorify God on this behalf" (1 Pet. 4:16).

Thought for Today: Our present sufferings won't be able to compare with God's glory and wonders that He has in store for us (Rom. 8:18; 1 Cor. 2:9). He is able to strengthen us to be faithful.

December 24: Read Revelation 3–5

Verses for Today: *"And to the angel of the church in Philadelphia write; These things saith he that is holy, he that is true, he that hath the key of David, he that openeth, and no man shutteth; and shutteth, and no man openeth; I know thy works: behold, I have set before thee an open door, and no man can shut it: for thou hast a little strength, and hast kept my word, and hast not denied my name"* (Rev. 3:7-8).

The church in Philadelphia probably seemed weak and insignificant as far as the world was concerned; their number was small, and they had only *"a little strength."* But notice! That small group of Christians in Philadelphia were not dependent upon their *"little strength"*; their faith was in Christ, who had opened a door that no one—not even Satan and all his dominion—was able to close.

Our Lord still opens doors, regardless of how great the opposition may be, or how impossible our situation may seem. God works through those who, like the people in Philadelphia, recognize the insufficiency of their strength and depend on Him to accomplish His good and glorious purposes.

The Lord has opened a door for believers to evangelize the world. It is an open door, which God, in His grace, has entrusted to us. We must not let Him down.

"Most gladly therefore will I rather glory in my infirmities, that the power of Christ may rest upon me. Therefore I take pleasure in infirmities, in reproaches, in necessities, in persecutions, in distresses for Christ's sake: for when I am weak, then am I strong" (2 Cor. 12:9-10).

Thought for Today: A Christian can lay up treasure in heaven, which no earthly power can destroy.

December 25: Read Revelation 6–8

Verse for Today: *"Blessing, and glory, and wisdom, and thanksgiving, and honour, and power, and might, be unto our God for ever and ever. Amen"* (Rev. 7:12).

Heaven echoes with praise and ceaseless adoration by the angels and living creatures that surround God's throne. These seven words of praise remind us about God's character and attributes, and they enable us to join with the angels of heaven in praise and worship of the Lord—now and for eternity.

"Glory" describes the splendor of His being.

"Wisdom" reveals the supremacy of His knowledge that becomes available to us through His Word, praying, and His Spirit (1 Cor. 1:30; Col. 2:3).

"Thanksgiving" is a natural expression of our gratitude to the Lord (1 Thess. 5:18).

"Honor" denotes that God alone is worthy of all recognition, adoration, and reverence (Ps. 96:4-9; 145:5; Isa. 25:1).

"Power" points out the supremacy of our God over all evil forces and every circumstance.

"Might" emphasizes His unlimited strength to perform His promises to all who call upon Him.

The concluding *"Amen"* expresses the full support and agreement of the innumerable angels, the mighty beings, and the host of all who stand before the throne. Praise God! We, too, can be included with that glorious kingdom and that innumerable host!

"Praise our God, all ye his servants, and ye that fear him, both small and great" (Rev. 19:5).

Thought for Today: Praise to the Lord comes from a heart that receives and experiences His grace, power, and glory.

December 26: Read Revelation 9–11

Verses for Today: *"And I will give power unto my two witnesses. . . . And when they shall have finished their testimony, the beast that ascendeth out of the bottomless pit shall make war against them, and shall overcome them, and kill them"* (Rev. 11:3, 7).

The Lord will call these two witnesses to face the fierce opposition of those who hate God. He will empower them to fulfill their calling, and they will be invincible until they *"have finished their testimony."* Then these witnesses of Christ will be martyred in the city *"where also our Lord was crucified"* (Rev. 11:8). Their dead bodies will be left in the street. Those who will have opposed the servants of God will be so happy over the deaths of the two witnesses that they will declare a celebration and refuse to allow them to be buried.

Satan works through other people—both believers and unbelievers—to oppose us and the work we are doing for Christ. But Jesus declares that *"ye shall be witnesses unto me"* (Acts 1:8).

We must take a stand. We have a commission to be His faithful witnesses, no matter the cost. We are His *"ambassadors"* (2 Cor. 5:20), and He is able to give us grace and strength for our task.

His Word must and will be preached *"in all the world for a witness unto all nations; and then shall the end come"* (Matt. 24:14). The message of God's divine love and truth cannot be defeated.

"Therefore, my beloved brethren, be ye stedfast, unmoveable, always abounding in the work of the Lord, forasmuch as ye know that your labour is not in vain in the Lord" (1 Cor. 15:58).

Thought for Today: Our work for the Lord does not end until He calls us home to be with Him.

December 27: Read Revelation 12–13

Verses for Today: *"And there appeared . . . a woman clothed with the sun. . . . And there appeared another wonder . . . a great red dragon, having seven heads and ten horns, and seven crowns upon his heads. . . . And I heard a loud voice saying . . . the accuser of our brethren is cast down. . . . And they overcame him by the blood of the Lamb, and by the word of their testimony; and they loved not their lives unto the death"* (Rev. 12:1, 3, 10-11).

Satan is *"the dragon"*—the perpetual enemy of Christ. He is as determined to destroy the work of Jesus now as he was to have Pharaoh kill all the Hebrew male children during the time of Moses, and to have Herod slaughter all the babies in Bethlehem, all in an effort to kill Christ.

The seven heads, ten horns, and crowns of the dragon indicate the great influence and the many forms of Satan's malicious, evil activities as he works through people to oppose the work of Christ.

But these verses assure us that Christ and His followers in every generation will overcome Satan *"by the blood of the Lamb, and by the word of their testimony."* Satan and his host of demons continually seek to destroy the likeness of Christ in every Christian, but we need not fear. We can overcome Satan through the power of Jesus, our testimony, and faithfully speaking God's Word. *The Spirit in us is greater than he [Satan] that is in the world* (1 John 4:4).

We have assurance of God's final, glorious triumph over all evil. We are to pray for Jesus's return and wait for it expectantly, patiently, and joyfully.

"Now is come salvation, and strength, and the kingdom of our God, and the power of his Christ: for the accuser of our brethren is cast down, which accused them before our God day and night" (Rev. 12:10).

Thought for Today: Satan thrives on the ignorance of saints concerning himself. God's Word reveals his tactics, along with our weapons, and our power in the Lord to defeat him.

December 28: Read Revelation 14–16

Verse for Today: *"And they sing the song of Moses the servant of God, and the song of the Lamb"* (Rev. 15:3).

Moses led the Israelites victoriously through the Red Sea—free from Egyptian bondage and Pharaoh's control. Pharaoh is a type of Satan, who influences unbelievers and attempts to hinder God's followers from being faithful to God. As Pharaoh's army pursued the Israelites, they were destroyed in the Red Sea.

The Israelites, filled with thanksgiving and praise to God, sang *"the song of Moses"* in gratitude for their merciful deliverance from death (Ex. 15).

Thousands of years have passed since that time, but the same song will be sung by Christians who remain faithful and choose to die rather than deny their faith in the Lord. They will also stand beside a sea—not the Red Sea, but *a sea of glass mixed with fire*—symbolic of the fiery trials they suffered on earth (Rev. 15:2). The rejoicing martyrs, however, will have no regrets about past sufferings. Instead, they will adore and praise God, saying, *Lord God Almighty, wonderful are Your works; King of nations, how just and true are Your ways!* (Rev. 15:3).

Christians may not be delivered from death, but they will one day be with the Lord and will understand God's wisdom and loving-kindness in allowing them to suffer for His sake, and will *"sing the song of Moses . . . and the song of the Lamb."*

The rewards God has in store for His people will far exceed any sacrifice we could make in serving Him. The suffering or death that we as Christians may encounter because of our faith in Jesus seems insignificant compared with the glorious, eternal future our Lord has prepared for us.

What God has prepared for those who love Him is beyond anything we have seen or heard and greater than anything we could ever imagine (Rom. 8:18; 1 Cor. 2:9).

Thought for Today: What a day of rejoicing our reunion with the Lord will be!

December 29: Read Revelation 17–18

Verse for Today: *"And upon her forehead was a name written, MYSTERY, BAB-YLON THE GREAT, THE MOTHER OF HARLOTS AND ABOMINATIONS OF THE EARTH"* (Rev. 17:5).

Old Testament Babylon, originally called Babel, was the first city where human government openly defied God (Gen. 11:1-9). Centuries later, Babylon became the most magnificent capital city of the ancient world. It was during this time that the Babylonians took the Israelites into captivity.

Babylon is symbolic of political, social, and economic systems that attempt to deceive, hinder, and enslave Christians. In Revelation, the harlot in alliance with the beast is called Babylon—a city. She pretends to represent God's church; but she is a deceiver, attempting to corrupt Christianity. To the unbelieving world, she is a *"mystery"* because the unsaved cannot discern the difference between true Christians and the counterfeit church, with all its worldly splendor and power.

The false church is not concerned with reaching a lost world with the Word of God—the message that Christ Jesus came into this world to save sinners. It is governed by humanistic principles, social issues, and material things. In these false churches, God's Word has been set aside, and lifeless formalism—and often good works—has taken its place.

It is only by reading God's Word, with a desire to know the truth, that we are protected against deception. God's Word and Spirit are able to prevent us from participating in the evil, unworthy things the world offers (Rev. 18:4). Instead, we are to know Him and serve Him faithfully.

"And I heard another voice from heaven, saying, Come out of her, my people, that ye be not partakers of her sins, and that ye receive not of her plagues" (Rev. 18:4).

Thought for Today: To reach our intended destination, it is not enough merely to be traveling; we must be on the right road. It is possible to be religious, but eternally lost. We must be walking with Christ on the road of salvation.

December 30: Read Revelation 19–20

Verses for Today: *"And I saw an angel come down from heaven, having the key of the bottomless pit and a great chain in his hand. And he laid hold on the dragon, that old serpent, which is the Devil, and Satan, and bound him a thousand years"* (Rev. 20:1-2).

There are many things in God's Word that we do not understand clearly. But one thing is plain: There is a devil, *"that old serpent,"* called Satan, who is behind all evil. He tries to destroy the work of God and all that is good (1 Pet. 5:8), and he seeks to deceive and ensnare everyone he can, especially Christians.

However, believers are to know God's Word and His Spirit, and be overcomers. Jesus defeated Satan by the very Word that we have in our hands today—the Bible (Matt. 4:4, 7, 10). We, too, can defeat the evil forces that surround us through the power of God's Word and His Spirit within us (1 John 4:4).

"Wherefore take unto you the whole armour of God, that ye may be able to withstand in the evil day. . . . And take . . . the sword of the Spirit, which is the word of God" (Eph. 6:13, 17).

Thought for Today: Satan is a deceiver and distorts the facts, but the Word of God is our truth and power.

December 31: **Read Revelation 21–22**

Verses for Today: *"And I saw a new heaven and a new earth: for the first heaven and the first earth were passed away; and there was no more sea. . . . And I heard a great voice out of heaven saying, Behold, the tabernacle of God is with men, and he will dwell with them, and they shall be his people, and God himself shall be with them, and be their God. And God shall wipe away all tears from their eyes; and there shall be no more death, neither sorrow, nor crying, neither shall there be any more pain: for the former things are passed away"* (Rev. 21: 1, 3-4).

What a blessed, exciting, trustworthy hope we have! There is a new day coming and a new city, which will be *full of the glory of God and the glory of Christ* (Rev. 21:23). It will be full of life and all that is beautiful. However, this glorious life is only for those who know Jesus as Lord and Savior and have been cleansed by Him. For *nothing impure, shameful, deceitful, or vile will enter it . . .* only those whose names *"are written in the Lamb's book of life"* (Rev. 21:27).

As beautiful as it will be for the believer, eternity will be forever filled with pain for the unbeliever and the sinful: *"The fearful, and unbelieving, and the abominable, and murderers, and whoremongers, and sorcerers, and idolaters, and all liars, shall have their part in the lake which burneth with fire and brimstone: which is the second death"* (Rev. 21:8).

Note the characteristics of the unsaved. God begins with *"the fearful"*—the coward who will not confess Jesus for fear of what others might say or do (Matt. 10:32-33; Rom. 10:9). Next are the *"unbelieving"*—though they may be morally good, they are still lost sinners who will be cast into *"the lake which burneth with fire."* To *not* believe God and to dismiss Him is a horrible sin (Ps. 78:22, 32; John 3:18; Heb. 3:12, 19). How solemn is the warning concerning *"all liars,"* the morally corrupt, whoremongers, fornicators, homosexuals, and those dealing in various forms of witchcraft, spiritualism, and idolatry. All will be cast into the lake of fire (Deut. 18:10-12; Eph. 5:3, 5; Col. 3:5-6; Heb. 13:4).

As wicked as these sins are, God is willing to forgive anyone—even the vilest sinner. His love reaches out to every repentant sinner who turns to Jesus. No one is ever good enough; each of us must trust the Lord to save us.

If you haven't yet received Jesus as your personal Savior—oh, friend—call on Him now. Do you believe that He died to save you from your sins and offers forgiveness? Ask Christ to save you and help you live for Him, for *"whosoever shall call on the name of the Lord shall be saved"* (Acts 2:21).

If you are a believer, ask the Lord to enable you to know Him more, strengthen you to live for Him, and empower you to share His good news of salvation with others.

Jesus, the Lamb of God, calls to us, *"And let him that is athirst come. And whosoever will, let him take the water of life freely"* (Rev. 22:17). *"Blessed are they that do his commandments, that they may have right to the tree of life, and may enter in through the gates into the city"* (Rev. 22:14). *"The grace of our Lord Jesus be with you all. Amen"* (Rev. 22:21).

Thought for Today: For the Christian, death is but a stepping-stone to everlasting life and to forever enjoying God and more of His glories, wonders, power, love, and blessings.

Appendix A
The Power of God's Evidence,
Promises, and Prophecy
to Build Our Faith

Note: This appendix on prophecy is referred to in the reading for May 10 (2 Kings 23–25).

~

God provides us with proof and evidence in a variety of ways because He wants us to believe Him, know Him, and heed His instructions for our good.

The first proof we have of God is through this created world. This fact is confirmed continually throughout the Bible, which declares God as the wonderful, mighty Creator of everything. The first book, Genesis, begins with the account of God creating the world, and the final book of Scripture, Revelation, states, *"Thou art worthy, O Lord, to receive glory and honour and power: for thou hast created all things, and for thy pleasure they are and were created"* (Rev. 4:11).[27]

Scripture boldly teaches that because the created world gives ample evidence for believing in God and His eternal power and divine nature, we are without excuse (Rom. 1:20). Each of us can easily comprehend that there is a God who is powerful, good, and glorious.

Before we discuss the next proof of evidence, prophecy, it helps to comprehend that God's Word contains power. The marvelous power of His Words is revealed in the first chapters of the Bible when God spoke all creation into existence. (He didn't snap His fingers or use any other method.) His Words hold such authority that He created the wonder of the heavens, earth, and mankind with them! Every time God declares something, it always happens as stated. This is true, as well, for Jesus and every word that He spoke. When Jesus declared someone was healed, or for the storm to *"Be still,"* it took place exactly in that manner.

All of God's Word and every promise of Scripture are filled with power and

---

27 A few other key verses regarding creation and God as Creator include Gen. 1:1; Ps. 19:1; Jer. 51:15; John 1:1-4; and Col. 1:15-17.

328 • Discovering God's Blessings

truth, which is why it can be trusted and why it changes lives. It is why we should heed all that God says, but also what can give us hope and faith to believe His promises. (If we trust Him and believe, we can count on His *good promises* being fulfilled for us in our lives, just as He says.)

Evidence of God's truth is additionally provided through prophecy. Prophecies are declarations about future events, which are fulfilled (sometime later) as stated. God's spokesmen in the Old Testament are called prophets. They declared God's instructions and warnings, as well as God-sized predictions, which seemed impossible to occur. Every time the promises came true, everyone was (and is) to know that the Lord spoke; that He has all knowledge; and that He always fulfills every word and promise He speaks (Isa. 46:10-11; Amos 4:13; 1 Thess. 5:20-21).

God's Word includes more than twenty-five hundred predictions regarding people, nations, and events. About two thousand predictions have been fulfilled as stated.[28] The remaining prophetic announcements, about five hundred, are still to take place and concern future events for this life, end times, and the next life.

Numerous detailed scriptural predictions in the Old Testament were given about a future, chosen, and anointed Savior-King and included specific facts about His birth, life, and death. The New Testament reveals Jesus as the Messiah-King, who fulfills all the promised details. Matthew's gospel is an encouraging read in that the writer brings a number of these to our attention with various phrases indicating, *"this is in fulfillment of prophecy."* Scripture states that proof regarding Jesus is also given through His miracles, signs, wonders, and resurrection (John 20:30-31; Acts 17:31; Heb. 2:3-4).

To read more on prophecy, the book *Why I Believe*, by D. James Kennedy, provides a faith-strengthening and enjoyable first chapter, "Why I Believe in the Bible." It explains prophecy by sharing a few remarkable predictions and how they came to be fulfilled.[29]

Verses on Proof, Prophecy, and Creation

I make known the end from the beginning, from ancient times; I declare what is still to come (Isa. 46:10-11).

He who forms the mountains, who creates the wind, and, who reveals His thoughts and plans to mankind . . . the Lord God Almighty is His name (Amos 4:13).

---

28 See https://reasons.org/explore/publications/articles/fulfilled-prophecy-evidence-for-the-reliability-of-the-bible.

29 D. James Kennedy, *Why I Believe* (Nashville, TN: Thomas Nelson, 1999). The first chapter, titled "Why I Believe in the Bible," can be read for free at Amazon.com with the "Look Inside" the book program (as of early 2022). The link is https://www.amazon.com/Why-Believe-D-James-Kennedy/dp/0849937396/.

Do not treat prophecies with contempt but test them all; hold on to them and to what is good (1 Thess. 5:20-21).

And many other signs truly did Jesus in the presence of His disciples, which are not written in this book: But these signs [miracles and wonders] *are written, that ye might believe that Jesus is the Christ, the Son of God; and that believing ye might have life through His name* (John 20:30-31).

He has fixed a day when He will judge the world with justice and equity by the Man He has chosen, and He has given proof and assurance of this to everyone by raising Him from the dead (Acts 17:31).

Appendix B

How I Came to Love Reading the Bible and to Publish This Book

Years ago I wanted to read the Bible, but struggled to do so. Jumping around in Scripture, or simply reading when I felt like it, didn't work for me. I would get lost or confused and give up. The plans that listed readings from several different places in Scripture overwhelmed me.

But one day at my local Christian bookstore, I purchased a book titled *The Best of Bible Pathway* (1993 edition). Dr. Hash's book helped me read the Bible, come to love the Bible, and begin having a daily quiet time with the Lord. As I grew in consistently (and persistently) reading God's Word, I was able to gain insights and strength from it, in ways I never would have without continuing to read all of it.

Admittedly, this journey took time. When I started utilizing this plan, I didn't like its use of calendar days (January 1, 2, etc.). I was certain that the days should be numbered "Day 1," "Day 2," and so on. Why did I have to read according to their schedule? Surprisingly, I discovered that the calendar days prodded me (actually forced me) to form a daily habit. When I would get behind in reading, I chose to catch up, rather than skip readings. At least once, I got several weeks behind and decided the best way to get back on track was to simply double up on daily readings. I knew I would eventually catch up and get back on course. Finally, I formed a daily habit.

Dr. John Hash's writing speaks with authority and gives a clear focus for each day's Bible reading. It prepared my mind and heart for God. The simplicity of this guide is its strength—staying with one segment of Scripture and reading it through. As I grew in reading the Bible, and in loving *Bible Pathway*, I began buying extra copies and sharing them with others. I even encouraged a women's Bible-study group with my story and this effective resource, and they used the plan for a yearlong study.[30]

---

30 I learned an interesting tip from the women. Each one took her book to an office-supply store where the spine edge was removed and the book was rebound with a spiral coil. This way, the book is able to lie open and flat for easier note-taking and daily use. The cost was less than ten dollars. Since no pages were copied, no copyright laws were violated.

God's Word Helps Me Hear Him

I've discovered that knowing God's Word helps me pray and hear from the Lord. Not only have I grown in asking God for help, comfort, encouragement, and direction, but I've found that He can more readily share with me what I need from His Word. The Lord brings phrases, passages, and stories to my mind, even if I haven't specifically memorized a particular portion. Truly the Lord is able to more freely talk and commune with those who know His Word.

The Miracle of How This Edition Came to Be

Eventually, Bible Pathway Ministry began updating their book edition, but I loved the 1993 version best. After two updates, I called the ministry in 2006, and asked one of their team members if they would consider reprinting the 1993 edition, so I could keep giving the books away. They generously gave me permission to republish it!

To this day, I feel blessed and thankful to Dr. John Hash and everyone at *Bible Pathway* for dedicating their lives to sharing the power of God's Word with others, and for generously allowing me the opportunity to reprint *The Best of Bible Pathway* (1993), which has been such a blessing in my life.

What you hold in your hands is a labor of love, as it took several years' work to retype and publish it. Because the first publishing house I contracted with went out of business, I am once again updating, retitling, and republishing this book. Not only do I still believe in the power of this book, but God has been strongly and persistently nudging me to update it one final time to bless more people.

My Prayer for You

My prayer for you is that you will grow in your relationship with God and know His goodness, proof, provisions, and the good plans He has for your life. Build a foundation of reading the Bible every day, and seek God in prayer. Ask the Lord to help you know Him.

Many blessings to you,

Robbi Cary

Appendix C

A Brief Overview of the Bible and Helpful Tips for Reading It

BY ROBBI CARY

The Bible reveals to us about God, ourselves, this life (and its real purposes), and the eternal life to come. Scripture provides truth and evidence so we may believe all that it shares. It explains and discloses about sin, evil, suffering, and death, and reveals to us Jesus, salvation, heaven, spiritual provisions, and blessings. It provides wisdom, instructions, and warnings. While we should desire to know it, apply it, and study it, we must begin with reading it.

To read all of God's Word, we will need to make a determined and persistent effort. We will need to develop a daily habit, carve out a consistent time of day, and choose a place to have our quiet time with God.

Learning basic facts about the Bible is helpful, for it is a unique book. In fact, it's a compilation of sixty-six different books written by forty men over a span of about 1,600 years—and yet all with a unified, singular message. Its authors include shepherds, fishermen, poets, scholars, and philosophers. All are God's representatives because the Bible reveals its ultimate author:

"All scripture is given by inspiration of God" (2 Tim. 3:16).

We can expect to enjoy amazing truth in our journey with God's Word. It offers us glimpses of God's glory, goodness, and greatness, while providing help, comfort, and hope. However, we can also expect to encounter difficulties. Struggles always occur in the pursuit of anything valuable and worthwhile. We will encounter mankind's brokenness and feel our own smallness and failings. We'll discover how far mankind (and ourselves) have strayed from God's plan and commands.

We'll be surprised at how God's character comprises two seeming contradictions: tender love, along with righteous judgment. God ordains and pours out great judgment and wrath on those who act against His holiness and commands. But He offers a way of salvation with grace, mercy, and loving-kindness, as He draws close to people whom He has created. He pursues us and offers us forgiveness, restoration, and new life through Jesus. God's righteous judgment and merciful love are a profound mystery that are resolved and understood in the life, death, and resurrection of Jesus.

So, the Bible is about God and about us. It's about our fallen condition versus an offer of new life. It is about Jesus, hope, and salvation.

Some passages we read will bring shock, fear, and questions, because God is greater than us—in wisdom, power, holiness, purity, and majesty. *His ways are higher and different from our ways* (Isa. 55:8–9). In fact, we need God's help, not just for new life, but for spiritual understanding as well (Luke 24:45).

We may want to read the Bible for knowledge, or simply to feel good, and then go about our lives, but the Bible is meant for more than just this kind of reading. God calls us to know Him, and His righteousness and mercy, and make choices. God's Word ruffles our placidness, our assumptions, our "goodness." It challenges and confronts our hearts, attitudes, and actions.

The Bible invites us to know and fellowship with its author, the Lord. It invites us to receive Him. When we read difficult parts of Scripture, we are to remember that we have hope and help in Jesus for every need (Ps. 46:1-3; 91:14-16; Heb. 4:14-16).

The Bible's Types of Literature and Layout

As we read through the Bible, we will encounter many types of literature. It's a history book and a how-to manual. It contains genealogies and facts. It reveals God's emotions and speaks to ours. It provides *practical* instructions for success regarding all areas of life, and it gives commandments. The Bible contains proverbs (succinct, memorable words of wisdom), poetry, songs, and an intimate love story. It includes examples of people who have walked with and loved God (and Christ), and those who have rebelled and fallen away. Controversial subjects are covered with the same amazing unity.

Mark Driscoll, a pastor and Christian author, once delightfully described the Bible's variety of literature, saying it contains "geographical surveys, architectural specifications, travel diaries, population statistics, family trees, inventories, and numerous legal documents."[31]

Scripture contains numerous God-sized predictions called prophecy. (God's spokesmen in the Old Testament were called prophets.) Prophecies are given to us to warn us, and to provide proof and evidence for us to believe and be blessed, and to have confident hope. Through the ages, God's prophecies seem impossible to occur; therefore, when they happen, we are to *know* God has spoken. They confirm God's promises, and tell us what is still to happen in the future.[32]

---

31 The article in which Driscoll's reflections appeared is no longer available online.
32 See Appendix A for more information regarding prophecy and evidence.

The Bible is given to us in two parts called testaments (the Old and New). The Old Testament lays the foundation for the New Testament, and the coming of Jesus Christ, our Savior. Every book of the Bible reveals Jesus (Luke 24:27, 44-45). He is the beginning and the climactic ending. He is the *Living* Word *of God* (John 1:1-5). Pastor Colin Smith, in his book *Unlocking the Bible*, states, "The Bible begins in a garden, ends in a city, and the whole of it is about Jesus Christ."[33]

The New Testament opens with four accounts called "gospels." The word "gospel" means "good news." These accounts reveal *the good news* of Jesus's life, death, and resurrection, through which we are able to receive salvation and blessings. These accounts were written by early followers—Matthew, Mark, Luke, and John—and bear their names. The first three accounts conclude with the Lord's instructions to His followers and His ascension into heaven.

Acts is the next book, which reveals the "acts" of the apostles and the church's miraculous growth following Jesus's ascension. The New Testament includes letters to churches and individuals, with instructions and warnings regarding our new life and end times.

Revelation, the last book of the Bible, is God's final disclosure to mankind about Jesus and all that is to come in the future. Revelation is full of prophecy, visons, and symbolism regarding past events and the final climactic battles between good and evil. It unveils the coming glorious reign of Jesus and His kingdom for all who have received Him into their lives.

Scripture's claims and truth are amazing—heart-pounding even. They detail God's plan, purposes, and promises since the beginning of creation; His plan and ability to make things right since sin entered the picture; and His numerous provisions and blessings for those who turn to Him.

Every type of literature is important to God's overall message, and to the message of that particular passage. We find poetry and beautiful imagery intended to stir our hearts, grab our imaginations, and enable us to receive and hold tight to its powerful truths. For example, John's gospel includes "simple" word pictures that declare great truth about Jesus. Among these, we are told that He is life, bread, and living water for those who receive Him.

Consider that the books of the Bible, particularly the four gospels about Jesus, pack a lot into a little space. The books are almost breathless in their pace. The information is given, but the interpretation is left to each of us. We must think on it. We get to choose. Jesus Himself challenged people to look at the evidence, then asked for their conclusion (Matt. 16:15). Some people followed Him; others rejected Him. We, too, have a choice.

---

33 Cited by Kevin Halloran, "Jesus in the Old Testament: Five Powerful Glimpses of Christ in Leviticus," *Unlocking the Bible*, September 17, 2012, https://unlockingthebible.org/2012/09/jesus-in-the-old-testament-five-powerful-glimpses-of-christ-in-leviticus/.

The Bible is simple, yet deep. We are given God's truth in various ways and from multiple authors. The Lord wants us to understand and grasp what He reveals concerning Himself and all that is to happen. God's Word is meant to comfort, encourage, and challenge us to make decisions. We must delve into it and interact with it. We are to study it, memorize it, and live it. Besides growing in knowledge and understanding, we're to grow in our relationship with the Lord and new life.

Reading with the Right Mind-set

There are many approaches to reading and studying Scripture. Each one has its place, purpose, and value. Gaining a grasp of the entirety of Scripture is valuable, as are studies on topics, themes, passages, and specific words. Even reading one of the gospels has great worth, for numerous people have received Jesus and been profoundly changed by the life-giving words in these accounts. Reading *through* the Bible is one of the ways to know and experience God through His Word.

Our approach and attitude when we read Scripture are important. We need to be careful (especially when using a reading plan, such as this one), and not simply feel we crossed it off our daily "to-do list." We don't want to read pridefully and think, "Well, I did that for the day," and put it down until the next day. As we read it, we want to interact with the Lord, know Him more, and allow its truth to transform our minds, hearts, lives, and actions. We want to be filled with the Lord's presence, wisdom, and power, so that our lives reflect Him.

On the other end of the spectrum, we can feel defeated if we view the Bible as simply a rule book. Certainly, the immenseness of God's righteousness and law, along with our smallness and inability to live righteously, can overwhelm us. These truths are meant to draw us to Jesus and His mercy, grace, help, and new life that He offers.[34]

God's Word declares both truth *and* grace.[35] God's truth includes amazing, serious, and hard aspects. He created us in His image, and for fellowship with Him. We are to honor God and are accountable to Him. He has high, righteous standards, and one day we will stand before God and give an account of our lives to Him.

Transgressing against God's commands is called sin, and He declared that the "sentence" for sin is death (Gen. 2:15-17; Rom. 6:23). All of us have sinned.

---

34 This concept is derived from a great article on the topic of how not to feel overwhelmed when you read your Bible: https://www.knowableword.com/2015/09/07/when-the-bible-over-whelms-you/. Another helpful article regarding this subject is located at: https://jazminnfrank.com/how-not-to-feel-overwhelmed-when-you-read-the-bible/.

35 This information on truth and grace is also shared in the introduction section, "A Few Tips for Reading the Bible and Using This Plan."

Because sin is brokenness from God, it also brings strife, pain, and difficult, un-foreseen consequences.

However, God loves us greatly. In God's love and mercy, He has provided a way of salvation for us through Jesus's life, death, and resurrection. As we turn to God and receive His Son, Jesus, into our lives, we are granted forgiveness, grace, new life, peace, and blessings! Scripture declares it this way:

"For the wages of sin is death; but the gift of God is eternal life through Jesus Christ our Lord" (Rom. 6:23).

"For God so loved the world, that he gave his only begotten Son, that whosoever believeth in him should not perish, but have everlasting life" (John 3:16).

God's law was given to us by Moses, but **grace and truth** *came by Jesus Christ* (John 1:17).

"The Word [Jesus] was made flesh, and dwelt among us, (and we beheld his glory, the glory as of the only begotten of the Father,) full of **grace and truth**" (John 1:14).

But now, through Jesus, we have been released from the law and all that had bound us—the law, its penalty of death, sin, and condemnation; now, we are able to serve God in a new way, with a new spirit (Rom. 7:6).

As you read God's Word, seek to recognize both truth and grace. Let yourself be moved by God's righteousness; His love and mercy; and His power to save and help.

Because the Bible can seem overwhelming, it helps to know that God's foundational truths are repeated and given to us in various ways, through various stories and examples, and through different kinds of literature in its pages.

A Love Story and Prayer

The Bible is much more than an instruction book and set of rules. It is a love story from God, a rescue story, a book rich with wonders and blessings. God is calling us to follow Him. To do this as He intends—joyfully and with love for Him—we must know our great need and His great love and provisions.

The Bible speaks to deep spiritual living, and for this we need God. In its introduction for reading the Bible, BibleStudyTools.com says it well: "Read the Bible for the sake of learning, not simply to accomplish your next reading. Say a short prayer to God before you begin, asking the Holy Spirit to give you wisdom and understanding, then be refreshed by the words you read!"[36]

---

36 From BibleStudyTools.com: https://www.biblestudytools.com/bible-reading-plan/book-order .html, accessed March 15, 2021. This is tip #3 under "Tips on Reading the Bible Daily."

The Bible is life-changing and joy-producing. It transforms lives and eternal destinies; it offers practical wisdom for life; it is great history and literature. No wonder God's Word is the best-selling book of all time, and available in nearly three thousand languages.[37]

The Lord is in the Bible's pages and words, and He wants to speak to you personally! How thrilling it is when God opens our eyes and hearts, and we see beyond our doubts, questions, and hardened assumptions to discover life, healing, hope, peace, and comfort—and, yes, instructions to us.

The Bible contains truth and wisdom apart from ourselves. Will we accept it and receive the Lord and His gift of salvation and new life? Will we let God's Word increase our faith and trust in Him? Will we heed and follow Him?

Start reading it today. Read it with a heart to know Him and His love, and what He wants to reveal to you. Ask the Lord to increase your understanding and love for Him. Continue to read, and reread, His Word.

---

37 This number is cited from https://www.wycliffe.org.uk/about/our-impact/ and comprises the fact that the Bible in its entirety has been translated into 717 different languages. Another 2,299 people groups have either the New Testament or a portion of the Bible in their language. While this number seems hard to believe, there are over six thousand languages in the world.

 Wycliffe Global Alliance (https://www.wycliffe.net/) is one of the key organizations and ministries working to translate the Bible for people groups. From humble beginnings, they have grown to include a number of separate organizations, which network together for different purposes of Bible translation (https://www.wycliffe.org/about/associated-organizations). Further information with two helpful and interesting articles can be found at https://www.wycliffe.org/about and https://www.sil.org/about/history.

Appendix D

The Blessings of God's Word

BY ROBBI CARY

The Bible reveals God to us and His great love, mercy, and power.
　　It shows us the way of salvation, new life, and blessings.
　　It provides us with evidence and proof for faith, and includes truth,
　　　　prophecies, and fulfillment.

The Bible gives authoritative promises, effectual guidance, and life-changing
　　　　direction.
　　It provides warnings and corrections, and great comfort and hope.
　　The Bible transforms the willing soul, as it gives help for every need.

The Bible provides assurance of eternal life and our blessed future with God in
　　　　His kingdom.
　　We are to know our Lord, along with the hope to which He calls us, and
　　　　the riches of our glorious inheritance.
　　Through its counsel and power, we are able to walk worthy of the Lord and
　　　　be fruitful in every good work.

The Bible reveals truth and righteousness, so that we might not fall away or be
　　　　deceived.
　　It is a mighty weapon and sword, enabling us to pull down strongholds.
　　God's Word brings health, healing, strength, success, and victory.

May the word of Christ dwell in you richly in all wisdom (Col. 3:16).

⌒

"He hath shewed thee, O man, what is good;
and what doth the LORD require of thee . . . to do justly,
and to love mercy, and to walk humbly with thy God?"
(Micah 6:8)

Appendix E

God's Love and Plan that We Are Saved, Blessed, and Fellowship with Him

(GOD'S WORD ON SALVATION)

God made all of creation wonderful, and He loves us dearly.

For I know the plans I have for you, declares the LORD; plans for good, not evil; plans to prosper you, and give you hope and a future (Jer. 29:11).

Every good and perfect gift is from above, coming down from the Father of the heavenly lights (James 1:17).

God has shown His love to us by sending His only Son into the world. God did this, so we might have life through Christ (1 John 4:9).

All the pain, suffering, and death in the world are the result of Satan's work and the sin of all people. Sin is falling short of God's ways and commands. Sin is harmful to ourselves and others; it shows a disregard for God; it separates us from God; and it brings punishment and death (physical and eternal). Death is not non-existence, it is being shut out from the life, presence, and glory of God (2 Thess. 1:7-10).

The thief, Satan, comes to steal, and to kill, and to destroy (John 10:10).

Your iniquities [sins and shortcomings] have separated you from your God; your sins have hidden His face from you (Isa. 59:2).

All have sinned and fall short of the glory of God (Rom. 3:23).

"For the wages of sin is death" (Rom. 6:23).

For those who are self-seeking and who reject the truth and who follow evil, there will be wrath and anger (Rom. 2:8).

We are all accountable to God and will one day stand before Him and answer for our thoughts, words, and actions.

Man is destined to die once, and after that to face judgment (Heb. 9:27).

We will all appear before Christ, and be judged by him; we will receive what we deserve for the good or evil that we have done while in this earthly body (2 Cor. 5:10).

On that day God will judge the secrets of each person through Jesus Christ (Rom. 2:16).

He has appointed a day, in which he will judge the world in righteousness by the man whom he has ordained; and he has given proof and assurance of this to all men by raising him from the dead (Acts 17:31).

Because God loves us greatly, He sent Jesus into the world to rescue us and give us new life.

For God so loved the world that He gave his one and only Son, so that whoever believes in Him shall not perish but have eternal life (John 3:16).

For the wages of sin is death, but the gift of God is eternal life in Christ Jesus our Lord (Rom. 6:23).

Whoever hears my word and believes Him who sent me has eternal life and will not be judged [condemned]; he has crossed over from death to life (John 5:24).

God gives us the choice to receive and accept Him, or reject Him.

"For whosoever shall call upon the name of the LORD shall be saved" (Rom. 10:13).

"If thou shalt confess with thy mouth the Lord Jesus, and shalt believe in thine heart that God hath raised him from the dead, thou shalt be saved" (Rom. 10:9).

And now what are you waiting for? Get up, be baptized, and wash your sins away, calling on His name (Acts 22:16).

Whoever believes and is baptized will be saved, but whoever does not believe will be condemned (Mark 16:16).

But to all who believed Him and receive Him, He gave the right [and blessing] to become children of God (John 1:12).

God gives us assurance concerning this new life, and He gives us His Spirit to help us.

These things have been written, so that you may believe that Jesus is the Christ, the Son of God, and that by believing, you may have life in His name (John 20:31).

And I will give you a new heart and spirit. I will put my Spirit in you. No longer will you have a heart of stone, but you will be able to follow my commandments. . . . You will be my people, and I will be your God! (Ezek. 36:26-28).

God gives us instructions for our new life in Him. With His help, we are to know Him, grow in Him, and grow in all that He has given us.

This is eternal life—that they know you, the only true God, and Jesus Christ, whom you have sent (John 17:3).

But grow in the grace and knowledge of our Lord and Savior Jesus Christ (2 Pet. 3:18).

If you love me, keep my commandments (John 14:15).

(A few key verses regarding our calling, inheritance, blessings, and provisions include Ps. 1:1-6; 103:1-6; Eph. 1:2-23; 3:18-20; 6:10-17).

God gives us important, difficult, and wonderful news concerning the future.

In the last days, there will be terrible days (2 Tim. 3:1). *Stand firm, and you will be saved* (Luke 21:19).

I heard a loud shout from the throne, saying, "Look, God's home is now among people! He will dwell with them, and they will live with Him and be His people. God Himself will be with them. He will wipe every tear from their eyes. There will be no more death or sorrow or crying or pain. All these things are gone forever (Rev. 21:3-4).

No eye has seen, no ear has heard, and no mind has imagined what God has prepared for those who love Him (1 Cor. 2:9).

How to Receive God's Gift of Salvation

If you have never received Jesus and salvation (or if you are unsure), and you desire to do so, know that the steps of salvation are as simple as A, B, C.

Accept (and understand) God's truth.
Believe on Jesus (and all that He offers to us).
Call on Jesus for salvation, and follow Him.

First, we must know and accept what God declares about:

◆ Himself (He is righteous and loves us greatly.)
◆ Life's purpose (God created us to know Him and love Him.)
◆ Ourselves (Every person falls short of God's ways, commands, and law. God declares this is sin, and the penalty is death. We lose the life He originally gave us, and our relationship with Him is broken.)
◆ God, with great love, offers us salvation as a free gift. (He has provided a way of salvation for us through Jesus, His Son. Jesus lived the perfect life that we couldn't live, and He died for us, taking the penalty for our sins; then, He was resurrected to life, in God's power. As we receive Jesus and His life, death, and resurrection, we are forgiven; restored back to God; and given new life, His Spirit, and His help.)

Salvation is a free gift that God gives to us if we will receive it.

It is by grace you have been saved through faith. This is not your own doing, but it is the gift of God; it is not the result of works, so that no one may boast (Eph. 2:8-9).

Everyone who calls on the name of the Lord will be saved (Acts 2:21).

If you desire salvation, simply talk to God (which is prayer). You can pray something like this prayer:

God, I know that I have sinned against You, and I need Your salvation and grace. I do believe that Jesus died for my sins, rose from the grave, and lives. Thank You that You love me and have provided for my salvation. Thank You that You hear my prayer. I want new life. Help me to know You, and Your love, kindness, peace, and joy. Help me to love You and live for You. In Jesus's name, Amen.

Be assured that God will begin to work in your life. Walk with God as He leads, including finding a Bible-believing church, being baptized, and acknowledging Jesus to others (Heb. 10:25; Mark 16:16; Rom. 10:9).

May God greatly bless you with faith, peace, and a bountiful life in Him.

Endorsements from
Bible Pathway *original* 1993

The Word and prayer go hand in hand in our relationship with God. I appreciate *Bible Pathway* because of its emphasis upon the whole counsel of God.

—Mrs. Vonette Bright
Chairman, National Day of Prayer Committee

The Bible is Christ-centered. So, read it, and read it again. The *Bible Pathway* method is an excellent aid [for] this.

—Dr. J. Sidlow Baxter
International author and lecturer

I fully recommend the *Bible Pathway* plan of reading the Scriptures.

—Dr. Luis Palau
Luis Palau Evangelistic Association

It's harvesttime. This is why the ministry of *Bible Pathway* is so important. Its emphasis is on the entire Word of God and getting it out to the whole world.

—Dr. Charles Stanley
President, In Touch Ministries;
Former President, Southern Baptist Convention

When viewers began calling our 25 counseling centers nationwide in Canada, giving their lives to Christ, we had no way of getting them into the Word of God daily until we came across *Bible Pathway*, which has blessed thousands of our viewers.

—Dr. David Mainse
President, One Hundred Huntley Street
Toronto, Ontario, Canada

I read through *Bible Pathway* and have nothing but praise to the Lord for its clarity and conciseness. The *Bible Pathway* guide is one of the best I have seen in helping toward regular, disciplined study of the Word of God, and I unreservedly commend it.

—Dr. Alan Redpath
Former Pastor of Moody Memorial Church

I have used *Bible Pathway* over the years, and it has been very helpful to me. This systematic plan gives a sense of "wholeness" to the Bible.

—Dr. Ted W. Engstrom
President Emeritus, World Vision

There are two things that in the entire history of Missions have been absolutely central: the one, most obviously, is the Bible itself. The other is the printed page. There is absolutely nothing else in terms of Mission Methodology that outranks the importance of the printed page. Meetings come and go. Personalities appear and are gone. But the printed page continues to speak. *Bible Pathway* combines these two essential tools. I just don't know of any other ministry that is doing this as effectively.

—Dr. Ralph Winter
Founder and General Director
of United States Center for World Mission

I think the *Bible Pathway* [guide] is a delightful and most effective program.

—James T. Draper Jr.
Baptist Sunday School Board

I am happy to recommend *Bible Pathway* for personal worship. I appreciate the brief comments under "Christ Revealed." [The guide] is appropriate for a broad evangelical audience.

—James W. Reapsome
Managing Editor, *Christianity Today*

"And now, brethren, I commend you to God, and to the word of his grace,
which is able to build you up, and to give you an inheritance"
(Acts 20:32).

Subject Index

Index of Books of the Bible

If you have grown spiritually and enjoyed *Discovering God's Blessings,* please tell others. Share a good review on Amazon, tweet and post online, and share with your friends and family.

Check out Robbi Cary's other books on Amazon and her website:

- *No Matter What, It's a Good Day When: Finding Blessings in Difficult Days* is a delightful, full-color gift book with brief encouraging prose and Scripture, and beautiful photographs.

- Robbi coauthored *Conspiracy of Grace: A Wild Tale of Transformation* with Dale Fiegland. Years in the making, Dale had become a gun-toting, knife-wielding, alcoholic Mafia runner. He had also been pursued by God for years. When Dale finally surrendered and asked God for help, miracles began to happen.

- Visit *RobbiCary.com* for a variety of posts to help you grow spiritually.

Made in the USA
Coppell, TX
19 December 2022